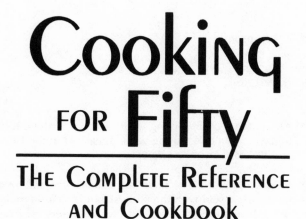

Cooking
FOR Fifty
The Complete Reference and Cookbook

Chet Holden

Produced by Alison Brown Cerier
Book Development, Inc.

John Wiley & Sons, Inc.
New York • Chichester • Brisbane • Toronto • Singapore

Senior Editor: Claire Thompson
Managing Editor: Janice Weisner
Production Coordination: Crane Typesetting
Interior Design: Mark Bergeron
Illustrations: Lori Neel

In recognition of the importance of preserving what has been written, it is a policy of John Wiley & Sons, Inc. to have books of enduring value published in the United States printed on acid-free paper, and we exert our best efforts to that end.

This publication is designed to provide accurate and authoritative information in regard to the subject matter covered. It is sold with the understanding that the publisher is not engaged in rendering legal, accounting, or other professional service. If legal advice or other expert assistance is required, the services of a competent professional person should be sought. FROM A DECLARATION OF PRINCIPLES JOINTLY ADOPTED BY A COMMITTEE OF THE AMERICAN BAR ASSOCIATION AND A COMMITTEE OF PUBLISHERS.

Copyright © 1993 by Chet Holden and Alison Brown Cerier Book Development, Inc.

All rights reserved. Published simultaneously in Canada.

Reproduction or translation of any part of this work beyond that permitted by section 107 or 108 of the 1976 United States Copyright Act without the permission of the copyright owner is unlawful. Requests for permission or further information should be addressed to the Permission Department, John Wiley & Sons, Inc.

Library of Congress Cataloging-in-Publication Data

Holden, Chet.
   Cooking for fifty : the complete reference and cookbook / Chet Holden.
      p.   cm.
   ''Produced by Alison Brown Cerier Book Development, Inc.''
   Includes index.
   ISBN 0-471-57015-X
   1. Quantity cookery.   I. Title.   II. Title: Cooking for 50.
TX820.H56   1992
641.5′7—dc20   92-27314
                                                                CIP

Printed in the United States of America

10 9 8 7 6 5 4 3 2 1

To Chris and Allison Holden

CONTENTS

Preface   xi

Acknowledgments   xiii

List of Tables   xv

PART ONE: REFERENCE   1

Cooking Methods: Techniques and Timetables   3
  ▲ **Dry-Heat Cooking Methods   5**
  Broiling   5
  Deep-Frying   9
  Panbroiling   11
  Panfrying   13
  Roasting   16
  Sautéing   21
  ▲ **Moist-Heat Cooking Methods   22**
  Braising   22
  Poaching   25
  Simmering   26
  Steaming   28
  ▲ **Meat Cooking Methods   32**

Equivalents, Ingredients, and Equipment   37
  ▲ **Weights to Measures Conversion Tables   39**
  Bakery Products   39

Dairy Products   40

Fruits   40

Grains   41

Spices and Herbs   42

Vegetables   43

▲ **U.S./Metric Conversion Tables   44**

Volume   44

Weight   45

▲ **Fahrenheit/Centigrade Conversions   45**

▲ **Microwave Time Conversions   46**

▲ **Temperature Guidelines for Food Safety   47**

▲ **Herbs and Spices Uses   48**

▲ **Flavor Substitutes   50**

▲ **Other Ingredient Substitutes   52**

▲ **Cheeses   52**

▲ **Equipment Sizes   55**

Standard Bowl Capacities   55

Insert Pan Dimensions and Capacities   55

Mixer Bowl Capacities   55

Standard Pot and Pan Capacities   56

Foodservice Scoop Capacities   57

Steam Kettle Capacities   57

▲ **Foodservice Can Sizes and Capacities   58**

Food Quantities   59

▲ **Amounts to Purchase for Fifty Portions   61**

Beverages   61

Cereal, Crackers, Grains   61

Dairy   62

Fruits   62

Beef   63

Lamb   63

Pork   64

Veal   65

Poultry   66

Seafood   66

Vegetables   67

▲ **Recipe Expansion and Reduction Tables   68**

Original Yield Four Portions   68

Original Yield Ten Portions   69

Original Yield Twenty-five Portions   70
Original Yield Fifty Portions   70

THE LANGUAGE OF FOOD   73

▲ **Menu Writer's Thesaurus**   75
▲ **American Regional Food Terms: Definitions and Origins**   88
▲ **International Food Terms: Definitions and Origins**   101
▲ **Food Word Translations**   120
▲ **French Food Words: Pronunciations and Definitions**   127
▲ **Italian Food Words: Pronunciations and Definitions**   142
▲ **Spanish Food Words: Pronunciations and Definitions**   153

FOODSERVICE PLANNING   161

▲ **Catering Equipment Checklist**   163
▲ **Table Skirting Requirements**   164
▲ **Full-Service Bar Requirements**   165
Liquor Yield Per Quart   165
Cost of Overpouring Liquor   166
Beer Yield Per Keg   166
▲ **Special Event Themes and Decor Ideas**   167
Early American   167
Southwestern United States   167
Mexico   168
Italy   168
The Orient   168
Medieval Times   168
Seven Seas Theme   169
▲ **Menu Concepts**   169
International Ethnic Sampler   169
American Regional Sampler   183
A World of Seafood   203
Hot and Spicy   204

PART TWO: RECIPES   209

APPETIZERS   211

▲ **Appetizers with Meat**   213
▲ **Appetizers with Poultry**   224
▲ **Appetizers with Seafood**   229
▲ **Appetizers with Vegetables**   235

Soups   245
  ▲ **Meat Soups**   247
  ▲ **Poultry Soups**   252
  ▲ **Seafood Soups**   255
  ▲ **Vegetable Soups**   257

Salads and Salad Dressings   271
  ▲ **Vegetable and Legume Salads**   273
  ▲ **Meat Salads**   284
  ▲ **Poultry Salads**   287
  ▲ **Seafood Salads**   298
  ▲ **Salad Dressings**   303

Seafood   311
  ▲ **Shellfish**   313
  ▲ **Finfish**   327

Meats   343
  ▲ **Beef**   345
  ▲ **Lamb**   355
  ▲ **Pork**   357
  ▲ **Veal**   368

Poultry   371
  ▲ **Chicken**   373
  ▲ **Turkey**   389

Pasta and Noodles   399
  ▲ **Hot Pastas**   401
  ▲ **Chilled Pastas**   413

Potatoes and Grains   421
  ▲ **Potatoes**   423
  ▲ **Rice**   437
  ▲ **Grains**   447

Vegetables and Legumes   453
  ▲ **Vegetables**   455
  ▲ **Legumes**   476

Breads, Muffins, and Biscuits   481

▲ Breads   483
▲ Muffins   492
▲ Biscuits   495

Desserts   501

▲ Fruit Desserts   503
▲ Cakes   514
▲ Pies   522
▲ Puddings   529
▲ Cookies   532

Breakfast and Brunch   537

▲ Eggs and Cheese   539
▲ Pancakes and Waffles   547
▲ Other Brunch Dishes   555

Index   562

PREFACE

My foodservice career began one summer night in 1974 when I accepted an invitation to observe a three-cook kitchen strut its stuff through a hectic Friday service. I was by then something of an accomplished home cook and had become friends with the chef. He thought I might get a kick out of watching the action.

I never got the chance: The pantry cook was a no-show, and I was asked to fill in. I did, and never looked back. I resigned a sales position and took my place behind the line. Six years of upscale hotel and restaurant kitchens later, I moved from the back of the house to the front of a typewriter with *Restaurants & Institutions Magazine*. In years since, I have developed recipes and menus, written cookbooks and commentary, and presented numerous cooking seminars. Throughout it all, I have developed a keen respect for the daily realities of professional cooking.

In writing *Cooking for Fifty*, my goal has been to compile a source book of references and recipes that reflect those realities. I wanted to produce a book that balances common sense with uncommon ideas.

In most cases, it makes very good sense for cooks to do some research even before they begin to cook. Thus, we begin *Cooking for Fifty* with an extensive Reference section that offers a broad range of resources with quick access to important numbers and facts. It begins, in the Cooking Methods section, with a brief refresher course on cooking techniques. There are conversion charts, food safety guidelines, flavoring substitutes, equipment capacity charts and a lot more. Charts will help guide you from weights to measures, and from U.S. to metric equivalents. I have also included a number of Food Quantity charts that indicate how much of several hundred foods one will need to buy to serve 50 portions. Then,

I included Recipe Expansion and Reduction charts to increase or reduce portion yields, based on recipes with multiple initial yields.

In our ever-changing industry, your patrons are looking for a world of dining pleasure. To help you offer it, I have provided a section on The Language of Food. There, you'll find a menu writer's thesaurus to help put more sizzle in your writing. When you write your next menu and decide "savory" doesn't quite strike your fancy, perhaps "zesty," "tangy," or "piquant" will. You'll discover definitions and origins of hundreds of American regional and international classics—as well as multilingual translations of common food terms. And you will find descriptions of hundreds of classic dishes from three of the universally popular cuisine styles: French, Italian, and Spanish.

The Reference section closes with ideas to support Foodservice Planning. You'll find important information that includes catering checklists, table skirting requirements, bar needs and portion yields—as well as Special Event Themes and Decor Ideas, and suggested Menu Concepts using the recipes that comprise the remainder of the book.

Cooking for Fifty contains more than three hundred recipes that reflect broad culinary trends that will likely continue for years to come. For example, you'll find numerous recipes for such contemporary favorites as pasta, grains, seafood, and fruits. To address the increasing demand for adventurous menus, I've included recipes from around the world as well as traditional favorites from American culinary regions.

Another consideration of contemporary reality is that the recipes reflect responsible nutritional balance: low in fat and sodium; high in complex carbohydrates, fruits, vegetables and protein. To fill a practical need in many foodservice settings, a nutrient analysis is included for each recipe.

The recipes use convenience products when sensible (who batter dips eight hundred pounds of chicken anymore?). They use contemporary equipment where feasible. Their food costs are realistic for a wide range of operations and budgets. Altogether, the recipes have been developed for the ways you work and the ways your patrons like to eat.

In both the Reference and the Recipe sections, one of my goals has been to provide you with as many tools as possible to practice the art of what I call "chameleon cookery": the ability to change quickly from one cuisine to another without retraining staff or retooling your kitchen. Culinary trends can be as fickle as your patrons, declining quickly from hot concept to fading fad. The key to success is flexibility. For example, try a favorite chicken recipe with pork. If an appetizer is a big hit, consider using it on the lunch or entree menu. To get you started, some variations are included with each recipe. And be sure to use the Flavor Substitutes table to transform a recipe just by changing seasonings; for example, if a recipe calls for curry, try it with cumin and chile powder instead, thus leaping from the Far East to the American Southwest.

It is within the context of adaptability that *Cooking for Fifty* was developed. It's fun to look at recipes not as mandates, but as roads on a map—each offering one of many ways to get from one point to another. I hope you'll enjoy exploring the alternate routes and byways on your road to professional success.

Acknowledgments

I'd like to acknowledge several people who contributed to the evolution and completion of *Cooking for Fifty*.

Alison Brown Cerier, who invited me to join her in the project. Phillip Cooke, who recommended me to Alison in the first place. Amber Dyer, a truly unique young woman who jumped with me into the research fires four years ago and hopefully will continue to stay close to the heat of cooking for years to come. Jim Fuqua, my unofficial partner in more than a decade of projects and my quite official friend through all of them. Larry Gess, who fifteen years ago did everything he could to entice me to teach outdoor cooking classes—and who since has done everything anyone ever could to support me just for being me. The Reverend Jack Noble, who invited me to prepare many of these recipes in the nicely appointed kitchen of our church and helped me learn that feeding the spirit is a life's work.

And finally, thanks to absolutely every cook and foodservice professional I've ever met. Writing about cooking can be tough work, but it doesn't hold a saucepan to those who do it for a living.

List of Tables

Table 1-1.   Timetable for Broiling Beef   6

Table 1-2.   Timetable for Broiling Veal   7

Table 1-3.   Timetable for Broiling Lamb   7

Table 1-4.   Timetable for Broiling Pork   8

Table 1-5.   Timetable for Broiling Smoked Ham   8

Table 1-6.   Timetable for Broiling Poultry   8

Table 1-7.   Timetable for Broiling Seafood   9

Table 1-8.   Timetable for Standard Deep-Frying   10

Table 1-9.   Timetable for Panbroiling Beef   12

Table 1-10.   Timetable for Panbroiling Veal   12

Table 1-11.   Timetable for Panbroiling Pork   12

Table 1-12.   Timetable for Panbroiling Seafood   13

Table 1-13.   Timetable for Panfrying Beef   13

Table 1-14.   Timetable for Panfrying Veal   13

Table 1-15.   Timetable for Panfrying Pork   15

Table 1-16.   Timetable for Panfrying Lamb   15

Table 1-17.   Timetable for Panfrying Poultry   15

Table 1-18.   Timetable for Panfrying Fish   16

Table 1-19.   Timetable for Roasting Beef   18

Table 1-20.   Timetable for Roasting Veal   18

Table 1-21.   Timetable for Roasting Lamb   19

Table 1-22.   Timetable for Roasting Pork   19

Table 1-23.   Timetable for Roasting Fully Cooked Ham   20

Table 1-24.   Timetable for Roasting Poultry   20

Table 1-25.   Timetable for Baking Seafood   20

Table 1-26.   Timetable for Braising Beef   23

Table 1-27.   Timetable for Braising Veal   24

Table 1-28.   Timetable for Braising Pork   24

Table 1-29.   Timetable for Braising Lamb   25

Table 1-30.   Timetable for Simmering Beef   27

Table 1-31.   Timetable for Simmering Veal   27

Table 1-32.   Timetable for Simmering Lamb   27

Table 1-33.   Timetable for Simmering Pork   28

Table 1-34.   Sample Timetable for Pressureless Steaming   30

Table 1-35.   Sample Timetable for 5 psi Pressure Steaming   30

Table 1-36.   Sample Timetable: 15 psi Pressure Steaming Fresh Vegetables   31

Table 1-37.   Sample Timetable: 15 psi Pressure Steaming Frozen Vegetables   31

Table 1-38.   Sample Timetable: 15 psi Pressure Steaming Canned Vegetables   31

Table 1-39.   Sample Timetable: 15 psi Pressure Steaming Seafood   32

Table 1-40.   Sample Timetable: 15 psi Pressure Steaming Meat and Poultry   32

Table 1-41.   Beef Cooking Methods   33

Table 1-42.   Lamb Cooking Methods   34

Table 1-43.   Pork Cooking Methods   35

Table 1-44.   Veal Cooking Methods   35

Table 1-45.   Bakery Products   39

Table 1-46.   Dairy Products   40

Table 1-47.   Fruits   40

Table 1-48.   Grains   41

Table 1-49.   Spices and Herbs   42

Table 1-50.   Vegetables   43

Table 1-51.   Volume   44

Table 1-52.   Weight   45

Table 1-53.   Microwave Time Conversions   46

Table 1-54.   Herbs and Spices Uses   48

Table 1-55.   Flavor Substitutes   50

Table 1-56.   Other Ingredient Substitutes   52

Table 1-57.   Cheeses   52

Table 1-58.   Standard Bowl Capacities   55

Table 1-59.   Insert Pan Dimensions and Capacities   55
Table 1-60.   Mixer Bowl Capacities   55
Table 1-61.   Standard Pot and Pan Capacities   56
Table 1-62.   Foodservice Scoop Capacities   57
Table 1-63.   Steam Kettle Capacities   57
Table 1-64.   Foodservice Can Sizes and Capacities   58
Table 1-65.   Beverages   61
Table 1-66.   Cereal, Crackers, Grains   61
Table 1-67.   Dairy   62
Table 1-68.   Fruits   62
Table 1-69.   Beef   63
Table 1-70.   Lamb   63
Table 1-71.   Pork   64
Table 1-72.   Veal   65
Table 1-73.   Poultry   66
Table 1-74.   Seafood   66
Table 1-75.   Vegetables   67
Table 1-76.   Original Yield Four Portions   68
Table 1-77.   Original Yield Ten Portions   69
Table 1-78.   Original Yield Twenty-five Portions   70
Table 1-79.   Original Yield Fifty Portions   70
Table 1-80.   American Regional Food Terms: Definitions and Origins   88
Table 1-81.   International Food Terms: Definitions and Origins   107
Table 1-82.   Food Word Translations   120
Table 1-83.   French Food Words: Pronunciations and Definitions   127
Table 1-84.   Italian Food Words: Pronunciations and Definitions   142
Table 1-85.   Spanish Food Words: Pronunciations and Definitions   153
Table 1-86.   Cost of Overpouring Liquor   166
Table 1-87.   Beer Yield Per Keg   166

PART ONE

REFERENCE

Cooking Methods: Techniques and Timetables....3

Equivalents, Ingredients, and Equipment.......37

Food Quantities 59

The Language of Food.......................73

Foodservice Planning.......................161

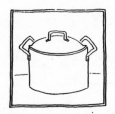

Cooking Methods: Techniques and Timetables

Dry-Heat Cooking Methods
- ▲ **Broiling**
- ▲ **Deep-Frying**
- ▲ **Panbroiling**
- ▲ **Panfrying**
- ▲ **Roasting**
- ▲ **Sautéing**

Moist-Heat Cooking Methods
- ▲ **Braising**
- ▲ **Poaching**
- ▲ **Simmering**
- ▲ **Steaming**

Meat Cooking Methods

Dry-Heat Cooking Methods

Broiling

Broiling is a dry-heat cooking method that is ideal for tender, relatively thin cuts of meat, poultry, seafood, and some vegetables. Because of the intense temperatures radiating from above the foods, broiling is a relatively short cooking process. The dry heat involved in broiling does nothing to break down internal connective tissues (collagen), thus only tender cuts of meats should be broiled. When foods have been broiled correctly, this cooking method yields moist, tender steaks, chops, or other foods and richly colored exterior surfaces. *Note:* With few exceptions, grilling is identical to broiling, but the heat source (heating elements, charcoal, etc.) are under the food rather than above it.

The Technique

1. Preheat Broiler. It is essential that cooking equipment be preheated so that surface browning begins almost immediately. Broiler racks can be oiled or sprayed to help reduce sticking.

2. Adjust Rack. Foods to be broiled should be positioned in accordance with their thickness: The thicker the cut, the farther it should be from the heat in order to prevent the outside surface from darkening too much before the inside is properly cooked. Generally, the correct distance from the heat source ranges from 2 to 6 inches. *Note:* When broiling frozen portion-control foods, increase the distance from the heat source and the cooking time roughly 30% to 50%.

3. Turn Cuts Only Once. When the top surface is nicely browned, turn the cut to expose the bottom surface to the heat. To enhance internal moisture, complete cooking without turning the cut again. *Note:* In grilling, cuts can be "rotated" to achieve aesthetically pleasing grid marks, but still only turned over once.

4. Do Not Use a Fork! When you turn or rotate broiled/grilled foods, never use a kitchen fork. Internal juices are highly pressurized during the cooking process and will use fork holes to quickly (often completely) "escape." The result will be overdone and highly unappreciated grilled foods. The best choice is long-handled kitchen tongs.

5. Test for Doneness. Countless methods have been used to determine doneness of broiled foods. For thicker cuts a quick-read thermometer can be used: Insert halfway into thickest part of the cut and read temperature.

Do not leave the thermometer in the cut during cooking. Another method employs the principle that as protein cooks, it tightens or firms. Therefore, gentle finger pressure will feel an increasingly firm "springiness."

6. Serve ASAP. Broiled foods are relatively thin, so they lose their internal heat quickly. Therefore, serve these foods as soon after cooking as your schedules permit. If you do need to hold broiled foods for extended times, undercook them by at least one level of doneness and store them in warming boxes.

A Note on Broiling Timetables

On the following charts, the designation "NR" in certain columns indicates that it is not recommended to cook particular cuts to certain degrees of doneness. Additionally, in some cases the time for well done cuts is not provided because of the difficulty of interpreting what individuals mean by "well done."

Table 1-1. Timetable for Broiling Beef

Beef Cut	Thickness (inches)	Distance from Heat (inches)	Approximate Total Cooking Time for Desired Degree of Doneness (minutes)	
			Rare	Medium
Shoulder steak	¾	2 to 3	12	14
	1	3 to 4	14	18
Rib steak	¾	2 to 3	8	12
	1	3 to 4	10	15
	1½	4 to 5	20	25
Ribeye steak	¾	2 to 3	8	12
	1	3 to 4	10	15
	1½	4 to 5	20	25
Top loin steak	¾	2 to 3	8	12
	1	3 to 4	10	15
	1½	4 to 5	20	25
Sirloin steak	¾	2 to 3	10	15
	1	3 to 4	16	21
	1½	4 to 5	21	25
Porterhouse steak	¾	2 to 3	8	12
	1	3 to 4	10	15
	1½	4 to 5	20	25
Filet mignon	1	2 to 3	8	12
	2	3 to 4	10	15

Beef Cut	Thickness (inches)	Distance from Heat (inches)	Approximate Total Cooking Time for Desired Degree of Doneness (minutes)	
			Rare	Medium
Beef patties	½ × 4	3 to 4	NR	10
	1 × 4	3 to 4	NR	14
Top round steak	1	3 to 4	15	18
	1½	4 to 5	20	25
Flank steak	1	2 to 3	12	14

NR = not recommended

Table 1-2. Timetable for Broiling Veal

Veal Cut	Thickness (inches)	Distance from Heat (inches)	Approximate Total Cooking Time for Desired Degree of Doneness (minutes)		
			Rare	Medium	Well
Loin/rib chop	1	4	NR	14 to 16	15 to 17
	1½	5	NR	21 to 23	23 to 25
Arm/blade steak	¾	4	NR	14 to 15	15 to 16
Veal patties	½ × 4	4	NR	8 to 10	10 to 12

NR = not recommended

Table 1-3. Timetable for Broiling Lamb

Lamb Cut	Thickness (inches)	Distance from Heat (inches)	Approximate Total Cooking Time (minutes) (medium-rare to medium)
Shoulder chop	¾ to 1	3 to 4	7 to 11 minutes
Loin/rib chop	1	3 to 4	7 to 11 minutes
	1½	4 to 5	15 to 19 minutes
Sirloin chop	¾ to 1	3 to 4	12 to 15 minutes
Leg steak	¾ to 1	3 to 4	14 to 18 minutes
Kabob cubes	1 to 1½	4 to 5	8 to 12 minutes
Lamb patties	½ × 4	3	5 to 8 minutes

Table 1-4. Timetable for Broiling Pork

Pork Cut	Thickness (inches)	Distance from Heat (inches)	Approximate Total Cooking Time (minutes) (Internal Temperature 160°F)
Loin/rib chop	¾	4	8 to 14
	1½	4	19 to 25
Butterfly chop	1	4	11 to 15
	1½	4	16 to 18
Blade chop, bone-in	¾	4	13 to 15
	1	4	26 to 29
Shoulder chop, bone-in	¾	4	16 to 18
	1	4	18 to 20
Kabob cubes, leg	1	4	9 to 13
Tenderloin	1	4	9 to 13
Pork patties	½ × 4	4	7 to 9

Table 1-5. Timetable for Broiling Smoked Ham

Smoked Ham Cut	Thickness (inches)	Distance from Heat (inches)	Approximate Total Cooking Time (minutes)
Ham slice	½	4	8 to 10
	1	4	14 to 16
Ham kabobs	1 to 1½	4	8 to 12
Loin chop	½ to 1	4	15 to 20
Canadian bacon	½	4	6 to 8

Table 1-6. Timetable for Broiling Poultry

Poultry Variety	Weight (pounds)	Distance from Heat (inches)	Approximate Total Cooking Time
Chicken, quarters	1 to 3	4 to 6	20 to 30 min
Chicken, parts	½ to 1	4 to 6	15 to 20 min
Duck, split	1 to 3	7 to 8	40 to 60 min
Turkey, parts	4 to 6	8 to 9	1 to 1½ hour

Table 1-7. Timetable for Broiling Seafood

Seafood Cut	Size	Distance from Heat (inches)	Approximate Total Cooking Time (minutes)
Flatfish, dressed	3 to 4 lb	NR	NR
Steaks	½ in	2 to 4	4 to 5
	¾ in	2 to 4	6 to 8
	1 in	3 to 4	8 to 10
	1½ in	3 to 4	12 to 15
	2 in	4	15 to 20
Fillets	½ in	2 to 4	4 to 5
	¾ in	2 to 4	6 to 8
	1 in	3 to 4	8 to 10
Shrimp, peeled	15/lb	3	5 to 8
Clams, shucked	—	4	5 to 8
Oysters, shucked	—	4	5 to 8
Lobsters			
Live, whole	1 lb	4	12 to 15
Tails, frozen	½ lb	4	10 to 15

NR = not recommended

Deep-Frying

Deep-frying is a dry-heat cooking method that is used for thin, often portion-size, cuts of tender meat, poultry, seafood, vegetables, and some pastries (e.g., doughnuts). It is common to use this process with fully cooked, frozen commercial products. When not prepared commercially, nearly all foods to be deep-fried (like their panfried counterparts) receive a preliminary dip into batter or breading. As the name implies, deep-frying requires enough cooking oil to completely and freely cover all foods being cooked. Deep-fried foods develop a delightful golden color and are moist and tender. They are often served with a sauce or gravy that is always prepared separately.

The Technique

1. Select Equipment. Deep-frying equipment is incredibly diverse. Gas, electric, standard, low-pressure, high-pressure, and automatic units are available in various capacities. The key to your choice is the workload the unit must carry.

2. Preheat Oil. The cooking oil must be preheated to proper temperature so that cooking begins immediately. If the oil is not hot enough, it will be absorbed by the food and not really deep-fry at all. If the oil is too hot, the outside surfaces will brown excessively before the inside cooks. The temperature setting for deep-frying should follow the general guideline that applies to all foods and cooking methods: The thicker the cut, the lower the temperature setting. The right temperature allows outside surfaces to brown nicely as the inside cooks to proper doneness.

3. Prepare Food for Deep-Frying. Unless commercially prepared foods are used, all foods should be cut into portion sizes and (with the exception of potatoes) normally coated with a batter or breading.

4. Add Food to Oil. Lower baskets into the hot oil and agitate slightly to prevent foods from sticking to the basket or each other. Follow recommended guidelines for cooking time.

5. Remove and Drain. When deep-fried foods are done, remove the basket and shake off excess oil. If desired, drain deep-fried foods on absorbent paper. Do not salt fried foods prior to service. Because salt draws moisture from the foods, adding it now will reduce breading quality.

6. Serve ASAP. Deep-fried foods lose heat quickly. In addition, as they rest after cooking, internal moisture tends to reduce the crispness of the golden brown breaded surface.

Table 1-8. Timetable for Standard Deep-Frying

Product	Fryer Temperature (°F)	Approximate Cooking Time (minutes)
Chicken portions		
Raw to done	325	9 to 11
Precooked, breaded	350	6 to 8
Fish fillets, frozen	375	4
Fish sticks	375	3 to 4
Fritters	375	3 to 5
Oysters	375	2 to 4
Scallops, fresh	370	4
Shrimp, frozen	350	3 to 5
Meat cutlets, ½-inch thick	350	4
French fries		
Raw to done, ¼ cut	350	5
Raw to done, ⅜ cut	350	6
Blanched, ¼ cut	350	2½
Blanched, ⅜ cut	350	3
Onion rings	350	3

Panbroiling

Panbroiling is a dry-heat cooking method that is used with thin cuts of tender meat, poultry, and seafood. Panbroiling can be done in skillets, flattop grills, and tilt kettles. Regardless of the equipment, heat is conducted directly to the bottom surface of panbroiled foods, which means the cooking process is very quick. The dry heat involved in panbroiling does not tenderize foods, so the cuts must be naturally tender. When foods have been panbroiled correctly, they are nicely seared and cooked to ideal internal doneness. Because the cuts are fairly thin, the range of degrees of doneness is not as great as that of other broil or grill methods.

The Technique

1. Preheat Pans/Equipment.   It is essential that cooking equipment be preheated so that searing and browning begin almost immediately. If desired, oil or nonstick sprays can be used to help prevent sticking.

2. Choose Appropriate Heat.   Foods to be panbroiled should be fairly thin, but because thickness varies, follow the general guideline that applies to all foods and cooking methods: The thicker the cut, the lower the temperature setting. This method allows outside surfaces to brown nicely as the inside cooks to proper doneness.

3. Turn Cuts Only Once.   When the top surface is nicely browned, turn the cut to expose the bottom surface to the heat. To enhance internal moisture, complete cooking without turning the cut again.

4. Do Not Use a Fork!   As in other broiling methods, internal juices are highly pressurized during the cooking process and will quickly (often completely) use fork holes to escape. The best choices are spatulas and long-handled kitchen tongs.

5. Do Not Add Liquid.   Panbroiling is a dry-heat cooking method. The introduction of any liquid will convert the dish from panbroiled to braised. If desired, sauces can be made after the panbroiling process.

6. Serve ASAP.   Panbroiled foods are relatively thin, so they lose their internal heat quickly. Therefore, serve these foods as soon after cooking as your schedules permit. If you need to hold broiled foods for extended times, undercook them by at least one level of doneness and store them in warming boxes.

Table 1-9. Timetable for Panbroiling Beef

Beef Cut	Thickness (inches)	Appropriate Temperature Setting	Approximate Total Cooking Time (minutes)
Ribeye steak	½	Medium-high	3 to 5
Top loin steak	¼	Medium-high	2 to 3
Eye round steak	½	Medium-high	2 to 4
	1	Medium	8 to 10
Tenderloin	¾ to 1	Medium	6 to 9
Round tip	⅛ to ¼	Medium-high	1
Sirloin, boneless	¾ to 1	Medium	10 to 12
Top round	1	Medium	13 to 16
Beef patties	½ × 4	Medium	7 to 8

Table 1-10. Timetable for Panbroiling Veal

Veal Cut	Thickness (inches)	Appropriate Temperature Setting	Approximate Total Cooking Time (minutes)
Loin/rib chop	¾ to 1	Medium	10 to 14
Blade steak	¾	Medium-low	13 to 15
Veal patties	½ × 4	Medium-low	6 to 9

Table 1-11. Timetable for Panbroiling Pork

Pork Cut	Thickness (inches)	Appropriate Temperature Setting	Approximate Total Cooking Time (minutes)
Loin/rib chop, bone-in	½	Medium	7 to 10
	1	Medium	12 to 17
Loin chop, boneless	½	Medium	7 to 10
	1	Medium	10 to 14
Butterfly chop	½	Medium	8 to 11
	1	Medium	12 to 17
Pork patties	½ × 4	Medium	7 to 9

Table 1-12. Timetable for Panbroiling Seafood

Seafood	Thickness (inches)	Appropriate Temperature Setting	Approximate Total Cooking Time (minutes)
Steaks	½	High	4 to 5
	¾	Medium-high	6 to 8
	1	Medium	8 to 10
Fillets	½	High	4 to 5
	¾	Medium-high	6 to 8
	1	Medium	8 to 10
Shrimp, peeled	15/lb	Medium-high	4 to 6
Clams, shucked	—	Medium-high	4 to 6
Oysters, shucked	—	Medium-high	4 to 6

Panfrying

Panfrying is a dry-heat cooking method somewhere between panbroiling and the sauté method. Like both, this cooking method is used for thin, often portion-size, cuts of tender meat, poultry, or seafood. A difference is that in panfrying, a preliminary dip into batter or breading is quite common. Panfrying requires more oil than the sauté method: For a general guideline, the oil should be high enough to measure about ⅓ to ½ of the thickness of the pieces being cooked. In the panfrying procedure, cuts develop a delightful golden color and are moist and tender. They are often served with a sauce or gravy, but unlike the sauté method and panbroiling, that sauce is rarely created in the same cooking pan or equipment.

The Technique

1. Select Equipment. As the term implies, panfrying can be done in individual pans. It also can be done in tilt or brazier kettles. If pans are your choice, they should be heavy enough to hold and maintain uniform heat and large enough to prevent overcrowding of cooking portions.

2. Preheat Oil. The cooking oil must be preheated to proper temperature so that cooking begins immediately. If the oil is not hot enough, the food will absorb it and not really panfry at all. If the oil is too hot, the outside surfaces will brown excessively before the inside cooks. For general purposes, the temperature setting for panfrying should follow the general guideline that applies to all foods and cooking methods: The thicker the cut, the lower the temperature setting. This procedure allows outside surfaces to brown nicely as the inside cooks to proper doneness.

3. Add Food to Oil. For appearance sake, place the presentation side of your panfried food in the oil first. Move the pan a bit from time to time to encourage even browning.

4. Turn Only Once. When the bottom surface is nicely browned (and a small amount of juice appears through the top batter layer) turn the cut to expose the uncooked surface to the oil. If you turn batter-coated or breaded panfried foods more than once, presentation quality is reduced.

5. Remove and Drain. When panfried foods are done, remove them with tongs or spatula (do not use a kitchen fork) and drain on racks or absorbent paper.

6. Serve ASAP. Panfried foods lose heat quickly. In addition, as they rest after cooking, internal moisture tends to reduce the crispness of the golden brown breaded surface.

Table 1-13. Timetable for Panfrying Beef

Beef Cut	Thickness (inches)	Optimum Heat Level	Approximate Total Cooking Time for Desired Degree of Doneness (minutes)	
			Rare	Medium
Flank strips	⅛ to ¼	High	1	2 to 3
Sirloin strips	⅛ to ¼	High	1	2 to 3
Top round strips	⅛ to ¼	High	1	2 to 3
Cutlets	⅛	High	NR	3 to 4
Beef patties	½	Medium	NR	5 to 6

NR = not recommended

Table 1-14. Timetable for Panfrying Veal

Veal Cut	Thickness (inches)	Optimum Heat Level	Approximate Total Cooking Time for Desired Degree of Doneness (minutes)
Cutlets	⅛	High	3 to 4
	¼	Medium	5 to 6
Veal patties	½	Medium	5 to 7

Table 1-15. Timetable for Panfrying Pork

Pork Cut	Thickness (inches)	Optimum Heat Level	Approximate Total Cooking Time for Desired Degree of Doneness (minutes)
Loin/rib chop,	¼	High	4 to 5
bone-in	½	Medium-high	5 to 6
	¾	Medium	8 to 10
	1	Med-Low	13 to 15
Loin chop, boneless	¼	Medium-high	4 to 5
Loin/butterfly chop,	½	Medium	5 to 8
boneless	¾	Medium	8 to 13
	1	Medium	13 to 18
Sirloin chop	¾	Medium	14 to 15
Tenderloin, sliced	¼	High	3 to 4
	½	High	4 to 5
Pork patties	½	Medium	7 to 9
Sirloin cutlet	¼	Medium-high	4 to 5
Cubed steak	½	Medium	6 to 7

Table 1-16. Timetable for Panfrying Lamb

Lamb Cut	Thickness (inches)	Optimum Heat Level	Approximate Total Cooking Time for Desired Degree of Doneness (minutes)		
			Rare	Medium	Well
Leg, sliced	⅛ to ¼	High	2	2 to 3	NR

NR = not recommended

Table 1-17. Timetable for Panfrying Poultry

Poultry Cut	Weight (ounces)	Optimum Heat Level	Approximate Total Cooking Time for Desired Degree of Doneness (minutes)
Breast, fresh	6	Medium-high	15 to 20
Breast, frozen	6	Medium	20 to 30
Leg/thigh, fresh	6	Medium-high	20 to 30
Leg/thigh, frozen	6	Medium	30 to 40
Quarters, fresh	12	Medium-high	20 to 30
Quarters, frozen	12	Medium	30 to 40

Table 1-18. Timetable for Panfrying Fish

Fish Variety	Thickness	Optimum Heat Level	Approximate Total Cooking Time for Desired Degree of Doneness (minutes)
Steaks	½ in	Medium	5 to 6
	¾ in	Medium	7 to 9
	1 in	Medium	10 to 11
	1½ in	Medium	15 to 17
	2 in	Medium	20 to 22
Fillets	½ in	Medium	5 to 6
	¾ in	Medium	7 to 9
	1 in	Medium	10 to 11
Shrimp, peeled	15/lb	Medium	8 to 10
Clams, shucked	—	Medium	4 to 5
Oysters, shucked	—	Medium	4 to 5

Roasting

Roasting is a dry-heat cooking method that is used with larger cuts of relatively tender meat, poultry, and seafood. In the cases of flatfish and other seafood, the generally used term is not *roasting* but *baking*, yet the process is the same.

In roasting, oven heat gradually penetrates the cut at the same time it develops a delightfully colored, flavorful outside surface. The dry heat of roasting does not tenderize foods, so the cuts must be tender naturally. One key to successful roasting is a postcooking resting period that permits internal juices to redistribute throughout the cut. When foods have been roasted and rested correctly, they carve nicely and retain moisture excellently. Although slow-roast, conventional, and convection ovens are normally used, the same principles of roasting apply to spit-turned rotisseries and dome-covered charcoal cookers.

Roasting is a flexible cooking method. A variety of preparation and holding equipment is available, and foods prepared in this way can be completed well in advance of service.

The Technique

1. Select Appropriate Foods.   As stated, roasting is used for larger cuts of tender meats.

2. Select Appropriate Oven Temperature.   Generally speaking, the optimum temperature for roasted foods follows this traditional guideline: The correct temperature permits simultaneous internal cooking and outer browning.

3. Option: Bard or Lard.   These processes can be used to increase the fat level of very lean meats. Barding is a process in which thin slices of fat are wrapped around the outside of the cut. Larding calls for thin strips of fat to be inserted directly into the cut.

4. Option: Tie or Truss.   Occasionally it will be desirable to secure the cut with cotton twine, particularly with some poultry and with roasts that are formed and rolled.

5. Select Proper Pan.   Roasting pans should be shallow, not deep, permitting the entire outer surface to receive uniform exposure to oven heat, and thus cook (and brown) evenly.

6. Place Cuts on Racks.   It is very important that cuts not touch the surface of the roasting pan. If they do, heat will be conducted directly onto the cut, greatly accelerating cooking on that surface, which will lead to irregular internal cooking and excessive surface darkening. Use pan racks or line roasting pans with carrots, celery and/or sliced or chopped onions. Do not let cuts touch each other on the roasting pans. Do not cover cuts: Covering creates excess moisture that interferes with browning and the roasting method.

7. Option: Insert Meat Thermometer.   If desired, a meat thermometer (not the quick-read variety) can be inserted into the fleshiest part of the cut so that the tip rests in the middle of the cut. In poultry, the thermometer should be inserted in the thickest part of the thigh.

8. Remove Before Completely Cooked.   It is very important to remove roasted cuts before they reach their final degree of doneness. Cover the cuts and allow them to rest. Roasted cuts continue to cook after removal from the oven, and juices will distribute evenly throughout. The amount of resting time necessary varies with the size of the cut: The larger the cut, the longer the resting period. *Note:* If adequate resting time is not permitted, much of the internal juice will purge from the roasted cut, reducing product quality and portion yield.

9. Carve Immediately Before Service.   When feasible, do not carve roasted cuts until just before service. If it is necessary to carve well before service, layer the carved cuts, ladle with juices and cover.

Roasting Frozen Cuts

Cuts can be roasted from the frozen state as well as directly from the refrigerator. Generally, the amount of time required to roast from the frozen state will be 30% to 50% longer than for chilled or defrosted cuts.

Table 1-19. Timetable for Roasting Beef

Beef Cut	Weight (pounds)	Oven Temperature (°F)	Approximate Minutes Per Pound for Desired Degree of Doneness		
			Rare	Medium	Well
Rib roast	6 to 8	300 to 325	23 to 25	27 to 30	32 to 35
	4 to 6	300 to 325	26 to 32	34 to 38	40 to 42
Ribeye roast	4 to 6	350	18 to 20	20 to 22	22 to 24
Rump roast	4 to 6	300 to 325	NR	25 to 27	28 to 30
Round tip roast	3½ to 4	300 to 325	30 to 35	35 to 38	38 to 40
	6 to 8	300 to 325	22 to 25	25 to 30	30 to 35
Top round roast	4 to 6	300 to 325	20 to 25	25 to 28	28 to 30
Tenderloin roast					
Whole	4 to 6	425		45 to 60	
Half	2 to 3	425		35 to 45	
Ground beef loaf	1½ to 2½	300 to 325		1 to 1½ hours	

NR = not recommended

Table 1-20. Timetable for Roasting Veal

Veal Cut	Weight (pounds)	Oven Temperature (°F)	Approximate Minutes Per Pound for Desired Degree of Doneness		
			Rare	Medium	Well
Rib roast	4 to 5	300 to 325	NR	25 to 27	29 to 31
Loin roast					
Bone-in	3 to 4	300 to 325	NR	34 to 36	38 to 40
Boneless	2 to 3	300 to 325	NR	18 to 20	22 to 24
Crown roast	7½ to 9½	300 to 325	NR	19 to 21	21 to 23
Ribeye roast	2 to 3	300 to 325	NR	26 to 28	30 to 33
Rump roast	2 to 3	300 to 325	NR	33 to 35	37 to 40
Shoulder roast	2½ to 3	300 to 325	NR	31 to 34	34 to 37

NR = not recommended

Table 1-21. Timetable for Roasting Lamb

Lamb Cut	Weight (pounds)	Oven Temperature (°F)	Approximate Minutes Per Pound for Desired Degree of Doneness		
			Rare	Medium	Well
Leg roast					
Whole, bone-in	7 to 9	325	15 to 20	20 to 25	25 to 30
Whole, bone-in	5 to 7	325	20 to 25	25 to 30	30 to 35
Boneless	4 to 7	325	25 to 30	30 to 35	35 to 40
Shank half	3 to 4	325	30 to 35	40 to 45	45 to 50
Sirloin half	3 to 4	325	25 to 30	35 to 40	45 to 50
Shoulder roast,					
boneless	3½ to 5	325	30 to 35	35 to 40	45 to 50
Rib rack	1½ to 2	375	30 to 35	35 to 40	40 to 45
Rib rack	2 to 3	375	25 to 30	30 to 35	35 to 40

Table 1-22. Timetable for Roasting Pork

Pork Cut	Weight (pounds)	Oven Temperature (°F)	Approximate Minutes Per Pound to Reach 160°F Internal Temperature
Loin roast			
Center, bone-in	3 to 5	300 to 325	26 to 31
Sirloin, boneless	2½ to 3½	300 to 325	33 to 38
Top (double)	3 to 4	300 to 325	33 to 38
Top (single)	2 to 4	300 to 325	30 to 40
Crown roast	6 to 10	300 to 325	20 to 25
Leg roast			
Whole, bone-in	12	300 to 325	23 to 25
Top (inside)	3½	300 to 325	38 to 42
Bottom (outside)	3½	300 to 325	40 to 45
Boston, boneless	3 to 4	300 to 325	40 to 45
Tenderloin roast	½ to 1	425	27 to 32
Ground pork loaf	1 to 1½	350	55 to 60
Ham, fresh			
Whole, boneless	8 to 12	300 to 325	17 to 21
Whole, bone-in	14 to 16	300 to 325	18 to 20
Half, bone-in	7 to 8	300 to 325	22 to 25
Portion, bone-in	3 to 5	300 to 325	35 to 40

Table 1-23. Timetable for Roasting Fully Cooked Ham

Fully Cooked Ham Cut	Weight (pounds)	Oven Temperature (°F)	Approximate Minutes Per Pound to Reach 140°F Internal Temperature
Whole, boneless	8 to 12	300 to 325	13 to 17
Whole, bone-in	14 to 16	300 to 325	12 to 14
Half, bone-in	6 to 8	300 to 325	17 to 20
Half, boneless	6 to 8	300 to 325	14 to 17
Portion, boneless	3 to 4	300 to 325	20 to 23

Table 1-24. Timetable for Roasting Poultry

Poultry (thawed)	Dressed Weight (pounds)	Oven Temperature (°F)	Approximate Time (hours) to Reach 170°F Internal Temperature
Chicken, whole	2½ to 4	325	1 to 1½
Duck	4 to 7	325	1 to 2
Goose	6 to 8	325	2½ to 3½
	8 to 12	325	3½ to 4½
Turkey, whole	6 to 8	325	3 to 3½
	8 to 12	325	3½ to 4½
	12 to 16	325	4½ to 5½
	16 to 20	325	5½ to 6½
	20 to 25	325	6½ to 7½
Turkey, halves	3 to 8	325	2 to 3
and pieces	8 to 12	325	3 to 4
Turkey breast, boneless	4 to 10	325	3 to 4

Table 1-25. Timetable for Baking Seafood

Seafood (thawed)	Weight and/or Thickness	Oven Temperature (°F)	Approximate Total Time to Bake Completely (minutes)
Flatfish, dressed	3 to 4 lb	350 to 400	45 to 60
Steaks	½ in	350 to 400	5 to 6
	¾ in	350 to 400	7 to 9
	1 in	350 to 400	10 to 11
	1½ in	350 to 400	15 to 17
	2 in	350 to 400	20 to 22

Seafood (thawed)	Weight and/or Thickness	Oven Temperature (°F)	Approximate Total Time to Bake Completely (minutes)
Fillets	½ in	350 to 400	5 to 6
	¾ in	350 to 400	7 to 9
	1 in	350 to 400	10 to 11
Sticks, breaded, frozen	1 oz	400	15 to 20
Shrimp, peeled	15/lb	350	12 to 15
Clams, shucked	—	450	12 to 15
Oysters, shucked	—	450	12 to 15
Lobsters			
Live, whole	1 lb	400	15 to 20
Tails, frozen	½ lb	450	20 to 30

Sautéing

The sauté cooking process is a dry-heat cooking method that is used for thin cuts of tender meat, poultry, seafood, and vegetables. Foods are prepared in very hot pans (or other appropriate equipment—tilt kettles, flattop grills, woks, etc.) in a small amount of heated oil. The sauté procedure develops crisp surfaces and moist, tender interiors. Sautéed proteins are normally served with a sauce that is often prepared in the same cooking pan or equipment. Based on a French term meaning "to skip and jump," the sauté method often includes a familiar flipping and tossing motion during cooking. The sauté method is an extremely fast cooking process that yields a world of culinary creations.

The Technique

1. Appropriate Foods. Foods to be sautéed simply must be thin and tender. High heat means the outer searing occurs rapidly, so thicker cuts do not have time to cook completely.

2. Prepare Foods. Because the sauté process is a dry-heat cooking method, all foods should be thoroughly dry before cooking. A light dredging in flour or sometimes cornstarch helps accomplish this crucial step.

3. Select Equipment. An ideal sauté pan has sloping sides to control flipping and turning foods. Woks are actually larger, round-bottom versions of sauté pans. A straight-sided, single-handled sauté pan is known by the French term *sautoir* (saw-TWAW). Pans should ideally be heavy enough to retain heat throughout the cooking process and large enough to prevent overcrowding cooked foods. Alternate equipment for the sauté process is tilt or brazier kettles.

4. Preheat Equipment and Oil. For successful sauté procedures, both the pan or equipment and the cooking oil must be preheated to proper temperature. Preheating helps prevent the food from sticking and prevents the oil from being absorbed by the food. Cooking oil is hot enough to sauté when it appears to shimmer but not smoke.

5. Add Food to Oil. A definite sizzling sound should be heard immediately. If the food does not sizzle when it hits the oil, the oil is not hot enough for the sauté process to occur. Agitate the pan or toss the food to encourage even browning. Because the sauté procedure is always extremely fast, cooking timetables are of no real use.

6. Serve ASAP. Sautéed foods lose heat quickly and should in every possible case be served immediately, especially when preliminary breading or dredging has created a crisp outside surface.

Moist-Heat Cooking Methods

Braising

Braising is a moist-heat cooking method that is ideal for less tender, often economical cuts of meat and poultry. Braising yields characteristically hearty menu items, such as ragouts, stews, and pot roasts. Typically, braising is a rather long process because it slowly breaks down the internal connective tissues (collagen) that make proteins tough. Although braising can certainly be used with naturally tender proteins (such as chicken breasts), its *purpose* is to produce succulent, fork-tender specialties with cuts that otherwise would be tough to eat. When done correctly, braising yields delightful, flavorful results.

The Technique

1. Cooking Equipment. Choose fairly heavy pots with tightly fitting covers. Alternatives to stove top pots are large oven brazier pans, steam kettles, and tilt kettles.

2. Initial Searing. Lightly brown the food you are going to braise before you braise it. This procedure is not, as is commonly thought, to seal in the juices, but rather to add flavor and color to the finished dish.

3. Liquid. Because moisture is required to break down connective tissues, all braising procedures call for the addition of liquid (water, stock, wine). The question is: How much? A general guideline is: Add enough liquid to cover no more than one third the height of the food to be cooked. At this level, the surfaces become glazed and sealed, giving the food an appealing color. At the same time, because moisture is present constantly, the food will become tender.

4. Cover the Pot. All braised preparations must be done *under cover!* Moisture is mandatory for tenderization, and a covered cooking vessel helps make the sauce that is part of the braising process.

5. Gentle Cooking. Braising does not occur if the cooking temperature is too high. The word braising implies no more than slow bubbling, not boiling. If you even think *boil*, the cut will become tough, dry, and unpalatable. Stovetop cooking temperatures should be adjusted to ensure a gentle simmer. If you plan to braise in the oven, a temperature range of 300°F to 325°F is recommended.

6. Complete Cooking. Braised food is done when a cooking fork inserts and comes out easily. It is a function of connective tissues breaking down under ideal conditions. At first those tissues will "grasp" (or connect to) the fork's tines. As tenderization occurs, the connective tissues relax and let go.

Table 1-26. Timetable for Braising Beef

Beef Cut	Approximate Thickness (inches)	Approximate Weight (pounds)	Approximate Cooking Time
Blade pot roast	—	3 to 5	1½ to 2½ hours
Arm pot roast	—	3 to 5	2 to 3 hours
Chuck roast	—	3 to 5	2 to 3 hours
Short ribs	2 × 2 × 4	—	1½ to 2½ hours
Flank steak	—	1½ to 2	1½ to 2½ hours
Round steak	¾ to 1	—	1 to 1½ hours
Swiss steak	1½ to 2½	—	2 to 3 hours

Table 1-27. Timetable for Braising Veal

Veal Cut	Approximate Thickness (inches)	Approximate Weight (pounds)	Approximate Cooking Time
Boneless breast (stuffed)	—	2 to 2½	1¼ to 1½ hours
Boneless breast (rolled/tied)	—	2 to 3	1½ to 2½ hours
Riblets	—	—	50 to 70 min
Arm steak	¾ to 1	—	45 to 60 min
Blade steak	¾ to 1	—	45 to 60 min
Round steak	¼	—	30 min
Round steak	½	—	45 min
Shoulder roast	—	3½ to 4	2 to 2½ hours
Loin/rib chop	½	—	8 to 10 min
Loin/rib chop	¾ to 1	—	20 to 25 min

Table 1-28. Timetable for Braising Pork

Pork Cut	Approximate Thickness (inches)	Approximate Weight (pounds)	Approximate Cooking Time
Shoulder steak	¾	—	40 to 50 min
Cubes	1 to 1¼	—	45 to 60 min
Leg steak	⅛ to ¼	—	5 to 7 min
Sirloin	—	2½ to 3½	1½ to 2½ hours
Chops			
Rib/loin	¾	—	30 min
Boneless loin	1½	—	45 min
Ribs			
Spareribs	—	—	1½ hours
Backribs	—	—	1½ hours
Country style	—	—	1½ to 2 hours
Tenderloin			
Whole	—	½ to 1	40 to 45 min
Slices	½	—	25 min
Boston blade			
Boneless	—	2½ to 3½	2 to 2½ hours
Bone-in	—	3 to 4	2¼ to 3 hours
Picnic shoulder			
Boneless	—	2 to 4	2½ to 3 hours
Bone-in	—	4 to 8	2¼ to 3 hours

Table 1-29. Timetable for Braising Lamb

Lamb Cut	Approximate Thickness (inches)	Approximate Weight (pounds)	Approximate Cooking Time
Breast			
Stuffed	—	2 to 3	1½ to 2 hours
Rolled	—	1½ to 2	1½ to 2 hours
Riblets	—	¾ to 1	1½ to 2 hours
Neck slices	¾	—	1 hour
Shanks	—	¾ to 1	1 to 1½ hours
Shoulder chop	¾ to 1	—	45 to 60 min
Stew cubes	1½	—	1½ to 2 hours

Poaching

Poaching is a moist-heat cooking method that is ideal for large or small cuts of tender meat, poultry, and seafood. Similar to simmering and braising, poaching calls for foods to be gently cooked (stove top or oven) in liquid that might or might not completely cover the foods. One key point that distinguishes poaching from simmering and braising is a slightly lower temperature. Poaching liquid should never bubble on the surface; the temperature at which this condition exists is approximately 170°F. Poaching is a healthy cooking choice since it does not add fats to food.

The Technique

1. Choose the Right Cuts. Poaching can be used with various sizes of tender proteins. Although typically used for seafood and chicken, poaching procedures do exist for tender red meats.

2. Cooking Equipment. Poaching can be done in a variety of equipment: special poaching pans, stock pots, roasting pans, sauté pans, brazier pans, steam kettles, and tilt kettles. The key is to have enough room not only to cook the food, but to easily remove it.

3. Prepare Cooking Equipment. It is a good idea to rub the surface of cooking equipment with oil or butter and to sprinkle it with minced aromatic vegetables. This process helps prevents foods from sticking, and contributes to the flavor of the final dish.

4. Choose Cooking Liquid. Appropriate cooking liquids include water, stocks, and occasionally beer. An acid such as citrus juice, wine, or vinegar is often added to help set up tender proteins. Depending on the recipe, the amount of poaching liquid will vary from completely covering foods to only partially covering them. In the latter case, cover the cooking equipment with a lid, or cover exposed surfaces of food with parchment or buttered paper. In any case, poaching liquid should start out cold.

5. Cook Gently. Poaching demands gentle, slow cooking. Bubbles should barely leave the bottom surface of the cooking equipment.

6. Test for Doneness. Poaching is complete when the cooked food springs back firmly when pressed. As when prepared with other cooking methods, poached fish will flake easily. Timetables are of little use in determining appropriate poaching times.

7. Serve Hot or Cold. If poached foods are to be served hot, remove them from the liquid and serve as soon as possible. If you serve poached foods cold, allow them to cool completely in the cooking liquid: They absorb tremendous flavor as they cool.

Simmering

Simmering is a moist-heat cooking method ideal for smaller cuts of less tender, often economical cuts of meat and poultry. Often called "stewing," simmering is usually a long process because it slowly breaks down the internal connective tissues (collagen) that make proteins tough. Although simmering can certainly be used with naturally tender proteins (e.g., chicken breasts), it is more commonly used to tenderize cuts that otherwise would be tough when prepared in dry-heat cooking methods. When done correctly, simmering produces flavorful soups and stews.

The Technique

1. Choose the Right Cuts. Simmering calls for small cuts of less tender proteins. The size of the cuts (and amount of cooking liquid) distinguishes simmering from braising. In some cases (e.g., corned beef brisket) the cuts are larger, but generally cubes no larger than 1 inch are desirable.

2. Cooking Equipment. Choose fairly heavy pots, brazier pans, steam kettles, and tilt kettles.

3. Initial Searing. Lightly brown the food you are going to simmer before proceeding. As is the case with braising, this step adds critical (and delightful) flavor and color to the finished dish.

4. Liquid. Because moisture is required to break down connective tissues, all simmering procedures call for the addition of liquid (water, stock, wine). Add enough liquid to completely cover the food to be cooked.

5. Do Not Cover the Pot.   Because some of the intense flavor of simmered dishes is developed by liquid reduction, you should not cover the cooking container.

6. Cook Gently.   Like braising, simmering calls for gentle, slow bubbling—not boiling.

7. Complete Cooking.   Simmered foods are done when a cooking fork inserts and comes out easily. It is a function of connective tissues breaking down under ideal conditions: At first those tissues will "grasp" (or connect to) the fork's tines. As tenderization occurs, the connective tissues relax and let go.

Table 1-30. Timetable for Simmering Beef

Beef Cut	Approximate Thickness (inches)	Approximate Weight (pounds)	Approximate Cooking Time (hours)
Corned beef	—	4 to 6	3½ to 4½
Shank, sliced	—	3	2½ to 3½
Beef cubes	1 × 1 × 1	—	2 to 3

Table 1-31. Timetable for Simmering Veal

Veal Cut	Approximate Thickness (inches)	Approximate Weight (pounds)	Approximate Cooking Time (hours)
Breast, boneless	1	—	1¼ to 1½
Shank, sliced	1½	—	1 to 1¼
Veal cubes	1 to 1½	—	¾ to 1

Table 1-32. Timetable for Simmering Lamb

Lamb Cut	Approximate Thickness (inches)	Approximate Weight (pounds)	Approximate Cooking Time (hours)
Lamb cubes	1 to 1½	—	1 to 1½

Table 1-33. Timetable for Simmering Pork

Pork Cut	Approximate Thickness (inches)	Approximate Weight (pounds)	Approximate Cooking Time (hours)
Spareribs	—	—	2 to 2½
Country ribs	—	—	2 to 2½
Pork cubes	1 × 1 × 1	—	¾ to 1
Smoked Ham			
Ham, whole	—	10 to 16	4½ to 5
Ham, half	—	5 to 8	3 to 4
Picnic shoulder	—	5 to 8	3½ to 4
Shoulder roll	—	2 to 4	1½ to 2
Ham hocks	—	—	2 to 2½

Steaming

Steaming is a moist-heat cooking method ideal for smaller cuts of tender meat, poultry, seafood, and vegetables. In this process food cooks at higher temperatures than boiling water for a short time. Because of the relatively short cooking times, steaming retains more nutrients than other moist-heat methods (e.g., poaching or boiling). The short cooking times also mean that steaming does not provide the environment necessary for breakdown of the internal connective tissues (collagen) that make proteins tough, so the food must be tender naturally. Steaming equipment varies greatly: pressureless, low pressure, and high pressure. The higher the pressure obtainable, the shorter the cooking times. In addition, steaming can be done on top of the stove.

The Technique: Stovetop Steaming

1. Choose the Right Foods.   Steaming calls for small pieces of tender proteins and vegetables.

2. Choose Equipment.   Stovetop steamers consist of a large pot with an inner perforated pot or rack.

3. Place Liquid in Steamer.   Add enough liquid (water, stock, etc.) to level that will not touch bottom of rack or insert. Heat liquid to a boil.

4. Place Food on Racks in Pans.   Steamer pans are ordinarily perforated to permit drainage of excess moisture. To permit adequate exposure to all surfaces, do not overcrowd foods. Put racks or inserts in steamer.

5. Cover Steamer.   To create the proper environment for steam to form and cook food, the cover should be heavy and fit securely.

6. Maintain Proper Temperature.   The liquid in the pot should be maintained at a gentle boil to ensure a steaming environment. Follow recipe guidelines for steaming times.

7. Remove Cover Carefully.   Always take care when removing the cover from a steaming container: As you lift the cover, tilt the bottom surface away from your face to allow steam to escape away from you.

The Technique: Pressure Steaming

When you use a pressurized steamer, internal temperatures increase in direct proportion to the amount of pressure maintained. With no pressure, steam is barely higher than 212°F (100°C); at 5 pounds of pressure (psi) steam temperature is 227°F (108°C); at 10 psi steam registers 240°F (116°C); and at 15 psi steam reaches 250°F (121°C). Obviously, at higher temperatures foods cook dramatically faster.

1. Choose the Right Foods.   Pressurized steaming calls for the same sorts of foods as outlined above.

2. Prepare Equipment.   Follow manufacturers' guidelines for water reservoir, pressure maintenance, and so forth.

3. Place Food on Racks or Pans.   Steamer pans are ordinarily perforated to permit drainage of excess moisture. To permit adequate exposure to all surfaces, do not overcrowd foods. Put racks or inserts in steamer.

4. Close and Secure Door.   Make sure doors are completely closed.

5. Set Timer and Operate.   Follow manufacturer and recipe guidelines.

6. Vent Steamer or Open Door Carefully.   Follow manufacturers' guidelines for venting. Open door very carefully and slowly.

Table 1-34. Sample Timetable for Pressureless Steaming

Food Product	Quantity	Approximate Steaming Time (minutes)
Broccoli, frozen	6 lb	3 to 4
Green beans, fresh	5 lb	10 to 15
Vegetables, canned	7 lb	5 to 10
Chicken, cut up	8 lb	25
Lobster tails, frozen	8 lb	15 to 25
Lobster, 1½-pound	10 to 20	12 to 15
Shrimp, frozen	10 lb	8 to 11
Fish fillets	3 lb	6 to 10
Steamer clams	10 lb	12 to 14
Crabs, whole	4 lb	15 to 20

Note: Countertop, single tray (12″ × 20″ × 2½″)

Table 1-35. Sample Timetable for 5 psi Pressure Steaming

Food Product	Portion Size (ounces)	Steaming Time (minutes)	Portions Per Compartment Per Hour
Fish fillets/steaks*	5	10 to 20	200
Lobster*	16	7 to 9	250
Carrots, fresh*	3	20 to 30	500
Cauliflower, fresh*	3	10 to 20	500
Peas, defrosted*	3	5 to 10	800
Corn, canned*	3	10 to 15	1350
Potatoes, whole*	4	20 to 30	500
Pasta†	8	20 to 25	200
Rice†	3	20 to 25	650
Eggs, in shell†	1 each	8 to 10	2000
Custard†	5	10 to 12	1000

*Pan dimensions: 12″ × 20″ × 2½″
†Pan dimensions: 12″ × 20″ × 4″

Table 1-36. Sample Timetable: 15 psi Pressure Steaming
Fresh Vegetables

Food Product	Approximate Steaming Time (minutes)
Asparagus spears	2 to 2½
Beans, green	2 to 3
Cabbage, shredded	2 to 2½
Corn, cob, small	3 to 4
Onions, sliced	3 to 4
Potatoes, sliced	4 to 5
Spinach, leaf	1

Note: Pan dimensions: 12″ × 20″ × 2½″

Table 1-37. Sample Timetable: 15 psi Pressure Steaming
Frozen Vegetables

Food Product	Approximate Steaming Time (minutes)
Beans, green	1
Broccoli spears	1 to 1½
Brussels sprouts	2½ to 4
Carrots, baby, whole	2½ to 3
Cauliflower	1 to 1½
Corn, whole	½ to 1
Mixed vegetables	1
Peas	1
Snow peas	¼ to ½
Yam patties, 2 ounce	5 to 6

Note: Pan dimensions: 12″ × 20″ × 2½″

Table 1-38. Sample Timetable: 15 psi Pressure Steaming
Canned Vegetables

Food Product	Approximate Steaming Time (minutes)
Beans, green	½
Carrots, sliced	½
Potatoes, small, whole	2 to 2½

Note: Pan dimensions: 12″ × 20″ × 2½″

Table 1-39. Sample Timetable: 15 psi Pressure Steaming Seafood

Food Product	Approximate Steaming Time (minutes)
Clams, soft shell	1½ to 2
Crab legs, claws	3
Lobster tails, 5 oz.	3 to 4
Lobster, whole, 1–1½ lbs.	7 to 9
Fish fillets	1 to 3
Shrimp, 10/12 per lb.	4

Note: Pan dimensions: 12″ × 20″ × 2½″

Table 1-40. Sample Timetable: 15 psi Pressure Steaming Meat and Poultry

Food Product	Approximate Steaming Time (minutes)
Beef, ½-inch cubes	30 to 35
Chicken breast, boned	7 to 8
Spareribs	12 to 15
Hot dogs	1½ to 2
Eggs, whole	6½

Note: Pan dimensions: 12″ × 20″ × 2½″

Meat Cooking Methods

A tremendous variety of meat cuts are available from your suppliers. A common challenge is to know which cuts work best with each cooking method. The following charts offer guidelines for cuts of beef, lamb, pork, and veal, along with the subprimal cuts from which they are taken and appropriate cooking methods for each.

Table 1-41. Beef Cooking Methods

Beef Cut	Subprimal	Cooking Method
Arm steak, roast	Chuck	Braise, stew
Blade steak, roast	Chuck	Braise, stew
Bottom round	Round	Roast, sauté
Chateaubriand	Tenderloin	Roast, broil, sauté
Chicken fried steak	Round	Panfry, sauté
Chipped beef	Any	Simmer
Chuck roast	Chuck	Braise, simmer
Chuck steak	Chuck	Braise
Chuck tender roast	Chuck	Braise, roast
Club steak	Loin/rib	Broil, sauté
Corned beef	Brisket	Braise, simmer
Cube/minute steak	Round	Sauté, broil
Delmonico steak	Loin/rib	Sauté, broil
Eye of round	Round	Braise, sauté, broil
Filet mignon	Tenderloin	Broil, sauté
Flank steak	Flank	Braise, broil
Ground beef	Chuck, round, sirloin	Sauté, broil, panfry, roast
Heart	Organ	Simmer, braise
Heel of round	Round	Braise, simmer
Kansas City strip	Loin	Broil, sauté
Kabobs	Sirloin/round	Broil
Kidney	Organ	Braise then sauté
Liver	Organ	Sauté, braise
London broil	Flank	Broil
New York strip	Top loin	Broil, sauté
Oxtails	Tail	Braise, simmer
Pastrami	Brisket	Braise, simmer
Plate	Plate	Braise, simmer
Porterhouse	Short loin	Broil, sauté
Pot roast	Chuck/round	Braise
Prime rib	Rib	Roast
Ribeye roast	Rib	Roast
Round steak	Round	Sauté, broil, braise
Rump roast	Round/rump	Roast, braise, broil
Salisbury steak	Round	Sauté, braise
Short loin	Loin	Sauté, broil
Short ribs	Chuck/rib/plate	Braise, simmer, broil
Sirloin	Loin	Roast, broil, sauté
Sirloin tip	Loin	Roast, broil, sauté
Skirt steak	Rib/plate	Braise, broil
Standing rib roast	Rib	Roast
Standing rump roast	Rump	Roast
Stew beef	Chuck	Braise, simmer

Beef Cut	Subprimal	Cooking Method
Strip loin steak	Short loin	Broil, sauté
Sukiyaki	Round	Simmer
Swiss steak	Round/chuck	Braise
T-bone steak	Short loin	Broil, sauté
Tenderloin steak	Tenderloin	Broil, sauté
Tongue	Organ	Braise, simmer
Top round roast	Round	Roast, braise
Top sirloin	Sirloin	Roast, broil
Tournedo	Tenderloin	Broil, sauté

Table 1-42. Lamb Cooking Methods

Lamb Cut	Subprimal	Cooking Method
Arm chops	Shoulder	Braise, broil
Baby lamb	Whole	Roast
Breast/pocket roast	Breast	Braise
Blade chops	Shoulder	Braise, broil
Crown roast	Rack/rib	Roast
Cushion shoulder	Shoulder	Roast
English chops	Loin	Broil, sauté
French rib chops	Rack/rib	Broil
Kabobs	Leg	Broil
Kidney	Organ	Braise, simmer
Kidney chops	Loin	Broil, sauté
Leg	Leg	Roast, sauté, broil
Leg chops	Leg	Braise, broil
Liver	Organ	Sauté, broil, roast
Loin	Loin	Broil, roast, sauté
Loin chops	Loin	Broil, sauté
Neck	Shoulder	Simmer
Noisettes	Loin	Broil, sauté
Rack/rib roast	Loin	Roast
Riblets	Breast	Braise, simmer
Rolled roast	Loin	Roast
Shank	Leg	Braise, simmer
Shoulder square	Shoulder	Roast, braise
Sirloin roast	Leg	Roast
Sirloin chops	Loin	Broil, sauté
Saddle	Loin	Roast

Table 1-43. Pork Cooking Methods

Pork	Subprimal	Cooking Method
Arm chops	Shoulder	Braise, broil
Arm roast/ham	Shoulder	Braise, roast
Bacon slab	Side	Sauté
Blade chops	Loin	Braise
Blade roast	Loin	Roast
Blade steak	Shoulder	Braise, broil
Boneless butt	Shoulder	Braise, roast
Boston butt	Shoulder	Braise, roast
Center loin roast	Loin	Roast
Canadian bacon	Loin	Sauté, broil
Center-cut roast	Leg	Roast, braise
Country-style rib	Loin (blade)	Braise then broil
Country ham	Leg	Simmer then roast
Ham butt	Leg	Roast, braise
Ham shank	Leg	Braise, simmer
Ham steak	Leg	Sauté, broil
Hocks	Neck/shoulder	Braise, simmer
Kidney	Organ	Braise, broil, sauté
Liver	Organ	Braise, broil, sauté
Loin chop	Loin	Broil, sauté
Loin roast	Loin	Broil, roast
Picnic ham	Shoulder	Braise, simmer, roast
Pigs feet/hocks	Leg	Simmer, braise
Rib chops	Center loin	Broil, sauté
Rolled roast	Center loin	Roast, braise
Sirloin chops	Center loin	Broil, sauté, braise
Spareribs	Loin	Braise, broil
Tongue	Organ	Braise, simmer
Tenderloin	Loin	Roast, broil, sauté

Table 1-44. Veal Cooking Methods

Veal Cut	Subprimal	Cooking Method
Arm steak, roast	Shoulder	Braise, stew
"Birds" (rolls)	Leg	Braise
Blade steak	Shoulder	Braise, stew, panfry
Boned shoulder	Shoulder	Braise, simmer
Breast	Breast	Braise, simmer
Center leg	Rib	Slow roast

Veal Cut	Subprimal	Cooking Method
Crown roast	Rib	Roast
Cutlet	Leg	Sauté, panfry
Foreshank	Shoulder	Braise
Ground	Various	Sauté, panfry, roast
Hind shank	Shoulder	Braise, simmer
Liver	Organ	Sauté, broil, braise
Loin chops	Loin	Sauté, broil, braise
Loin roast	Loin	Roast, braise
Neck	Shoulder	Simmer
Rack	Rib	Roast
Shank (leg)	Leg	Braise
Saddle	Rib/loin	Roast
Sweetbreads	Organ	Simmer, sauté

Equivalents, Ingredients, and Equipment

Weights to Measures Conversion Tables
- ▲ **Bakery Products**
- ▲ **Dairy Products**
- ▲ **Fruits**
- ▲ **Grains**
- ▲ **Spices and Herbs**
- ▲ **Vegetables**

U.S./Metric Conversion Tables
- ▲ **Volume**
- ▲ **Weight**

Fahrenheit/Centigrade Conversions

Microwave Time Conversions

Temperature Guidelines for Food Safety

Herbs and Spices Uses

Flavor Substitutes

Other Ingredient Substitutes

Cheeses

Equipment Sizes
- ▲ **Standard Bowl Capacities**
- ▲ **Insert Pan Dimensions and Capacities**
- ▲ **Mixer Bowl Capacities**
- ▲ **Standard Pot and Pan Capacities**
- ▲ **Foodservice Scoop Capacities**
- ▲ **Steam Kettle Capacities**

Foodservice Can Sizes and Capacities

WEIGHTS TO MEASURES CONVERSION TABLES

Table 1-45. Bakery Products

Food Description	Weight	Measure
Baking powder	1 lb	2⅓ c
	1 oz	2⅓ T
Baking soda	1 lb	2¼ c
	1 oz	2¼ T
Bran, all-bran	1 lb	2 qt
Bran flakes	1 lb	3 qt
Brown sugar	1 lb	3 c lightly packed
	1 lb	2 c firmly packed
Cake crumbs, soft	1 lb	1½ qt
Chocolate, baker's	1 lb	16 squares
Chocolate, chips	1 lb	2½ c
Chocolate, grated	1 lb	3½ c
Chocolate, melted	1 lb	2 c
Cornmeal	1 lb	3½ c
Cornstarch	1 lb	3½ c
	1 oz	3½ T
Corn syrup	1 lb	1½ c
Cream of tartar	1 oz	3 T
Flour, whole wheat	1 lb	3½ c
Flour, cake, sifted	1 lb	1 qt
Flour, bread, sifted	1 lb	1 qt
Flour, white, unsifted	1 lb	1 qt
Gelatin, unflavored	1 lb	3 c
	1 oz	3 T
Honey	1 lb	1½ c
Jam/jelly	1 lb	1½ c
Nutmeats, chopped	1 lb	1 qt
Shortening	1 lb	2¼ c
Sugar, granulated	1 lb	2¼ c
Sugar, powdered	1 lb	3¼ c sifted
Tapioca, quick cooking	1 lb	2⅔ c raw
	1 lb	7 c cooked
Water	1 lb	2 c
Yeast, dry	1 oz	3⅓ T
Yeast, dry	1 lb	3⅓ c

Table 1-46. Dairy Products

Food Description	Weight	Measure
Butter/margarine	1 lb	2 c
Eggs, boiled, chopped	1 lb	2½ c (3½ c per dozen)
Eggs, shelled, large	1 lb	2 c (9 to 11 each)
Egg whites	1 lb	2 c (17 to 20 each)
Egg yolks	1 lb	2 c (19 to 23 each)
Cheese, diced	1 lb	1 qt
Cheese, grated	1 lb	3½ c to 1 qt
Cottage cheese	1 lb	2¼ c
Cream cheese	1 lb	2 c
Light cream	1 lb	1¾ c
Heavy cream	1 lb	2 c or 1 qt whipped
Milk, condensed	1 lb	1½ c
Milk, dry, instant	1 lb	5¾ c
Milk, dry, regular	1 lb	1 qt
Milk, evaporated	1 lb	1⅞ c
Milk, fresh	1 lb	2 c
Sour cream	1 lb	2 c

Table 1-47. Fruits

Food Description	Weight	Measure
Apples, fresh	1 lb	3 medium
Apples, diced	1 lb	1 qt
Apples, sliced	1 lb	1 qt
Applesauce	1 lb	2 c
Apricots, dried	1 lb	3 c raw or 5 c cooked
Avocados, canned	1 lb	2 c
Avocados, medium	1 lb	2 to 3
Bananas, medium	1 lb	3
Bananas, peeled	1 lb	2½ c diced
Blackberries, canned	1 lb	3 c
Blackberries, fresh, IQF	1 lb	1 qt
Blueberries, fresh, IQF	1 lb	3 c
Cantaloupe	1 lb	1 small
Cherries, candied	1 lb	3 c or 120
Cherries, canned, drained	1 lb	3 c
Citron, chopped	1 lb	2½ c
Cranberries, fresh, IQF	1 lb	1 qt or 3¼ c cooked
Currants	1 lb	3½ c
Dates, pitted	1 lb	2¾ c

Food Description	Weight	Measure
Figs, dry	1 lb	3 c
Grapefruit	1 lb	12 segments
Grapes	1 lb	1 qt or 2½ c sliced
Orange rind, grated	1 oz	3 T
Oranges	1 lb	2¼ c diced
Peaches, fresh, IQF	1 lb	4 medium
Peaches, canned, drained	1 lb	2½ c diced
Pineapple	1 lb	2½ c diced
Prunes	1 lb	3 c or 6 c cooked
Pumpkin	1 lb	2 c puree
Raisins	1 lb	3 c
Raspberries, fresh, IQF	1 lb	3½ c or 2 c cooked
Rhubarb	1 lb	1 qt or 2½ c cooked
Strawberries, fresh, IQF	1 lb	3 c
Strawberries, sliced	1 lb	2 c

Table 1-48. Grains

Food Description	Weight	Measure
Barley	1 lb	2½ c
Bran, all-bran	1 lb	2 qt
Bran flakes	1 lb	3 qt
Bread crumbs, dry	1 lb	5 c
Bread crumbs, fresh	1 lb	2½ qt
Bread crumbs, dry, sifted	1 lb	1 qt
Bread, soft, cubes	1 lb	2 qt
Bread, ⅝" slices	1 lb	16 slices
Cracker crumbs	1 lb	5 c
Crackers, crumbled	1 lb	2 qt
Crackers, graham	1 lb	40
Crackers, saltine	1 lb	108
Cracked wheat, raw	1 lb	3½ c raw
	1 lb	1½ qt cooked
Cornflakes	1 lb	5 qt
Cornmeal	1 lb	3½ c raw
	1 lb	3 qt cooked
Cornstarch	1 lb	3½ c
	1 oz	3½ T
Flour, all types	See Bakery Products table	
Hominy grits	1 lb	3 c raw
	1 lb	3 qt cooked

Food Description	Weight	Measure
Macaroni, 1"	1 lb	4 c raw
	1 lb	2½ qt cooked
Oats, rolled	1 lb	4¾ c raw
	1 lb	2¼ qt cooked
Rice	1 lb	2 c raw
	1 lb	2½ qt cooked
Spaghetti, 2"	1 lb	5 c raw
	1 lb	2½ qt cooked
Tapioca, quick cooking	1 lb	2⅔ c raw
	1 lb	2 qt cooked
Tapioca, pearl	1 lb	2¾ c raw
	1 lb	2 qt cooked
Wheat, shredded	1 lb	20 each

Table 1-49. Spices and Herbs

Herb/Spice (dried)	Weight	Measure
Allspice, ground	1 oz	5½ T
Basil	1 oz	½ c
Bay leaf	1 oz	7 T
Caraway seed	1 oz	5½ T
Cardamom seed	1 oz	5½ T
Celery seed	1 oz	¼ c
Cinnamon	1 oz	5½ T
Cloves, ground	1 oz	5½ T
Coriander seed	1 oz	6¾ T
Cumin seed	1 oz	6 T
Dill seed	1 oz	4½ T
Dill weed	1 oz	6 T
Fennel seed	1 oz	4½ T
Garlic powder	1 oz	6⅓ T
Ginger	1 oz	6 T
Mace	1 oz	5¼ T
Marjoram	1 oz	½ c
Mustard, dry	1 oz	6⅓ T
Nutmeg, ground	1 oz	5 T
Onion powder	1 oz	4½ T
Oregano	1 oz	6 T
Paprika	1 oz	5 T
Parsley flakes	1 oz	½ c + 1½ t
Pepper, black	1 oz	½ c
Pepper, chili	1 oz	½ c + 1½ t

Herb/Spice (dried)	Weight	Measure
Pepper, red	1 oz	½ c + 1½ t
Pepper, white	1 oz	½ c
Poppy seeds	1 oz	3¾ T
Rosemary	1 oz	½ c
Sage	1 oz	½ c + 1½ T
Savory	1 oz	6¾ T
Sesame seed	1 oz	5 T
Tarragon	1 oz	6¾ T
Thyme	1 oz	6⅓ T
Turmeric	1 oz	5 T

Table 1-50. Vegetables

Food Description	Weight	Measure
Asparagus, canned tips	1 lb	18 stalks
Asparagus, canned stalks	1 lb	2½ c
Asparagus, fresh, IQF	1 lb	18 stalks
Bean sprouts	1 lb	2¼ c
Beans, kidney, dried	1 lb	2⅓ c raw
	1 lb	1½ qt cooked
Beans, lima, dried	1 lb	2⅓ c raw
	1 lb	1½ qt cooked
Beans, lima, fresh, IQF	1 lb	2¼ c shelled
Beans, navy, dried	1 lb	2⅓ c raw
	1 lb	1¾ qt cooked
Beans, string, cut, IQF	1 lb	5½ c
	1 lb	3 c cooked
Beets, diced	1 lb	2¼ c
Beets, sliced	1 lb	2⅔ c
Brussels sprouts, IQF	1 lb	1 qt
Cabbage, shredded	1 lb	7 c raw
	1 lb	3½ c cooked
Carrots, diced	1 lb	3¼ c
Carrots, fresh	1 lb	4 medium
Celery, diced	1 lb	3¼ c
Corn, cream style	1 lb	2 c
Corn, kernel, IQF	1 lb	2⅓ c
Cucumber, diced	1 lb	2½ c
Eggplant, diced	1 lb	1 qt
Eggplant, sliced	1 lb	8 slices
Lettuce, shredded	1 lb	2 qt
Mushrooms, fresh	1 lb	1⅓ c cooked

Food Description	Weight	Measure
Onion, A.P.	1 lb	4 medium
Onion, chopped	1 lb	3 c
Onion, minced	1 lb	3¼ c
Parsley	1 lb	6 c chopped
Parsnips, A.P.	1 lb	4 medium
Parsnips, diced	1 lb	3 c
Parsnips, mashed	1 lb	2 c
Peas, dried, split	1 lb	2⅓ c raw
	1 lb	5½ c cooked
Peas, fresh, E.P., IQF	1 lb	2 c
Peppers, bell	1 lb	5 medium
Peppers, bell, chopped	1 lb	3½ c
Potatoes, A.P.	1 lb	3 medium raw
Potatoes, cooked, diced	1 lb	2 c mashed
Potatoes, sweet	1 lb	3 c
Pumpkin, cooked	1 lb	3 medium
Radishes, trimmed	1 lb	2 c
Sauerkraut	1 lb	1 qt
Spinach, canned, drained	1 lb	1½ c cooked
Spinach, fresh	1 lb	3 c cooked
	1 lb	5 c loose
Tomatoes, canned	1 lb	2 c
Tomatoes, dried	1 lb	3½ c
Tomatoes, fresh	1 lb	3 medium
Tomatoes, fresh, diced	1 lb	3 c
Turnips, A.P.	1 lb	4 medium
Turnips, raw, diced	1 lb	3½ c

U.S./METRIC CONVERSION TABLES

Table 1-51. Volume

U.S. Volume	Metric Volume	U.S. Volume	Metric Volume
1 t	5 ml	¾ c	180 ml
2 t	10 ml	1 c	240 ml
1 T	15 ml	2 c	480 ml
2 T	30 ml	3 c	720 ml
3 T	45 ml	1 qt	950 ml
¼ c	60 ml	2 qt	1.9 L
⅓ c	80 ml	3 qt	2.9 L
½ c	120 ml	1 gal	3.8 L
⅔ c	160 ml		

TAblE 1-52. WeiqhT

U.S. Weight	Metric Weight	U.S. Weight	Metric Weight
½ oz	14 g	2 lb	908 g
1 oz	28 g	4 lb	1.8 kg
2 oz	56 g	5 lb	2.3 kg
4 oz	114 g	10 lb	4.54 kg
8 oz	227 g	15 lb	6.8 kg
1 lb	454 g	20 lb	9.1 kg

FAhRENhEiT/CENTiqRAdE CONVERSiONS

The following list provides conversions from Fahrenheit temperatures to Centigrade, and from Centigrade to Fahrenheit. To convert any temperature from one style to the other, simply follow these guidelines:

To convert any Fahrenheit temperature to Centigrade:

Subtract 32 from the Fahrenheit amount and multiply result by .556.

Example: 212°F

212 − 32 = 180

180 × .556 = 100°C

To convert any Centigrade temperature to Fahrenheit:

Multiply the Centigrade amount by 1.8 and add 32.

Example: 100°C

100 × 1.8 = 180

180 + 32 = 212°F

Fahrenheit Temperature	Centigrade Temperature
0	−18
10	−12
20	−7
30	−1
32	0
40	4
50	10
100	37
120	48
140	59

Fahrenheit Temperature	Centigrade Temperature
160	70
180	81
200	92
212	**100**
225	106
250	120
275	134
300	147
325	161
350	175
375	189
400	202
425	216
450	230
475	244
500	257
550	285
600	312

Table 1-53. Microwave Time Conversions

Use the following chart as a guide when using your microwave oven with recipes developed in more, or less, powerful units. For example, if you have a 650-watt microwave and the recipe calls for 20 seconds cooking time in a 400-watt oven, reduce your cooking time to 15 seconds. Wattage ratings for ovens can be found in the owner's manual and on the oven's serial number plate.

600–700 Watts	500–600 Watts	400–500 Watts
15 seconds	18 seconds	20 seconds
30 seconds	35 seconds	45 seconds
1 minute	1 minute, 15 seconds	1 minute, 30 seconds
2 minutes	2 minutes, 30 seconds	2 minutes, 50 seconds
3 minutes	3 minutes, 30 seconds	4 minutes, 15 seconds
4 minutes	4 minutes, 50 seconds	5 minutes, 45 seconds
5 minutes	6 minutes	7 minutes
6 minutes	7 minutes, 15 seconds	8 minutes, 30 seconds
8 minutes	9 minutes, 30 seconds	11 minutes, 15 seconds
10 minutes	12 minutes	14 minutes

Temperature Guidelines for Food Safety

It is imperative to follow guidelines for proper handling and holding of food. The general rule: Keep foods below 40°F (4°C) or above 140°F (60°C). The following chart shows the key temperatures for retardation, growth, and destruction of bacteria that cause food spoilage and foodborne illness.

A key consideration: Because refrigeration does not kill bacteria but merely retards its growth, bacteria will multiply rampantly *every time* food reaches a temperature in the danger zone. So, if a food product stays in the danger zone for even one hour, and is then chilled to safe temperatures, bacteria have already multiplied rapidly—and are waiting to do it again as soon as they get the right conditions.

	°C	°F	Bacterial Activity
	121	250	Resistant spores killed
	100	212	
	71	160	Resistant salmonella killed
	84	148	Vegetative cells killed
	58	137	Trichina killed
DANGER ZONE!!	50	122	
BACTERIA GROW RAPIDLY	32	90	Bacteria double every 30 minutes
RAPID SPOILAGE	21	70	Bacteria double every hour
AND	18	60	Bacteria double every 2 hours
FOOD POISONING	10	50	
	4	40	Bacteria double every 6 hours
	0	32	Bacteria double every 20 hours
	−2	28	Bacteria double every 60 hours
	−10	14	Lower limit of bacterial growth

Table 1-54. Herbs and Spices Uses

Herb or Spice	Forms	Especially Suited for Use In
Allspice	Whole/ground	Meat, fish, fowl, spinach, turnips, peas
Anise	Whole/ground	Pastry, pie filling, shellfish, carrots
Basil	Fresh, dried	Meat, fish, fowl, tomato dishes, sauces
Bay leaf	Whole leaves	Meat, fish, fowl, stews, chowders, marinades
Caraway	Whole/ground	Beans, cabbage, soup, breads, cheese spread
Cardamom	Whole/ground	Pastry, pies, yams, pumpkin, fruit compote
Cayenne	Ground	Casseroles, curries, sauces, Mexican
Chervil	Fresh	Soup, salad, eggs, sauces, dressing
Chili powder	Ground	Meats, stews, sauces, soups, Mexican
Chives	Fresh, dried	Any dish complemented by onion
Cinnamon	Sticks, ground	Fruits, pork, chicken, yams, carrots, squash
Cloves	Whole, ground	Pork, soup, baked beans, candied yams
Coriander	Whole, ground	Pastry, cookies, cream soups, Spanish food
Cumin	Whole, ground	Chili, stews, beans, cabbage, Oriental and Mexican cuisine
Curry powder	Ground	Meat, fish, fowl, stews, eggs, creamed vegetables, dressings, cottage cheese
Dill	Fresh, dried, whole, ground	Meat, fish, fowl, cream cheese, breads, potato salad, chowders
Fennel	Whole, ground	Breads, cookies, apples, pork, squash, sausage, sauces, cabbage, Italian
Ginger	Fresh, dried	Pastry, pie, chutney, curries, stews, yellow vegetables, beets, dressings, Oriental
Mace	Whole, ground	Chicken, creamed shellfish, cakes, cookies, poundcake, yellow vegetables, desserts
Marjoram	Fresh, dried	Pork, lamb, seafood sauces, chowder, stews, salads, green beans, omelets
Mint	Fresh, dried	Lamb, veal, fish, beans, carrots, potatoes
Mustard	Ground	Dressings, eggs, potatoes, soups, vegetables
Nutmeg	Whole, ground	Desserts, stews, cream dishes, potatoes
Oregano	Fresh, dried	Italian and Mexican cooking; tomato sauces, fish, poultry, salads, mushrooms
Paprika	Ground	Sausage, chowders, marinades, stews, sauces
Parsley	Fresh, dried	Meat, fish, fowl, stews, sauces, breads
Pepper, black/white	Whole, ground	Almost anything!
Pepper, crushed red	Dried	Stews, sauces, chowders, vegetables
Peppercorns, green	Brined, dried	Sauces, marinades, dressings, seafood
Pickling spice	Whole, dried	Marinades, meat, fish, fowl, boiled shellfish
Poppy seeds	Whole, dried	Breads, cookies, cheese dishes, pasta, fruits
Rosemary	Fresh, dried	Meat, game, poultry, soups, stews, marinades, green beans, dumplings
Saffron	Dried, ground	Rice, potatoes, seafood, stews, veal, curries, cream sauces

Herb or Spice	Forms	Especially Suited for Use In
Sage	Fresh, dried	Pork, veal, poultry, dressings, chowders, cream sauces, soups
Savory	Fresh, dried	Eggs, salads, seafood, soups, tomatoes, beans, lentils, squash, grilled meats
Sesame	Whole	Bread, cookies, seafood, pork, chicken, noodles, salads, Chinese, African, Hispanic
Tarragon	Fresh, dried	Eggs, salads, lamb, seafood, marinades, soups, chowders, beans, broccoli, sauces
Thyme	Fresh, dried	Seafood, veal, fowl, sauces, tomatoes, beans, mushrooms, onions, carrots, potatoes
Turmeric	Ground	Curries, soups, rice, dressings, seafood
Watercress	Fresh	Salads, sauces, omelets

Table 1-55. Flavor Substitutes

Every international cooking style is based on a selection of specific herbs, spices, and other key ingredients. These ingredients largely distinguish Mexican from German, Chinese from Greek, cuisines. By substituting the ingredients of one culinary style for those of another, any base recipe can be converted into a virtual United Nations of options. For example, to shift from Chinese to Mexican, substitute cumin for anise, and lime juice for soy sauce.

Chinese	French	German	Greek	Hungarian	Indian
Ginger	Tarragon	Caraway seed	Oregano	Paprika	Curry
Anise seed	Shallots	Dill seed	Mint	Poppy seed	Cumin seed
Garlic	Chives	Onion	Bay leaf	Caraway seed	Coriander
Onion	Fines herbes	Paprika	Garlic	Garlic	Turmeric
Red pepper	Marjoram	Ginger	Onion	Dill seed	Red pepper
Fennel seed	Thyme	Rosemary	Cinnamon	Onion	Black pepper
Cloves	Black pepper	Nutmeg	Fennel	Cinnamon	Ginger
Cinnamon	Rosemary	White pepper	Pepper	White pepper	Cardamom seed
Sesame oil	Garlic		Lemon		
Scallions	Vinegar				
Soy Sauce					

Indonesian	Italian	Mexican	Spanish	Swedish	African
Curry	Garlic	Chili pepper	Saffron	Cardamom seed	Pepper
Garlic	Basil	Cumin seed	Paprika	Nutmeg	Cumin
Red pepper	Oregano	Oregano	Garlic	Dill seed	Coriander
Ginger	Onion	Garlic	Onion	Bay leaf	Mint
Cinnamon	Sage	Onion	Parsley	Allspice	Saffron
Nutmeg	Fennel	Coriander seed	Bay leaf	Black pepper	Anise
Cloves	Pepper	Sesame seed	Cumin seed	Mustard	Cinnamon
Caraway seed	Marjoram	Sweet pepper	Cinnamon	Cinnamon	
		Lime			

Table 1-56. Other Ingredient Substitutes

Food Product Needed	Acceptable Substitute
Baking powder, 1 t	¼ t baking soda plus ½ t cream of tartar
Brown sugar, 1 c	1 c sugar plus 2 T molasses
Buttermilk, 1 c	1 T vinegar plus milk to make 1 c
Butter (or margarine), 4 oz	7 T vegetable oil
Chocolate, unsweetened, 1 oz	3 T cocoa powder plus 1 T butter, margarine, or vegetable oil
Corn syrup, 1 c	1 c sugar plus ¼ c liquid
Flour (to thicken)	½ volume cornstarch
Herbs (fresh)	⅓ volume dried herbs
Honey, 1 c	1¼ c sugar plus ¼ c liquid
Lemon juice	¼ volume vinegar
Tomato sauce, 2 c	¾ c tomato paste plus 1 c water
Tomato juice	equal parts tomato sauce and water

Table 1-57. Cheeses

Name	Flavor	Texture	Description	Uses
Domestic U.S. Cheeses				
American	Mild	Semisoft	Cow milk	Sandwiches, snacks
Brick	Mild, sweet	Firm	Cow milk	Sandwiches, salads
Colby	Mild	Firm to hard	Cow milk	Sandwiches, sauces
Cottage	Mild	Soft, loose	Cow milk	Salads
Cream	Mild, sweet	Soft, creamy	Cow milk	Sandwiches, spreads
Monterey Jack	Mild, snappy	Firm	Cow milk	Snacks, cooking
Stirred curd	Mild, cheddary	Semisoft to hard	Cow milk	Base for process cheese
Dutch Cheeses				
Edam	Mild, salty	Semisoft	Cow milk	Fruits, snacks
Gouda	Mild, nutty	Firm	Cow milk	Fruits, snacks, cooking
English Cheeses				
Cheddar	Mild to sharp	Firm to hard	Cow milk	Sandwiches, cooking
Stilton	Semisoft to hard	Piquant	Cow milk	Dessert, sauces
French Cheeses				
Beaufort	Mild	Soft	Whole, lowfat cow, or goat milk	Fondues and gratins

Name	Flavor	Texture	Description	Uses
Bleu	Piquant, tangy	Semisoft	Whole, lowfat cow or goat milk	Salads and dressings, desserts
Brie	Mild to pungent	Soft, creamy	Whole cow milk	Dessert, fruit
Camembert	Mild to pungent	Soft, creamy	Whole cow milk	Dessert, fruit
Cantal	Sweet, nutty	Firm	Whole cow milk	Dessert, fruit, souffles, soups
Chablou	Mild to strong	Firm	Goat milk	Dessert, fruit, hors d'oeuvre
Coulommiers	Mild	Soft	Cow milk	Dessert, fruit
Maroilles	Full	Soft	Cow milk	Dessert
Mont-d'Or	Delicate	Soft	Goat milk	With red wine
Munster	Full	Firm	Cow milk	Wine, steamed potatoes
Murol	Mild	Firm	Cow milk	Dessert
Neufchâtel	Mild	Soft, creamy	Whole or skim cow milk	Dips, salads, fruits, spreads, dessert baking
Olivet	Spicy	Soft	Cow milk	Nuts, wine
Petit-Suisse	Full	Soft	Cow milk and cream	Desserts, sauces
Port-Salut	Mild	Semisoft	Cow milk	Spreads, dips, dessert, toast
Reblochon	Sweet, nutty	Creamy	Cow milk	Dessert, fruit
Roquefort	Sharp, spicy	Semisoft	Sheep's milk	Salads, fruit, dessert
Saint-Marcellin	Sweet, acidic	Soft	Cow milk	Light red wine
Saint-Nectaire	Earthy, musty	Soft	Cow milk	Fruit, bread
Saint-Paulin	Sweet	Soft, smooth	Cow milk	Salad, dessert, sandwiches
Tomme de Savoie	Nutty	Semisoft to firm	Cow milk	Dessert, sandwiches
Vacherin	Mild	Soft	Cow milk	Spread, dessert, sandwiches
German Cheeses				
Fruhstuk	Strong	Soft, smooth	Cow milk	Dessert, spreads, sandwiches
Muenster	Mild	Semisoft	Cow milk	Sandwiches
Schloss	Strong	Soft	Cow milk	Spreads, sandwiches
Italian Cheeses				
Asiago	Sharp	Semisoft to hard	Whole or lowfat cow milk	Sliced, with fruit; grated in pasta, soups, and sauces

Name	Flavor	Texture	Description	Uses
Bel Paese	Mild to full	Soft, smooth	Whole cow milk	With fruit, as spread
Caciocavallo	Sharp	Hard, firm	Cow, sheep, or goat milk	Grated, with sauces/ pastas
Fontina	Mild	Creamy	Whole cow milk	With fruits; in sauces, soups
Gorgonzola	Sharp, like French *bleu*	Semisoft	Cow or goat milk or mixture	Salads, with fruits
Mascarpone	Mild	Creamy	Cow milk	As a spread, in desserts
Mozzarella	Mild	Semisoft	Cow milk, whole/lowfat	Grated, sliced for cooking
Parmesan	Sharp	Hard	Cow milk	Grated; salads, soup, sauces, pasta
Provolone	Sharp, smoky	Hard	Goat milk	Grated; salads, soup, sauces, pasta
Ricotta	Soft, moist	Cottage cheese	Cow's milk, curd, and whey	Baked pasta
Romano	Sharp	Hard	Cow or goat milk	Grated; salads, soup, sauces, pasta
Norwegian Cheeses				
Gammelost	Sharp	Semisoft	Cow milk	Cooking
Gjetost	Sweet	Hard	Goat milk	Snacks, crackers
Jarlsberg	Mild	Firm to hard	Cow milk	Snacks, sauces
Primost	Mild to full	Semisoft	Cow milk	Cooking
Swiss Cheeses				
Emmental	Mild, nutty	Firm	Cow milk	Sandwiches, salads, fondue
Gruyère	Mild, sweet	Hard	Cow milk	Dessert, fondue
Miscellaneous International Cheeses				
Feta (Greece)	Sharp, acidic	Semisoft	Cow, goat, or sheep milk	Salads, cooking
Limburger (Belgium)	Strong, aromatic	Soft, smooth	Cow milk	Snacks, spreads
Queso blanco (Latin America)	Salty	Soft, crumbly	Cow milk	Salads, topping for cooking

EQUIPMENT SIZES

Table 1-58. Standard Bowl Capacities

Diameter (inches)	Volume	Diameter (inches)	Volume
5	10 oz	12	1 gal
6	14 oz	15	2 gal
8	1¼ qt (5 c)	18	3¾ gal
10	2 qt	23	9 gal

Table 1-59. Insert Pan Dimensions and Capacities

Pan Size	Depth (inches)	Capacity (quarts)	Portions (4 ounces)
12" × 20"	2½	9	70
	4	15	120
	6	22	175
½ size	2½	4	30
	4	7	55
	6	10	80
⅓ size	2½	3	20
	4	4½	35
	6	6½	50
¼ size	2½	2	16
	4	3	24
	6	4½	35

Table 1-60. Mixer Bowl Capacities

The following chart serves as a guide to determine the maximum load of certain foods in mixer bowls of various sizes.

Product	5 qt	10 qt	12 qt	20 qt	30 qt	60 qt	80 qt	140 qt
Mashed potatoes	3 lb	8 lb	10 lb	15 lb	23 lb	40 lb	60 lb	100 lb
Mayonnaise	1½ qt	3 qt	4½ qt	10 qt	3 gal	4½ gal	7½ gal	12½ gal
Pancake batter	2 qt	1 gal	5 qt	2 gal	3 gal	6 gal	8 gal	NR
Cake batter, creaming	3 lb	10 lb	12 lb	20 lb	30 lb	60 lb	90 lb	165 lb
Cake batter, sponge	2 lb	4 lb	5 lb	8 lb	12 lb	24 lb	40 lb	75 lb

Product	5 qt	10 qt	12 qt	20 qt	30 qt	60 qt	80 qt	140 qt
Cake icing	2 lb	6 lb	7 lb	12 lb	18 lb	36 lb	65 lb	100 lb
Dough, light	4 lb	11 lb	13 lb	25 lb	45 lb	80 lb	170 lb	210 lb
Dough, heavy	NR	NR	NR	15 lb	30 lb	60 lb	140 lb	175 lb
Dough, pie	3 lb	9 lb	11 lb	18 lb	27 lb	50 lb	75 lb	125 lb
Dough, pizza	NR	NR	NR	NR	NR	40 lb	85 lb	130 lb

Note: All estimated portions are based on mixers operating at maximum capacity.
NR indicates foods not recommended for mixers of the designated size.

TABLE 1-61. STANDARD POT AND PAN CAPACITIES

Diameter (inches)	Depth (inches)	Volume (quarts)	Portion Yield (4 ounce)*
	Single-Handled Sauce Pans		
6	5¼	1½	10
7¾	6½	2¾	20
8¾	7⅛	3¾	30
9⅛	7½	4½	35
9⅞	7⅝	5½	40
10⅝	8⅝	7	50
11¼	9¾	8½	65
11¾	10¼	10	75

Diameter (inches)	Depth (inches)	Volume (quarts)	Portion Yield (8 ounce)*
	Double-Handled Sauce Pots		
8¾	6	6	20
10	6⅜	8½	30
11	7½	12	45
12	7½	14	55
13	8⅞	20	75
14	9⅞	26	100
16	10	34	130
18	10	44	170
20	11	60	230
	Stockpots		
9	8⅝	9	30
10	9	12	45
10	11	15	55
11	12¼	20	75
12	13	25	95

Diameter (inches)	Depth (inches)	Volume (quarts)	Portion Yield (8 ounce)*
Stockpots			
13	14⅜	32	120
14	15¼	40	155
16	17½	60	230
18	18¼	80	300
20	18½	100	375

*Yield based on pots not being completely filled.

Table 1-62. Foodservice Scoop Capacities

By understanding how much scoops hold, you can more closely control portion size and food cost. Please note that the scoop number tells the number of portions per quart of food.

Scoop Number	Volume Yield
4	1 c
6	⅔ c
8	½ c
12	⅓ c
16	¼ c
24	1½ oz

Table 1-63. Steam Kettle Capacities

Kettle Size (gal)	8 oz	6 oz	5 oz	4 oz	3 oz	2 oz
10	128	170	205	256	340	512
20	256	340	410	512	680	1024
30	384	510	615	768	1020	1536
40	512	680	820	1024	1360	2048
60	768	1020	1230	1536	2040	3072
80	1024	1360	1640	2048	2720	4096
100	1280	1700	2050	2560	3400	5120
150	1920	2550	3075	3840	5100	7680

Note: All estimated portions are based on kettles operating at 80% of total capacity.

Table 1-64. Foodservice Can Sizes and Capacities

Can Size	Measure (approx.)	Weight (approx.)	Needed to Equal #10 Can
6 oz	¾ c	6 oz	18 cans
8 oz	1 c	8 oz	13 cans
No. 1	1¼ c	10½ oz	10 cans
No. 300	1¾ c	15½ oz	7 cans
No. 303	2 c	1 lb	6½ cans
No. 2	2½ c	1¼ lb	5¼ cans
No. 2½	3½ c	1¾ lb	4 cans
No. 3 cyl	5¾ c	2⅞ lb	2½ cans
No. 10	3 qt	6½ lb	—

Food Quantities

Amounts to Purchase for Fifty Portions
- ▲ **Beverages**
- ▲ **Cereal, Crackers, Grains**
- ▲ **Dairy**
- ▲ **Fruits**
- ▲ **Beef**
- ▲ **Lamb**
- ▲ **Pork**
- ▲ **Veal**
- ▲ **Poultry**
- ▲ **Seafood**
- ▲ **Vegetables**

Recipe Expansion and Reduction Tables
- ▲ **Original Yield Four Portions**
- ▲ **Original Yield Ten Portions**
- ▲ **Original Yield Twenty-Five Portions**
- ▲ **Original Yield Fifty Portions**

AMOUNTS TO PURCHASE FOR FIFTY PORTIONS

During trimming, preparation and cooking, many foods lose weight, which means the amount purchased (A.P.) and edible portion (E.P.) weights for a given food often differ dramatically. You can use the following tables to determine the necessary amount of food for fifty servings of each food at the portion size suggested.

Table 1-65. Beverages

Food Product	Portion Size (ounces)	Purchase Amount for Fifty Portions
Beverages	4	1¾ gal
	6	2½ gal
	8	3¼ gal
	12	5 gal
Coffee, ground	6	1½ lb
Coffee, instant	6	4 oz

Table 1-66. Cereal, Crackers, Grains

Food Product	Portion Size	Purchase Amount for Fifty Portions
Bread, ⅝" slices	2	3 lb
Cereals, dry	½ c	3 lb
Crackers, graham	2	2 lb
Crackers, saltines	4	2 lb
Cornmeal, cooked	5 oz	2 lb
Hominy grits	½ c	2 lb
Macaroni	4 oz	6 lb
Oats, rolled	½ c	2 lb
Rice	½ c	3½ lb
Spaghetti	4 oz	6 lb
Tapioca, quick cooking	3 oz	3 lb
Wheat, shredded	2	5 lb

Table 1-67. Dairy

Food Product	Portion Size	Purchase Amount for Fifty Portions
Butter/margarine, pats	1	1 lb
Eggs, large	2	9 doz
Cottage cheese	2 oz	7 lb
Cream cheese, spread	1 oz	4 lb
Light cream, beverages	1 oz	2 qt
Heavy cream, whipped	¼ c	1½ qt
Sour cream	1 oz	3¼ lb

Table 1-68. Fruits

Food Product (edible portion 3 oz)	Estimated Trim Loss (%) from Preparation	Purchase Amount for Fifty Portions (pounds)
Apples, peeled, cored, diced	25	13
Avocado, peeled, seeded	35	15
Bananas, sliced	35	15
Blueberries	5	9
Cantaloupe, peeled, diced	50	20
Cherries, pitted	15	11
Cranberries	5	9
Grapefruit, sectioned	50	20
Grapes, seedless	5	9
Honeydew melon, peeled, diced	55	21
Mangoes, peeled, pitted	30	14
Nectarines, pitted	10	11
Oranges, sectioned	60	24
Peaches, peeled, pitted	25	13
Pears, peeled, cored	25	13
Pineapple, peeled, diced	50	20
Plums, pitted	5	9
Strawberries, hulled	15	11
Watermelon, rind removed	45	17

Table 1-69. Beef

Beef Cut (edible portion 3 oz)	% Loss from Preparation and Cooking (includes bone weight)	Purchase Amount for Fifty Portions (pounds)
Brisket, boneless	60	24
Brisket, corned	55	21
Beef cubes (stewing)	45	18
Ground beef (25% fat)	25	13
Roasts		
Pot roast, boneless	40	16
Pot roast, bone-in	55	21
Prime rib, boneless	40	16
Prime rib, bone-in	55	21
Ribeye	40	16
Round, boneless	40	16
Rump, boneless	40	16
Sirloin, boneless	40	16
Tenderloin, trimmed	20	12
Short ribs	75	38
Steaks		
Cubed (3 oz)	35	15
Filet mignon (4 oz)	10	15
Flank (3 oz)	35	15
Porterhouse (8 oz)	25	34
Ribeye (6 oz)	25	25
Round (3 oz)	40	16
Sirloin (6 oz)	25	25
T-bone (6 oz)	40	32

Table 1-70. Lamb

Lamb Cut (edible portion 3 oz)	% Loss from Preparation and Cooking (includes bone weight)	Purchase Amount for Fifty Portions (pounds)
Chops		
Arm	55	22
Blade	55	22
English	55	22
French rib	55	22
Leg	40	16
Loin	40	16
Sirloin chops	55	22

Lamb Cut (edible portion 3 oz)	% Loss from Preparation and Cooking (includes bone weight)	Purchase Amount for Fifty Portions (pounds)
Roasts		
Baby lamb	55	22
Breast	45	18
Crown roast	50	19
Leg, boneless	40	16
Leg, bone-in	55	22
Loin	30	15
Rack/rib	50	19
Rolled	40	16
Sirloin	40	16
Kabobs	35	15
Noisettes	10	11
Riblets	60	25
Shank	60	25
Saddle	55	22

Table 1-71. Pork

Pork Cut (edible portion 3 oz)	% Loss from Preparation and Cooking (includes bone weight)	Purchase Amount for Fifty Portions (pounds)
Blade Steaks	45	18
Chops		
Arm	45	18
Blade	45	18
Loin, boneless	25	13
Rib	45	18
Cutlets	10	11
Country-style rib	65	15
Cubes	25	13
Ham		
Boneless butt	37	15
Boston butt	40	16
Ham butt	45	18
Ham steak	35	15
Pullman, cooked	10	11
Shoulder, picnic, boneless	25	13
Hocks	70	32

Pork Cut (edible portion 3 oz)	% Loss from Preparation and Cooking (includes bone weight)	Purchase Amount for Fifty Portions (pounds)
Roasts		
Arm/ham	63	26
Blade	63	26
Center loin	35	15
Center-cut	35	15
Rolled roast	35	15
Tenderloin	25	13
Spareribs	75	38

Table 1-72. Veal

Veal Cut (edible portion 3 oz)	% Loss from Preparation and Cooking (includes bone weight)	Purchase Amount for Fifty Portions (pounds)
Cubes	25	13
Cutlet	25	13
Ground	25	13
Loin chops	62	25
Rib chops	62	25
Roasts		
Boned shoulder	45	18
Boned breast	45	18
Center leg	45	18
Crown	65	27
Shank		
Foreshank	65	27
Hind shank	65	27
Steaks		
Arm	55	22
Round	55	22

Table 1-73. Poultry

Poultry Cut (edible portion 3 oz)	% Loss from Preparation and Cooking (includes bone weight)	Purchase Amount for Fifty Portions (pounds)
Chicken		
Breast half	35	15
Drumstick	50	19
Drumstick and thigh	50	19
Thigh	50	19
Whole	55	21
Whole, stewing	55	21
Wings	63	25
Duck, whole	55	21
Turkey		
Boneless roll, raw	35	15
Boneless roll, cooked	10	11
Breast, whole	45	18
Drumstick	55	21
Leg quarters	55	21
Whole	50	19

Table 1-74. Seafood

Seafood Type (edible portion 3 oz)	% Loss from Preparation and Cooking (includes bone and shell weight)	Purchase Amount for Fifty Portions (pounds)
Finfish		
Whole	70	32
Whole, dressed	65	27
Fillets and steaks	30	14
Shellfish		
Crab, blue	85	63
Crab, Dungeness	75	38
Crab, picked	15	12
Crab, king	50	19
Crab, soft shell	35	15
Clams, hard shell	85	63
Clams, soft shell	72	34
Clams, shucked	55	21
Lobster, picked	15	12
Lobster, tails	50	19

Seafood Type (edible portion 3 oz)	% Loss from Preparation and Cooking (includes bone and shell weight)	Purchase Amount for Fifty Portions (pounds)
Lobster, whole	75	38
Oysters, shucked	55	21
Scallops, breaded IQF	0	10
Scallops, raw	40	16
Shrimp, peeled	40	16
Shrimp, unpeeled	50	19
Shrimp, breaded IQF	0	10
Shrimp, cooked, peeled	15	12

Table 1-75. Vegetables

Vegetable (edible portion 3 oz)	% Loss from Preparation and Cooking	Purchase Amount for Fifty Portions (pounds)
Asparagus	45	17
Beans, string	15	12
Beets	25	13
Broccoli	20	12
Brussels sprouts	25	13
Cabbage, green	15	12
Cabbage, red	30	14
Carrots	30	14
Cauliflower	35	15
Celery	15	12
Chard	10	11
Cucumbers, peeled	15	12
Eggplant	20	12
Endive, curly	20	12
Lettuce, head	25	13
Lettuce, leaf	35	15
Lettuce, romaine	35	15
Mushrooms, trimmed	10	11
Okra, trimmed	15	12
Onions, peeled	15	12
Parsnips	15	12
Peas	60	24
Peppers, bell, seeded	20	12
Potatoes, peeled	20	12
Radishes, trimmed	10	11
Rutabaga	15	12

Vegetable (edible portion 3 oz)	% Loss from Preparation and Cooking	Purchase Amount for Fifty Portions (pounds)
Spinach, trimmed	15	12
Squash, acorn	15	12
Squash, butternut	15	12
Squash, hubbard	35	15
Squash, summer	5	10
Squash, zucchini	5	10
Sweet potatoes	20	12
Tomatoes	5	10
Turnips	20	12

RECIPE EXPANSION AND REDUCTION TABLES

To use these convenient tables, find the column that shows the portion yield of your original recipe. Then, to expand or reduce the portion yield, move to the right or left to find your desired production yield. For example, if a particular recipe yields fifty portions and calls for 1 quart of an ingredient, to prepare four portions of that same recipe you should use approximately ⅓ cup. If you want to prepare 500 servings, you should use approximately 2½ gallons.

TAble 1-76. ORiGiNAL YiELd FOUR PORTiONS

4	10	25	50	75	100	250	500
⅛t	⅓t	¾t	1½t	2⅓t	1T + ⅛t	2T + 2½t	¼c + 1¼T
¼t	⅔t	1½t	3⅛t	1½T	2T + ¼t	¼c + 1½T	½c + 2¼T
½t	1⅓t	1T	2T	3T	¼c + ½t	½c + 2½T	1¼c + 2½t
1t	2½t	2T	¼c + ½t	¼c + 2T	½c + 1t	1¼c + 2t	2½c + 1½T
1½t	4t	3T + ¼t	6T + ½t	½c + 1½T	¾c + 1t	2c	1qt
2t	5t	¼c + ½t	½c + 1t	¾c + 1½t	1c + 2t	2½c + 1½T	1qt + 1¼c
2½t	2¼T	⅓c	⅔c	1c	1¼c + 1T	3¼c	1qt + 2½c
1T	2½T	¼c + 2T	¾c + ½T	1c + 3T	1½c + 1½T	3½c + 2½t	1qt + 3½c
1½T	3¾T	½c + 1T	1c + 1t	1¾c	2c + 2t	1qt + 1¾c	2qt + 3½c
2T	¼c + 1T	¾c + ¼t	1½c + ½t	2⅓c	3c + 1t	1qt + 3½c	3qt + 3½c
3T	¼c + 3½T	1c + ⅛t	2c + ¼t	3½c	1qt + ½t	2qt + 3½c	5qt + 3½c
¼c	½c + 2T	1½c + 1T	3c + 2T	1qt + ⅔c	1qt + 2¼c	3qt + 3½c	1gal + 3½qt
⅓c	½c + 3T	2c + 1T	1qt + 2T	1qt + 2c	2qt + ¼c	5qt + 2½c	2gal + 2½qt
½c	1¼c	3c + 2T	1qt + 2¼c	2qt + 1¼c	3qt + ½c	7qt + 3½c	3gal + 3½qt
⅔c	1½c + 2½t	1qt + 2T	2qt + ⅔c	3qt + ½c	1gal + ¾c	2gal + 2½qt	5gal + 1qt
¾c	1⅞c	1qt + ⅓c	2qt + 1¼c	3½qt	1gal + 2¾c	2gal + 3¼qt	5½gal + 6c

4	10	25	50	75	100	250	500
1c	2½c	1qt + 2¼c	3qt + ½c	1gal + 2¾c	1gal + 2¼qt	3gal + 3¼qt	7½gal + 5c
1¼c	3c + 2T	2qt	1gal	1gal + 7½c	2gal	4gal + 3¼qt	9½gal + 1qt
1½c	3¾c	2qt + ⅔c	1gal + 2½c	1gal + 3qt	2gal + 1¼qt	5gal + 3¼qt	11½gal + 2c
1¾c	1qt + ½c	2qt + 3c	1gal + 1¼qt	2gal + ¾c	2gal + 3qt	6gal + 3¼qt	13½gal + 2c
2c	1qt + 1c	3qt + ½c	1gal + 2¼qt	2gal + 1¼qt	3gal + 2c	7gal + 3¼qt	15½gal + 2c
3c	1qt + 3½c	1gal + 2½c	2gal + 1¼qt	3½gal	4gal + 3½qt	11gal + 3qt	23gal + 7c
1qt	2½qt	1gal + 2¼qt	3gal + 2c	4gal + 2½qt	6gal + 1qt	15½gal + 2c	31gal + 1qt
2qt	1gal + 1qt	3gal + 2c	6gal + 1qt	9gal + 1½qt	12gal + 2qt	31gal + 1qt	62½gal
3qt	1gal + 3½qt	4gal + 3qt	9gal + 1½qt	14gal + 1c	18gal + 3qt	46gal + 3½qt	93gal + 3qt
1gal	2½gal	6gal + 1qt	12gal + 2qt	18gal + 3qt	25gal	62gal + 2qt	125gal

Table 1-77. Original Yield Ten Portions

4	10	25	50	75	100	250	500
pinch	**⅛t**	⅓t	⅝t	⅞t	1¼t	1T + ⅛t	2T + ¼t
⅛t	**¼t**	⅔t	1½t	1¾t	2½t	2T + ¼t	¼c + ½t
¼t	**½t**	1¼t	2½t	1T + ¾t	1T + 2t	¼c + ½t	½c + 1t
½t	**1t**	2½t	1T + 2t	2T + 1½t	3T + 1t	½c + 1t	1c + 2t
⅔t	**1½t**	1T + ⅛t	2T + 1½t	3T + 2¼t	¼c + 1T	¾c + 1½t	1½c + 1T
¾t	**2t**	1T + 2t	3T + 1t	¼c + 1t	⅓c + 1T	1c + 2t	2c + 1½T
1t	**2½t**	2T + ¼t	¼c + 1t	⅓c + 2½t	½c + 1t	1¼c + 2½t	2⅔c
1¼t	**1T**	2½T	¼c + 1T	⅓c + 1T	½c + 2T	1½c + 1T	3c + 2T
1¾t	**1½T**	3T + 2¼t	⅓c + 2T	⅔c	¾c + 3T	2¼c + 2¼t	1qt + ¾c
2½t	**2T**	¼c + 2T	½c + 2T	¾c + 3T	1¼c	3c + 2T	1½qt + ¼c
1T + ½t	**3T**	¼c + 3½T	¾c + 3T	1⅓c	1⅞c	1qt + ⅔c	2qt + 1½c
1½T	**¼c**	⅔c	1¼c	1⅞c	2½c	1qt + 2¼c	3qt + ½c
2T	**⅓c**	¾c + ½t	1⅔c	2½c	3⅓c	2qt + ⅔c	1gal + 1½c
3T + ½t	**½c**	1¼c	2½c	3¾c	1qt + 1c	3qt + ½c	1½gal + 1c
¼c	**⅔c**	1½c + 1t	3⅓c	1qt + 1c	1qt + 2½c	1gal + ⅔c	2gal + 1½c
¼c + 1½T	**¾c**	1¾c + 1t	3¾c	1qt + 1½c	1qt + 3½c	1gal + 2½c	2¼gal + 1c
⅓c + 1T	**1c**	2½c	1¼qt	1qt + 3½c	2qt + 2c	1½gal + 1c	2gal + 2c
½c	**1¼c**	3c + 2T	1qt + 2¼c	2qt + 1½c	3qt + ½c	1½gal + 7c	4gal
½c + 1½T	**1½c**	3¾c	1qt + 3½c	2qt + 3¼c	3qt + 3c	2gal + 1¼qt	4gal + 2½qt
⅔c	**1¾c**	1qt + ⅓c	2qt + ¾c	3qt + 1c	1gal + 1½c	2gal + 3qt	5½gal
¾c + 1T	**2c**	1qt + 1c	2qt + 3c	3qt + 3c	1gal + 1qt	3gal + 2c	6¼gal
1c + 3T	**3c**	1qt + 3½c	3qt + 3c	1gal + 1½qt	1gal + 3½qt	4½gal + 3c	9gal + 6c
1½c + 1T	**1qt**	2½qt	1gal + 1qt	1gal + 3½qt	2gal + 2qt	6gal + 1qt	12½gal
3c + 3T	**2qt**	1gal + 1qt	2gal + 2qt	3gal + 3qt	5gal	12½gal	25gal
1qt + ¾c	**3qt**	1gal + 3½qt	3gal + 3qt	5gal + 2½qt	7gal + 2qt	18gal + 3qt	37½gal
1qt + 2½c	**1gal**	2½gal	5gal	7gal + 2qt	10gal	25gal	50gal

Table 1-78. Original Yield Twenty-five Portions

4	10	25	50	75	100	250	500
pinch	pinch	⅛t	¼t	⅜t	½t	1¼t	2½t
pinch	⅛t	¼t	½t	¾t	1t	2½t	2T + 2t
pinch	¼t	½t	1t	1½t	2t	1T + 2t	3T + 1t
⅛t	⅓t	1t	2t	1T	1T + 1t	3T + 1t	¼c + 3T
¼t	½t	1½t	1T	1T + 1½t	2T	¼c + 1½T	½c + 3T
⅓t	¾t	2t	1T + 1t	2T	2T + 2t	⅓c + ½t	⅔ + 1t
½t	1t	2½t	1T + 2t	2T + 1½t	3T + 1t	½c + 1t	1c + 2t
½t	1¼t	1T	2T	3T	¼c	⅔c	1⅓c
¾t	1¾t	1½T	3T	¼c + 1T	¼c + 2T	¾c + 1½T	1½c + 3T
1t	2½t	2T	¼c	¼c + 2T	½c	1¼c	2½c
1½t	1T + ½t	3T	¼c + 2T	½c + 1T	¾c	¾c + 1½t	3¾c
2t	1½T	¼c	½c	¾c	1c	2½c	1qt + 1c
2½t	2T + ½t	⅓c	⅔c	1c	1⅓c	3⅓c	1½qt + ½c
1T + ¾t	3T + 1t	½c	1c	1½c	2c	1qt + 1c	2½qt
1T + 2t	¼c	⅔c	1⅓c	2c	2⅔c	1qt + 2½c	3qt + 1c
1T + 2½t	⅓c	¾c	1½c	2½c	3c	1qt + 3½c	3qt + 3c
2T + 1½t	⅓c + 1½T	1c	2c	3c	1qt	2½qt	1gal + 1qt
3T + ½t	½c	1¼c	2½c	3¾c	1qt + 1c	3qt + ½c	1gal + 2¼qt
3T + 2½t	½c + 1½t	1½c	3c	1qt + ½c	1½qt	3qt + 3c	1gal + 3½qt
¼c + 1½t	⅔c	1¾c	3½c	1qt + 1¼c	1qt + 3c	1gal + 1½c	2gal + 3c
¼c + 1T	¾c + 2½t	2c	1qt	1½qt	2qt	1gal + 1qt	2½gal
½ + 3½T	1c + 3½T	3c	1½qt	2¼qt	3qt	1gal + 3½qt	3gal + 3qt
⅔c	1½c + 1½T	1qt	2qt	3qt	1gal	2½gal	5gal
1½c + 1½t	3c + 3T	2qt	1gal	1½gal	2gal	5gal	10gal
1⅞c	1qt + ¾c	3qt	1½gal	2gal + 1qt	3gal	7½gal	15gal
2½c + 1T	1½qt + ¼c	1gal	2gal	3gal	4gal	10gal	20gal

Table 1-79. Original Yield Fifty Portions

4	10	25	50	75	100	250	500
2t	1T + 2t	¼c	½c	¾c	1c	2½c	1qt + 1c
2½t	2T + ½t	⅓c	⅔c	1c	1⅓c	3⅓c	1qt + 2½c
2¾t	2T + 1¼t	⅓c + 2t	¾c	1c + 1½t	1½c	3¾c	1qt + 3½c
1T + 1t	3T + ½t	½c	1c	1½c	2c	1qt + 1c	2½qt
1T + 1½t	¼c	½c + 2T	1¼c	1½c + 2¼t	2½c	1qt + 2¼c	3qt + ½c
2T	¼c + 2½t	¾c	1½c	2¼c	3c	1qt + 3½c	3qt + 3c
2¼T	¼c + 1½T	¾c + 2T	1¾c	2½c + ¾t	3½c	2qt + ¾c	1gal + 1½c
2½T	¼c + 2½T	1c	2c	3c	1qt	2½qt	1gal + 1qt
¼c	½c + 1½T	1½c	3c	1qt + ½c	1½qt	3qt + 3c	1gal + 3½qt
⅓c	¾c + 2½t	2c	1qt	1½qt	2qt	1gal + 1qt	2½gal
⅔c	1½c + 1½T	1qt	2qt	3qt	1gal	2½gal	5gal
1c	2¼c + 2½T	1½qt	3qt	1gal + 2c	1½gal	3gal + 3qt	7½gal
1¼c	3c + 3T	2qt	1gal	1½gal	2gal	5gal	10gal
pinch	pinch	pinch	⅛t	⅛t	¼t	⅔t	1¼t

4	10	25	50	75	100	250	500
pinch	⅛t	⅛t	¼t	⅓t	½t	1¼t	2½t
pinch	⅛t	¼t	½t	¾t	1t	2½t	1T + 2t
⅛t	¼t	½t	1t	1½t	2t	1T + 2t	3T + 1t
⅛t	⅓t	¾t	1½t	2¼t	1T	2T + 1½t	¼c + 2T
⅛t	⅓t	1t	2t	1T	1T + 1t	3T + 1t	¼c + 2½T
¼t	½t	1¼t	2½t	1T + 1¼t	1T + 2t	¼c + ½t	½c + 1t
¼t	½t	1½t	1T	1T + 1½t	2T	¼c + 1½t	½c + 2T
½t	1t	2¼t	1½T	2T + ¾t	3T	⅓c + 2T	¾c + 3T
½t	1¼t	1T	2T	3T	¼c	½c + 2T	1½c
¾t	1¾t	1T + 1½t	3T	¼c + 1½t	¼c + 2T	¾c + 1T	1⅞c
1t	2½t	2T	¼c	¼c + 2T	½c	1½c	2½c
1¼t	1T + ½t	2T + 2t	⅓c	½c	⅔c	1⅔c	3⅓c

The Language of Food

Menu Writer's Thesaurus

American Regional Food Terms: Definitions and Origins

International Food Terms: Definitions and Origins

Food Word Translations

French Food Words: Pronunciations and Definitions

Italian Food Words: Pronunciations and Definitions

Spanish Food Words: Pronunciations and Definitions

Menu Writer's Thesaurus

Menu writers often find themselves, quite literally, at a loss for words. Whether your objective is to create a new menu, write the dinner specials board, or promote a special event, the words you choose can add power to your pen. The following list offers several hundred words that have culinary uses, every one accompanied by related alternatives.

A

alcohol	liquor, spirits, booze, firewater, white lightning
alternative	choice, option, preference, pick
amazing	astounding, miraculous, incredible, unprecedented
ambrosial	savory, delicious, flavorful, fragrant, divine, heavenly, ethereal
amenity	courtesy, grace, geniality, protocol, pleasantry
ample	plentiful, bountiful, abundant, numerous, profuse, luxuriant
apex	summit, pinnacle, acme, zenith, peak, crest
appetite	hunger, thirst, craving, desire
appetizer	canapé, starter, bite, dainty, tidbit, morsel, antipasto, *pu pu*, hors d'oeuvre, *bonne bouche*
appetizing	savory, luscious, flavorful, delectable, delicious, ambrosial, appealing, enticing, tantalizing, seductive
applause	salvo, bravo, ovation, encore, acclaim, kudos, accolades
aquatic	maritime, oceanic, nautical
arctic	polar, frigid, ice-cold, frosty, chilly, snowy, wintry, glacial
aroma	scent, smell, bouquet, fragrance, savor, breath
aromatic	fragrant, scented, perfumed, spicy, savory, pungent, piquant
arouse	incite, kindle, ignite, electrify, rally, revive, whet, invigorate
art	skill, dexterity, mastery, ingenuity, talent, flair, genius, touch
artful	ingenious, clever, inventive
artistic	beautiful, exquisite, magnificent, harmonious, brilliant, masterful, tasteful, cultivated, original, virtuoso
artistry	brilliance, genius, talent, skill, knack, feel, gift
assorted	varied, mixed, diverse, miscellaneous, motley
assortment	collection, mixture, mélange, medley, potpourri, hash
assure	assert, affirm, pledge, promise, certify, warrant, strengthen
astounding	amazing, astonishing, wonderful, startling, surprising
atmosphere	environment, setting, surroundings, ambience, aura, tone, mood, character, spirit, feeling
auburn	reddish-brown, copper, bronze, rust, cinnamon, golden-brown, chestnut, russet

au courant	up-to-date, contemporary, current, stylish, trendy, hip, with it, vogue, modern, up-to-the-minute
authentic	reliable, trustworthy, realistic, genuine, real, bona fide, real life, the real McCoy, authoritative, confirmed
autumn	fall, harvest time, harvest gold
avant-garde	new, current, fashionable, explorative, innovative, modern, unique, novel, creative
awaken	arouse, animate, activate, enliven, excite, kindle, spark
awesome	impressive, marvelous, fantastic, noble, regal, awe-inspiring

B

backwater	country, frontier, retreat, rustic, seclusion
bait	lure, entice, intrigue, bewitch, tantalize, charm, stimulate, arouse
balmy	mild, calm, fair, pleasant, soothing, fragrant, aromatic, scented
banquet	feast, repast, dinner, spread, revelry, carnival, bacchanalia
barbecue	spit-roast, cookout, picnic, grill, broiler, al fresco
basic	fundamental, essential, vital, traditional, familiar
beer	malt, ale, porter, stout, lager, bock, suds
befitting	suitable, proper, relevant, appropriate
best	unsurpassed, superior, foremost, preeminent, consummate, superlative, sterling, first-class
bevy	multitude, galaxy, host, number, array, collection, sea, assembly
bewitch	lure, tantalize, seduce, enchant, captivate, fascinate, mesmerize
biscuit	bun, scone, cracker, rusk
bit	piece, touch, trace, smidgen, shadow, shaving, sprinkle
bitter	acrid, pungent, sour, tart, acid, vinegary
bizarre	strange, uncommon, quaint, eccentric, weird, absurd, fantastic
black	ebony, raven, sable, pitch, inky, jet
bland	mild, suave, calming
blithe	cheerful, happy, pleased, contented, merry, gleeful
blue	sky-blue, baby-blue, powder-blue, deep-blue, azure, sapphire, aquamarine, turquoise, marine, navy, indigo
blush	flush, redden, scarlet, glow, hint, hue, suggestion
bonbon	candy, fondant, confection, sweet, mint, nougat, toffee
bottle	glass, vial, flask, decanter, carafe, pitcher, flagon
brine	pickle, marinate, steep, soak
broad	wide, extensive, immense, vast, unlimited, boundless, infinite
broil	grill, barbecue, spit-roast, sear, panbroil, singe, blacken

brown	bay, chestnut, brunette, auburn, coffee, chocolate, mahogany, walnut, cinnamon, ginger, tawny, tan, khaki

C

cabaret	nightclub, discotheque, disco, casino, honky-tonk, bistro, rathskeller, beer garden, bar, juke joint
café	coffeehouse, bistro, restaurant, diner, automat, bar and grill
cake	fritter, torte, *dacquoise*
candied	glacé, sugared, honeyed, sugar-coated
candy	confection, sweets, fondant, *confit*, sweetmeat, butterscotch, caramel, peppermint, dainty, tidbit
carafe	decanter, bottle, flask, flagon, carboy, jug
cask	keg, barrel, vat, vessel, hogshead
casserole	terrine, baking dish
cater	furnish, supply, indulge, humor, gratify, satisfy, attend, entertain, regale, wine and dine
celestial	sublime, heavenly, glorious, golden, olympian
char	sear, toast, broil, grill, blacken, charcoal
china	porcelain, stoneware, ironstone, pottery, crocks, terracotta
coffee	espresso, capuccino, café au lait, java
coin	copper, silver, gold, change, doubloon, jinglers, pin money, chicken feed, petty cash
concoction	mixture, drink, creation, invention, potion
confection	sweet, candy, bonbon, sweetmeat, dainty, preserve, confit
cook	prepare, create, concoct, combine, compose, improvise, brew up, broil, grill, roast, sauté, boil, simmer, poach, braise, steam, fry, stir-fry, panfry, panbroil
cool	timely, stylish, vogue, hip, nippy, icy
copious	ample, bountiful, extensive, abundant, teeming, lavish, luxuriant
creative	innovative, inspired, talented, artistic, formative, trend-setting, clever, imaginative
crimson	burgundy, wine, scarlet, red, ruby, cardinal, cranberry
cup	mug, stein, demitasse, saucer, chalice, tankard, wineskin, tumbler, goblet, beaker

D

dash	bit, touch, tinge, trace, suggestion, hint, smack, sprinkling, tad, smidgen
dinner	banquet, repast, feast, refection, table d'hote
dish	container, tureen, vessel, tray, platter, crock, porringer

E

eat	dine, nosh, graze, bolt, nibble, scarf, consume, chew, devour, crunch, break bread, gobble
eclectic	broad-based, liberal, varied, grab bag, comprehensive, multifaceted
embers	coals, charcoal, barbecue, spit-roast, gray, hot, glowing
epicure	connoisseur, gourmet, libertine, gourmand
epicurean	stylish, refined, cultivated, fine, polished, tasteful, noble

F

fabled	legendary, historic, fabulous, storied, famous
fad	style, chic, vogue, trend, craze, mania, rage, furor, last word
festival	fete, banquet, carnival, Mardi Gras, anniversary, gala, festivity, feast, wassail, reception, hilarity
festive	joyous, jolly, convivial, mirthful, gleeful, hospitable
fizz	champagne, bubbles, sputter, ferment, sparkling, effervescence, spray, foam
flagon	mug, stein, demitasse, saucer, chalice, tankard, wineskin, tumbler, goblet, beaker, decanter, carafe
flaming	flambé, afire, ablaze, glow, radiate, spark, luminous
flask	mug, stein, demitasse, saucer, chalice, tankard, wineskin, tumbler, goblet, beaker, decanter, carafe
flavor	taste, savor, essence, spirit, sense, soul, style, tang, character
flavorful	tasty, delicious, satisfying, delectable, luscious, ambrosial, pleasant, appetizing
food	nourishment, comestible, victuals, vittles, sustenance, rations, chow, mess, provisions, menu
fowl	hen, chicken, duck, broiler, roaster, turkey, guinea hen, partridge, quail, pheasant
fresh	new, bright, garden-fresh, vibrant, keen, original, vogue, chic, modern, au courant

G

gaiety	élan, cheer, gladness, felicity, delight, joy, merrymaking, joviality, merriment, laughter, dancing, exultation
gala	jubilee, celebration, banquet, fete, carnival, happening, extravaganza, ritual, pageant
gem	stone, jewel, crown, priceless, diamond, ruby, sapphire, masterpiece, bijou, ornament, pearl, work of art, wonder, pièce de résistance
glacial	icy, ice-cold, polar, frozen, frosty, freezing, Siberian, arctic

gourmet	connoisseur, libertine, gourmand
green	verdant, lincoln, jade, kelly, aqua, turquoise, olive, grassy, fresh
grill	barbecue, broil, spit-roast, coals, hot, blacken, gridiron

H

hallmark	pinnacle, peak, acme, apex, top, stamp, seal, cachet
haunch	leg, loin, thigh, side, flank, round, rump
hazel	nutbrown, acorn, cinnamon, beige, khaki, tawny, russet
heady	strong, full, aromatic, robust, intoxicating, exciting, thrilling, stimulating, electrifying, invigorating
healthful	salubrious, wholesome, nutritious, invigorating, bracing, stimulating, beneficial, tonic
hearth	fireside, fireplace, chimney, homestead, rustic
hearty	vigorous, lusty, strong, stout, substantial, nutritious, nourishing
heat	zest, bite, tang, piquancy, warmth, intensity, fire
heavenly	blissful, delightful, savory, sublime, enchanting, flawless, ideal
hefty	sizeable, heavy, substantial, mammoth, ample, mighty, colossal, enormous, gigantic
heighten	intensify, sharpen, increase, augment, magnify, deepen
heritage	tradition, legacy, history, ancestry, background
highlight	feature, focus, essence, pith, meat, gist, substance, distinction
hint	trace, tinge, touch, trace, lace, sprinkle, whisper, dash, speck, touch
hip	cool, in, chic, vogue, stylish, trendy, hot
holiday	festival, fete, banquet, carnival, Mardi Gras, anniversary, gala, festivity, feast, wassail, reception, hilarity
homemade	natural, rustic, domestic, native, homey, rural, simple, basic, down-home, folksy, warm
honey	nectar, syrup, molasses, sorghum, peachy, sweet
honeyed	sweetened, charming, sugary, candied, nectared, rich
hors d'oeuvre	starter, tidbit, nosh, canapé, aperitif, relish, smorgasbord, tapas, zensai
hospitality	warmth, grace, charm, kindness, amicability, cordiality
hot	zesty, piquant, heated, spicy, curry, chili, blazing, scorching, steaming, torrid, searing, sultry, peppery, pungent
hot	up-to-date, contemporary, current, stylish, trendy, hip, with it, vogue, modern, up-to-the-minute
hotel	inn, motel, motor inn, tavern, B&B, rooming house, lodge, hostel
huge	gigantic, gargantuan, enormous, herculean, monumental, massive, towering, prodigious
hunger	appetite, desire, yen, craving, thirst, hankering, urge, itch, covet, crave

hungry	ravenous, starving, famished
hunk	chunk, slab, portion, wedge, serving, share, portion

I

icing	frosting, glaze, fondant
icy	freezing, arctic, glacial, Siberian, wintry, frosty, zippy, snappy
ignite	flame, touch off, alight, kindle, glow, inflame, flambé
imbibe	drink, savor, take part, quaff, sip
immerse	plunge, dunk, steep, douse, drench
incense	perfume, aroma, fragrance, scent, redolence, bouquet
induce	entice, elicit, lure, bait, persuade, convince, sway, inspire, nudge
indulge	satisfy, gratify, appease, satiate, fulfill, pamper, fawn
informal	casual, natural, comfortable, at ease, unpretentious, homespun, down-home, unassuming, bohemian
infuse	steep, permeate, submerge, marinate, season, flavor
inky	raven, sable, black, ebony, jet
inn	hotel, motel, motor, tavern, B&B, rooming house, lodge, hostel
inspired	animated, enlivened, fresh, aroused, excited, awake, alert, alive
instill	infuse, saturate, permeate, steep
interlace	weave, mesh, crisscross, zigzag, entwine, mingle, twist
inventive	innovative, inspired, talented, artistic, formative, trend-setting, clever, imaginative
inviting	enticing, alluring, tempting, tantalizing, seductive, stimulating, captivating, appetizing
iridescent	shimmery, pearly, glimmering, opalescent, sparkling, shiny, flickering, lustrous

J

jam	preserves, conserves, marmalade, jelly, confit, confection
jelly	aspic, blancmange, pudding, preserves, conserves, marmalade, jam, confit, confection
jewel	stone, gem, crown, priceless, diamond, ruby, sapphire, masterpiece, bijou, ornament, pearl, work of art, wonder, pièce de résistance
jubilee	fete, banquet, carnival, Mardi Gras, anniversary, gala, festivity, feast, wassail, reception, hilarity

K

keg	cask, barrel, vat, vessel, hogshead
kernel	nugget, core, seed, grain, center

kettle	pot, pan, stewpot, cauldron, crucible
kipper	cure, smoke, salt, brine, preserve
kitchen	cookhouse, cookroom, galley, scullery, *cocina*, larder, bakehouse, chuck-wagon
knead	work, manipulate, press, form, massage
kudos	accolades, applause, salvo, bravo, ovation, encore, acclaim

L

lacy	light, filigree, webbed, gossamer, thin, meshed, translucent
lagniappe	bonus, extra, baker's dozen, dividend, fringe, perc
larder	kitchen, pantry, chamber, scullery, storeroom, stockroom, buttery, stillroom
legendary	fabled, storied, famous, immortal, marvelous, fabulous, heroic, prominent, exalted, touted, acclaimed
lemon	citrus, fruit, acid, tart, sour, yellow, tangy
lightly	brightly, easily, flittingly, gently, merrily, saucily, gladly
liqueur	cordial, nightcap, after-dinner drink
liquor	spirits, booze, firewater, white lightning, hooch
lively	brisk, sprightly, fresh, invigorating, nimble, spry, vivacious, vivid, flashy, peppy, zingy
lounge	café, bistro, nightclub, disco, taproom, barroom, cabaret
luster	sheen, shine, gloss, polish, twinkle, brilliance, dazzle
lustrous	shiny, glossy, radiant, gleaming, dazzling, brilliant, superb, rich, renowned, distinguished
lusty	bold, vigorous, stout, hearty, heady, heavy, substantial, satisfying
luxuriant	copious, ample, bountiful, abundant, lavish

M

macaroni	pasta, noodle, spaghetti, elbows, butterfly, shells
macerate	steep, soak, marinate, soften
magenta	reddish purple, fuchsia, crimson, red, scarlet, carmine
marvelous	wondrous, remarkable, superb, splendid, a-one, first class, top drawer, astounding
masterly	artful, supreme, excellent, superior, peerless, expert, distinguished
meal	repast, breakfast, lunch, dinner, nosh, brunch, fare, menu, board, table d'hote, tiffin
mélange	mixture, medley, olio, miscellany, salmagundi, cluster, symphony
menu	table d'hote, à la carte, bill of fare, carte, card
milky	white, creamy, translucent, opalescent, iridescent, frosted, ivory, alabaster

mince	dice, chop, hash, crumb, fragment
miniature	bantam, lilliputian, teeny, wee, little, minute
mist	cloud, vapor, haze, gauze, fog
mixture	mélange, potpourri, composition, ragout, hodgepodge, jumble, hash, pastiche, pasticcio
morsel	tidbit, bite, hint, crumb, piece, sliver, shaving, smidgen, speck, suggestion, hint, tinge
mug	tankard, stein, chalice, schooner, pilsner, glass
myriad	host, mass, legion, innumerable, limitless, endless, scillions and zillions, gobs, torrent
mystique	aura, atmosphere, essence, spell, charm, delight, character, mood

N

native	homegrown, local, domestic, indigenous, authentic
noble	superior, sublime, lofty, choice, prime
nonstop	ceaseless, constant, continuous, around the clock
nosh	snack, eat between meals, nibble, peck, morsel, tidbit
noticeable	conspicuous, notable, remarkable, unforgettable, special, momentous
nourishing	healthful, healthy, wholesome, nurturing, supporting
novel	new, innovative, hot off the fire, avant-garde
nuance	subtlety, shade, hint, suggestion, trace, tinge, touch, distinction
nut	kernel, grain, pip, seed
nutbrown	brown, tan, hazel, coffee, cinnamon
nutritious	healthful, wholesome, beneficial

O

oasis	watering hole, haven, retreat, refuge, resort, asylum
odor	aroma, scent, perfume, essence, bouquet
olio	mixture, hash, stew, chowder, hodgepodge, potpourri
opaque	dense, murky, hazy, foggy, dark, dull
opening	kickoff, birth, premiere, dawn, threshold, debut
optimum	finest, best, acme, pinnacle, paragon, phoenix
opulence	wealth, riches, fortune, bounty
opulent	abundant, profuse, teeming, lavish, luxuriant
original	primary, novel, new, creative, innovative, source, genesis
ornate	elegant, frilly, elaborate, baroque, arabesque, rococo, flamboyant
outdoor	al fresco, barbecue, picnic, open air, open spaces

ovation	salvo, bravo, encore, acclaim, kudos, accolades, plaudits, stomping, rooting, cheering
overtone	hint, suggestion, shadow, innuendo, sense, spirit

P

pacify	quiet, calm, lull, soothe, relieve, comfort
pageantry	flourish, revelry, gala, grandeur, splendor, flair
palate	taste, appetite, tongue, appreciation, delight
pan	kettle, pot, cauldron, casserole, chafing dish
panache	brilliance, glitter, splendor, flamboyance, chic, elan, style
pancake	crepe, flapjack, griddle cake, hotcake, buttercake, flannelcake, blini, latke, blintz, tortilla, chapati
paramount	superlative, outstanding, greatest, champion, superior, premier
parboil	blanch, precook, scald
party	fete, banquet, carnival, Mardi Gras, anniversary, gala, festivity, feast, wassail, reception, hilarity
pastel	shade, tint, subtle, shaded, pale, subdued, delicate
pastry	pie, tart, puff, vol-au-vent, paté choux, eclair, Danish
patio	terrace, piazza, flagstone, porch, court, courtyard, cloister
peak	pinnacle, summit, top, crest, apex, zenith, supremacy, perfection
pearly	creamy, milky, snowy, iridescent, opalescent
penetrating	deep, sharp, pointed, keen, acute
pepper	condiment, spice, chilies
peppery	hot, burning, spicy, racy, nippy, piquant, seasoned, stimulating
peppy	energetic, vigorous, bubbly, dynamic, electric, alive
perfect	ideal, flawless, pure, supreme, incomparable, exquisite, champion, polished, seasoned
perfume	scent, smell, bouquet, fragrance, savor, breath
perky	lively, pert, sprightly, dynamic, chipper, buoyant, frolicsome
peruse	read, study, scan, eye, scrutinize, wade into
pickle	brine, steep, marinade, preserve, cure, kipper
pickle	gherkin, chowchow, chutney, condiment, piccalilli
pick-me-up	refreshment, shot in the arm, tonic, bracer, stimulant, cordial
picnic	al fresco, outing, barbecue, clambake, oyster roast, luau, spree, excursion, fish fry
pie	tart, pasty, turnover, quiche
pinch	tinge, hint, sprinkling, suggestion, shade, trace
piquant	pungent, spicy, zesty, peppery, curried, sharp, tantalizing, snappy, spiced, piercing

pitcher	carafe, urn, samovar, tankard, stein, crock, toby, jar
pleasure	enjoyment, satisfaction, contentment, jubilation, joy
plentiful	ample, bountiful, abundant, copious, profuse, abounding, lavish
plush	luxurious, posh, swanky, classy, elegant, sumptuous, opulent
polite	courteous, civil, respectful, refined, gracious, suave, sophisticated
posh	deluxe, elegant, grand, baroque, showy, flowery
potent	strong, heady, powerful, intense, packs a wallop, forceful
potpourri	mixture, hash, stew, chowder, hodgepodge
powder	dust, sprinkle, spray, flour, scatter, dabble
premiere	debut, opening, principal, first, highest, earliest
prepare	make, create, fix, cook, bake, concoct, whip up, compose, invent
preserve	brine, steep, marinade, preserve, cure, kipper
preserve	conserves, marmalade, jelly, confit, confection
pretty	pleasing, delightful, beautiful, delicate, appealing, bonny, cute as a button
promotion	advertising, publicity, heralding, blurb, placard, notice, flyer, leaflet, broadside, fanfare
provender	feed, fodder, nourishment, food, sustenance, munchies, snack, nosh, tidbit, comestibles
pudding	custard, flummery, rennet, bombe, mousseline, blancmange, souffle, mousse
pungent	biting, bitter, acid, tangy, sour, stinging, burning

Q

quaff	drink, imbibe, gulp, swallow, guzzle, belt
quality	distinction, superiority, eminence, nobility, value, worth, supremacy
quantity	amount, sum, share, portion, dole, batch, quota
quench	satisfy, satiate, sate, hit the spot, soothe

R

radiant	shining, bright, dazzling, brilliant, sparkling, shimmering, scintillating, luminous
rare	uncommon, unique, notable, singular, excellent, extraordinary, exquisite, preeminent, precious
raven	black, glossy, jet-black, coal-black, ebony, sable
red	scarlet, crimson, ruby, cardinal, port, claret, russet, cherry, cranberry, vermillion, salmon, lobster, coral
red-hot	burning, scorching, blistering, spicy, racy, nippy, piquant, seasoned, stimulating

refreshing	quenching, exhilarating, inviting, rejuvenating, revitalizing, bracing
region	area, location, territory, section, zone, locale, province, district, quarter, realm
relax	loosen, calm, tranquilize, soothe, unwind, unbend, lay back, hang loose, loosen up, lounge
relish	pleasure, gusto, zest, desire, wish, delight
relish	piccalilli, chowchow, sauce, condiment, chili sauce
repast	meal, banquet, feast, snack
reputation	name, renown, notoriety, respect, esteem, celebrity, eminence
restaurant	inn, tavern, bistro, cafeteria, brasserie, coffeehouse, beanery, cabaret, automat, drive-in, deli, lunch counter
revelry	élan, cheer, gladness, felicity, delight, joy, merrymaking, joviality, merriment, laughter, dancing, exultation
rich	opulent, lavish, lush, fragrant, aromatic, ambrosial, savory, strong, pungent
ripe	mature, aged, mellow, bloomed, full-grown, golden, seasoned
ritzy	elegant, posh, luxurious, snazzy, swell, flashy, elaborate, swank, chic, stylish
roast	barbecue, grill, spit-roast, bake, broil, sear
romantic	original, inventive, creative
rosy	salmon, coral, pink, cherry, cerise, cheerful, bright, sunny
rustic	rural, down-home, sylvan, plain, unassuming, peasant, bucolic

S

sable	black, glossy, jet-black, coal-black, ebony
salmagundi	mixture, hash, stew, chowder, hodgepodge, potpourri
salty	saline, briny, piquant, pungent, sharp, biting, spicy
sauce	condiment, dressing, relish, chutney, seasoning, velvet
savor	essence, spirit, enjoy, indulge, appreciate, treasure, prize
savory	delicious, tasty, flavorful, piquant, pungent, tangy, epicurean
scent	smell, bouquet, fragrance, savor, breath
scorching	burning, blistering, spicy, racy, nippy, piquant, seasoned, stimulating
scrumptious	delicious, mouth-watering, tasty, splendid, magnificent, wonderful, terrific, delectable
sea	ocean, briny deep, bounding main, open sea, the drink
seasoned	pungent, spicy, zesty, peppery, curried, sharp, tantalizing, snappy, spiced, piercing
seasoning	spice, herb, flavor, zest, aromatic, condiment
sensational	exciting, arousing, bracing, rousing, electrifying, marvelous, amazing, astounding

serenity	tranquility, peacefulness, quiet, calm, stillness, quiescence
sharp	pungent, spicy, zesty, peppery, curried, sharp, tantalizing, snappy, spiced, piercing
shimmer	glow, gleam, glimmer, shine, glisten, sparkle, iridescence
shiny	glossy, glowing, lustrous, gleaming, radiant, brilliant, beaming, shimmering
silken	delicate, elegant, fragile, diaphanous, smooth, sleek
silvery	glossy, glowing, lustrous, gleaming, radiant, brilliant, beaming, shimmering
simmer	stew, poach, bubble, seethe
singe	char, blacken, grill, broil, spit-roast, brown
slice	slab, wedge, hunk, sliver, rasher, shaving, collop, cutlet
slow	gradual, moderate, leisurely, unhurried, measured, methodical, deliberate
smell	scent, perfume, bouquet, fragrance, savor, breath
smoky	hazy, foggy, frosty, blackened, brown
snack	nosh, tidbit, bite, canapé, hors d'oeuvre, morsel, munchy
soft	plush, smooth, silken, satiny, velvety, fleecy, furry, gentle, calm, temperate, warm
soup	bisque, chowder, stew, puree, potage, bouillon, broth, consommé, gumbo, mulligatawny
sour	acid, tart, vinegary, bitter
spacious	open, free, roomy, vast, immense, gigantic, mammoth, expansive
spice	herb, flavor, zest, aromatic, condiment, bite
spicy	pungent, spicy, zesty, peppery, curried, sharp, tantalizing, snappy, spiced, piercing
spirited	animated, lively, vivacious, energetic, hearty, stout, bubbling, dynamic, spunky
spit	charcoal, barbecue, rotisserie, skewer
splash	dash, hint, trace, lace, sprinkle, spray
stew	ragout, salmagundi, slumgullion, hodgepodge, fricassee, chowder, olla podrida, salmi, soup
stuffing	dressing, forcemeat, farce
stylish	chic, dapper, fashionable, trend, fad, tone, spirit, zest, character, panache, élan, avant-garde
sugary	sweetened, charming, honeyed, candied, nectared, rich
superb	distinguished, excellent, first-rate, top drawer, noteworthy, exemplary, choice, prime, glorious
superior	distinguished, excellent, first-rate, top drawer, noteworthy, exemplary, choice, prime, glorious

supper	banquet, repast, feast, refection, table d'hote
sweet	sugary, honeyed, confection, candy, bonbon

T

tab	check, bill, charge, tally, score
table	stand, counter, buffet, sideboard, banquette, dinner, banquet, two-top, four-top
talent	skill, dexterity, mastery, ingenuity, flair, genius, touch
tan	bay, chestnut, brunette, auburn, coffee, chocolate, mahogany, walnut, cinnamon, ginger, tawny, khaki
tart	pie, torte, quiche, pasty, turnover
tart	sharp, sour, acid, lemony, acerbic, acrid, bitter, harsh, piquant
taste	savor, relish, nibble, nosh, flavor, savor, spice, tang
tasteful	chic, dapper, fashionable, trend, fad, tone, spirit, character, panache, élan, avant-garde
tasty	savory, delightful, palatable, pleasing, yummy, luscious, scrumptious, ambrosial
tavern	inn, cabaret, disco, bar, barroom, brasserie, taproom, lounge, watering hole, gin mill, honky-tonk, speakeasy
tender	butterlike, delicate
thin	lean, spare, scant, lanky, svelte, slim, lithe
tinge	touch, trace, lace, sprinkle, whisper, dash, speck
tint	hue, color, pastel, shade, tone, cast, subtle
tiny	diminutive, bantam, lilliputian, teeny, wee, little, minute
trace	touch, hint, suggestion, lace, sprinkle, whisper, dash, speck

U

ultimate	maximum, most, supreme, paramount, greatest, superlative
ultra	max, extreme, radical, notable, extraordinary, exceptional, remarkable
uncommon	unique, notable, singular, excellent, extraordinary, exquisite, preeminent, precious

V

valued	prized, esteemed, respected, treasured, revered, venerated, adored
vanguard	forefront, cutting edge, avant-garde, innovation, creativity, trailblazer, trend-setter
variation	departure, alternative, divergence, change of pace, option
variety	choice, selection, assortment, mélange, medley, potpourri, pastiche, patchwork

verdant	green, fresh, sylvan, grassy, pastoral
version	rendition, interpretation, conception, rendering
vibrant	alive, animated, lively, vivacious, energetic, hearty, stout, bubbling, dynamic, spunky
vogue	new, current, fashionable, explorative, innovative, modern, unique, novel, creative

W

waiter	waitress, server, maitre d'hotel, steward, butler, valet, attendant, checker, sommelier
warm	tepid, lukewarm, heated, toasty, snug, cordial, inviting, glowing
wassail	toast, pledge, salutation, cheer, gala, festival
whisper	touch, trace, lace, sprinkle, dash, speck

Y

yeast	ferment, mold, leaven, rise, foam, bubble, effervesce, brew
yellow	golden, gold, autumn, gilt, honey, butter, quince, banana, canary, tawny, amber, blond, flaxen, buff, straw
yule	Christmas, Christmastide, Noel, Advent

Z

zany	comical, crazy, ridiculous, amusing, merry, mirthful, jolly, batty, wacko, cuckoo, goofy
zeal	fervor, passion, fire, enthusiasm, intensity, excitement, gusto, energy, elation
zenith	summit, pinnacle, top, crest, apex, supremacy, perfection
zest	zeal, fervor, passion, fire, enthusiasm, intensity, excitement, gusto, energy, elation, trace, tinge, touch, lace, sprinkle, whisper, dash, speck

TABLE 1-80. AMERICAN REGIONAL FOOD TERMS: DEFINITIONS AND ORIGINS

Because our country is so rich in both natural food resources and international food heritage, our menus feature the best of both. The following listings highlight some of the foods and terms that have found their ways into our American culinary vocabulary and into the evolving history of our cuisine. In many instances the origins of our foods are clear; in others, they are far from clear. Every attempt has been made to give the proper credit where it is due, but as you will see, sometimes the source is widespread (termed "General"), basically unknown (termed "Indefinite"), or occasionally the subject of argument (termed "Debated").

Food Term	Description	Origin
akule	dried salted fish	Pacific
albondiga	meatball flavored with vegetables and sauce	Hispanic
ambrosia	cocktail made with lemon juice, brandy, applejack, Cointreau, and champagne	New Orleans
ambrosia	fruit and coconut dessert	South
Anadama bread	dense cornmeal bread sweetened with molasses	Northeast
andouille	seasoned smoked pork sausage	Cajun
angel food cake	light, puffy cake with many beaten egg whites	General
apee	cookie made from butter, sugar, and sour cream	Philadelphia
apple butter	pureed apples with cider	Pennsylvania Dutch
apple dumpling	baked dessert made of apples in pastry dough	Midwest
apple fritter	apple slice covered with batter and fried	Midwest
apple snow	dessert of egg whites, sugar, applesauce, and whipped cream	Indefinite
apple brown Betty	layered dessert of apples and buttered crumbs	Indefinite
apple Charlotte	dessert made of cooked apples and bread slices	France
applejack	apple cider or brandy	New England
apple pandowdy	sliced apples covered with crust	Northeast
apple pie	apples baked in a pie crust	General
applesauce	pureed apples	General
arroz con pollo	steamed rice with chicken	Hispanic
Ashley bread	batter bread with rice flour	South
Awenda bread	batter bread with grits	South
Bacardi Cocktail	cocktail of lime juice, grenadine, and rum	Miami
bachelor's button	cookie with a cherry set on top	Indefinite
bagel	poached yeast bun with a hole in the center	Jewish
Baked Alaska	baked meringue-covered cake with ice cream core	Debated
banana bread	cakelike bread	General
bananas Foster	sautéed banana slices with brown sugar and cinnamon; flamed with banana liqueur and rum	New Orleans
bannock	cornmeal cake derived from Scottish barley cakes	New England
Baptist cake	doughnut variation	New England
batter bread	cornbread variation	Virginia
beef-on-weck	sliced beef on caraway roll with horseradish	New York

Food Term	Description	Origin
beignet	deep-fried yeast-raised dough balls dusted with powdered sugar	France
billi-bi	soup made from mussels, cream, and seasonings	France
bird's nest pudding	apple pudding	New England
biscuit	small leavened and shortened bread	General
bishop's bread	quick bread with dried fruits	Midwest
black bottom pie	chocolate custard topped with rum custard and whipped cream	Indefinite
black cake	rich butter cake with molasses and dried fruit	Virginia
blintz	crepe-like pancake	Jewish
Bloody Mary	cocktail made with tomato juice, vodka, celery seeds, and worcestershire	Paris
blue lagoon	cocktail made with blue curacao, vodka, and lemon juice	Paris
bobotee	savory puddinglike mixture of milk, bread crumbs, almonds, onions, and Tabasco	Indefinite
bongo bongo soup	oyster-and-spinach soup	New Zealand
boova shenkel	dumpling stew	Pennsylvania Dutch
borscht	soup made of beets and often cabbage	Russia
Boston baked beans	navy beans made with molasses and salt pork or bacon	New England
Boston brown bread	molasses-sweetened bread with rye, whole wheat, and graham flours; normally with raisins	New England
Boston cream pie	yellow cake with pastry cream filling and chocolate icing	Boston
boudin	sausages of several sorts	Louisiana
bounce	fermented beverage; rum or brandy poured over fruit, with sugar, spices, and water	Northeast
Brandon puff	muffin of flour and cornmeal	South Carolina
brandy Alexander	cocktail made with brandy, cream, and a chocolate cordial	Indefinite
Bronx cocktail	cocktail made with gin, sweet and dry vermouths, and orange juice	New York
brownie	rich chocolate cake cut into squares	General
buck	drink made with gin, gingerale, and lemon juice	Indefinite
Buffalo wings	deep-fried chicken wings served with a hot sauce and blue cheese dressing	Buffalo, New York
bullshot	cocktail made with vodka, beef bouillon, and spices	Detroit
buñuelo	deep-fried round pastry sprinkled with sugar	Southwest
burgoo	meat and vegetable stew	Kentucky

Food Term	Description	Origin
burrito	wheat flour tortilla rolled with various fillings and usually fried	Mexico
butterscotch	confection made from butter, brown sugar, and lemon juice	Scotland
caesar salad	salad of romaine lettuce, garlic, olive oil, croutons, Parmesan cheese, Worcestershire sauce, and anchovies	Tijuana, Mexico
café brulot	dark coffee mixed with the flavors of citrus rind and brandy	New Orleans
calas	breakfast bread made with rice mixed with flour, spices, and sugar; deep fried	New Orleans
candy apple	confection made by immersing an apple in red syrup that forms a hard shell on the fruit	Indefinite
Cape Cod turkey	cod, seasonings, bread crumbs, eggs, and butter; baked	New England
caramel	confection made of sugar, cream, butter, and flavorings	General
carrot cake	made with carrots, sugar, butter, flour, and spices	General
challa	shaped loaf of white, slightly sweetened bread coated with an egg-white glaze	Jewish
chaudin	stuffed pig's stomach; browned and cooked in a kettle	Cajun
cheesecake	dessert cake or pie made with cream, cottage, or ricotta cheese, with a graham cracker crust	Northeast
chicken a la king	chicken in cream sauce garnished with pimentos	New York
chicken cacciatore	chicken cooked with mushrooms and tomato sauce	Italy
chicken fried steak	beef steak tenderized by pounding, coated with flour or batter, and fried crisp	Southwest
chicken-in-the-shell	chicken in creamed mushroom sauce served in a shell	San Francisco
chicken tetrazzini	chicken in cream sauce, served over spaghetti and browned in the oven with bread crumbs and Parmesan cheese	Debated
chiffon	very light, sweet, fluffy filling for a pie, cake, or pudding	General
chiles relleños	fried stuffed chili peppers	Hispanic
chili con carne	beef stew seasoned with cumin and chili peppers	Texas
chili con queso	appetizer dip made of chili peppers and cheese	Southwest
chimichanga	deep-fried wheat tortilla stuffed with minced beef, potatoes, and seasonings	Mexico
chipped beef	dried beef	England

Food Term	Description	Origin
chitterlings	hog's intestines either fried or boiled	South
chocolate velvet cake	richly textured chocolate cake	New York
chop suey	bamboo shoots, water chestnuts, bean sprouts, celery, soy sauce, and pork or chicken	Chinese-American
chowchow	relish of pickles or other vegetables	Chinese-American
chowder	hearty seafood or corn soup	General
chow mein	vegetable and meat stew with fried noodles	Chinese-American
Christy Girl	cocktail made with peach brandy, dry gin, grenadine, egg white, and ice cubes	New York
cinderella	muffin flavored with wine or sherry and nutmeg	Indefinite
cioppino	tomato-based fish and shellfish stew	San Francisco
clam fritter	deep-fried clam in batter	New England
clams posillipo	clams cooked with garlic, tomatoes, and seasonings	Italian-American
cole slaw	shredded cabbage, mayonnaise, and seasonings	Dutch
cookie	small, flat, sweet cake	Dutch
coquina soup	soup of periwinkle clams	Florida
corn dog	sausage in cornbread on a stick	Texas
corned beef	beef that has been cured in salt	Indefinite
cottage pudding	plain cake that is smeared with a sweet sauce	Indefinite
country captain	curried chicken with rice and condiments	Georgia
crabmeat Louis	chilled crabmeat with a zesty dressing of mayonnaise, chili sauce, grated onion, and various other seasonings	San Francisco
crabmeat Remick	crabmeat, chili sauce, mayonnaise, and seasonings	New York
crab Norfolk	baked crab seasoned with vinegar, Tabasco, and Worcestershire sauce	Virginia
Cuba libre	cocktail made with rum, cola, and lime juice	Cuba
curaçao	cordial based on the flavor of green oranges	Curaçao
cush	cornmeal pancake	Africa
cushaw	squash; cut, boiled, and drained; the pulp is mashed with butter, sugar, milk, eggs, nutmeg, allspice, and salt then baked	Cajun
cyclone candy	sweet confection of sugar, molasses, vinegar, and butter	New England
daiquiri	cocktail made with rum, sugar, and lime juice	Cuba
Danish pastry	variety of yeast-dough pastries rolled and filled with cheese, prunes, almond paste or fruit preserves	East
dirty rice	rice cooked with chicken livers and herbs	Cajun

Food Term	Description	Origin
doughnut	deep-fried yeast pastry with a hole in the middle	General
Dresden	cold sauce, made with hard-boiled eggs, onions, mustard, and other seasonings	Germany
egg cream	soft drink made with milk, chocolate syrup and soda water	New York
Eggs Benedict	English muffins topped with a slice of Canadian bacon, poached eggs, and hollandaise sauce	New York
Eggs Sardou	poached eggs with artichoke hearts, anchovies, chopped ham, truffles, and hollandaise sauce	New Orleans
election cake	yeast-raised fruitcake with sherry and spices	New England
empanada	fried turnover pastry with savory fillings	Mexico
enchilada	tortilla stuffed with various fillings of meat, cheese, pepper sauce, chorizo sausage, and other ingredients	Mexico
English muffin	round, flat muffin made from white flour, yeast, malted barley, vinegar, and farina	Indefinite
fettuccine Alfredo	fettuccini noodles mixed with butter, Parmesan cheese, and cream	Rome
Fish House punch	punch made of lemon juice, brandy, and peach brandy	Philadelphia
floating island	dessert made with fluffs of meringue set in a custard sauce	France
fondue	method of fast cooking by which bite-size pieces of meat, fruit, or bread are impaled on skewers and dipped into a cooking liquid to be cooked or coated	Switzerland
Franconia potatoes	boiled potatoes baked with butter	New Hampshire
french fry	method of cooking potatoes or other vegetables cut into narrow strips or rounds	American
French toast	bread dipped in an egg-and-milk mixture, fried in butter, and served with syrup or powdered sugar	Debated
fry bread	bread of Southwest Indians, it is deep-fried and sometimes served with honey or powdered sugar	Southwest
fudge	semisoft candy made from butter, sugar, and various flavorings; the most usual being chocolate, vanilla, and maple	New England
funeral pie	pie traditionally baked before the imminent death of a family member	Pennsylvania Dutch
funnel cake	deep-fried pastry made from batter dripped through a funnel	Pennsylvania Dutch
gazpacho	cold tomato soup with chunky vegetables	Andalusia, Spain

Food Term	Description	Origin
gefilte fish	fish loaf or cake seasoned with chopped eggs, onion, and pepper	Jewish
gimlet	cocktail made with gin and lime juice	Indefinite
gingerbread	made from ginger, flour, cream, butter, brown sugar, molasses, an egg, baking soda, and boiling water	Indefinite
ginger beer	nonalcoholic beverage flavored with fermented ginger	England
gingersnap	cookie made from ginger and molasses	Germany
golden Cadillac	cocktail made with crème de cacao and heavy cream	Indefinite
goulash	meat and vegetable stew seasoned with paprika	Hungary
grasshopper pie	made with green crème de menthe, gelatin, and whipped cream	South
Green Goddess	salad or salad dressing made from anchovies, mayonnaise, tarragon, vinegar, and other seasonings	San Francisco
grillade	veal or beef slices braised with seasonings and served with grits	Louisiana
grits	finely ground, dried, hulled corn kernels	South
grunt	dessert with berries and a dough steamed in a kettle	New England
guacamole	dip made from avocados and chili pepper	Southwest
Hangtown Fry	fried oysters with scrambled eggs and bacon	San Francisco
Harvard beets	beets cooked in vinegar, sugar, and cornstarch	Indefinite
Harvard cocktail	cocktail made with brandy, sweet vermouth, sugar, and orange bitters	Massachusetts
Harvey Wallbanger	cocktail made with vodka, Galliano, orange juice, and sugar	California
heavenly hash	dessert made with vanilla wafers and whipped cream	Midwest
hopping john	seasoned cowpeas and rice	South
hot brown	hot sandwich with chicken, turkey, bacon and/or ham topped with cheese sauce	Louisville, Kentucky
huevos rancheros	fried eggs on tortillas with tomato sauce	Southwest
hurricane	cocktail made with passion fruit flavoring, dark rum, and citrus juices	New Orleans
hush puppy	deep-fried cornmeal dumpling	South
icebox pie	crusted, creamy pie that is frozen or chilled firm	General
Indian pudding	cornmeal dessert pudding made with milk and molasses	New England
Ingwer kuche	rich cake with ginger and molasses	Pennsylvania Dutch

Food Term	Description	Origin
Irish coffee	blend of hot coffee, Irish whiskey, and whipped cream	San Francisco
jambalaya	rice, pork, ham, chicken, sausage, shrimp, crayfish, and seasonings	Cajun
Johnny Marzetti	ground beef, tomato, and macaroni	Ohio
jolly boy	nineteenth century fried cake split in half, buttered, and served with maple syrup	New England
jumble	cookie with nuts "jumbled" up in the dough	General
kamikaze	cocktail made with citrus juices, Cointreau, and vodka	Debated
ketchup	variety of condiments, the most common containing tomato, vinegar, brown sugar and spices	Indonesia
knish	pastry stuffed with mashed potato, cheese, buckwheat groats, or chopped liver	Jewish
kreplach	dumpling containing chopped meat or cheese, often served in soup	Jewish
kugel	noodle or potato pudding served on the Jewish Sabbath	Jewish
Lady Baltimore cake	white cake filled with nuts and raisins and covered with a vanilla-and-egg-white frosting	South Carolina
ladyfinger	light sponge-cake biscuit	General
Lafayette bread	cakelike ginger-and-spice bread	Virginia
leather	confection made from dried-fruit butters or purees baked slowly and cut in long strips resembling leather	Native American
Lebkuchen	spice cake	Germany
Lee cake	white cake flavored with citrus rind and juice	Southern
limpin' Suzan	red beans and rice	Southern
Little Joe's	ground meat and spinach	Indefinite
lobscouse	beef-and-potato stew	New England
lobster americaine	lobster prepared with a sauce of tomatoes, brandy, white wine, cayenne pepper, and seasonings	France
lobster Newburg	lobster meat, sherry, egg yolks, cream, and cayenne pepper	New York
lomi-lomi salmon	salted salmon	Hawaii
low mull	meat-and-vegetable stew	New England
McGinty	pie made from dried apples	Oregon
maid of honor	custard tart made with plums or other fruit	New England
mai tai	cocktail made with lime, curacao, and rum	California

Food Term	Description	Origin
Manhattan	cocktail made with bourbon or blended whiskey with sweet vermouth and bitters	Washington, D.C.
Margarita	cocktail made with tequila, Triple Sec or Cointreau, and lime juice	Tijuana, Mexico
Marlborough pie	apple-and-cream pie	Debated
Miami grill	grilled veal chops, orange slices, bananas, and tomatoes	Miami, Florida
mint julep	cocktail made with bourbon, sugar, and mint	Kentucky
miracle	nineteenth century fried cookie	New England
mock turtle soup	soup made from calves' brains to resemble true turtle soup	England
monkey bread	sweet yeast bread, sometimes mixed with currants, formed from balls of dough, placed next to and on top of each other	Indefinite
moonshine	dessert made of egg whites and fruit preserves	New England
mulacolong	stewed chicken	Southern
Naples biscuit	light biscuit similar to a ladyfinger	Italy
New Bedford pudding	pudding made from cornmeal, flour, eggs, and molasses	Massachusetts
New England dinner	poached meats and vegetables	New England
nun's toast	hard-boiled eggs with gravy on toast	Indefinite
Ohio pudding	sweet potato pudding with carrots and brown sugar	Ohio
old-fashioned cocktail	cocktail made with whiskey, sugar, and bitters	Kentucky
orange blossom	cocktail made with orange juice and gin	New York
Oxford John	mutton stew	England
oysters Bienville	oysters in cream sauce with green pepper, onion, cheese, and bread crumbs	New Orleans
oysters Kirkpatrick	baked oysters, green pepper, and bacon	San Francisco
oysters Rockefeller	oysters cooked with watercress, scallions, celery, anise, and other seasonings	New Orleans
Palace Court salad	salad of lettuce, tomato, and artichoke with a dressing of mayonnaise and crabmeat	San Francisco
parfait	frozen dessert from eggs, cream, sugar, and flavorings	France
Parker House roll	puffy yeast roll with a creased center	Boston
pasta primavera	pasta with cream sauce and spring vegetables	New York
pasty	savory turnover that may contain a variety of meats and fillings	Michigan
pepper pot	tripe soup with black pepper and seasonings	Philadelphia

Food Term	Description	Origin
Philly cheese-steak	sandwich made with thin slices of beef topped with cheese and other condiments and served on a crisp Italian-style roll	Philadelphia
Philadelphia eggs	split muffins topped with cooked chicken white meat, poached eggs, and hollandaise sauce	Philadelphia
philpy	rice bread	South Carolina
picadillo	mincemeat stew	Southwest
pilau	any of a variety of steamed rice dishes made of meat, chicken, fish, or vegetables in a broth	Louisiana
piña colada	cocktail made with light rum, coconut cream, and pineapple juice	Puerto Rico
pink lady	cocktail made by mixing grenadine, lime or lemon juice, apple brandy, gin, and one egg white	Indefinite
pink sauce	sauce served with shrimp	Undetermined
pinole	dried, ground, spiced, and sweetened corn	Southwest
pommes soufflés	potatoes are sliced thin and deep-fried twice to give them a puffy, crisp texture	France
Pompey's head	roll of meat with a sauce of tomatoes and green pepper	Undetermined
popover	light, hollow muffin made from an egg batter	Oregon
Portuguese bread	white bread sweetened with sugar and sometimes baked with slices of sausage	Northeast/Hawaii
potato salad	cold or hot potatoes with diverse seasonings	General
potpie	crusted pie made with poultry or meat and usually chopped vegetables	General
pound cake	plain white-cake loaf whose name derives from the weight of ingredients	General
praline	confection made from almonds or pecans in caramel	Southern
quiche	pie or tart having an egg filling and a variety of other ingredients	France
railroad cookie	cookie swirled on the inside with cinnamon and brown sugar	Missouri
Ramos gin fizz	cocktail made with cream, gin, lemon juice, orange flower water, and egg whites	New Orleans
rankins	cheese pudding	Indefinite
red beans and rice	kidney beans and rice flavored with a ham bone	Southern
redeye gravy	gravy made from ham drippings, often flavored with coffee	Southern
red snapper Vera Cruz	red snapper cooked with chili peppers, tomatoes, and other seasonings	Mexico

Food Term	Description	Origin
refried beans	mashed, cooked pinto beans	Southwest
rickey	drink whose basic ingredients are lime juice and soda water	Debated
Rob Roy	cocktail made with Scotch, sweet vermouth, and bitters	Scotland
rock and rye	liqueur with a blended whiskey base, to which is added rock candy syrup and sometimes fruits	Undetermined
rocky road	confection of milk or dark chocolate mixed with marshmallows and nuts	Undetermined
rollmops	marinated herring fillet that is stuffed and rolled	Germany
Roquefort dressing	mayonnaise with Roquefort or blue cheese	France
rumrousal	New England milk punch made by combining Jamaican rum, milk, honey, and bourbon	New England
rum tum tiddy	New England blend of tomato soup and Cheddar cheese served as a main course	New England
Russian dressing	salad dressing made from mayonnaise, pimento, chili sauce, green pepper, and chives	Undetermined
Salisbury steak	patty made from ground beef and seasonings and usually broiled	England
Sally Lunn	bread made from flour, yeast, eggs, and sugar	England
salmagundi	chopped meat, eggs, anchovies, onions, and vinegar served on lettuce	France
sangria	drink made with red wine, fruits, and sometimes brandy	Spain
Saratoga potatoes	thinly sliced, deep-fried potatoes	New York
Schichtkuche	Pennsylvania Dutch "layer cake"	Pennsylvania Dutch
scrapple	cornmeal mush with pork; fried in slices	Pennsylvania Dutch
screwdriver	drink made with vodka and orange juice	Indefinite
scripture cake	cake made with ingredients as listed in certain Bible verses	Baptist
seed cake	nineteenth century cake made from caraway seed	General
semmel	yeast roll	Pennsylvania Dutch
Senate bean soup	white bean soup in the U.S. Senate restaurant	Washington, D.C.
she-crab soup	soup made from blue crabs, crab roe, sherry, and vegetables	Southeast
Shirley Temple	nonalcoholic beverage with grenadine, ginger ale, and a maraschino cherry	General
shoofly pie	made with molasses and brown sugar	Pennsylvania Dutch
shortnin' bread	southern quick bread made with butter or lard	Southern
shrimper's sauce	tomato sauce	Southern
shrimps de Jonghe	shrimp with garlic, oil, and bread crumbs	Chicago

Food Term	Description	Origin
sidecar	cocktail made with brandy, orange-flavored liqueur, and lemon juice	Paris, France
Singapore sling	cocktail made with gin, cherry brandy, Cointreau, Benedictine, and citrus juices	Singapore
sloppy Joe	ground beef, onions, green peppers, and ketchup or tomato sauce made in a skillet and served on a hamburger bun	General
slump	cooked fruit and yeast-raised dough balls	New England
sole Marguery	fillets of sole served in a sauce made with egg yolks, butter, and white wine cooked with mussels and shrimp	France
sopaipilla	deep-fried fritter usually served with honey	Mexico
sour	drink made with liquor, sugar, and citrus juices usually shaken with cracked ice	Indefinite
sourdough	white bread made with a sour starter made from flour, water, and sugar	General
spoon bread	soft, custardlike cornmeal bread	Native American
squirt	drink of liquor or wine, fresh fruit syrup, and seltzer or club soda	General
sticky	sweet pastry	South Carolina
sticky bun	bun flavored with cinnamon and brown sugar	General
stone fence	alcoholic drink made from apple cider or applejack and a liquor such as rum	New England
strawberry shortcake	dessert made with a biscuit pastry, strawberries, and whipped cream	General
streusel	crumb topping of flour, butter, and spices that is sprinkled and baked on breads, cakes, and muffins	Germany
strudel	rolled pastry filled with nuts, streusel mixture, fruit, or cheese	Germany
stuffing	packed combination of meats, vegetables, grains, fats, or other ingredients inserted into meat, poultry, or fish	General
succotash	corn and lima beans	Native American
sukiyaki	meat and vegetables simmered together	Japan
Swedish meatball	meatball covered with brown gravy	Sweden
Swiss steak	sliced beef baked with tomatoes, onions, peppers, and sometimes thyme, rosemary, basil, or chili	England
switchel	colonial drink made with molasses, rum, and water	New England
syllabub	eggnog made with wine	England/France

Food Term	Description	Origin
taffy	confection made from sugar, butter, and flavorings that has a chewy texture obtained by twisting and pulling the cooked ingredients into elasticity	England
tamale pie	cornmeal mush filled with chopped meat and a hot chili sauce	Southwest
tansy	pudding made from the tansy plant or any such confection made with tart fruit	England
tequila sunrise	cocktail made with tequila, orange juice, and grenadine	Mexico
Toll House cookie	cookie made from flour, semisweet chocolate chips, brown sugar, and nuts	Massachusetts
Tom and Jerry	cocktail made with eggs, sugar, brandy or bourbon, and whiskey, topped with milk or boiling water	England
Tom Collins	cocktail made with gin, citrus juice, and soda water	Debated
tortilla	flat, unleavened cake made of cornmeal or white flour	Mexico
tostada	deep-fried corn chip	Mexico
turnover	pastry filled with fruit preserves, chopped meat, or cooked sauce	General
twin mountains	New England muffin	New England
upside-down cake	cake that is baked with its filling or flavoring on the bottom and then inverted before serving	General
vichyssoise	potato and leek cream soup	France
waffle	light batter cake cooked on a griddle with a special weblike pattern	Dutch
Waldorf salad	salad with a mayonnaise dressing, apples, and celery	New York
Washington pie	cake of several layers with fruit or marmalade	Virginia
whip	dessert of whipped cream with sugar and lemon juice	General
Yale boat pie	layers of meat, poultry, and shellfish set in a pastry crust	Massachusetts
Yorkshire pudding	puffy bread made by cooking an egg-and-milk batter in the hot fat pan drippings from a roast beef	England
zephyrina	light and airy cookie	North Carolina
zombie	drink made from various rums and citrus juices	Los Angeles
zwieback	dry toasted bread slices	Germany

Table 1-81. International Food Terms: Definitions and Origins

In foodservice there are always ethnic trends. If the cuisine of choice today is Mexican, tomorrow it might be Chinese or Italian—or Egyptian! The following listings present a global overview of international culinary classics, offered in the hope that you will find intriguing menu options to satisfy whatever cuisine patrons demand.

Term	Definition	Origin
abbachio al forno	roast leg of lamb with herbs	Italy
acini de pepe	tiny round or square pasta	Italy
adobo	two-step cooking method: initial simmering in spicy marinade, followed by deep frying; used with chicken, meat, and fish	Pacific
aeppel-flask	casserole of smoked bacon, onions, and apples	Sweden
agnolotti	dumplings stuffed with meat and vegetables; translates "little lambs"	Italy
aillade	mayonnaise prepared with garlic, walnuts, and hazelnuts; served with seafood	France
aioli	garlic and olive oil sauce	France
ajinomoto	monosodium glutamate	Japan
akee	fruit of an evergreen tree that, when cooked, resembles scrambled eggs	Jamaica
à la carte	menus that present prices for each specific dish or course	France
à la minute	restaurant dishes that are prepared at the moment they are ordered	France
ali-oli	garlic and oil sauce	Spain
allumettes	literally "matches"; refers to foods that are cut to resemble sticks; also refers to thin puff pastry strips that are covered with cheese or icing	France
amaretti	macaroons made from almond paste	Italy
ambigu	French-Creole term for buffet	France
anna potatoes	prepared by tiering a heavy casserole with alternate layers of thinly-sliced potatoes, plus clarified butter and seasonings; cooked until crisp and brown	France
annatto	yellowish-red dyes prepared from pulp found around seeds of a tropical tree; used for color and flavoring	Lat. Amer.
antipasto	appetizer	Italy
antojitos	literally "snacks"	Mexico
apfelpfannkuchen	apple pancakes	Germany

Term	Definition	Origin
arrostino annegato	thick veal chunks that are skewered, seasoned, and fried, then braised with white wine, lemon juice, and brown stock	Italy
Arista de Vitello	roast loin of veal flavored with white wine, herbs, and seasonings	Italy
Arista Fiorentina	roast pork loin flavored with garlic; served cold	Italy
assiettes parisiennes	hors d'oeuvres	France
au jus	natural meat juices	France
avgolemono soup	thick, cold, tangy chicken soup	Greece
baba	small yeast cake saturated with hot syrup, flavored with rum and topped with whipped cream	France
bacalao	dried, salted codfish	Spain
Bagatelle, sole	rolled fillets of sole served on chopped tomatoes and mushrooms covered in Mornay and grilled	France
baglawa/baklava	baked, buttered layers of phyllo pastry sheets with nuts, honey, sugar, and cinnamon	Middle East
bagna cauda	anchovy and garlic dip	Italy
baguettes	crisp, crunchy, long loaves of bread	France
ballekes	fried meatballs	Belgium
balletjes	spicy vegetable meatballs	Holland
ballotine	boned meat, game, fowl, or fish that is stuffed and cooked	France
banquet menu	starting with a rich clear soup, then a fish course, then a main course, accompanying vegetables and a salad, and finally dessert	General
barbacoa	barbecue	Spain
barding	process of wrapping meats with fat before cooking	General
barquettes	small boat-shaped pastries that are baked and used for holding various fillings	France
bastila	pigeon pie	Arabia
bavarois, creme	delicate custard flavored with liqueurs and topped with fruit	France
bavarois, sauce	hollandaise sauce added to peppercorns, horseradish, thyme, and vinegar and flavored with crayfish butter	France
béarnaise sauce	strained vinegar, chopped shallots and seasonings added to hollandaise	France
béchamel sauce	classic white "mother sauce" base for other cream sauces	France
beignets	meats, fish, vegetables, and fruits cut in pieces, dipped in beer batter and deep-fried	France
beluga caviar	finest caviar	Russia

Term	Definition	Origin
berner platte	smoked pork, pig's feet, sausages, boiled and wine-cooked sauerkraut and boiled potatoes	Switzerland
beurre manie	thickener of butter and flour kneaded together	France
beurre noir	sweet butter cooked brown with wine vinegar, capers, and parsley added	France
beurres composes	compound butters made from a multitude of flavorful foods, condiments, and herbs	France
biersuppe	beer mixed with roux and spices and simmered; heavy cream added; served on toast	Germany
billi bi	mussel soup	France
bird's nest soup	made by adding a nest to a rich chicken broth with water chestnuts, chicken, and an egg white	China
biscotto	twice-baked biscuit, wafer, or cookie	Italy
biscuit tortoni	frozen mousse	Italy
bisque	thick pureed soup from shellfish bound with heavy cream	France
bitki	fried meatballs served with sour cream or tomato sauce	Russia
blancmange	pudding made with almond paste	France
blanquette	sauce that coats thickly	France
bleu, truite au	live trout plunged into boiling court bouillon which produces a blue tint	France
blini	yeast pancake cooked in butter and often served with caviar and sour cream	Russia
blintz	small pan-fried batter-cake rolled with meat, potato, cheese, or fruit filling	Jewish
boeuf à la mode	marinated meat; browned in olive oil, marinated again, and simmered	France
bok choy	chard cabbage	China
bollito misto	boiled meats and poultry cooked together and served in a rich vegetable broth	Italy
Bombay duck	dried tropical fish	Asia
bonne femme	phrase indicating that a dish has been cooked simply	France
bordelaise, à la	prepared with white or red wine	France
boreks	dumplings made from superthin sheets of dough filled with meat, cheese, chicken, or spinach	Turkey
borracha, salsa	pasilla chilies, garlic and pulque chopped in a blender with olive oil until smooth	Mexico
borracho, pollo	chicken in wine	Spain
borsch/borscht	soup made with beets, meat stock, onions and cabbage	Russia
bouchée à la reine	small puff pastry served as an appetizer	France

Term	Definition	Origin
boudin blanc	sausage made from ground pork and veal or chicken with eggs, breadcrumbs, and onions	France
boudin noir	blood sausage	France
bouillabaisse	stew of eel, haddock, sea bass, red snapper, lobster, mussels, tomatoes, and seasonings	France
bouquet garni	herb bundle added to simmering foods	France
bouquetière	variety of colorful vegetables uniformly cut and arranged	France
bourguignonne	designation for a dish that is prepared with red wine	France
bourride, la	fish stew	France
bracioli	individual slices of beef spread with a stuffing, rolled up, and braised	Italy
Braciuola de Maiale	pork chops with flour, egg, breadcrumbs, and sautéed in olive oil; baked with white wine	Italy
brado fogada	shrimp and spinach preparation	Italy
brandade	boiled, boned salt cod cut in small pieces and sautéed, ground up, pounded, and mixed with heavy cream and seasonings	France
brasserie	where beer and cider are made and sold; café or restaurant also	France
bratwurst	sausage made from pork, herbs, and spices	Germany
bretonne, à la	garnished with beans	France
brioche	light yeast cake	France
brochet, quenelles de	pike dumplings	France
brochette, en	method of cooking food over the fire "on a skewer"	France
brunoise	vegetables that are finely chopped or diced	France
bul-kogi	thinly sliced beef or chicken breast that is marinated and grilled over hot charcoal	Korean
bully beef	creamed beef	England
burgoo	rich stew including hen meat, squirrels, pork, beef, lamb, vegetables, and herbs	USA
burrida	thick fish soup of various fish in a fish stock flavored with white wine, seasonings, and tomatoes	Italy
burritos	small tortillas filled with various mixtures	Mexican
cacciatora, alla	Italian version of Hunter's Style: chicken braised with onions, garlic, and mushrooms in red or white wine sauce	Italy
caesar salad	salad of romaine lettuce, croutons, grated Parmesan cheese, and seasonings	Mexico
calabaza	green pumpkin squash	West Indies
calalou	stew of pork, veal, beef, or fowl simmered in broth with fresh corn, peppers, okra, celery, and seasonings	Caribbean

Term	Definition	Origin
calzone	crescent-shaped turnover stuffed with cheese, ham, salami, and herbs baked in an oven	Italy
camerones, arroz con	white rice and shrimp preparation	Mexico
caneton a l'orange	young duckling braised and served with an orange-flavored sauce	France
cannoli	deep-fried dough rolls; filled with pastry cream	Italy
cannelloni	stuffed tubes of pasta	Italy
capers	green flower buds of the caper bush that are pickled	Madagascar
cappellitti	hat-shaped pasta	Italy
capsicum	various kinds of peppers	General
carbonara, spaghetti alla	pasta dish with ham or bacon	Italy
carbonnade à la flamande	meat stew	France
Caribbean pepperpot	stew of chicken, cubed pork, calf's foot, oxtail, and seasonings	Jamaica
cassareep	juice of the grated cassava root	Latin America
cassata	layers of sponge cake filled with sweet ricotta cheese filling	Italy
cassava	tropical root vegetable with edible starchy flesh	Tropics
cassia	leaves and bark of the cassia tree; closely related to cinnamon	Indonesia
cassoulet	dried white bean dish with chunks of pork, mutton or lamb, poultry, sausage, and seasonings	France
cervelat	highly spiced and smoked sausage	Germany
challah	Jewish braided bread	Middle East
champignons	mushrooms	France
chapatis	skillet-cooked flat bread	India
charlotte russe	chilled dessert made by filling a mold with biscuits and Bavarian cream	France
chateaubriand	fillet of beef	France
château potatoes	potato balls baked in butter, oil, and bouillon	France
chaud-froid, sauce	"hot-cold" sauce often used in classical buffets	France
chayote	green or white pear-shaped fruit	Mexico
chervil	herb used in French and Italian cooking	Europe
chiffonade	French method of cutting vegetables into fine strips or ribbons	France
chipolata	small sausage made with onions	Italy
chorizo	red sausage made from pork liver, meat, and fat with peppers, juniper berries, and seasonings	Spain
choron, sauce	sauce béarnaise with tomato puree	France
choucroute garni	sauerkraut cooked in white wine with ham, smoked goose, sausages, and bacon	France

Term	Definition	Origin
clabber	curds	Ireland
clafoutis	open-faced cherry tart	France
cocido	meat and vegetable stew or soup	Spain
cock-a-leekie soup	chicken and leek soup	Scotland
concasser	to chop and pound or shred	France
conchiglie	tiny shell-shaped pasta	Italy
confit	preserved goose, duck, or pork	France
consommé	clear soup made from beef, chicken, or veal	France
contorni	Italian side dishes	Italy
coppa	finely ground pork salami sausage	Italy
coq au vin	chicken cooked in red or white wine	France
Coquilles St. Jacques	poached scallops that are breaded, placed in their shells, topped with garlic butter and white wine with bacon pieces	France
cornet	small, conical pastry filled with cream	France
cornichons	very tiny sweet-sour pickles or gherkins	France
costoletta	cutlet or chop of veal, pork, or mutton	Italy
coulis	rich meat sauce made from juices out of meats, or a finely pureed sauce	France
couscous	cereal grain	Africa
crème a l'anglaise	sweet, thick sauce for desserts	France
crème brûlée	chilled custard with a layer of brown sugar that is broiled until caramelized	England
crème caramel	chilled custard with light caramel sauce	France
crème pâtissière	thick custard for filling cream puffs	France
crepe	very light sweet or savory pancake	France
crepinettes	small cakes of seasoned ground meats, truffles, mushrooms, garlic, and thick cream	France
crespelle	thin crepes	Italy
croissant	flaky butter-rich roll	France
croquembouche	puff paste balls or fruit dipped into sugar syrup to harden, assembled in stacks or towers	France
croquettes	deep-frying ground meat, fish, or vegetables	France
crostini	small slices of white bread served with cheese, liver paste, anchovies, ham, salami, and tomatoes	Italy
croustade	crisp shell of bread or pastry	France
croûte	hard crust of bread or pastries	France
croutons	bread cubes sautéed in butter or oil	France
cruda, salsa	tomatoes, serrano chilies, onions and coriander finely chopped	Mexico
crudités	raw vegetables cut into strips	France

Term	Definition	Origin
crumpet	round teacake with holes on top; served toasted and buttered	England
csirke paprikas	chicken paprika	Hungary
cucculli	small dumplings made from potatoes, nuts, and marjoram; breaded and fried crisp	Italy
daikon	Japanese or Chinese red radish	Japan
dampfknodel	yeast dumplings cooked in sugared milk and sweet butter and served with vanilla sugar and apricot puree	Germany
danoise, sauce	rich sauce made from tart apple puree, grated horseradish and heavy cream; served with fish	France
dariole	small cylindrical mold that is buttered, lined with puff pastry, filled with frangipane cream, baked, and sprinkled with sugar	France
darne	sliced fish steak	France
dartois	layers of puff pastry filled with almond cream, covered with a piece of pastry, baked, and iced	France
dashi	fish stock	Japan
daube, en	stewed food	France
dauphine potatoes	cream puff paste mixed with mashed potatoes and egg yolks until light; rolled, cut into pieces, dipped in batter and deep-fried	France
dauphinoise, à la	anything made with dairy products	France
degraisser	to skim off fat from stocks or sauces	France
dejeuner	lunch	France
demitasse	half a cup	France
dente, al	medium-cooked, literally done "to the tooth"	Italy
Devonshire cream	heavy clotted cream	England
dim sum	bite-size dumplings made from a mixture of wheat starch and tapioca flour and stuffed with forcemeats; steamed or deep-fried	China
dobos torte	six layers of sponge cake filled and iced with a light chocolate custard and coated with hard caramel	Hungary
dolce/dolci	sweet	Italy
dolmades	stuffed grape leaves filled with rice and meat	Greece
doree	term for food that has a golden tint from frying, sautéing, or broiling	France
durum wheat	hard wheat flour for pasta	
duxelles	chopped mushrooms, parsley, onions, seasonings, and shallots sauteed in butter	France
eau de vie	distilled spirit; literally "water of life"	France
éclair	pastry made from pâté à choux dough, filled with flavored crème patissière	France

Term	Definition	Origin
écrevisse	fresh water crab, crayfish	France
eiswein	wine made from fully ripe "frozen" grapes	Germany
émincé	mincemeat hash	France
empanada	pastry turnover made from dough circles; filled	Spain
enchiladas	corn flour tortillas filled with various mixtures	Mexico
entrecote	sirloin steak; translates "between the ribs"	France
entremets	between dishes	France
escabeche	pickled fish	Spain
escargots	snails	France
estouffade	stew	France
estragon	tarragon	France
estouffer	to steam	France
faggot	small bundle of herbs used to flavor soups, stews, and sauces	France
fagioli	dried beans	Italy
farce/farci	stuffing/stuffed	France
farfellette	ribbon-shaped bow pasta	Italy
fecule/fecula	flour derived from potatoes	France
felafel	fried dish made with chick-peas	Middle East
fettuccine	long egg noodles	Italy
feuilletage	leaf or sheet of puff pastry dough	France
fines herbes, sauce aux	fresh herbs simmered in dry white wine	France
finnan haddie	smoked haddock	Scotland
flan	caramel custard	Spain
fleurons	crescent-shaped flaky pastry garnish	France
florentine, à la	indicates spinach used in a dish	France
fondant, glace au	icing made from granulated sugar	France
fondantes, potatoes	potatoes cut in olive shapes; sautéed in butter	France
forno, al	baked in an oven	Italy
fraîche, crème	thick simmered cream of sour cream, yogurt, or buttermilk added to cream	France
frangipane	thick pastry cream flavored with macaroons	Italy
frappé	mixed or beaten with shaved ice	France
friandises	small pastry or sweetmeat served after desserts	France
fricadelles	meatballs	France
fricandeau	loin of veal that is larded with salt pork, braised, and roasted	France
fricassee	white meat or poultry stew	France
frittata/frittate	flat Italian omelette	Italy

Term	Definition	Origin
fromage	cheese	France
frumenty	pudding-type dish of oatmeal or wheat	England
fugu	blowfish; extremely poisonous	Japan
fumet	highly reduced extract of fish, meat, poultry, or vegetables	France
funghi	mushrooms	Italy
galantine	meat or fowl that has been boned, stuffed, and rolled	France
garam masala	mixture of spices known as curry	India
garbanzo	chick-pea	Spain
gaufres	light sweet waffles	France
gaufrettes, pommes	deep-fried potato slices	France
gazpacho	cold tomato soup	Spain
gefilte fish	dumpling made from ground pike or whitefish	Jewish
gelato	ice cream	Italy
ghee	clarified butter	India
gigot	leg of lamb or sheep	France
gnocchi	potato dumplings made with mashed potato mixture	Italy
gorda	tortilla filled with refried beans and then deep-fried	Mexico
granita	sherbet	Italy
gratin	crust formed on top of foods by baking or broiling	France
gravlax	very fresh salmon that is boned, cut in half and marinated; served raw	Sweden
grenadine	sweet, red syrup made from the pomegranate	France
grenadins	fillets of veal or the white meat of turkey	France
grenouilles	frogs' legs	France
grissini	hard-baked crunchy breadsticks	Italy
guacamole	avocado dip, sauce or salad	Mexico
gulyas/goulash	stew made with a lot of paprika	Hungary
haggis	sheep's stomach stuffed with chopped organ meats, oatmeal, fat, and seasonings	Scotland
halva/halvah	dessert of semolina flour, syrup, almonds, and sautéed butter	Turkey/ Greece
haricots	beans	France
harissa	hot sauce	Morocco
harusame	bean threads	Japan
hasenpfeffer	wild hare stew	Germany
hiyamugi	thin noodles	Japan
hoisin sauce	dark brown sauce	China
hors d'oeuvre	course served before the meal	France
hotchpotch	sautéed flank steak with vegetables and spices	Holland

Term	Definition	Origin
hummus	dip made with chick-peas and sesame	Middle East
hush puppies	fried cornmeal balls	S. America
ichaban dashi	soup stock	Japan
imu	underground oven	Polynesia
insalata mista	mixed salad	Italy
Irish stew	stewed breast and shoulder of mutton	Britain
jao-tze	dumpling filled with seasoned meat	China
jardinière	served with a variety of vegetables	France
jerky	dried strips of round steak	USA
jicama	brownish root	Mexico
julienne	small thin strips of vegetables	France
kabinett	classification for wine	Germany
kalb	veal	Germany
kanten	gelatinous substance from seaweed	Japan
kari	curry	Indonesia
katsuobushi	dried bonito	Japan
kedgeree	normally refers to stews or casseroles	East Indian
kibbeh	ground lamb and lentils	Middle East
kielbasa	generic term for sausage	Poland
Kiev, chicken à la	flattened chicken breast rolled around seasoned butter, breaded, and deep-fried	France
kim-chee	pickled cabbage	Korea
kipper	smoked herring	Britain
klosse	light, fluffy dumplings	Germany
knackwurst/knockwurst	sausage made from ground pork, beef and pork	Germany
knish	mashed potato dough wrapped around cheese, liver, meats, hard-boiled eggs, or chicken	Russia
knödel	dumpling	Germany
kobe beef	well-marbled beef	Japan
koulibiac	puff pastry layered with fish and other ingredients	Russia
koyatofu	dried soybean curd	Japan
kreplach	square-shaped noodle dough filled with meat and cheese	Jewish
kugel	pudding made with potatoes or noodles	Jewish
kugelhopf	yeast cake	France
langosta	lobster	Spanish
langostino	crawfish	Spanish
langouste	crawfish	France
lapin	rabbit	France

Term	Definition	Origin
latke	potato pancakes	Jewish
lavash	thin, crisp bread	Russia
leberwurst	liver sausage	Germany
lebkuchen	richly spiced cake or gingerbread	Germany
legumi	vegetables	Italy
île flottante	custard with meringue	France
limousine, à la	preparation of red cabbage and often chestnuts	France
linguini	narrow, flat noodles	Italy
loquat	small yellow fruit	China
lotus buns	yeast buns	China
lot yow	hot oil	China
lox	smoked salmon	Jewish
lutefisk	salted codfish	Norway
lyonnaise, à la	term indicating presence of cooked onions	Provence
macaroni	tube-shaped pasta	Italy
macédoine	mixture of fruits or vegetables	France
mafalde	twisted, long ribbon-noodles	Italy
mai jing	monosodium glutamate	China
maltaise sauce	hollandaise sauce with juice and rind of blood oranges	France
mandarin pancake	Chinese pancake	China
mango chutney	spicy condiment	India
manicotti	"little muffs" of pasta filled with ricotta cheese, meat, and sauce	Italy
manioc	cassava plant	Haiti
manzo	beef	Italy
marchand de vin sauce	red wine with chopped shallots, chives, and many spices	France
marinade	spiced liquid mixture used to flavor meats, fowl, fish, or vegetables	General
marinara sauce	red sauce	Italy
marrons	chestnuts	France
marzipan	ground almond paste with sugar and egg whites	Spain
masa	cornmeal prepared by soaking corn in lime water	Mexico
matelote, à la	fresh-water fish stew	France
matignon, à la	vegetable, meat, and herb coating used to add aroma and flavor to meat or fowl	France
matzo	crisp, unleavened bread	Jewish
melanzane	eggplant	Italy
melba	thin, small bread toasts	France

Term	Definition	Origin
mettwurst	smoked pork sausage	Germany
meunière, à la	fish fillet dusted with flour and sautéed in sweet butter	France
meurette, eggs	eggs gently poached in red wine; served on toast	France
mezzani	smooth, tubular pasta	Italy
milanese, alla	foods dusted with flour, dipped in egg yolk, bread crumbs and Parmesan cheese	Italy
mille-feuille	delicate baked puff pastry	France
minestrone	soup of cut vegetables, macaroni or rice and Parmesan cheese	Italy
mirepoix	mixture of onions, celery, carrots sautéed in butter and seasoned	France
mirin	sweet sake (rice wine)	Japan
miso	fermented soybean paste	Japan
miso shiru	mild white soybean paste	Japan
moelle, à la	dish served with beef marrow	France
mole	chili sauce	Mexico
morilles	mushrooms	France
mortadella	lightly smoked sausage	Italy
mostoccioli	smooth, tubular pasta	Italy
moules	bivalve mollusks or mussels	France
mousse	sweet or savory puree mixed with egg whites and heavy cream	France
mousseline	rich forcemeat made from finely ground meat, poultry, fish, game, or shellfish with cream and egg whites	France
mu-er	black tree fungus	China
mulligatawny soup	soup that uses a variety of meats, vegetables, and spices	Anglo-Indian
mung	translucent cellophane noodles	China
mung bean	green bean half the size of a pea	India
muscoli	mussels	Italy
nabemono	one-pot cookery	Japan
napoleon	puff pastry filled with crème pâtissière	France
nappe	coated with a sauce or a jelly	France
nasi goreng	Indonesian smorgasbord	
natur schnitzel	veal cutlet	Germany
navarin	stew made from mutton or lamb	France
nesselrode	refers to presence of chestnuts	France
nicoise, à la	garnish of garlic, tomatoes, anchovies, black olives, capers, and lemon juice	France

Term	Definition	Origin
nimono	foods simmered or boiled	Japan
nockerl, salzburger	creamy, light dumplings	Austria
noir, beurre	browned butter	France
noki	egg noodles	Hungary
norvégienne	ice cream enclosed within a sponge cake and coated with meringue then baked	France
nougat	confection made with roasted almonds or walnuts mixed with honey and sugar	France
O'Brien potatoes	fried diced potatoes with onions and sweet green peppers	Ireland
oeuf	egg	France
oie	goose	France
orrechietti	ear-shaped pasta	Italy
ortolan	tiny birds	France
orzo	barley-shaped pasta	Greece
ossi bucchi alla milanese	veal shanks	Italy
paella	saffron-flavored rice	Spain
pagnotta del cacciatore	game birds wrapped in a dough and baked	Italy
paillarde	piece of meat that has been pounded flat before cooking	France
pain perdu	French toast	France
paistettu lohi	baked salmon cakes	Finland
pakora	batter-fried vegetables	India
panada	flours, breadcrumbs, rice, or potatoes mixed with egg yolks	Spain
papillote	meat or fish that is wrapped in wax paper or cooking parchment and baked	France
pappadums	spicy pancakelike breads	India
parillada	mixed grill	Argentina
parisienne, potatoes	ball-shaped potatoes sautéed in butter and herbs	France
parkin	ginger and oatmeal cake	England
pastina	tiny disks of pasta used in soups	Italy
pastina al uovo	same as pastina, but with eggs	Italy
pastitsio	casserole of baked meat and macaroni	Greece
pastrami	spicy, pepper-hot, marinated sirloin beef	Jewish
paupiettes	thinly sliced pieces of meat or fish	France
peking duck	roasted duck	China
peperoncini	very small red sausage	Italy
peperoni	bell peppers	Italy
perciatelli	tubular, long pasta slightly larger than spaghetti	Italy

Term	Definition	Origin
périgourdine	with a garnish of black truffles	France
persillade	seasoning of minced fresh parsley and raw garlic	France
pesto alla genovese	herb-and-cheese paste	Italy
petite marmite	small earthenware bowl	France
petits fours	delicate cakes	France
phoenix-tailed shrimp	deep-fried shrimp	China
phyllo	paper-thin sheets of pastry dough	Greece
piacere, à	phrase meaning "done to your pleasure"	Italy
piatti del giorno	specials of the day	Italy
piccata milanese	slice of veal pounded flat	Italy
pilaf	baked rice	Turkey
piperade	tomatoes and peppers cooked with seasonings and mixed with scrambled eggs	France
pirog/piroshki	yeast-dough pastry	Russia
pistou	soup of beans, potatoes, leeks, and seasonings	France
pita	pocket bread that is filled	Yugoslavia
plantains	large green cooking bananas	Mexico
poele	type of covered roast cooked in butter	France
poi	vegetable paste	Polynesia
poisson	fish	France
poivrade, sauce	peppercorn sauce	France
poivre, entrecote au	peppered steak	France
polenta	cornmeal mixture	Italy
pollo	chicken	Italy
pollo	chicken	Spain
polonaise, à la	garnished with hard-boiled eggs and fresh parsley mixed with breadcrumbs fried in butter	France
polpette di manzo	fried beef meatballs	Italy
polpettine	tiny meatballs	Italy
polpettone	meat loaf made	Italy
polpo	octopus	Italy
pomme	apple	France
pomme de terre	potato	France
pomodoro	tomato	Italy
pomodoro salsa	tomato sauce	Italy
potage	thick soup	France
pot-au-feu	beef and vegetable soup	France
potee	thick stew or soup	France
poulet	chicken that is more than three months old	France

Term	Definition	Origin
poussin	young chicken	France
prairie eel	rattlesnake steak	USA
praline	nut and sugar combination blended	France
prawns	large shrimp	General
primavera	fresh spring vegetables	Italy
printanier	dish made with fresh green produce	France
prix fixe	list of prepared dishes served at a meal for one price	France
profiteroles	cream puff pastry	France
prosciutto di parma	ham cured by salting and drying	Italy
provencale, à la	cooked with garlic and olive oil	France
pulque	drink made from the fermented sap of the maguey plant	Mexico
pu pu	appetizers	Polynesia
quenelle	dumplings made from chicken, fish, meat, or game	France
quesadilla	corn flour tortillas folded over various fillings	Mexico
quiche	savory custard	France
raclette	heated cheese	Switzerland
ragout	stew	France
ragu	meat and tomato sauce	Italy
raki	liquor flavored with aniseed	Turkey
ramequin	baked cheese or small pastry that is filled with a cheese mixture	France
rarebit	toast with sauce made with beer, butter, cheese, milk, pepper, and salt	Wales
ratatouille nicoise	vegetable stew	France
ravioli	small filled pasta	Italy
red-cooking	browning food in soy sauce	China
reine, à la	any dish made with plump chicken	France
rellenos, chiles	stuffed chile peppers	Mexico
retsina	wine flavored with resin	Greece
rigati	ribbed and tubular pasta	Italy
rigatoni	ribbed, large tubular pasta, cut into 3-inch segments	Italy
ris de veau	sweetbreads	France
risi e bisi	rice dish with green peas, minced onions, ham or pork	Italy
risotto	creamy rice dish	Italy
rissole potatoes	browned potato balls	France
roestbraten	roasted boneless cut of beef or pork loin	Germany
roesti	process of sauteing until crisp and golden	Switzerland

Term	Definition	Origin
roesti potatoes	potatoes that have been shredded, seasoned, and cooked in butter	Switzerland
rouille	garlic and breadcrumb paste	France
roulade	meat that has been flattened, stuffed, and rolled before cooking	France
rouladen, beef	pounded sliced beef	Germany
roux	butter and flour mixture used to thicken sauces and soups	France
rumaki	chicken livers wrapped around water chestnuts; wrapped with bacon	Polynesia
sabayon	egg yolk custard	Italy
sachertorte	rich chocolate cake	Austrian
sake	wine made from rice, malt, and water	Japan
salame/salami	sausage	Italy
salisbury steak	hamburger steaks	England
salmis	game stew	France
salpicon	one or more ingredients diced and bound with a sauce	France
salsify	oyster plant: root vegetable	France
saltfish and akee	simmered saltcod with sautéed pork fat, hot peppers, scallions, tomatoes, and thyme	Jamaican
saltimbocca	veal dish with sage and thin sliced ham	Italy
sambals	vegetables cooked in a sauce	India
samosas	turnovers filled with vegetables or meat	India
sashimi	thinly sliced raw fish	Japan
satay	small pieces of mutton, beef, and chicken barbecued with a sharp peanut sauce	Indonesia
sate manis	sweetly marinated beef cubes that are skewered and broiled	Indonesia
sauerbraten	marinated beef	Germany
sauerkraut	shredded, fermented cabbage	Austria
savarin	baba-type cake filled with whipped cream, cherries or fruits flavored with liqueur	France
savoury	highly seasoned dish served at the end of a dinner	England
scallopine	thin slices of veal	Italy
scampi	prawns or large shrimp	Italy
schlacht platte	platter of German specialities served at a restaurant	Germany
schlag	whipped cream mixed with vanilla sugar	Germany
schnitzel	veal dipped in egg yolk, breaded, and sautéed in butter	Austria
schwartzwalder kirschtorte	chocolate cake with cherries	Germany

Term	Definition	Origin
scungilli	squid	Italy
semolina	hard wheat flour	Italy
seviche	fish marinated in lime juice and many other seasonings	Mexico
shiitake	large black tree mushroom	Japan
shish kebab	meat barbecued on skewers	Arabia
shiu mai	steamed meat dumplings	China
shoo-fly pie	molasses pie	Holland
shoyu	all-purpose soy sauce	Japan
smorgasbord	rich and varied foods on a table to sample	Sweden
smorrebrod	open-face sandwich	Sweden
sofrito	seasoned tomato sauce	Spain
somen	thin wheat noodles	Japan
sommelier	wine steward	France
sorbet	fruited ice	France
sourdough	bread dough with a starter	Egypt
souvarou, à la	pheasant dish	France
spaghetti	long, thin strands of pasta	Italy
spaghettini	thin spaghetti	Italy
spanakopitta	spinach-filled pie with a phyllo crust	Greece
spatlese	wine made from grapes left on the vine	Germany
spaetzle	tiny dumpling	Germany
spezzatino	meat stew	Italy
spiedo, allo	skewered on a spit and roasted	Italy
spumoni	dessert consisting of a layer of chocolate ice cream and a layer of vanilla ice cream between which is rum-flavored whipped cream with nuts and candied fruits	Italy
steak and kidney pie	savory pie	England
stefado	stew of hare, veal, or beef	Greece
stollen, dresdener	festive fruit loaf	Germany
stracciatella	soup made from both chicken and beef consommé	Italy
strudel	flaky pastry that is covered with fruits, cream cheese or cottage cheese	Austria
stufato	boiled or stewed	Italy
sukiyaki	chicken, beef, or pork stew	Japan
supremes de volaille	breasts of chicken	France
sushi	any of a number of seafood and rice mixtures	Japan
suzette, crepes	thin pancakes served with orange sauce	France
Tabasco	spicy sauce	Mexico

Term	Definition	Origin
table d'hote menu	menu featuring a complete meal at a fixed price	France
tacos	tortillas stuffed with various mixtures	Mexico
tafelspitz	boiled beef brisket	Germany
tagliarini	very narrow egg noodles	Italy
tagliatelle	fettuccini	Italy
tahini	crushed sesame seeds	Indonesia
tamales	coarse cornmeal dough	Mexican
tamarind	seeds of an Asiatic tree used to add a fruity flavor	India
tandoor	clay oven	India
tapenade	deviled eggs	France
thermidor, lobster	lobster meat with sauce of heavy cream, eggs, white wine, cheese, and seasonings; replaced in the shells and broiled	France
thousand-year-old eggs	eggs wrapped in rice husks; soaked in tea, salt, lime, and ashes	China
timbale	round mold	France
tofu	soybean curd	Japan
tomatillos	husk-covered green vegetables	Mexico
tonno	tuna	Italy
torte	rich cake	Germany
tortellini	ring-shaped pasta	Italy
tortilla	thin, flat corn or wheat pancake	Mexico
tostada	crisp-fried filled tortilla	Mexico
tostones de platano	fried plantains	Spain
tournedos	slices of the fillet of beef	France
treacle	molasses	England
trencherman	hearty eater	England
tripe	third stomach of a cow	general
trockenbeerenauslese	dessert wine	Germany
truffles	fungus that grows near the roots of oak and chestnut trees	France
tubettini	tiny tubular pasta	Italy
tutti-frutti	vanilla and pistachio ice cream with candied fruits	Italy
udon	thick noodle	Japan
umido	stewed or boiled meats	Italy
vacherin	dessert made of baked meringue	France
variniki	ravioli-type preparation	Russia
vatroushki	tartlets made from puff pastry and filled with cream cheese seasoned with salt and sugar	Russia
veloute, sauce	cream sauce	France

Term	Definition	Origin
verde, salsa	green sauce	Mexico
vermicelli	very thin spaghetti	Italy
veronique, à la	garnish of seedless white grapes	France
vichyssoise soup	cold soup made from chicken stock, potatoes, leeks and cream	France
vitello	veal	Italy
Vitello al Barolo	pot roast of veal	Italy
vol-au-vent	puff pastry shells	France
wakame	dried seaweed	Japan
wasabe	green horseradish	Japan
waterzooi	Belgian stew made with fish or chicken	Belgium
wellington, beef	filet of beef wrapped in puff pastry	England
wienerschnitzel	breaded veal cutlet	Germany
wonton	dumpling wrapper	China
wood ears	charred-looking mushroom	Italy
wurst	sausage	Germany
yaki	grill	Japan
yakitori	skewered chicken grilled over charcoal fire	Japan
yorkshire pudding	puffy bread pancake served with roast beef	England
yosenabe	casserole dish with various kinds of seafood, bean curd, and vegetables	Japan
zabaglione	sweet dessert custard with Marsala	Italy
zakouski/zakuski	appetizer assortment	Russia
zampone	meat from a pig's leg	Italy
zarzuela de mariscos	seafood stew	Spain
zensai	appetizers	Japan
ziti	large tubular pasta, cut into 3-inch segments	Italy
zuppa inglese	rum cake topped with a custard cream and slivered almonds	Italy
zwieback	type of toast or rusk that has been baked twice	Germany

Table 1-82. Food Word Translations

As your menu takes on more international flavor, your cooks and service staff will encounter strange new words, and often difficult challenges in pronouncing them. The following pages contain the foreign-to-English translations of common French, Italian, and Spanish terms.

English	Spanish	French	Italian
		Fruits	
apple	manzana	pomme	mela
apple cider	sidra	cidre	sidro
apricot	albricoque	abricot	albicca
banana	platano	banane	banana
black currant	grosella	cassis	more
blueberry	arandano	myrtille	mirtillo
cherry	ceriza	cerise	ciliega
cranberry	arandano	airelles rouge	mirtillo rosso
currant	pasa di corinto	raisins di corinthe	uva di corinto
date	datil	datte	dattero
fig	higo	figue	fico
fruit	fruta	fruit	frutta
fruit, dried	fruta seca	fruits seches	frutta secca
fruit plate	compotera	compotiere	recipiente per frutta
gooseberry	grosella	groseille verte	uva spina
grape	uva	raisin	uva
lemon	limon	citron	limone
lemonade	limonada	limonade	limonata
lemon juice	jogo de limon	jus de citron	sugo di limone
marmalade	marmelada	marmelade	marmellata
medlar	nispole	nefle	nespola
melon	melon	melon	mellone
mixed fruit	frutas varidas	fruits panaches	frutta mista
morello	guindilla	griotte	marasche
mulberry	moras	mures	more
orange	naranja	orange	arancia
peach	alberchigo	peche	pesca
pear	pera	poire	pera
pepper, sweet	pimiento	poivron doux	peperoni
pineapple	pina tropical	ananas	ananasso

English	Spanish	French	Italian
Fruits			
plum	ciruela	prune	prugna
pomegranate	granada	grenade	mela grana
pumpkin	calabaza	potiron	zucca
quince	membrillo	coing	cotogna
raspberry	frambuesa	framboise	lampone
red currant	grosella	groseille rouge, de bar	ribes rosso
rhubarb	ruibarbo	rhubarbe	rabarbaro
stewed fruit	compota	compote	composta di frutta
strawberry	fresa	fraise	fragole
tangerine	mendarina	mandarine	mandarino
tomato	tomate	tomate	pomodoro
watermelon	sandia	pasteque	cocomero
Vegetables			
artichoke	alcachofa	artichaut	carciofo
asparagus	esparrago	asperge	asparago
barley	cebada	orge	orzo
beet root	remolacha	betterave	barbabietola
cabbage	col	chou	cavola
caper	alcaparra	capre	capperi
cardoon	cardon	cardon	cardo
carrot	zanahoria	carotte	carote
cauliflower	coliflor	choufleur	cavolfiori
celery	apio	celeri	sedano rapa
chick-pea	garbanzos	pois chiche	ceci
cos lettuce	ensalada romano	laitue romaine	lattuga romana
cucumber	pepino	concombre	cetriolo
gherkins	pepinillos	cornichons	cetriolini
green cabbage	repollo	chou vert	verza
indian corn	maiz	mais	grano turco
lettuce	lechuga	laitue	lattuga
mushroom	champignon	champignon	funghi
olive	aceituna	olive	oliva
onion	cebolla	oignon	cipolla
peas	guisantes	petits pois	piselli
pepper	pimienta	poivre	pepe
pickle	caustico	marinade	mainata

English	Spanish	French	Italian
Vegetables			
pickled cabbage	berzas	choucroute	crauti
potato	patata	pomme te terre	patata
radish	rabanito	radis	rapanello
rice	arroz	riz	riso
spinach	espinaca	epinards	spinaci
truffle	trufa	truffle	tartufi
turnip	nabos	navets	navone
vegetables	legumbre	legumes	legumi
Meats			
bacon	lardo	lard	lardo
beef	carne de vaca	boeuf	manzo
beef tenderloin	lomo	filet de boeuf	filetto di bue
beef tea	jugo de carne	jus de viande	sugo di carne
belly	vientre	ventre	pancia
brains	sesos	cervelle	cervella
braised meat	carne estofado	viande braise	brasato
breast	pecho	poitrine	petto
breast of veal	pecho de ternera	poitrine de veau	petto di vitello
brisket	pecho	poitrine	petto
brisket of beef	pecho de vaca	poitrine de boeuf	petto di manzo
calf's liver	manos de ternera	pieds de veau	zempetto di vitello
calf's head	cabeza de ternera	tete de veau	testina di vitello
calf's liver	higado de ternera	foi de veau	fegato di vitello
calf's pluck	asa lura de ternera	fraise de veau	rete di vitello
chitterlings	asa dura	fraise, fressure	trippa
cold meat	fiambres	viande froide	carne fredda
collop	escalopin	escalope	braciola
cutlet, chop	chuleta	cotellete	costoletta
deer	ciervo	cerf	cervo
forcemeat	relleno	farce	ripieno
ham	jamon	jambon	prosciutto
hare	liebre	lievre	lepre
hash	salpicon	hachis	trito, carne tritata
haunch	pernil	cuissot	coscia
haunch, venison	asada de corzo	gigot de chevreuil	coscia di capriolo
head	cabeza	tete	testa

English	Spanish	French	Italian
Meats			
kidney	rinones	rognon	rognone
lamb	cordero	agneau	agnello
lamb cutlet	costillas di cordero	côte d'agneau	costolette do agnello
leg	oierna	gigot	cosciotta
leg of lamb	pierma di cordero	gigot d'agneau	coscia d'agnello
leg of mutton	pierna di carnero	gigot de mouton	cosciotto di castrato
leg of veal	maza de ternera	cuisseau de veau	coscia di vitello
liver	higado	foie	fegato
loin of veal	rinonada de ternera	longe de veau	lombata di vitello
meat	carne	viande	carne
mutton	cordero	mouton	montone
mutton cutlet	chuletas de cordero	côte de mouton	braciola di montone
ox tail	rabo de vaca	queu de boeuf	coda di bue
ox tongue	lengua de vaca	langue de boeuf	lingua di bue
pork	cerdo	cochon, porc	porco, maiale
pork chop	chuleta de cerdo	côte de porc	costolette di maiale
pork trotters	manos de cerdo	pieds de porc	zampetti di porco
rabbit	conejo	lapin	coniglio
roast	asado	rotis, rots	arrosto
roast pork	asado de cerdo	porc roti	arrosto di maiale
roast loin of veal	asado de ternera de rinones	longe de veau rotie	lombata di vitello
roebuck	corzo	chevreuil	capriolo
saddle of venison	lomo de corzo	selle de chevreuil	lombo di capriole
sausage	salchichon	saucisse	salsiccia
smoked beef	carne ahumado	boeuf fumé	carne affumicata
stomach	estoago	estomac	stomace
veal, calf	ternera	veau	vitello
veal cutlet	costila de ternera	côte	costolette di vitello
venison, game	caza	gibier	selvaggina
wild boar	jabali	sanglier	cinghaile
young wild boar	jabato	marcassin	cinghialetto
Seafood			
anchovy	anchoa	anchois	acciuga
bass	lubina	bar	pesce

English	Spanish	French	Italian
Seafood			
carp	carpa	carpe	carpione
caviar	cavial	caviar	caviale
clams	coquillas	clovisses	conchiglie
cod	bacalao fresco	cabillaud	merlusso fresco
collop	escalopin	escalope	braciola
crab	camarones	crabe	granchio
crayfish	cangrejo	ecrevisse	gambero
eel	anguila	anguille	anguilla
eel pout	lota	lotte	lasca
fish	pescado	poisson	pesce
flounder	lenguado	flet	passera
frog	rana	grenouille	rana
haddock	besugo	aiglefin	nasello
head	cabeza	tete	testa
herring	arenque	hareng	aringa
liver	higado	foie	fegato
lobster	langosta	homard	astice
mackerel	verdel	maquereau	sgombro
mussel	almejas	moule	muscoli
oyster	ostra	huitre	ostriche
perch pike	lucio	sandre	luccioperca
pike	lucio	brochet	luccio
salmon	salmon	saumon	salmone
sardine	cerdena	sardine	sardine
snail	caracole	escargot	lumache
sole	lenguado	sole	sogliola
sturgeon	esturion	esturgeon	storione
trout	trucha	truite	trota
tuna	atun	thon	tonno
turbot	rodaballo	turbot	rombo
turtle	tortuga	tortue	tartaruga
Poultry			
baby chicken	pollito	poussin	pulcino
breast	pecho	poitrine	petto
chicken	pollo	poulet	pollo
chicken liver	higado de pollo	foie de volaille	fegato di polla

English	Spanish	French	Italian
Poultry			
chitterlings, pluck	asa dura	fraise, fressure	trippa
collop	escalopin	escalope	braciola
cutlet, chop	chuleta	cotellete	costoletta
duck	pato	canard	anitra
fattened chicken	pollo	poularde	pollastra
forcemeat	relleno	farce	ripieno
fowls	aves de corral	volaille	pollame
giblets	memudillos	abats de volaille	frattaglie
goose	ganso, oca	oie	oca
goose liver	higado de oca	foie gras	fegata de oca
guinea fowl	pintada	pintade	gallina
hash	salpicon	hachis	trito, carne tritata
head	cabeza	tete	testa
kidney	rinones	rognon	rognone
lark	alondra	mauviette	allodola
leg	oierna	gigot	cosciotta
liver	higado	foie	fegato
ortolan	verderon	ortolan	ortolano
partridge	perdix	perdreau	pernice
peacock	pavo real	paon	pavone
pheasant	faisan	faisan	fagiano
pigeon	paloma	pigeon	piccione
plover	avefria	vanneau	vannello
quail	codorniz	caille	quaglia
sausage	salchichon	saucisse	salsiccia
snipe	becada	becasse	beccaccia
teal	cerceta	sarcelle	arzavola
turkey	pava	dinde	tacchino
wing	ala	aile	ali
wing of chicken	ala de pollo	aile de poulet	ala di pollo
woodcock	becada	becasse	beccaccia
Spices and Herbs			
allspice	pimienta	piment	paprika
angelica	angelica	angelique	angelica

English	Spanish	French	Italian
Spices and Herbs			
aniseed	anis	anis	anice
basil	basilico	basilic	basilico
bay leaf	laurel	laurier	alloro
caper	alcaparra	capres	capperi
cayenne pepper	pimienta de cayenne	poivre de cayenne	pepe di caienna
chervil	perifollo	cerfeuil	cerfoglio
chicory	achicoria	chicoree	cicoria
chive	cebolleta	ciboulette	porrino
cinnamon	canela	cannelle	cannella
cloves	clavos	girofles	chiodi di garofani
curry	curry	currie	curry
dandelion	diente de leon	pissenlit, dent-de-lion	dente di leone
garlic	ajo	ail	aglio
ginger	jengibre	gingembre	zenzero
herbs	hierbe	herbes	erbe
horseradish	rabeno	raifort	rafano
leek	puerro	poireau	porro
marjoram	mejorana	marjolaine	maggiorana
mint	menta	menthe	menta
mustard	mostaza	moutarde	senape
nutmeg	nuez moscada	muscade	noce moscata
parsley	perejil	persil	prezzemolo
poppy	adormidera	pavot	papavero
saffron	azafran	safran	zafferano
sage	salvia	sauge	salvia
sorrel	acedera	oseille	acetosella
spice	especie	epices	spezie
tarragon	estragon	estragon	serpentaria
watercress	berros	cresson	crescione

Table 1-83. French Food Words: Pronunciations and Definitions

French Term	Pronunciation	Definition
abricot	ah-bree-COE	apricot
agneau	on-YO	lamb
ail	eye	garlic
aioli	eye-o-LEE	garlic mayonnaise served with seafood
airelle rouge	eye-REL ROOS	cranberry
Albufera	al-bue-FAIR-aw	supreme sauce with meat glaze and pimento butter
allemande	al-ay-MOND	cream sauce
allumette	al-oo-MET	strip of puff pastry with either a sweet or savory filling or garnish
aloyau	ah-lo-YO	sirloin
amandine	aw-mon-DEEN	garnished with almonds
ananas	an-aw-NOSS	pineapple
anchois	on-SCHWAW	anchovy
andouille	an-DOO-we	pork sausage
anguille	on-GHEE	eel
appareil	ap-air-A	mixture of ingredients ready for preparation
arachide	air-aw-SHEED	peanut
artichaut	ar-tee-SHOW	artichoke
asperge	ess-PAIRJ	asparagus
aubergine	oh-bare-ZHEEN	eggplant
aurore, àl'	oh-ROAR	bechamel sauce with tomato puree
aveline	ah-vaw-LEEN	hazelnut or filbert
baguette	baa-GET	long loaf of French bread
bain marie	bane maw-REE	container of warm water in which another container is nested
ballotine	bal-o-TEEN	large piece of poultry that is boned, stuffed, rolled or shaped, and braised or roasted

French Term	Pronunciation	Definition
banane	ban-NAN	banana
bar	BAR	sea bass
baraquille	bar-aw-KEY	triangular stuffed pastry hors d'oevre
baton, batonnet	baa-TONE, baa-toe-NET	shaped like a little stick
bavarois	baw-var-WAW	Bavarian cream
bavette	baa-VET	tip of sirloin
bearnaise	bare-NAYZ	hollandaise-style sauce with vinegar, shallots and tarragon
Beaufort	bo-FOR	soft, unpressed blue cheese
bécasse	bay-CASS	woodcock
beignet	ben-YAY	food dipped in batter and fried in deep fat
beurre	burr	butter
beurre blanc	burr blonk	sauce made by reducing white wine and shallots; then swirling in cold butter
beurre noir	burr nwar	sauce made by cooking butter until browned
blanc de blancs	blonk duh blonk	white sparkling wine from white grapes
blanquette	blawn-KET	veal, chicken, or lamb stew
Bleu d'Auvergne	bluh day-VAIR-nyuh	soft, unpressed blue cheese
blond de veau	blond duh VO	white veal stock
bombe	BOME	ice cream layers packed in a mold
bonbon	bon-BON	candy
boudin noir	BOO-don NWAW	blood sausage
bouillon	boo-YON	stock or broth
bouquet garni	boo-KAY gar-NEE	bundle of herbs
bourride	bore-REED	fish stew
brioche	bree-OCHE	rich yeast pastry
brochette	bro-SHET	skewer
cabillaud	ca-bee-YO	fresh cod
café au lait	ca-FAY o LAY	coffee with hot milk
cahors	caw-OR	red wine

French Term	Pronunciation	Definition
caille	ky-YEE	quail
calmar	cal-MAR	squid
Camembert	cam-em-BARE	soft, creamy cheese with white mold rind
canapé	ca-na-PAY	bread garnished with savory food
canard sauvage	caw-NARD so-VOZH	wild duck
caneton	can-a-TONE	duckling
canneberge	can-BEARJH	cranberry
Cantal	can-TALL	raw, cured cheese
caroline	care-o-LEEN	savory éclair
carré d'agneau	car don-YOU	loin or rack of lamb
cassis	cah-SEES	black currant
cerfeuil	sir-FWEE	chervil
cerise	sir-EESE	cherry
cervelas	sir-VELL-oss	pork sausage
cervelles	sir-VELL	brains
Chabichou	shaw-bee-SHOO	soft, mild goat cheese
champignon	sham-peen-YONE	mushroom
Chantilly	shan-tee-YEE	sweetened whipped cream
chapelure	shap-aw-LURE	brown breadcrumbs
charcuterie	shar-KOO-tear-ee	sausage making
charlotte	shar-LOT	classic apple compote in bread-lined buttered mold
Chavignol	shaw-vin-YOL	soft French goats' milk cheese
chiffonnade	shiff-o-NOD	vegetables sliced into thin strips
chinois	sheen-WAW	fine-mesh sieve
chou	shoo	cabbage
choucroute	shoo CROOT	sauerkraut
choufleur	shoo FLOOR	cauliflower
choux de Bruxelles	shoo duh broox-EL	brussels sprouts
ciboulette	sib-oo-LET	chives
citron	sit-TRONE	lemon
civette	siv-ET	chives
cocotte	ko-KOT	casserole
coing	kewn	quince

French Term	Pronunciation	Definition
composé	com-po-ZAY	typically, an arranged salad
compote	com-POTE	fresh fruit stewed in syrup
concasser	cone-kaw-SAY	roughly chopped vegetables
concombre	cone-cone-BRUH	cucumber
confit	cone-FEE	duck or goose cooked slowly in its own fat
confiture	cone-fee-TYURE	preserve or jam
consommé	cone-so-MAY	ultra-clear broth of meat, chicken, game, or fish
coquillage	ko-kee-YAWJ	shellfish
coquille Saint-Jacques	ko-KEE sawn ZHOCK	scallop
Cote Rotie	coat ro-TEE	red wine from the Rhone Valley
cotriade	ko-tree-ODD	fish soup from Brittany
côte	coat	rib or chop
côtelette	ko-taw-LET	cutlet
Coulommiers	koo-lum-mee-A	creamy white aged cheese
courge	coorzh	marrow or squash
creme brulée	krem brew-LAY	custard dessert caramelized under broiler before service
creme anglaise	krem on-GLACE	custard
crepe	krep	thin, light pancake
crepinette	krep-en-ET	small sausage wrapped in caul rather than casing
crevette	cruh-VET	shrimp
croquembouche	crow-kem-BOOSH	small cream puffs piled into a pyramid and drizzled with caramel glaze
Crottin de Chavignol	cro-TEN duh shaw-veen-YOL	goats' milk cheese
croustade	crew-STOD	hollowed bread or pastry used as a base for savory foods
crouton	CREW-tawn	small piece of bread or dough used for garnish

French Term	Pronunciation	Definition
dacquoise	dah-KWAZ	baked merignue disks with ground nuts; layered with whipped cream and berries
darne	darn	fish steak
degustation	day-goo-staw-see-OWN	tasting or sampling
demi, demie	dem-EE	half
demi-sec	dem-ee SEK	wine term meaning literally "half dry"
diable	dee-AW-bluh	meat or poultry seasoned with mustard, vinegar, or hot seasoning
dinde	DIN-day	turkey hen
duxelles	duke-SELL	paste of finely chopped mushrooms and shallots
échalote	esh-aw-LOTE	shallot
éclair	ay-KLARE	finger-shaped, cream-filled pastry
ecrevisse	ay-cray-VEECE	freshwater crayfish
émincé	ay-MONCE	thinly sliced cooked meat
entrecôte	on-tray-KOTE	steak
épice	ay-PEECE	spice
épinard	ep-ee-NARD	spinach
escalope	ess-kal-OPE	scallop of meat or fish
escargot	ess-car-GO	snail
espagnole	ess-spon-YOLE	basic brown sauce
estragon	ess-straw-GAWN	tarragon
faisan	fy-ZAWN	pheasant
farce	farse	stuffing, forcemeat
fines herbes	feen urb	mixture of chopped parsley, chervil, tarragon, and chives
flagolet	fla-zho-LAY	small pale green bean
flambé	flaum-BAY	to flame or ignite
fleuron	floor-OWN	flaky pastry garnish
foie gras	fwaw GRAW	goose liver
fond d'artichaut	fon du ar-tee-SHOW	artichoke heart
fondant	fon-DON	confectionery sugar

French Term	Pronunciation	Definition
fraise	frez	strawberry
framboise	fram-BWAZ	raspberry
frangipane	fran-juh-PAN	almond-flavored confection
friandise	free-on-DEEZ	petits four
fricassee	frik-aw-SAY	white meat stew
frit	freet	fried
froid	fwaw	cold
fromage	fro-MAWZH	cheese
fruits de mer	fwee de MAIR	seafood
fumé	foo-MAY	smoked
fumet	foo-MAY	concentrated liquid
galantine	gal-awn-TEEN	poultry, fish, or meat is boned, stuffed and rolled; poached in stock
ganache	gaw-NOSH	chocolate pastry filling
garbure	gar-BEOUR	thick soup
garde manger	gar mon-JAY	cold buffet
garniture	gar-nee-TURE	garnish
gateau	gah-TOE	cake
gaufre	GO-fruh	waffle
gelée, en	on zhel-AY	in aspic
genièvre	zhen-ee-EV	juniper berry
genoise	zhen-WAZ	basic sponge cake
gibier	zhee-bee-AY	game
gigot	zhee-GO	leg of mutton
gigue	zhee-GAY	haunch of venison or boar
gingembre	gin-gem-BRUH	ginger
glacage	glaw-SAUZH	browning or glazing
glacé	gloss	ice cream or cake icing
gougère	goo-ZHAIR	baked puff paste with cheese
goujonette	goo-zho-NET	thin strips of fish
Grand Marnier	gran mar-GNAY	orange liqueur
grecque, à la	a law GREK	flavored with olive oil and lemon juice
grenouille	grawn-WEE	frog
gribiche	gree-BEESH	herby mayonnaise sauce for chilled fish

French Term	Pronunciation	Definition
groseille	gro-ZAY	currant
haricot	air-ee-KO	bean
haricot blanc	air-ee-KO blonk	white kidney bean
haricot flageolet	air-ee-KO fla-zho-LAY	pale green bean
haricot rouge	air-ee-KO roozh	red kidney bean
haricot verte	air-ee-KO vair	green string bean
homard	o-MAR	lobster
huile	we	oil
huitre	WE-truh	oyster
ile flottante	eel flo-TAUNT	poached meringue served in custard sauce
jalousie	jah-loo-SEE	puff pastry strip with a sweet filling
jambon	zhan-BONE	ham
julienne	zhool-ee-EN	"matchstick" cut
jus	zhoo	juice
lait	lay	milk
laitue	lay-TYEW	lettuce
langouste	lan-GOOSE-tuh	rock or spiny lobster
langoustine	lan-goo-STEEN	small lobster or saltwater crayfish
langue	LONG-guh	tongue
lapin	lah-PAN	rabbit
lard de poitrine fumé	lar du pwah-TREEN foo-MAY	bacon
larder	lar-DARE	to insert slivers of fat or garlic into meat
legumes	lay-GOOM	vegetables
leveret	luh-vair-ET	young rabbit
liason	lee-ay-ZONE	bind or thicken soup or sauce with egg yolks or starch
lier	lee-AY	to blend
lièvre	lee-EV-ruh	rabbit
limande	lee-MOND	lemon sole
livarot	lee-vaw-RO	whole-milk cheese
lyonnaise, à la	lee-o-NAYZ	with onions
longe de veau	long du VO	loin of veal
lotte	lot	monkfish
loup	loo	sea bass

French Term	Pronunciation	Definition
macedoine	mah-suh-DWAWN	mixture of sliced fresh fruits
mache	mash	lamb's lettuce
madeleine	mah-dah-LEN	small, shell-shaped cake
madrilene	mah-draw-LEN	beef consommé flavored with tomato
magret, maigret	mah-GRET	breast of duck
maitre d'hotel	MET-tru do-TEL	person in charge of a restaurant dining room
mais	my-EESE	corn
manderine	man-daw-REEN	tangerine
maquereau	MAH-CAH-row	mackerel
marignan	mar-een-YAWN	rich yeast dough soaked in rum-flavored syrup and filled with creme Chantilly
marinière, à la	mair-in-YAIR	seafood cooked in white wine with shallots, parsley, and butter
marjolaine	mar-zho-LAYN	almond dacquoise layered with chocolate, praline, and buttercream
marmelade	mar-mah-LAID	thick sweetened fruit puree
marmite	mar-MEET	large covered pot
Maroilles	maw-ROY	soft, creamy whole milk cheese
marquise	mar-KEEZE	fruit ice folded with whipped cream
marron	maw-ROAN	chestnut
matelote	maw-taw-LOT	fish stew
medaillon	may-dye-YONE	small round slice of meat
mélanger	mel-on-ZHAIR	to mix
menthe	menth	mint
merlan	mair-LAWN	whiting
meunière, à la	mun-YARE	sauteed fish served with butter and lemon

French Term	Pronunciation	Definition
miel	me-YELL	honey
mignonette	min-yo-NET	coarsely ground pepper
mijoter	me-zho-TARE	to simmer
mille-feuille	me-FWEE	puff pastry
mirepoix	meer-ah-PWAW	mixture of diced vegetables used for flavor in cooking
miroton	meer-ah-TONE	brown meat stew
mise en place	meez on PLAUCE	assembly of all ingredients necessary for cooking
mode, à la	ah law MODE	braised beef with vegetables
moelle	mo-EL	beef marrow
moka	MO-kaw	mocha
Mont Blanc	mone BLONK	chestnut puree topped with creme Chantilly
morille	mor-EEL	morel
Mornay	mor-NAY	cream sauce with cheese
morue	MO-roo	salt cod
moulange	moo-LAZH	molding
moule	MOOL	mussel
mousse	moose	sweet or savory dish lightened with beaten egg whites or cream
mousseline	moose-ah-LEEN	sauce made by folding unsweetened whipped cream into hollandaise
mousseux	moose-UH	sparkling or effervescent
moutarde de Meaux	moo-TARD du meu	grainy mustard
mouton	moo-TAWN	mutton
Munster	MUN-stir	pasteurized whole-milk cheese
Murol	mu-ROLL	hard cows' milk cheese
mure	moo-RAY	blackberry
myrtille	meer-TEEL	blueberry
nage, à la	ah lah NAZH	cooked in white wine court bouillon
napolitain	naw-pole-ee-TEN	cornmeal cake

French Term	Pronunciation	Definition
napper	nah-PAY	to coat or mask with sauce
nature	nah-TEUR	plain, ungarnished
navarin	naw-VARE-ee-aw	mutton stew
navarraise	nah-vare-AIZE	tomato sauce
navet	nah-VAY	turnip
Neufchâtel	noof-chaw-TEL	soft uncooked cheese
nicoise, à la	ah la nee-SWAUSE	tomatoes chopped and sautéed in olive oil with garlic, capers, sliced lemon, anchovies, and black olives
noisette	nwaw-ZET	hazelnut
noix	NWAW	nut, walnut
nonpareille	known-pare-AY	small pickled capers
normande	nor-MOND	fish veloute with mushrooms
nouilles	NOO-yaw	noodles
oeuf	oof	egg
oie	waw	goose
oignon	own-YONE	onion
Olivet	all-ee-VET	whole or partially skimmed-milk cows' cheese
ortolan	or-toe-LAWN	small bird
oseille	oh-ZAY	sorrel
oursin	or-SAWN	sea urchin
paillarde de veau	pie-YARD doo VO	grilled veal scallop
paillettes	pie-YET	pastry straws
pain	PEN	bread loaf
palmier	pal-mee-AY	puff pastry sprinkled with sugar
palourde	paw-LOORD	clam
pamplemousse	PAM-pill-moose	grapefruit
panache	paw-NOSH	mixed or multicolored
panais	pah-NAY	parsnip
panure	pah-NYOOR	golden breadcrumb crust
papillon	pah-pee-YONE	butterfly-shaped pastry
papillote	pah-pee-YOTE	paper frill

French Term	Pronunciation	Definition
parfait	par-FAY	mousselike dessert
Paris-Brest	PAIR-ee bress	pastry ring of paté à choux topped with sliced almonds and filled with creme praline
parmesan, à la	aw law par-muh-ZHAN	with grated Parmesan cheese
passer	pah-SAY	to strain through a sieve
pasteque	pah-STEK	watermelon
pastis	pah-STEECE	anise liqueur
patate douce	paw-TOT dooce	sweet potato
pâte	pot	pastry, paste, dough, or batter
pâté	paw-TAY	meat, poultry, game or seafood cooked in pastry
pâte à choux	pot o shoe	cream puff paste
pâte sucrée	pot soo-CRAY	sweet pastry
pêche Melba	pesh MEL-baw	peaches poached in vanilla syrup, served on vanilla ice cream with raspberry puree
persil	pair-SEE	parsley
petite marmite	peh-TEET mar-MEET	clear consommé
petit four	peh-tee FOR	small, garnished cake
Petit-Suisse	peh-tee SWEECE	pasteurized cows' milk cheese
pigeonneau	pee-zhen-O	young squab
piment doux	pee-men DOE	sweet pepper
pintade	pen-TAD	guinea hen
piperade	pee-pair-ODD	tomatoes cooked in olive oil with bell peppers and onions
piquante	pee-KAUNT	sauce of chopped shallots reduced with white wine and vinegar
Pithiviers	pee-thee-vee-AY	large round puff pastry filled with almond paste
pluvier	ploo-VAIR	plover

French Term	Pronunciation	Definition
pocher	po-SHAY	to poach
poeler	pwaw-LAY	to cook food with a little butter
poire	pwahr	pear
poireau	pwa-RO	leek
pois	pwah	pea
poisson	pwah-SONE	fish
poitrine de porc	pwah-TREEN de PORK	pork belly
poivrade	pwah-VRODD	game sauce with crushed pepper and herbs
poivre	pwauv	pepper
pomme	pume	apple
pomme de terre	pume du TARE	potato
pommes Anna	pume anna	potato slices baked brown and crisp
pommes paille	pume pi-EE	deep-fried potato straws
Port-Salut	port saw-loot	uncooked, pressed, pasteurized cows' milk cheese
potage	po-TAWZH	soup
pot-au-feu	po taw FEW	meat and vegetable stew
pot de creme	po du KREM	small, individual custard, mousse
potiron	po-teh-RONE	pumpkin
poularde	poo-LARD	fat hen or chicken
poulet	poo-LAY	young spring chicken
poussin	pwaw-SAWN	very young chicken
primeur	pree-MUER	early or forced fruit or vegetable
profiteroles	pro-fee-tare-OLS	small puffs of choux paste often filled with cream or creme pâtissière
provencal	pro-ven-SAWL	garnish or sauce with chopped tomatoes sauteed in olive oil with garlic and parsley
prune	prewn	plum

French Term	Pronunciation	Definition
pyramid	peer-ah-MEED	generic name for fresh chevre cheese
quatre-épices	kwaw-tra peece	mixture of finely ground white pepper, nutmeg, clove, and ginger
quenelle	kuh-NELL	dumpling made of seafood, chicken, game, or veal
quiche	keesh	custard tart
radis	rah-DEE	radish
raffinade	rah-fee-NOD	refined sugar
ragout	rah-GOO	meat, poultry, or fish stew
raie	ray	skate
raifort	ray-FOR	horseradish
raisin	ray-ZEN	grape
ratatouille	rah-tah-TOO-ee	diced eggplant, tomatoes, zucchini, green peppers, onions, and garlic sautéed in olive oil
rave	rawv	turnip or other root vegetable
ravigote	raw-vee-GOAT	vinaigrette with capers, chopped onions, and herbs
Reblochon	reh-blo-SHONE	rich, soft cows' milk cheese
recette	reh-SET	recipe
rechauffé	reh-SHOFE	food that is reheated or made with leftovers
remoulade	reh-mo-LAWD	mayonnaise mixed with mustard, anchovy, gherkins, capers, parsley, chervil, and tarragon
renverser	ren-vair-SAY	to unmold
rigodon	ree-go-DOAN	brioche custard tart
ris de veau	ree duh VO	veal sweetbread
rissoler	ree-zo-LAY	to brown in hot fat
riz	reece	rice
rognons	roan-YONES	kidneys

French Term	Pronunciation	Definition
romarin	ro-mair-EN	rosemary
Roquefort	ROKE-for	blue cheese
rosbif	roce-BIF	roast beef
roti	ro-TEE	roasted or a roast
rouget	roo-ZHAY	red mullet
roulle	roo-YUH	round slice of meat
rouille	roo-EE	spicy red pepper and garlic mayonnaise
roulade	roo-LAWD	sliced meat or fish rolled around a savory stuffing
roux	roo	flour and butter mixture used to thicken
royale	roy-AL	unsweetened custard
royan	ro-YAWN	fresh sardine
sablé	saw-BLAY	shortbread
Sainte-Maure	sent MOR	goats' milk cheese
Saint-Marcellin	sent mar-suh-LEN	raw goat cheese
Saint-Nectaire	sent nek-TARE	unpasteurized, raw, pressed cows' milk cheese
Saint-Paulin	sent po-LAN	uncooked, pressed cows' milk cheese
saisir	sy-SEAR	to sear
saucisse	so-SEECE	fresh sausage
saumon	so-MONE	salmon
sauté	so-TAY	to cook food quickly in hot fat
savarin	sah-vah-REN	ring-shaped baba filled with creme Chantilly, creme patissière, or fresh fruit
sec	sek	wine term meaning dry
sel	sell	salt
selle	sell	saddle
serviette	sir-vee-ET	napkin; food served in a folded napkin
sommelier	so-mel-YAY	wine steward, wine waiter
sorbet	sor-BAY	sherbet

French Term	Pronunciation	Definition
soufflé	soo-FLAY	classic fluffy beaten egg dish; sweet or savory; hot or cold
soupe	soo-puh	hearty and robust peasant soup
sucre	SOO-kruh	sugar
tapenade	tap-en-ODD	capers, anchovies, and olives thinned with olive oil
tarte	tart	tart, tartlet
terrine	tare-EEN	mixture of meat, game, poultry, or vegetables and seasonings, cooked in mold lined with pork or bacon
tete de veau	TET de vo	calf's head
thé	tay	tea
thon	tone	tuna
timbale	tim-BALL	food prepared in a conical mold
Tomme de Savoie	tum duh sah-VWAW	uncooked, pressed cows' milk cheese
tortue	tor-TOO	turtle
tourné	tor-NAY	vegetable that is shaped to resemble miniature footballs
tournedos	TOR-naw-doze	slices from the middle of the beef filet
toute-épice	toot ay-PEECE	allspice
Trappiste	tra-PEEST	semihard cheese
tuile	tweel	crisp almond cookie
vacherin	vah-share-AN	stacked disks of meringue
Vacherine Mont-d'Or	vah-share-AN mon-DOR	uncooked, unpressed whole cows' milk cheese
vapeur	vah-POOR	steam
veau	vo	veal
velouté	vel-oo-TAY	"velvet" white sauce
viande	vee-OND	meat
vinaigrette	vin-ah-GRET	basic sauce or dressing of oil and vinegar

French Term	Pronunciation	Definition
volaille	vo-LYE	poultry, fowl, or chicken
vol-au-vent	vool-o-VANT	puff pastry cases
xérès	ZER-sees	sherry

Table 1-84. Italian Food Words: Pronunciations and Definitions

Italian Term	Pronunciation	Definition
abbacchio	ah-BAH-kee-o	very young suckling lamb
acciuga	ah-CHEW	anchovy
aceto	ah-CHAY-tho	very fine, dark, mellow vinegar made in Modena, Italy
aceto-dolce	ah-CHAY-tho DULL-chay	sweet-and-sour mixture of fruits and vegetables used as an antipasto
aglio	ah-YEE-oh	garlic
agnello	AN-yell-o	lamb
agnolotti	on-yo-LOW-tee	meat-stuffed pasta (ravioli)
amaretti	ah-maw-RET-tee	small, light almond cookie
anitra	ON-ee-tra	duck
antipasto	on-tee-PAWS-taw	appetizer
aragosta	aw-raw-GO-staw	lobster
arància	aw-RAWN-chaw	orange
Arborio	awr-BO-ree-oh	short, fat-grained rice
aringa	ah-REEN-gaw	herring
arista	ah-REE-staw	roast loin of pork
arsella	are-SELL-la	mussel
arugula	are-ROO-go-law	aromatic salad herb
Asiago d'Allevo	aw-see-AW-go dee awl-LAY-vo	scalded-curd cheese made from cows' milk
bagna calda	BON-yaw CALL-duh	hot sauce
bagna cauda	BON-yaw COW-duh	sauce of garlic and anchovies; served warm with raw vegetables
balsamella	ball-saw-MELL-la	onion flavored white sauce of milk stirred into a roux
basilico	baw-zee-LEE-ko	basil
battuto	baw-THOO-toe	base for stews and soups

Italian Term	Pronunciation	Definition
Bel Paese	bell paw-EE-say	semisoft, mild uncooked Italian cheese
bietola	bee-ET-ol-la	Swiss chard
bollito	bowl-LEE-toe	mixed boiled meats
bolognese, alla	bowl-low-NEE-say	see ragu Bolognese
braciola	braw-chee-O-luh	cutlet or chop
brasato	braw-SAW-toe	braised
bresaola	bre-SAW-oh-law	dried salt beef sliced from the fillet
brodo	BRO-doe	broth or bouillon
bronzino	brawn-TSEE-no	sea bass
bruschetta	brew-SKET-taw	toasted bread topped with garlic and olive oil
burrida	bu-REE-daw	fish stew from Genoa
burro	BORE-row	butter
cacciagione	kaw-chaw-GO-oh-nee	game
cacciatora	kaw-chee-ah-TOR-ah	sauce of mushrooms, onions, tomatoes, and herbs with wine
Caciocavallo	kaw-chee-oh-caw-VAWL-lo	spindle-shaped whole cows' milk cheese
calamari	caw-law-MAW-ree	squid
caldo	CALL-doe	hot
calzone	call-TZO-nee	pizza turnover
campagnola	cawm-pawn-YO-law	country style: onions and tomatoes
cannella	cawn-EL-la	cinnamon
cannellini	can-ay-LEE-nay	white kidney beans
cannelloni	can-ay-LO-nay	pasta squares baked in sauce
cannoli	can-O-lee	pastry tubes filled with ricotta cheese, chocolate, and candied citron
capelli d'angelo	caw-PELL-ee dee AN-gel-o	angel hair pasta
capitone	cap-ee-TOE-nee	large conger eel
caponata	cap-o-NOT-ah	Silician vegetable salad
cappelletti	cap-el-LET-tee	hat-shaped, stuffed pasta
cappone	cap-PO-nee	capon
cappuccino	cap-poo-CHEE-no	espresso coffee with frothy milk
capretto	cap-PRET-o	kid

Italian Term	Pronunciation	Definition
carbonara, alla	car-bo-NAR-aw	spaghetti sauce of bacon, eggs, Parmesan cheese, and cream
carciofo	car-CHAW-foe	artichoke
carne	CAR-nee	meat
carpaccio	car-PAW-chee-o	raw beef fillet sliced very thin
casalinga	caw-saw-LEEN-gaw	homemade
cassata	caw-SAW-taw	layers of cake filled with ice cream or ricotta cheese and candied fruits
castagna	caw-STAW-nee-ya	chestnut
cavolfiore	caw-vol-fee-OR-ay	cauliflower
cavolo	caw-VO-lo	cabbage
ceci	CHEH-chee	chick-peas
cervo	CHAIR-vo	venison
cetriolo	chet-TREE-o-lo	cucumber
Chianti	kee-ON-tee	red table wine
Chiaretto	kee-aw-RET-toe	rosé wine
ciliega	cheel-YAY-jaw	cherry
cioccolata	chee-o-ko-LAW-taw	chocolate
cipolla	chee-PO-law	onion
coda di bue	KO-daw dee BOO-ay	oxtail
conchiglia	cone-KEE-glee-aw	shellfish shaped pasta
coniglio	cone-EEL-yo	rabbit
coratella	ko-raw-TELL-aw	organ meats
coscetto	ko-SHET-o	leg of lamb
coscia	KO-shaw	chicken thigh
cosciotto	ko-SHOW-tho	leg of lamb
costata	ko-STAW-taw	rib chop
costoletta	ko-sto-LET-taw	chop or cutlet
cotechino	ko-tay-KEE-no	large pork sausage
cotto	CAW-toe	cooked
cozza	KO-tza	mussel
crespella	kress-PEL-law	pancake
crosta	CROW-staw	crust
crostacei	crow-staw-CHE-ee	shellfish
crostata	crow-STAW-taw	pie
crostatina	crow-staw-TEEN-aw	tart
crostino	crow-STEEN-o	crouton
crudo	CREW-doe	raw, fresh

Italian Term	Pronunciation	Definition
cuore	KOO-oh-ray	heart
dattero	daw-TEAR-o	date
dente, al	all DEN-tay	pasta or vegetables cooked just until firm and crunchy
disossato	dee-so-SAW-toe	boned
dolce	DULL-chay	sweet
Dolcetto	dull-CHET-o	red wine grapes from Piedmont
dorato	doe-RAW-toe	egg battered and fried golden
dragoncello	draw-gawn-CHEL-o	tarragon
espresso	ess-PRESS-o	strong coffee
fagioli	faw-jee-O-lee	white haricot or kidney beans
farcito	far-CHEE-to	stuffed
farfalle	far-FALL-eh	butterfly-shaped pasta
farina	faw-REE-naw	flour
fatto in casa	FAW-toe een CAW-saw	homemade
fegato	fay-GAW-toe	liver
ferri, ai	FAIR-ree	grilled over open fire
fetta	FET-taw	slice, fillet
fettuccine	fet-too-CHEE-nay	"ribbons" of egg pasta
fiasco	fee-AW-sko	wine bottle with straw covering
fico	FEE-ko	fig
finocchio	feen-O-kee-o	fennel
Fior di Latte	FEE-or dee LAW-tay	cows' milk cheese
fiorentina, bistecca alla	bee-STEK-caw aw-la fee-o-ren-TEE-na	grilled T-bone steak served with olive oil
fiori di zucca	FEE-o-ree dee ZOO-kaw	squash blossoms battered and fried
Fior sardo	FEE-o-raw SAWR-doe	goat milk cheese
focaccia	fo-CAW-shee-o	flat, round bread
fonduta	fawn-DOO-taw	melted Fontina cheese with eggs, butter, milk, sliced truffles, and white pepper
Fontina	fawn-TEE-naw	semicooked and pressed raw cows' cheese
formaggio	for-MAW-jee-o	cheese
fragola	fraw-GO-law	strawberry
freddo	FRED-do	cold
fresco	FREH-scoe	fresh

Italian Term	Pronunciation	Definition
frittata	free-TAW-taw	open-faced omelet
frittella	free-TELL-law	fritter
fritto mista	FREE-toe MEE-staw	mixed food, deep-fried in batter
frizzante	freed-ZAWN-tay	wine term meaning effervescent
frutta fresca de stagione	FRU-ta FRE-scaw day staw-jee-O-nay	fresh seasonal fruit
frutti di mare	FROO-tee dee MAW-ray	seafood, usually shellfish
funghi	FOONG-jee	mushroom
fusilli	few-SILL-ee	thin, spiral-shaped pasta
gambero	gawn-BEAR-o	shrimp
garganelli	gar-gaw-NEL-lee	egg pasta macaroni
gelato	juh-LAW-toe	ice cream
genovese, alla	jen-o-VAY-say	cuisine using fresh herbs, vegetables, and fish
ghiaccio	ghee-AH-kee-o	ice
giardiniera, alla	jee-ar-dee-nee-AIR-ah	with mixed sliced vegetables
giorno, del	jee-OR-no	of the day
glassato	glahs-SAW-toe	glazed
gnocchi	nee-O-kee	small potato or flour dumplings
Gorgonzola	gor-gon-ZOLE-ah	Blue cheese
grana	GRAW-naw	hard granular cheese
granchio	GRAWN-kee-o	crab
granita	graw-NEE-taw	fruit ice or sherbet
grappa	GRAWP-paw	Italian brandies
gremolada	grem-o-LAW-daw	chopped parsley, garlic, and lemon
griglia, alla	GREEL-yaw	grilled
grissino	gree-SEE-no	breadstick
guarnito	goo-ar-NEE-toe	garnished
imbottito	im-bo-TEE-toe	stuffed
impanato	eem-paw-NOT-taw	breaded
insalata	een-so-LAW-taw	salad
involtine	een-vol-TEE-nay	stuffed meat rolls
jota	JO-taw	soup with beans, sauerkraut, potatoes, and bacon
lampone	lam-PO-nay	raspberry
lardo	LAR-doe	salt pork
lasagne	law-ZAWN-yaw	ribbons of pasta

Italian Term	Pronunciation	Definition
latte	LAW-tay	milk
lattuga	law-TOO-gaw	lettuce
lauro	law-OOH-row	bay leaf
legumi	lay-GOO-mee	vegetables
lenticchie	len-tee-KEE-ee	lentils
lepre	LEH-pray	hare
lesso	LESS-so	boiled
limone	lee-MO-nay	lemon
lingua di bue	lee-GWAY dee BOO-ay	ox tongue
lingue di passera	leen-GOO-ay dee paw-SAY-raw	thin eggless pasta
linguine	leen-GWEE-nay	thin, flat, eggless pasta
lombo	LOME-bow	loin
luganeaga	loo-gaw-NEE-aw-gaw	mild, fresh pork sausage
lumaca	loo-MAW-kaw	snail
maccarello	maw-kaw-RELL-o	mackerel
maccheroni	maw-care-O-nee	macaroni
mafalde	maw-FALL-dee	long pasta strips with fluted edges
maggiorana	maw-jee-o-RAW-naw	marjoram
maiale	maw-ee-AW-lee	pork
maionese	maw-ee-o-NAY-zay	mayonnaise
maltagliati	mall-taw-YAW-tee	"badly cut" pasta
manicotti	maw-nee-KO-tee	flat, tube-shaped stuffed pasta
Manteca	mawn-TAY-kaw	cows' milk cheese
manzo	mawn-ZO	beef
marinara, alla	maw-ree-NAR-aw	tomato sauce with garlic and herbs
mascarpone	maw-skar-PO-nay	cows' cheese served with fruits and pastries
mela	MAY-law	apple
melagrana	may-law-GRAW-naw	pomegranate
melanzana	may-lawn-TZAW-naw	eggplant
mezzani	may-TSAW-nee	long, narrow pasta shaped like a tube
midollo	mee-DULL-o	marrow
minestra	mee-NES-traw	hearty soup served as a first course
misto	MEE-stow	mixed
Montasio	mown-TAW-see-o	firm, whole cow's milk cheese
montone	mown-TOE-nay	mutton

Italian Term	Pronunciation	Definition
mostardo di frutta	mow-STAR-doe dee FROO-taw	fruits in mustard flavored syrup; like chutney
Mozzarella	mote-saw-RELL-aw	white buffalos' milk; cheese
napoletana, alla	naw-pole-aw-TAW-naw	meatless spaghetti sauce
nocchette	no-KET-taw	pasta "bow ties" for soup
noce	NO-chay	nut
nostrale	no-STRAWL-ay	native or homegrown
oca	O-kaw	goose
olio	o-LEE-o	oil
olivette di vitello	ol-lee-VET-tay dee vee-TELL-o	veal birds
orecchiette	o-ray-kee-ET-tay	earshaped eggless pasta
orzo	OR-zo	barley
ossobuco alla milanese	o-so-BOO-ko AW-law mee-law-NAY-say	veal shanks braised with vegetables
ostrica	o-STREE-kaw	oyster
pagello	paw-JEL-o	red snapper
paglia e fieno	paw-YEE-aw A fee-A-no	"straw and hay" fettuccine
panato	paw-NAW-toe	fried in breadcrumbs
pancetta	pawn-CHET-taw	Italian bacon
pan de Spagna	pawn day SPAWN-yaw	sponge cake soaked in liqueur and filled with cream or jam
pandorato	pawn-do-RAW-toe	bread dipped in egg and milk; deep-fried
pane	PAW-nay	bread
panettone	paw-nay-TONE-a	light yeast breakfast cake
panforte	pawn-FOR-tay	fruitcake
panna	PAN-naw	cream
Pannerone	paw-nay-RONE-ay	pale cheese with holes from Lombardy
panzanella	pawn-zaw-NEL-law	salad of vegetables and anchovies with stale bread
panzarotti	pawn-zaw-RAW-tay	pastry crescents stuffed with cheese
pappardelle	paw-par-DEL-lay	long, flat, crimped egg noodles
Parmigiano Reggiano	par-mee-jee-AW-no rej-ee-AW-no	partially-skimmed cows' milk cheese with tiny holes
passata	paw-SAWT-aw	puree
passatelli in brodo	paw-saw-TELL-ee een BRO-doe	Parmesan, eggs, and breadcrumbs mixed and pressed to form strands
pasta	PAW-staw	dough or paste

Italian Term	Pronunciation	Definition
pasta asciutta	PAW-staw ah-shee-OOH-taw	"dry" pasta
pasta e fagioli	PAW-staw A faw-jee-O-lee	pasta soup with white beans and salt pork
pasticcio	paw-STEE-kee-o	layered pasta with a savory filling
pastina	paw-STEE-naw	small pasta for soup
patata	paw-TAW-taw	potato
Pecorino Romano	peck-o-REE-no row-MON-o	dense, white, cooked cheese
Pecorino Siliano	peck-o-REE-no sill-ee-ON-o	dense, white, uncooked cheese
penne	PEN-ay	quill-shaped pasta
pepe nero	pay-PAY NAY-ro	black pepper
peperonata	pay-pay-ro-NAW-taw	sweet peppers, tomatoes, onions, and garlic cooked in olive oil and served cold
peperoncino	pay-pay-ro-CHEE-no	hot red chili pepper
peperoni	pay-pay-RO-nee	Italian beef and pork sausage
pera	PAY-raw	pear
pernice	pair-NEECH	partridge
pesca	PAY-skaw	peach
pesce	PAY-shay	fish
pesto	PAY-stow	crushed basil, garlic, pine nuts, and Parmesan or Pecorino in olive oil
petto	PAY-toe	breast, chest or brisket
pezzo	PAYZ-doe	piece
piacere, a	aw pee-aw-CHAIR-ay	cooked "to please"
piccante	pee-KAWN-tay	piquant or spicy
piccata	pee-KOT-aw	veal scallop
pignoli	peen-YOL-ay	pine nuts
pinzimonio	peen-tzee-MO-nee-o	dipping sauce of oil, salt, and pepper
piselli	pee-ZEL-lee	peas
pizza	PETE-zaw	open-faced tart
pizzaiolo	pete-zy-O-lo	tomato sauce served with garlic and herbs
polenta	poe-LEN-taw	cornmeal pudding
pollame	po-LAW-may	poultry
pollo	PAUL-lo	chicken
polpetta	pole-PAYT-taw	meat patty
polpo	POLE-poe	squid or octopus

Italian Term	Pronunciation	Definition
pomodoro	pom-o-DOE-roe	tomato
popone	po-PO-nay	melon
porchetta	por-CHET-taw	roast suckling pig
porcino	po-CHEE-no	wild mushroom
porro	POR-row	leek
prezzemolo	pred-zay-MO-lo	parsley
primavera, alla	pree-maw-VAY-raw	pasta dish made with fresh ham
Provolone	pro-vo-LO-nay	cooked and kneaded spun-curd cheese from cows' milk
prugna	PROON-yaw	plum
quadrucci	kwaw-droo-CHAY	"little squares" of egg pasta
quaglia	kwaw-YEE-aw	quail
Quartirolo	kwawr-tee-RO-lo	soft, uncooked, pressed, cheese
radicchio	raw-DEE-kee-o	chicory with red or pinkish leaves
rafano	raw-FAW-no	horseradish
ragu Bolognese	RAW-goo bowl-low-NEE-say	meat sauce from Bologna
Ragusano	raw-GOO-saw-no	spun-curd cheese
rapa	RAW-paw	turnip
ravanello	raw-vaw-NAIL-lo	radish
ravioli	raw-vee-O-lee	small filled pasta squares
ribes	REE-bess	gooseberry, currant
ribollita	ree-bowl-LEE-taw	soup of white beans, vegetables, bread, cheese, and olive oil
ricotta	ree-KO-taw	cheese made from leftover whey from other cheeses
rigaglie	ree-gaw-YEE-ay	giblets
rigatoni	ree-gaw-TOE-nee	fat-ribbed macaroni
ripieno	ree-pee-EEN-o	stuffed
riso	REE-sew	rice
risotto	ree-SEW-toe	rice cooked in butter with chopped onion and slowly added stock
risotto milanese	ree-SEW-toe mee-law-NAY-say	risotto flavored with saffron
Robiola	ro-bee-O-law	soft, uncooked cheese
role	RO-lay	stuffed and rolled meat slice
rosmarino	ro-so-maw-REE-no	rosemary
ruote	roo-O-tay	wheel-shaped pasta

Italian Term	Pronunciation	Definition
rustica, alla	roo-STEE-kaw	spaghetti sauce of anchovies, garlic, oregano, and Pecorino cheese
salami	saw-LAW-mee	sausage
salsa	SAUL-saw	sauce
saltare	saul-TAW-ray	to sauté
saltimbocco	saul-teem-BO-kaw	veal scallop braised in butter and Marsala
salvia	saul-VEE-aw	sage
sangue, al	sawn-GOO-ay	rare
scaloppina di vitello	skal-o-PEE-nay dee vee-TEL-lo	thinly cut veal scallop
Scamorza	skaw-mor-TZAW	cheese similar to Mozzarella
scampi	SKAM-pee	saltwater crayfish
scarola	skaw-RO-law	escarole
scungilli	skwin-JEE-lee	gastropod mollusk
sedano	say-DON-o	celery
semifreddo	say-mee-FRAY-doe	frozen mousselike dessert
sfogliata	sfol-YAW-taw	puff pastry
sgombro	ze-GOME-bro	mackerel
soffrito	so-FREE-toe	tomatoes, onions, garlic, and herbs cooked in olive oil
sogliola	so-yee-O-law	sole
spaghettini	spaw-get-TEE-nee	thin spaghetti
spezie	spet-TSEE-ay	spices
spezzatino	speds-aw-TEE-no	stew
spiedo	spee-A-doe	spit for roasting meat
spuma	SPOO-maw	fruit or water ice with Italian meringue
spumante	spoo-MAWN-tay	sparkling wine
Stracchino	straw-KEE-no	uncooked cheese
stracciatella	straw-chee-aw-TAY-law	chicken or beef stock thickened with egg, cheese, and semolina
stracotto	straw-KO-toe	pot roast or braised meat
stufa	STOO-faw	stove
sugo	SOO-go	sauce
tacchino	taw-KEE-no	turkey
tagliatelle	taw-yee-aw-TELL-ay	long thin flat strips of pasta
tagiolini	taw-jee-o-LEE-nee	very thin noodles
Taleggio	taw-LAY-jee-o	uncooked, cheese; very delicate and buttery

Italian Term	Pronunciation	Definition
tartufo	tar-TOO-fo	truffle
te	tay	tea
timo	TEE-mo	thyme
Tomino	toe-MEE-no	uncooked cheese from the Italian Alps
tonno	TOE-no	tuna
torrone	toe-RO-nay	nougat
torta	TOR-taw	Italian tart, pie, or cake
tortellini	tor-taw-LEE-nee	small rounds of filled egg pasta
Toscanello	toe-skaw-NAY-lo	cooked cheese from Tuscany and Sardinia
trenette	tray-NAY-tay	flat pasta
triglia	tree-YEE-aw	red mullet
trota	TRO-taw	trout
tutti-frutti	TOO-tee FROO-tee	mixed preserved fruits
uccello	oo-CHAY-lo	bird
umido, in	oo-MEE-doe	stewed
uovo	WO-vo	egg
vellutata	vel-loo-TAW-taw	soup thickened with egg yolk
verdura	vair-DOO-raw	vegetable
vermicelli	ver-mee-CHAY-lee	very thin pasta
Vezzena	veds-AY-nah	hard cheese from skim milk
vitello	vee-TELL-o	veal
vongola	vone-GO-law	clam
zabaglione	zab-ee-YONE-ay	dessert custard flavored with Marsala and sugar
zafferone	zaf-A-ro-nay	saffron
zampone	zam-PO-nay	lightly seasoned pork sausage
zenzero	zen-ZAIR-o	ginger
ziti	ZEE-tee	large tube pasta
zucchero	zoo-KAY-ro	sugar
zuppa	ZOO-paw	soup
zuppa inglese	ZOO-paw een-GLAY-say	rum-soaked sponge cake layered with custard and cream

Table 1-85. Spanish Food Words: Pronunciations and Definitions

Spanish Term	Pronunciation	Definition
aceite	ah-say-EE-tay	oil
aceituna	ah-say-ee-TOO-nah	olive
achiote	ah-chee-O-tay	annatto
agrio	ah-GREE-o	sour
aguacate	ah-gwa-KAW-tay	avocado
aguardiente	ah-gwar-dee-EN-tay	strong Spanish liqueur
ajo	AH-hoe	garlic
albondigas	all-bone-DEE-gaws	spicy meatballs
alcachofa	all-kaw-CHO-faw	artichoke
aliolo	all-ee-O-la	garlic mayonnaise for seafood
almeja	al-MAY-haw	clam
almendra	al-MAIN-draw	almond
arenque	ah-RAIN-kay	herring
arroz	ah-ROCE	rice
asado	ah-SAW-do	roasted or broiled
Asturias	ah-STEW-ree-ahs	strong, sharp cheese
azafran	ah-saw-FRAWN	saffron
azucar	ah-soo-CAR	sugar
batata	bah-TAW-taw	sweet potato
bodega	bo-DAY-gaw	wine cellar or store
bogavante	bo-gaw-VON-tay	large-clawed lobster
boqueron	bo-care-OWN	anchovy or whitebait
borrachos	bor-RAW-chos	sponge cakes sprinkled with wine and cinnamon
botifarra	bo-tee-FAR-rah	blood sausage
broa	BRO-ah	cornbread
budin	boo-DEEN	pudding
bullabesa	boo-ya-BASE-ah	fish stew of Catalonia
buñuelo	boon-YAY-lo	fritter
Burgos	boor-GOSE	mild, fresh ewes' milk cheese
burrito	boor-EE-to	filled, rolled wheat tortilla
cabra	caw-BRAW	goat
Cabrales	caw-braw-LAYS	blue-veined goat cheese
cabrito	caw-BREE-to	kid
calabacita	caw-law-bah-CEE-to	zucchini
calabaza	caw-law-BAH-saw	pumpkin
calderada	cawl-day-RAW-dah	thick Galician fish stew
caldereta	cawl-day-RAY-taw	meat fish or stew

Spanish Term	Pronunciation	Definition
caliente	cawl-ee-EN-tay	hot
camaron	caw-mah-RONE	shrimp
camote	caw-MO-tay	sweet potato
cangrejo	cawn-GRAY-ho	crab
capeado	caw-pay-AH-do	dipped and batter fried crab
carbonado	car-baw-NAW-doe	beef stew from Argentina
carne	CAR-nay	meat
cazuela	caw-SWAY-law	earthenware casserole
cebiche	say-BEE-chay	raw fish cooked by marination in citrus juice
cebolla	say-BO-ya	onion
Cebreto	say-BREE-toe	creamy blue-veined cheese
ceci	SAY-see	chick-peas
cena	SAY-naw	supper
cerdo	SAIR-doe	pork
cerveza	sair-VAY-suh	beer
chayote	chy-YO-tay	pear-shaped vegetable
chilindron	chee-LEAN-drone	chicken braised in sweet red peppers, onions, garlic, and ham
chipolata	chee-poe-LAW-tah	sausage flavored with chives
chongos	CHONE-gose	custard pudding with lemon and cinnamon
chorizo	chore-EAT-so	spicy pork sausage
chuleta	chew-LAY-taw	chop
cigala	see-GAW-law	saltwater crayfish
cilantro	see-LAWN-tro	fresh coriander leaf
Cincho	SEEN-cho	ewes' milk
cocado	coe-CAW-doe	coconut custard
cochino	coe-CHEE-no	pig
cocido	coe-SEE-doe	stew or cook
codorniz	coe-dorn-YEEZ	quail
col	COLE	cabbage
coliflor	coe-lee-FLOR	cauliflower
conejo	cone-YAY-hoe	rabbit
cordero	core-DAIR-oh	lamb
crema	CREM-ah	custard or cream
crudo	CREW-doe	raw fish
deshebrar	day-shay-BRAR	to shred

Spanish Term	Pronunciation	Definition
dulce	dull-CHAY	sweet
durazno	door-AWCE-no	peach
empanada	em-paw-NAW-daw	savory pie with various fillings
empandita	em-pawn-DEE-taw	small empanada
ensalada	en-saw-LAW-daw	salad
entremeses	en-tray-MAY-sayz	appetizers
escabeche	es-caw-BAY-chay	cooked fish or poultry marinated in wine vinegar; served cold
escalibada	es-caw-lay-BAW-daw	sweet peppers, eggplants, and tomatoes grilled over charcoal
estilo de	es-TEE-lo day	in the style of
estofado	es-toe-FAW-daw	stew
fabada asturiana	fa-BAW-daw ahs-too-ree-AHN-ah	hearty peasant bean stew
fiambre	fee-OM-bray	cold cuts
flameado	fla-may-AH-doe	flamed with heated liqueur
frambuesa	from-boo-AY-saw	raspberry
fresa	FRAY-saw	strawberry
fresco	FRES-coe	fresh
frijoles	free-HOLE-ays	beans
frio	FREE-oh	cold
frito	FREE-toe	fried
gallina	gah-YEEN-ah	hen
gamba	GOM-bah	shrimp
garbanzo	gar-BON-so	chick-pea
gazpacho	gawz-PAW-cho	chilled thick tomato soup
granada	graw-NAW-da	pomegranate
guisantes	gwee-SAWN-tays	peas
guiso/guisado	GWEE-zo/gwee-ZAW-doe	stew or stewed
haba	AH-baw	fava
harina	ah-REE-naw	flour
helado	ay-LAW-do	ice cream
hervir	air-VEER	to boil
higado	ee-GAW-doe	liver
higo	EE-go	fig
hinojo	ee-NO-hoe	fennel
horchata	or-CHAW-taw	drink of pumpkin seeds or almonds
horno	OR-no	oven
huevos	WAY-voce	eggs

Spanish Term	Pronunciation	Definition
jamon	haw-MONE	ham
judia	who-DEE-ah	kidney bean or string bean
leche	LAY-chay	milk or custard
lechecillas	lay-chay-SEE-yas	sweetbreads
lechuga	lay-CHOO-gaw	lettuce
legumbres	lay-GOOM-brays	vegetables
lengua	LAIN-gwa	calf's tongue
lenguado	lain-GWA-doe	sole
licuado	lee-CWA-doe	citrus fruit drink
lima	LEE-maw	lime
limon	lee-MOAN	lemon
linguica	lean-GWEE-caw	pork sausage with garlic
longanzia	loan-gwa-ZEE-ah	large pork sausage with garlic, marjoram, and pimiento
lubina	loo-BEEN-ah	sea bass
Manchego	mon-CHAY-go	golden cheese
mantecado	mon-tay-CAW-doe	rich vanilla ice cream with whipped cream
mantequilla	mon-tay-KEE-ya	butter
manzana	mon-ZON-ah	apple
mariscos	maw-REECE-coes	shrimp or scallops
mejillone	may-hee-YO-nay	mussel
mejorana	may-hor-ON-ah	marjoram
melocoton	may-low-co-TAWN	peach
menestra	may-NAY-straw	stew
menudo	may-NOO-doe	tripe stew
merluza	mair-LOO-saw	hake
mero	MAIR-oh	rock bass
morcilla negra	more-SEA-yaw NAY-graw	blood sausage
moscada	mo-SCAW-do	nutmeg
naranja	naw-RON-haw	orange
nispola	nee-SPOW-law	persimmon
nuez	new-ACE	nut, walnut
olla podrida	oh-YA po-DREE-daw	generic term for stew
oloroso	oh-lo-ROW-so	Spanish sherry
ostra	oh-STRAW	oyster
paella	pie-EE-yaw	rice dish with a variety of meats, fish and vegetables
parrilla	pawr-REE-yaw	grill

Spanish Term	Pronunciation	Definition
pastel	paw-STALE	pie, cake, or pastry
patata	paw-TAW-taw	potato
pato/pata	PAW-toe/PAW-taw	duck
pavo	PAW-vo	turkey
pechuga de pollo	pay-CHEW-gaw day PO-yo	chicken breast
pepino	pay-PEE-no	cucumber
pepita	pay-PEE-taw	seed used in cooking
pepitoria, en	pay-PEE-toe-ree-ah	sauce with almonds, garlic, herbs, saffron, and wine
pera	pay-RAW	pear
peregrinos	pay-ray-GREE-noce	scallops
Perilla	pay-REE-yaw	firm, mild cheese
pescado	payce-CAW-do	fish
pez espada	payce ess-PAW-daw	swordfish
picadilla	peek-ah-DEE-ya	ground, minced, or shredded meat
pichon	pee-CHONE	squab
pierna de cordero	pee-AIR-naw day cor-DAIR-oh	leg of lamb
pimienta	pee-mee-EN-taw	black pepper
pina	PEE-naw	pineapple
pisto	PEE-stow	chopped tomatoes, red or green peppers, zucchini, and onions stewed
platano	plaw-TAWN-oh	fruit related to the banana
pollo	po-YO	chicken
pollo a la chilindron	po-YO ah law chee-lean-DRONE	braised chicken with sweet red peppers, tomatoes, onions, garlic, and ham
postre	PO-stray	dessert
pringar	preen-GAR	to baste
puchero	poo-CHAIR-oh	pot
puerco	poo-AIR-co	pig or pork
puerro	poo-AIR-row	leek
queso	KAY-so	cheese
rabano	raw-bawn-o	radish
rallado	raw-YAW-do	grated
ranchero	rawn-CHAIR-o	country style
rapé	raw-PAY	monkfish or angler
raya	RAW-ya	skate

Spanish Term	Pronunciation	Definition
relleno	ray-YAIN-o	stuffing or stuffed
remol	ray-MOLE	brill (flounder)
remolacha	ray-mo-LAW-chaw	beet
repollo	ray-PO-yo	cabbage
riñones	reen-YO-nays	kidneys
rodaballo	row-daw-BUY-yo	turbot
Roncal	roan-CALL	cheese from Navalle
salchicha	saul-CHEE-chaw	sausage
salmonette	saul-MO-net	red mullet
salsa	SAUL-saw	sauce
sangria	sawn-GREE-ah	red or white wine with brandy, soda water, sugar, and sliced orange or lemon peel
San Pedro	sawn PAY-dro	saltwater fish
semilla	say-MEE-yaw	seed
sesos	SAY-sose	brains
seviche	say-VEE-chay	raw fish or shellfish marinated in citrus juice and seasonings
solera	sow-LAIR-ah	process wherein sherry and other fortified wines are blended and matured consistency
sopa	SO-paw	soup
tapas	TAW-paws	Spanish appetizers
té	TAY	tea
ternera	tear-NAY-raw	veal
Tetilla	tay-TEA-ya	soft creamy goat cheese
tocino	toe-SEE-no	bacon
torta	TOR-taw	cake, loaf, or roll of bread
tortilla	tor-TEE-ya	flat corn or wheat pancake/bread
tostada	toe-STAW-daw	toast
trigo	TREE-go	wheat
trucha	TRU-chaw	river trout
turron	tour-ROAN	chewy candy like nougat
uva	oo-VAW	grape
verdura	vair-DOOR-ah	vegetable
Villalon	vee-YA-LONE	even-textured and salty cheese
xato	SAW-to	Belgian endive with red chili peppers, almonds, garlic, oil, and vinegar

Spanish Term	Pronunciation	Definition
yemas de San Leandro	YAY-moss day sawn lay-YAWN-dro	egg-yolk poured into hot syrup and twisted into sweets
zanahoria	zaw-naw-OR-ee-ah	carrot
zarzamora	zar-zaw-MO-raw	blackberry
zarzuela	zar-SWAY-law	seafood stew

Foodservice Planning

Catering Equipment Checklist

Table Skirting Requirements

Full-Service Bar Requirements
- ▲ **Liquor Yield Per Quart**
- ▲ **Cost of Overpouring Liquor**
- ▲ **Beer Yield Per Keg**

Special Event Themes and Decor Ideas
- ▲ **Early American**
- ▲ **Southwestern United States**
- ▲ **Mexico**
- ▲ **Italy**
- ▲ **The Orient**
- ▲ **Medieval Times**
- ▲ **Seven Seas Theme**

Menu Concepts
- ▲ **International Ethnic Sampler**
  Mexican
  Italian
  Oriental
- ▲ **American Regional Sampler**
  Northeastern United States
  Pacific Coast United States

Southern United States
Southwestern United States

▲ **A World of Seafood**

▲ **Hot and Spicy**

Catering Equipment Checklist

When planning your equipment needs for off-premise catering functions, remember this key point: If you don't take it with you, you probably won't have it! Use the following list as a check for typical types of equipment and tools you will need. Quantities of each will vary with the number of patrons served.

- ▲ Table skirts (see chart)
- ▲ Tablecloths
- ▲ Napkins
- ▲ Water, wine, and cocktail glasses
- ▲ Cocktail picks
- ▲ Bar condiments
- ▲ Ice
- ▲ Silverware
- ▲ China
- ▲ Plate covers
- ▲ Serving forks and spoons
- ▲ Service trays and platters
- ▲ Chafing dishes
- ▲ Burner fuel
- ▲ Candelabra
- ▲ Candles
- ▲ Salt and pepper shakers
- ▲ Oil and vinegar cruets
- ▲ Coffee pots
- ▲ Tea bags
- ▲ Water pitchers
- ▲ Bus tubs
- ▲ Flowers and/or other centerpieces
- ▲ Trash cans
- ▲ Plastic trash bags

Table Skirting Requirements

Round Tables: Fully Skirted

Diameter (inches)	Skirting Required (feet)
48	13
60	16
66	18
72	19

Rectangular Tables: ¾ Skirted

Dimensions (inches)	Skirting Required (feet)
30 × 72	12
30 × 96	14
36 × 72	13
36 × 96	15

Rectangular Tables: Fully Skirted

Dimensions (inches)	Skirting Required (feet)
30 × 72	18
30 × 96	22
36 × 72	19
36 × 96	23

Full-Service Bar Requirements

The following list recommends equipment to serve each 100 patrons at a full-service beer and liquor bar.

Equipment Needed	Number Recommended
Blenders	2
Condiment containers	2
Corkscrews	3
Cutting boards	2
Cocktail shakers	4
Cocktail strainers	2
Fruit knives	2
Fruit peelers	2
Ice scoops	2
Jiggers	4
Mixing spoons	2
Muddlers	2
Water pitchers	4

Liquor Yield Per Quart

Use the following chart to calculate alcoholic beverage requirements.

Ounces Per Pour	Pours Per Quart
⅝	51
¾	42
⅞	36
1	32
1⅛	28
1¼	25
1½	21
2	16

Table 1-86. Cost of Overpouring Liquor

Even a slight overpour per drink adds up. Use the following chart as a reminder of the way careless drink preparation can reduce profits. Calculations are based on 1 U.S. quart (950 ml) per bottle and a very conservative profit of $1.00 per drink served.

Cases Used (12 bottles/case)	Profitability Loss 2 oz/bottle overpour	Profitability Loss 4 oz/bottle overpour	Profitability Loss 6 oz/bottle overpour
1	¾ qt $24	1½ qt $48	2¼ qt $72
5	3¾ qt $120	7½ qt $240	11¼ qt $360
10	7½ qt $240	15 qt $480	22½ qt $720
20	15 qt $480	30 qt $960	55 qt $1,480

Table 1-87. Beer Yield Per Keg

Use the following charts to calculate the portion yield for dispensing draft beer from ½-barrel size kegs. 1 keg = 1,984 fluid ounces; 165 12-ounce bottles or cans; 6.9 24-can cases.

	KEG YIELD BY GLASS		
Service Style	1" Head	¾" Head	½" Head
Mugs			
10 oz	248	233	223
12 oz	203	189	176
14 oz	169	158	153
16 oz	149	140	134
Pilsners			
8 oz	325	292	280
9 oz	282	259	245
10 oz	250	233	215

KEG YIELD BY PITCHER		
Pitcher Volume (ounces)	1" Head	1½" Head
54	47	50
60	39	42
64	35	38

Special Event Themes and Decor Ideas

To add a touch of class to your themed functions and special events, consider some of the following decor suggestions.

Early American

Copper pots
Barrels
Wagon wheels
Lanterns
Pistols and rifles
Powder horn
Fife and drum
Revolutionary era flags

Reproduction newspapers
Colonial-style uniforms
Puritan-style hats and jackets
Hay bales
Canvas
Split logs
Milking stools
Butter churn

Southwestern United States

Coffee grinder
Chuck wagon
Longhorns
Steer hides
Chaps
Boots
Lanterns
Campfire setup
Wagon wheels
Pork or flour barrels
Pot belly stove

Tools
Reins and tack
Horseshoes
Western signs
Restoration wanted posters
Indian blankets
Telegraph keys
Beer barrels
Covered sidewalks
Player piano
Red, white, and blue bunting

Mexico

Serapes
Blankets
Sombreros
Bullfight posters
Matador costumes
Mariachi music
Cactus
Mexican flag
Wrought iron fence gates
Aztec calendars

Reproduction Mayan sculpture
Conquistador armor
Lottery tickets
Travel posters
Red, white, and green bunting
Palm fronds
Chile peppers
Corn
Pottery

Italy

Dried pasta
Italian flag
Wicker Chianti bottles
Sausages and cheese
Fishing nets
Travel posters
Gondola
Herb bunches

Crates of roma tomatoes
Tower of Pisa
Street side tables
Umbrella tables
Baskets of purple grapes
Marzipan fruits
Olive barrels

The Orient

Bamboo
Paper umbrellas
Paper dragons
Fortune cookies
Chopsticks
Travel posters
Reproduction jade
Bamboo steamers
Porcelain bowls and spoons
Woks and tools

Fish nets
Glass net floats
Mongolian hot pot
Sheepskin blankets
Coolie hats
Hibachi
Chile peppers
Whole spices
Carved melons

Medieval Times

Crossbow
Armor

Trencher bread loaves
Wine pitchers

Thatch
Coat of arms
Robin Hood memorabilia
Battle axes
St. George and the dragon
Stained glass
Candelabra
Metal goblets

Tapestries
Swords
Battering ram
Whole roast of beef, lamb or
  suckling pig
Platters of fruit
Court jesters

Seven Seas Theme

Fishing nets
Glass net floats
Harpoons
Cork
Coils of rope
Sail canvas
Nautical compass
Sextant
Reproduction maritime maps
Life preservers
Cruise posters

Steamer trunks
Divers' helmets
Block and tackle
Buoys
Lighthouse posters
Lobster traps
Clam shovel and buckets
Oars
Brass telescope
Models of sailing ships

MENU CONCEPTS

To help you with menu planning, the following recipe titles from *Cooking for Fifty* have been arranged in ethnic and American Regional categories. In some cases, recipes might not have originated in the designated area, but will still complement that ethnic or American Regional cooking style.

International Ethnic Sampler

Appetizers

▲ Argentine Spiced Beef Empanadas
Chimichurri Sauce
Greek Herbed Cocktail Meatballs
Mexican Stuffed Beef Nachos Campeche

Quesadillas Con Carne

Mexican Carne Picadillo

Oriental Flank Steak Spirals

Skewered Swedish Meatballs

Grilled Pork Toasts with Mango Chutney

Polynesian *Pu Pu* Appetizer Pork

Spicy Indonesian Pork Sates

Chicken Drumsticks with Jalapeño Jelly

Grilled Chicken Strips with Red Chile Marinade

Shanghai Chicken Wings

Two-Alarm Chinese Chicken Wings

Yakitori

Ceviche of Scallops Veracruz

Baked Shrimp Italiano

Chinese Fried Shrimp

Cheese Calzone

Grilled Crostini with Caponata

Guacamole Pancho Villa

Pita Wedges with Red Lentil Hummus

Spiced Cocktail Pecans

Spicy Marinated Mushrooms

Sicilian Vegetarian Pizza

Vegetable Fritatta

Salads

▲ Spiced Black Bean Salad

Fiesta Hot Three Bean Salad

Indian Coleslaw with Orange Mayonnaise

Catalonian Tomato Salad with Lentils and Olives

Green Lentil Salad with Red Wine Vinaigrette

Mediterranean Lentil Salad with Grilled Peppers

Mediterranean New Potato Salad

Mandarin Beef with Sesame-Mustard Dressing

Thai Beef Salad

Venetian Pork Salad with Walnuts

Arabian Nights Chicken Salad

Chicken Salad Bali Hai with Mango Chutney Dressing

Chicken Salad Bombay with Curry and White Grapes

Mexican Fiesta Chicken Salad

Moroccan-Style Turkey Salad

Smoked Turkey Salad Calypso

Smoked Turkey Salad with Honey and Soy Sauce

Turkey Salad with Wild Rice and Mandarin Orange

Chilled Shrimp with Rotini and Olives

"Light Lunch" Warm Caribbean Shrimp Salad

Paella Salad

Warm Shrimp Salad with Sesame Vinaigrette

Provençale Salade Nicoise

Mexican Emperor French Dressing

Orange Yogurt Sauce

Red Wine Vinaigrette Salad Dressing

Russian-Style Salad Dressing

Sesame-Mustard Salad Dressing

Yogurt Vinaigrette with Cumin and Cilantro

Soups

▲ Calalou

Caribbean Red Bean and Lentil Soup

Creme Senegalaise

Light Fresh Mushroom Soup with Vermouth

Mexican Gazpacho

Minestrone

Pistou Provençale

Tortilla Soup Monterey

Autumn Beef Ragout
Hungarian Goulash Stew
Chinese Eggdrop Soup

Seafood

▲ Broiled Scallops with Spiced Orange Sauce
Spiced Orange Sauce
Curried Scallops with Spiced Apple Relish
Spiced Apple Relish
Beer-Batter Coconut Shrimp with Orange Sauce
Orange Sauce
Broiled Shrimp with Chinese Basting Sauce
Glazed Shrimp with Chilies and Sesame
Shrimp and Vegetable Teriyaki
Mixed Seafood Paella
Broiled Cod with Jalapeño Onion Marmalade
Szechuan Broiled Flounder
Baked Haddock with Indonesian Curry Sauce
Oriental Barbecued Haddock
Polynesian Baked Monkfish with Sweet 'n' Sour Sauce
Red Snapper Veracruz
Baked Turban of Sole Florentine
Baked Trout Romano
Cantonese Sweet and Sour Trout
Italian-Style Baked Trout
Sweet and Sour Whitefish Fillets
Sweet and Sour Sauce

Poultry

▲ Blue Mountain Barbecued Chicken
Braised Chicken, Mexican Style
Chicken Chili with Tortilla "Pasta"
Chicken Tetrazzini Milano
Chicken with Orange Sauce Orlando

Orange Sauce Orlando

Sesame Chicken with Mild Chilies

Szechuan Velvet Chicken

Tandoori Roasted Chicken Breasts

Thai Chicken Legs

Chinese-Style Roasted Turkey Breast

Grilled Turkey for Fajitas

Medallions of Turkey in Mustard Sauce

Turkey Marsala with Mushrooms

Meats

▲ Bavarian Meat Loaf with Ginger Glaze

Ginger Glaze Basting Sauce

Bracciole

Bul-Kogi

Jamaican Marinated Flank Steak

Oriental Smoke-Roasted Beef Tenderloin

Roestbraten

Sukiyaki

Roast Lamb with Ginger Baste

Skewered Lamb with Cinnamon-Pepper Marinade

Chinese Firecracker Pork Loin

Pork Medallions Barcelona

Roast Pork Loin Florentine

Szechuan Pork with Peanuts

Tuscan Pork with Herbed Lentils

Velvet Pork Ribbons with Spinach

Braised Veal Saltimbocca

Veal Piccata Milanese

Pasta and Noodles

▲ Cheese Tortellini with Roma Tomato Sauce

Creamy Fettuccine with Smoked Chicken

Fettuccine Pasta with Tomato and Capers

Fusilli with Meatless Marinara Sauce
Linguine with White Clam Sauce
Manicotti Pasta Rolls with Pine Nuts and Spinach
Mixed Cheese Manicotti with Pimento Cream Sauce
Pimento Cream Sauce
Oriental Noodles with Beef Broth
Spaghetti with Mixed Herbs
Spaghettini Porcini with Garlic and Herbs
Stir-Fried Noodles with Ginger and Scallions
Chilled Linguine with Ginger and Peanuts
Chilled Rainbow Pasta Primavera
Chinese Shrimp Shells with Broccoli Florets
Cold Cheese Tortellini with Mustard Yogurt Sauce
Cold Noodles with Shredded Vegetables
Pasta Salad Mexicana
Szechuan Noodles with Bean Sauce and Chicken
Vermicelli with Chili Oil and Cashews

Starches

▲ Cantonese Braised Potatoes
Gnocchi
Potato Croquettes with Garlic and Cheese
Potato Kugel with Golden Raisins
Potato Pancakes *Roesti*
Roasted Potatoes with Garlic and Herbs
Swiss Mashed Potatoes with Pear
Jamaican Curried Yams
Fried Rice Espagnole
Golden Almond Rice Pilaf
Mediterranean Brown Rice with Almonds
New Delhi Curried Rice
Pistachio Pilaf with Golden Raisins
Orange Rice with Sweet Pepper

Steamed Rice with Water Chestnuts

Baked Jamaican Pepper-Herb Grits

Broiled Polenta Marinara

Almond Couscous with Currants

Red Pepper Couscous

Vegetables and Legumes

▲ Chinese Green Beans with Sesame Oil and Almonds

Dilled Green Beans

Steamed Broccoli with Sesame Seeds

Swedish Cabbage with Caraway

Red Cabbage with Apple and Cloves

Glazed Carrots Grand Marnier

Oriental Cucumbers with Shredded Carrots

Grilled Eggplant with Herbs and Cheese

Ratatouille Nicoise

Szechuan Barbecued Eggplant

Caribbean Sautéed Mushrooms

Roasted Onions with Rubbed Sage

Mexican Squash Succotash

Spaghetti Squash with Basil and Parmesan

Grilled Herbed Zucchini Wafers

Steamed Zucchini with Carrots and Mint

Egyptian-Style Red Lentil Puree

Herbed Lentils with Tofu

Breads

▲ Grilled Monkey Bread

Zucchini Bread with Walnuts and Lemon

Buttermilk Cinnamon Scones

Mexican Jalapeño Biscuits

Corn Muffins with Jalapeño and Bacon

Desserts

▲ Baked Pears with Toasted Almond Butterscotch Sauce
Toasted Almond Butterscotch Sauce
Fresh Apple Sampler with Gingered Yogurt
Fresh Fruit with Strawberry-Yogurt Creme Sauce
Strawberry-Yogurt Creme Sauce
Marinated Oranges with Mock Rum Cream
Strawberry Crepes Neapolitan
Cannoli Tarts with Strawberry Sauce
Clafouti
Spanish Flan

Brunch

▲ Baked Eggs with Ham and Jarlsberg Cheese
Breakfast Pizza with Sausage and Cheese
Brunch Blintzes
Huevos Rancheros
Mediterranean Scrambled Eggs with Mint Yogurt Sauce
Stuffed French Toast with Honey-Ricotta
Strawberry Sauce Grand Marnier
Blini
German Apple Pancakes
Broiled Citrus Melange
Strawberries and Oranges with Cointreau and Mint
Tropical Marinated Fruit Cocktail

MEXICAN

Appetizers

▲ Mexican Stuffed Beef Nachos Campeche
Quesadillas Con Carne
Mexican Carne Picadillo
Chicken Drumsticks with Jalapeño Jelly
Grilled Chicken Strips with Red Chile Marinade

Ceviche of Scallops Veracruz
Guacamole Pancho Villa
Spicy Marinated Mushrooms

Salads

▲ Spiced Black Bean Salad
Fiesta Hot Three Bean Salad
Mexican Fiesta Chicken Salad
Mexican Emperor French Dressing
Yogurt Vinaigrette with Cumin and Cilantro

Soups

▲ Mexican-Style Gazpacho
Tortilla Soup Monterey
Green Chile Beef Stew

Seafood

▲ Glazed Shrimp with Chilies and Sesame
Broiled Cod with Jalapeño Onion Marmalade
Red Snapper Veracruz

Poultry

▲ Braised Chicken, Mexican Style
Chicken Chili with Tortilla "Pasta"
Lime-Marinated Grilled Chicken
Grilled Turkey for Fajitas

Pasta

▲ Pasta Salad Mexicana

Starches

▲ Baked Chile-Cheese Rice
Fried Rice Espagnole
Mexican Squash Succotash

Bread

▲ Mexican Jalapeño Biscuits

Desserts

▲ Choco-Nut Layer Cakes
Baked Pears with Toasted Almond Butterscotch Sauce
Toasted Almond Butterscotch Sauce
Marinated Oranges with Mock Rum Cream
Spanish Flan

Brunch

▲ Huevos Rancheros
Broiled Citrus Mélange
Tropical Marinated Fruit Cocktail

ITALIAN

Appetizers

▲ Baked Shrimp Italiano
Cheese Calzone
Grilled Crostini with Caponata
Sicilian Vegetarian Pizza
Take-a-Break Mushroom Pizza Snacks
Vegetable Fritatta

Salads

▲ Herbed Broccoli with Mixed Peppers
Venetian Pork Salad with Walnuts
Chilled Shrimp with Rotini and Olives
Red Wine Vinaigrette Salad Dressing

Soups

▲ Minestrone

Seafood

▲ Baked Sole with Mixed Peppers and Fruit
  Baked Turban of Sole Florentine
  Baked Trout Romano
  Italian Baked Trout

Poultry

▲ Chicken Tetrazzini Milano
  Grilled Chicken Breast with Lemon and Capers
  Turkey Marsala with Mushrooms

Meats

▲ Bracciole
  Roast Pork Loin Florentine
  Tuscan Pork with Herbed Lentils
  Braised Veal Saltimbocca
  Veal Piccata Milanese

Pasta

▲ Cheese Tortellini with Roma Tomato Sauce
  Creamy Fettuccine with Smoked Chicken
  Fettuccine Pasta with Tomato and Capers
  Fusilli with Meatless Marinara Sauce
  Linguine with White Clam Sauce
  Manicotti Pasta Rolls with Pine Nuts and Spinach
  Mixed Cheese Manicotti with Pimento Cream Sauce
  Pimento Cream Sauce
  Spaghetti with Mixed Herbs
  Spaghettini Porcini with Garlic and Herbs
  Chilled Rainbow Pasta Primavera
  Cold Cheese Tortellini with Mustard Yogurt Sauce

Starches

▲ Gnocchi
Roasted Potatoes with Garlic and Herbs
Golden Almond Rice Pilaf
Mediterranean Brown Rice with Almonds
Pistachio Pilaf with Golden Raisins
Orange Rice with Sweet Pepper
Broiled Polenta Marinara

Vegetables

▲ Steamed Broccoli with Sesame Seeds
Sliced Carrots with Apricot Glaze
Grilled Eggplant with Herbs and Cheese
Spaghetti Squash with Basil and Parmesan
Grilled Herbed Zucchini Wafers

Breads

▲ Zucchini Bread with Walnuts and Lemon
Lemon-Pepper Whole Wheat Biscuits

Desserts

▲ Lemon Cheesecake
Baked Pears with Toasted Almond Butterscotch Sauce
Toasted Almond Butterscotch Sauce
Fresh Fruit with Strawberry-Yogurt Creme Sauce
Strawberry-Yogurt Creme Sauce
Marinated Oranges with Mock Rum Cream
Strawberry Crepes Neapolitan
Cannoli Tarts with Strawberry Sauce

Brunch

▲ Breakfast Pizza with Sausage and Cheese
Mediterranean Scrambled Eggs with Mint Yogurt Sauce

Stuffed French Toast with Honey-Ricotta

Strawberry Sauce Grand Marnier

Broiled Citrus Melange

Strawberries and Oranges with Cointreau and Mint

Tropical Marinated Fruit Cocktail

ORIENTAL

Appetizers

▲ Oriental Flank Steak Spirals

Grilled Pork Toasts with Mango Chutney

Polynesian *Pu Pu* Appetizer Pork

Spicy Indonesian Pork Sates

Shanghai Chicken Wings

Two-Alarm Chinese Chicken Wings

Yakitori

Chinese Fried Shrimp

Salads

▲ Herbed Broccoli with Mixed Peppers

Sweet Potato Salad with Pineapple and Ginger

Mandarin Beef with Sesame-Mustard Dressing

Thai Beef Salad

Smoked Turkey Salad with Honey and Soy Sauce

Turkey Salad with Wild Rice and Mandarin Orange

Warm Shrimp Salad with Sesame Vinaigrette

Sesame-Mustard Salad Dressing

Soups

▲ Chilled and Spiced Melon Soup

Squash Bisque with Ginger

Chinese Eggdrop Soup

Seafood

▲ Beer-Batter Coconut Shrimp with Orange Sauce
Orange Sauce
Broiled Shrimp with Chinese Basting Sauce
Glazed Shrimp with Chilies and Sesame
Shrimp and Vegetable Teriyaki
Szechuan Broiled Flounder
Oriental Barbecued Haddock
Cantonese Sweet and Sour Trout
Sweet and Sour Whitefish Fillets
Sweet and Sour Sauce

Poultry

▲ Sesame Chicken with Mild Chilies
Szechuan Velvet Chicken
Thai Chicken Legs
Chinese Roasted Turkey Breast
Bul-Kogi
Oriental Smoke-Roasted Beef Tenderloin
Sukiyaki
Roast Lamb with Ginger Baste
Chinese Firecracker Pork Loin
Pork Tenderloin with Orange and Ginger
Szechuan Pork with Peanuts
Velvet Pork Ribbons with Spinach

Pasta and Noodles

▲ Oriental Noodles with Beef Broth
Stir-Fried Noodles with Ginger and Scallions
Chilled Linguine with Ginger and Peanuts
Chinese Shrimp Shells with Broccoli Florets
Cold Noodles with Shredded Vegetables
Szechuan Noodles with Bean Sauce and Chicken
Vermicelli with Chili Oil and Cashews

Starches

▲ Cantonese Braised Potatoes

Roasted Potatoes with Garlic and Herbs

Golden Almond Rice Pilaf

Pistachio Pilaf with Golden Raisins

Orange Rice with Sweet Pepper

Steamed Rice with Water Chestnuts

Vegetables

▲ Chinese Green Beans with Sesame Oil and Almonds

Steamed Broccoli with Sesame Seeds

Sliced Carrots with Apricot Glaze

Oriental Cucumbers with Shredded Carrots

Szechuan Barbecued Eggplant

Desserts

▲ Baked Pears with Toasted Almond Butterscotch Sauce

Toasted Almond Butterscotch Sauce

Fresh Apple Sampler with Gingered Yogurt

Brunch

▲ Broiled Citrus Mélange

Strawberries and Oranges with Cointreau and Mint

Tropical Marinated Fruit Cocktail

American Regional Sampler

Appetizers

▲ Chicken Drumsticks with Jalapeño Jelly

Grilled Chicken Strips with Red Chile Marinade

Crabmeat Norfolk

Crabmeat Remick with Chile Mayonnaise

Louisiana Barbecued Shrimp

Spiced Cocktail Pecans

Spicy Marinated Mushrooms

Take-a-Break Mushroom Pizza Snacks

Vegetable Fritatta

Salads

▲ Spiced Black Bean Salad

Fiesta Hot Three Bean Salad

Green Beans with Dill and Garlic Vinaigrette

Herbed Broccoli with Mixed Peppers

Signature Potato Salad

Sweet Potato Salad with Pineapple and Ginger

Grilled Chicken Salad with Chopped Pecans

Southwestern Duck Salad with Melon and Pecans

Granny Smith's Turkey Salad

Turkey Salad with Wild Rice and Mandarin Orange

Apple-Walnut Vinaigrette Dressing

Light Vinaigrette Dressing

Orange Yogurt Sauce

Red Wine Vinaigrette Salad Dressing

Russian Salad Dressing

Sesame-Mustard Salad Dressing

Yogurt Vinaigrette with Cumin and Cilantro

Soups

▲ Chilled and Spiced Melon Soup

Creamy Corn Chowder with Grilled Pepper

Fresh Mushroom Cream Bisque

Harvest Peach Chilled Bisque with Brandy

Light Fresh Mushroom Soup with Vermouth

Squash Bisque with Ginger

Tortilla Soup Monterey

Wisconsin Cheese Soup

Green Chile Beef Stew

Philadelphia Pepper Pot Soup

Southwestern Herbed Meatball Soup

Cajun Chicken Jambalaya

Pistol Pete's Green Chicken Chili

Manhattan Clam Chowder with Dry Sherry

San Francisco Bayside Cioppino

Seafood

▲ Low Country White Corn Crab Cakes

Broiled Scallops with Spiced Orange Sauce

Spiced Orange Sauce

Beer-Batter Coconut Shrimp with Orange Sauce

Orange Sauce

Louisiana Shrimp Pilau

Shrimp Americaine

Shrimp Creole

Broiled Cod with Jalapeño Onion Marmalade

Baked Sole with Mixed Peppers and Fruit

Broiled Roughy with Orange Sauce and Pecans

Poached Salmon with Aromatic Vegetables

Poultry

▲ Austin Chicken Burritos

Chicken Chili with Tortilla "Pasta"

Chicken with Orange Sauce Orlando

Orange Sauce Orlando

Country Captain Chicken Breasts

Grilled Chicken with Apricot Glaze

Lime-Marinated Grilled Chicken

Peach-Basted Broiled Chicken Breasts

Broiled Turkey Breast with Black Currant Sauce

Black Currant Sauce

Grilled Turkey for Fajitas

Oven-Smoked Barbecued Turkey Breast

Roast Turkey with Spiced Cranberry Sauce
Spiced Cranberry Sauce

Meats

▲ Baked Meat Loaf with Creole Tomato Sauce
Creole Tomato Sauce
Barbecued Pork with Apricots
Grilled Pork Loin Santa Fe
Sautéed Pork with Bourbon and Mustard

Pasta

▲ Creamy Fettuccine with Smoked Chicken
Linguine with White Clam Sauce
Spaghetti with Mixed Herbs
Pasta Salad Mexicana

Starches

▲ Cheese 'n' Bacon Mashed Potatoes
Grilled Potatoes O'Brien
Roasted Potatoes with Garlic and Herbs
Saratoga Potato Crisps
Kentucky Sweet Potatoes
Praline Yams
Sweet Potatoes with Orange and Pecans
Baked Chile-Cheese Rice
Down South White Rice with Raisins
Orange Rice with Sweet Pepper
White Rice O'Brien
Baked Cheese Grits
Creole-Style White Hominy

Vegetables

▲ Cajun Barbecued Green Beans
Dilled Green Beans

Glazed Carrots Grand Marnier
Sliced Carrots with Apricot Glaze
Roasted Onions with Rubbed Sage
Acorn Squash with Honey and Maple
Grilled Yellow Squash
Pureed Squash with Apples and Cinnamon
Grilled Herbed Zucchini Wafers
Boston Baked Beans
Black-Eyed Peas with Spiced Sausage
Smoky Butter Beans with Chili Sauce

Breads

▲ Annie's Bakeshop Anadama Bread
Apple Bread
Bishop's Bread
Blueberry Corn Bread
Grilled Monkey Bread
Iroquois Spoon Bread
Nut-Rich Boston Brown Bread
Sweet Potato Nut Bread
Zucchini Bread with Walnuts and Lemon
Buttermilk Cinnamon Scones
Cheese and Bacon Biscuits
Lemon-Pepper Whole Wheat Biscuits
No-Rise Angel Biscuits
Pepper-Cheese Boarding House Biscuits
Carolina White Corn Hush Puppies
Corn Muffins with Jalapeño and Bacon
Lemon 'n' Walnut Muffins

Desserts

▲ Choco-Nut Layer Cakes
Cottage Pudding
Gingerbread Delight

Ginger Pound Cake

Hawaiian Sunset Grilled Pound Cake

Lemon Cheesecake

Lemon Pound Cake with Blueberry Sauce

Blueberry Sauce

Washington Pie

Choco-Mint Brownies

Gingersnap Giants

Kiss o' Chocolate Drop Cookies

Luscious Lemon Nutcrunch Bars

Oatmeal-Date Delights

Baked Pears with Toasted Almond Butterscotch Sauce

Toasted Almond Butterscotch Sauce

Fresh Apple Sampler with Gingered Yogurt

Fresh Fruit with Strawberry-Yogurt Creme Sauce

Strawberry-Yogurt Creme Sauce

Guilt-Free Jubilee Cherry Sauce

Mama Clements's Apple Brown Betty

Marinated Oranges with Mock Rum Cream

Peach and Pecan Pandowdy

Strawberry Shortcake

Blackbottom Pie

Grasshopper Pie

Pennsylvania Shoofly Pie

State Fair Blueberry Pie

Mohawk Valley Indian Pudding

New Bedford Corn and Sweet Potato Pudding

Brunch

▲ Breakfast Pizza with Sausage and Cheese

Brunch Blintzes

Huevos Rancheros

Southwestern Rarebit

Holiday Pumpkin-Nut Pancakes
Kentucky Griddle Cakes
New York Cheddar Pancakes
Whole Wheat Honey Pancakes
Golden Waffles with Nantucket Cranberry Syrup
Nantucket Cranberry Syrup
Broiled Citrus Mélange
Tropical Marinated Fruit Cocktail
Toasted Almond Granola
Peppered Roast Beef Hash
Philadelphia Scrapple

NORTHEASTERN UNITED STATES

Appetizers

▲ Greek-Style Herbed Cocktail Meatballs
Skewered Swedish Meatballs
Baked Shrimp Italiano

Salads

▲ Green Beans with Dill and Garlic Vinaigrette
Herbed Broccoli with Mixed Peppers
Signature Potato Salad
Granny Smith's Turkey Salad
Apple-Walnut Vinaigrette Dressing
Light Vinaigrette Dressing
Red Wine Vinaigrette Salad Dressing
Russian-Style Salad Dressing

Soups

▲ Creamy Corn Chowder with Grilled Pepper
Fresh Mushroom Cream Bisque
Light Fresh Mushroom Soup with Vermouth

Squash Bisque with Ginger
Philadelphia Pepper Pot Soup
Manhattan Clam Chowder with Dry Sherry

Seafood

▲ Shrimp Americaine
Baked Haddock with Herbs and Chablis
Baked Sole with Mixed Peppers and Fruit

Poultry

▲ Grilled Chicken with Apricot Glaze
Broiled Turkey Breast with Black Currant Sauce
Black Currant Sauce
Roast Turkey with Spiced Cranberry Sauce
Spiced Cranberry Sauce

Meat

▲ Grilled Pork with Ginger and Burgundy

Starches

▲ Grilled Potatoes O'Brien
Potato Croquettes with Garlic and Cheese
Potato Kugel with Golden Raisins
Roasted Potatoes with Garlic and Herbs
Saratoga Potato Crisps
Golden Almond Rice Pilaf
Orange Rice with Sweet Pepper
White Rice O'Brien
Broiled Polenta Marinara

Vegetables

▲ Dilled Green Beans
Glazed Carrots Grand Marnier
Sliced Carrots with Apricot Glaze

Roasted Onions with Rubbed Sage
Acorn Squash with Honey and Maple
Grilled Yellow Squash
Pureed Squash with Apples and Cinnamon
Boston Baked Beans

Breads

▲ Annie's Bakeshop Anadama Bread
Apple Bread
Bishop's Bread
Iroquois Spoon Bread
Nut-Rich Boston Brown Bread
Toasted Bagels with Apples and Cheddar
Zucchini Bread with Walnuts and Lemon
Buttermilk Cinnamon Scones
Lemon-Pepper Whole Wheat Biscuits
Pepper-Cheese Boarding House Biscuits
Lemon 'n' Walnut Muffins

Desserts

▲ Choco-Nut Layer Cakes
Cottage Pudding
Gingerbread Delight
Ginger Pound Cake
Lemon Cheesecake
Lemon Pound Cake with Blueberry Sauce
Blueberry Sauce
Washington Pie
Choco-Mint Brownies
Gingersnap Giants
Kiss o' Chocolate Drop Cookies
Luscious Lemon Nutcrunch Bars
Oatmeal-Date Delights
Baked Pears with Toasted Almond Butterscotch Sauce

Toasted Almond Butterscotch Sauce

Fresh Fruit with Strawberry-Yogurt Creme Sauce

Strawberry-Yogurt Creme Sauce

Guilt-Free Jubilee Cherry Sauce

Mama Clements's Apple Brown Betty

Peach and Pecan Pandowdy

Strawberry Shortcake

Grasshopper Pie

Pennsylvania Shoofly Pie

State Fair Blueberry Pie

Mohawk Valley Indian Pudding

New Bedford Corn and Sweet Potato Pudding

Brunch

▲ Baked Eggs with Ham and Jarslberg Cheese

Breakfast Pizza with Sausage and Cheese

Brunch Blintzes

Blini

German Apple Pancakes

Holiday Pumpkin-Nut Pancakes

New York Cheddar Pancakes

Whole Wheat Honey Pancakes

Golden Waffles with Nantucket Cranberry Syrup

Nantucket Cranberry Syrup

Broiled Citrus Mélange

Tropical Marinated Fruit Cocktail

Toasted Almond Granola

Peppered Roast Beef Hash

Philadelphia Scrapple

PACIFIC COAST UNITED STATES

Appetizers

▲ Oriental Flank Steak Spirals

Grilled Pork Toasts with Mango Chutney

Polynesian *Pu Pu* Appetizer Pork

Shanghai Chicken Wings

Two-Alarm Chinese Chicken Wings

Yakitori

Chinese Fried Shrimp

Grilled Crostini with Caponata

Sicilian Vegetarian Pizza

Take-a-Break Mushroom Pizza Snacks

Vegetable Fritatta

Salads

▲ Green Beans with Dill and Garlic Vinaigrette

Herbed Broccoli with Mixed Peppers

Signature Potato Salad

Sweet Potato Salad with Pineapple and Ginger

Mandarin Beef with Sesame-Mustard Dressing

Thai Beef Salad

Chicken Salad Bali Hai with Mango Chutney Dressing

Grilled Chicken Salad with Chopped Pecans

Granny Smith's Turkey Salad

Smoked Turkey Salad with Honey and Soy Sauce

Turkey Salad with Wild Rice and Mandarin Orange

Chilled Shrimp with Rotini and Olives

Apple-Walnut Vinaigrette Dressing

Light Vinaigrette Dressing

Orange Yogurt Sauce

Red Wine Vinaigrette Salad Dressing

Sesame-Mustard Salad Dressing

Yogurt Vinaigrette with Cumin and Cilantro

Soups

▲ Chilled and Spiced Melon Soup

Creamy Corn Chowder with Grilled Pepper

Fresh Mushroom Cream Bisque

Harvest Peach Chilled Bisque with Brandy

Light Fresh Mushroom Soup with Vermouth

Squash Bisque with Ginger

San Francisco Bayside Cioppino

Seafood

▲ Broiled Scallops with Spiced Orange Sauce

Spiced Orange Sauce

Curried Scallops with Spiced Apple Relish

Spiced Apple Relish

Beer-Batter Coconut Shrimp with Orange Sauce

Orange Sauce

Broiled Shrimp with Chinese-Style Basting Sauce

Glazed Shrimp with Chilies and Sesame

Shrimp and Vegetable Teriyaki

Baked Haddock with Herbs and Chablis

Polynesian Baked Monkfish with Sweet 'n' Sour Sauce

Baked Sole with Mixed Peppers and Fruit

Poached Salmon with Aromatic Vegetables

Poultry

▲ Chicken Chili with Tortilla "Pasta"

Grilled Chicken with Apricot Glaze

Lime-Marinated Grilled Chicken

Grilled Turkey for Fajitas

Meats

▲ Oriental Smoke-Roasted Beef Tenderloin

Sukiyaki

Barbecued Pork with Apricots

Grilled Pork with Ginger and Burgundy

Starches

▲ Grilled Potatoes O'Brien

Potato Croquettes with Garlic and Cheese

Potato Kugel with Golden Raisins
Potato Pancakes *Roesti*
Roasted Potatoes with Garlic and Herbs
Sweet Potatoes with Orange and Pecans
Baked Chile-Cheese Rice
Golden Almond Rice Pilaf
Orange Rice with Sweet Pepper
Steamed Rice with Water Chestnuts
White Rice O'Brien
Broiled Polenta Marinara
Almond Couscous with Currants
Red Pepper Couscous

Vegetables

▲ Chinese Green Beans with Sesame Oil and Almonds
Dilled Green Beans
Steamed Broccoli with Sesame Seeds
Glazed Carrots Grand Marnier
Sliced Carrots with Apricot Glaze
Oriental Cucumbers with Shredded Carrots
Grilled Eggplant with Herbs and Cheese
Roasted Onions with Rubbed Sage
Grilled Yellow Squash
Mexican Squash Succotash
Spaghetti Squash with Basil and Parmesan
Grilled Herbed Zucchini Wafers
Steamed Zucchini with Carrots and Mint
Herbed Lentils with Tofu

Breads

▲ Apple Bread
Grilled Monkey Bread
Zucchini Bread with Walnuts and Lemon
Buttermilk Cinnamon Scones

Lemon-Pepper Whole Wheat Biscuits

Lemon 'n' Walnut Muffins

Desserts

▲ Choco-Nut Layer Cakes

Gingerbread Delight

Ginger Pound Cake

Hawaiian Sunset Grilled Pound Cake

Lemon Cheesecake

Lemon Pound Cake with Blueberry Sauce

Blueberry Sauce

Choco-Mint Brownies

Gingersnap Giants

Luscious Lemon Nutcrunch Bars

Oatmeal-Date Delights

Baked Pears with Toasted Almond Butterscotch Sauce

Toasted Almond Butterscotch Sauce

Fresh Apple Sampler with Gingered Yogurt

Fresh Fruit with Strawberry-Yogurt Creme Sauce

Strawberry-Yogurt Creme Sauce

Guilt-Free Jubilee Cherry Sauce

Marinated Oranges with Mock Rum Cream

Strawberry Shortcake

Cannoli Tarts with Strawberry Sauce

Spanish Flan

Brunch

▲ Baked Eggs with Ham and Jarslberg Cheese

Breakfast Pizza with Sausage and Cheese

Brunch Blintzes

Huevos Rancheros

Mediterranean Scrambled Eggs with Mint Yogurt Sauce

Stuffed French Toast with Honey-Ricotta

Strawberry Sauce Grand Marnier

Southwestern Rarebit

Blini

German Apple Pancakes

Whole Wheat Honey Pancakes

Broiled Citrus Mélange

Strawberries and Oranges with Cointreau and Mint

Tropical Marinated Fruit Cocktail

Toasted Almond Granola

Peppered Roast Beef Hash

SOUTHERN UNITED STATES

Appetizers

▲ Crabmeat Norfolk

Crabmeat Remick with Chile Mayonnaise

Louisiana Barbecued Shrimp

Spiced Cocktail Pecans

Spiced Black Bean Salad

Signature Potato Salad

Sweet Potato Salad with Pineapple and Ginger

Grilled Chicken Salad with Chopped Pecans

Soups

▲ Chilled and Spiced Melon Soup

Creamy Corn Chowder with Grilled Pepper

Harvest Peach Chilled Bisque with Brandy

Light Fresh Mushroom Soup with Vermouth

Cajun Chicken Jambalaya

Seafood

▲ Low Country White Corn Crab Cakes

Louisiana Shrimp Pilau

Shrimp Creole

Broiled Roughy with Orange Sauce and Pecans

Poultry

▲ Chicken with Orange Sauce Orlando
Orange Sauce Orlando
Country Captain Chicken Breasts
Peach-Basted Broiled Chicken Breasts

Meats

▲ Baked Meat Loaf with Creole Tomato Sauce
Creole Tomato Sauce
Barbecued Pork with Apricots
Sautéed Pork with Bourbon and Mustard

Starches

▲ Cheese 'n' Bacon Mashed Potatoes
Grilled Potatoes O'Brien
Potato Croquettes with Garlic and Cheese
Roasted Potatoes with Garlic and Herbs
Kentucky Sweet Potatoes
Praline Yams
Sweet Potatoes with Orange and Pecans
Baked Chile-Cheese Rice
Down South White Rice with Raisins
Orange Rice with Sweet Pepper
White Rice O'Brien
Baked Cheese Grits
Creole White Hominy

Vegetables

▲ Cajun Barbecued Green Beans
Dilled Green Beans
Sliced Carrots with Apricot Glaze
Roasted Onions with Rubbed Sage
Grilled Yellow Squash

Grilled Herbed Zucchini Wafers
Black-Eyed Peas with Spiced Sausage
Smoky Butter Beans with Chili Sauce

Breads

▲ Apple Bread
Bishop's Bread
Blueberry Corn Bread
Sweet Potato Nut Bread
Cheese and Bacon Biscuits
No-Rise Angel Biscuits
Pepper-Cheese Boarding House Biscuits
Carolina White Corn Hush Puppies
Corn Muffins with Jalapeño and Bacon

Desserts

▲ Choco-Nut Layer Cakes
Gingerbread Delight
Ginger Pound Cake
Lemon Cheesecake
Lemon Pound Cake with Blueberry Sauce
Blueberry Sauce
Choco-Mint Brownies
Kiss o' Chocolate Drop Cookies
Luscious Lemon Nutcrunch Bars
Oatmeal-Date Delights
Baked Pears with Toasted Almond Butterscotch Sauce
Toasted Almond Butterscotch Sauce
Peach and Pecan Pandowdy
Strawberry Shortcake
Blackbottom Pie
Grasshopper Pie
New Bedford Corn and Sweet Potato Pudding

Brunch

▲ Holiday Pumpkin-Nut Pancakes
Kentucky Griddle Cakes
Broiled Citrus Mélange
Tropical Marinated Fruit Cocktail
Toasted Almond Granola
Peppered Roast Beef Hash

SOUTHWESTERN UNITED STATES

Appetizers

▲ Quesadillas Con Carne
Mexican Carne Picadillo
Chicken Drumsticks with Jalapeño Jelly
Grilled Chicken Strips with Red Chile Marinade
Guacamole Pancho Villa
Spiced Cocktail Pecans
Spicy Marinated Mushrooms

Salads

▲ Spiced Black Bean Salad
Fiesta Hot Three Bean Salad
Mexican Fiesta Chicken Salad
Southwestern Duck Salad with Melon and Pecans
Mexican Emperor French Dressing
Orange Yogurt Sauce

Soups

▲ Chilled and Spiced Melon Soup
Creamy Corn Chowder with Grilled Pepper
Mexican Gazpacho
Tortilla Soup Monterey
Green Chile Beef Stew
Southwestern Herbed Meatball Soup
Pistol Pete's Green Chicken Chili

Seafood

▲ Glazed Shrimp with Chilies and Sesame
Broiled Cod with Jalapeño Onion Marmalade
Broiled Roughy with Orange Sauce and Pecans

Poultry

▲ Austin Chicken Burritos
Chicken Chili with Tortilla "Pasta"
Lime-Marinated Grilled Chicken
Grilled Turkey for Fajitas
Oven-Smoked Barbecued Turkey Breast

Meats

▲ Barbecued Pork with Apricots
Grilled Pork Loin Santa Fe

Starches

▲ Pasta Salad Mexicana
Cheese 'n' Bacon Mashed Potatoes
Grilled Potatoes O'Brien
Praline Yams
Sweet Potatoes with Orange and Pecans
Baked Chile-Cheese Rice
Fried Rice Espagnole
Golden Almond Rice Pilaf
Orange Rice with Sweet Pepper
White Rice O'Brien
Baked Cheese Grits

Vegetables

▲ Sliced Carrots with Apricot Glaze
Roasted Onions with Rubbed Sage
Grilled Yellow Squash
Mexican-Style Squash Succotash

Grilled Herbed Zucchini Wafers
Black-Eyed Peas with Spiced Sausage
Smoky Butter Beans with Chili Sauce

Breads

▲ Blueberry Corn Bread
Sweet Potato Nut Bread
Cheese and Bacon Biscuits
Lemon-Pepper Whole Wheat Biscuits
Mexican Jalapeño Biscuits
No-Rise Angel Biscuits
Pepper-Cheese Boarding House Biscuits
Corn Muffins with Jalapeño and Bacon

Desserts

▲ Choco-Nut Layer Cakes
Lemon Cheesecake
Lemon Pound Cake with Blueberry Sauce
Blueberry Sauce
Choco-Mint Brownies
Gingersnap Giants
Kiss o' Chocolate Drop Cookies
Luscious Lemon Nutcrunch Bars
Oatmeal-Date Delights
Baked Pears with Toasted Almond Butterscotch Sauce
Toasted Almond Butterscotch Sauce
Marinated Oranges with Mock Rum Cream
Strawberry Shortcake
Blackbottom Pie
State Fair Blueberry Pie
Spanish Flan

Brunch

▲ Huevos Rancheros
Southwestern Rarebit

Whole Wheat Honey Pancakes
Broiled Citrus Mélange
Tropical Marinated Fruit Cocktail
Toasted Almond Granola
Peppered Roast Beef Hash

A World of Seafood

Appetizers

▲ Crabmeat Norfolk
Crabmeat Remick with Chile Mayonnaise
Ceviche of Scallops Veracruz
Baked Shrimp Italiano
Louisiana Barbecued Shrimp
Chinese Fried Shrimp

Salads

▲ Chilled Shrimp with Rotini and Olives
"Light Lunch" Warm Caribbean Shrimp Salad
Paella Salad
Warm Shrimp Salad with Sesame Vinaigrette
Provençale Salade Nicoise

Soups

▲ Manhattan Clam Chowder with Dry Sherry
San Francisco Bayside Cioppino

Entrees

▲ Low Country White Corn Crab Cakes
Broiled Scallops with Spiced Orange Sauce
Curried Scallops with Spiced Apple Relish
Beer-Batter Coconut Shrimp with Orange Sauce
Broiled Shrimp with Chinese-Style Basting Sauce
Glazed Shrimp with Chilies and Sesame
Louisiana Shrimp Pilau

Shrimp Americaine
Shrimp and Rice Creole
Shrimp and Vegetable Teriyaki
Mixed Seafood Paella
Broiled Cod with Jalapeño Onion Marmalade
Szechuan Broiled Flounder
Baked Haddock with Herbs and Chablis
Baked Haddock with Indonesian Curry Sauce
Oriental Barbecued Haddock
Polynesian Baked Monkfish with Sweet 'n' Sour Sauce
Red Snapper Veracruz
Baked Sole with Mixed Peppers and Fruit
Baked Turban of Sole Florentine
Broiled Roughy with Orange Sauce and Pecans
Poached Salmon with Aromatic Vegetables
Baked Trout Romano
Cantonese Sweet and Sour Trout
Italian-Style Baked Trout
Sweet and Sour Whitefish Fillets

Pasta

▲ Linguine with White Clam Sauce
Chinese Shrimp Shells with Broccoli Florets

Hot and Spicy

Appetizers

▲ Argentine Spiced Beef Empanadas
Chimichurri Sauce
Mexican Stuffed Beef Nachos Campeche
Quesadillas Con Carne
Mexican Carne Picadillo
Grilled Pork Toasts with Mango Chutney
Polynesian *Pu Pu* Appetizer Pork

Spicy Indonesian Pork Sates
Chicken Drumsticks with Jalapeño Jelly
Grilled Chicken Strips with Red Chile Marinade
Shanghai Chicken Wings
Two-Alarm Chinese Chicken Wings
Crabmeat Remick with Chile Mayonnaise
Ceviche of Scallops Veracruz
Louisiana Barbecued Shrimp
Chinese Fried Shrimp
Guacamole Pancho Villa
Spiced Cocktail Pecans
Spicy Marinated Mushrooms

Salads

▲ Spiced Black Bean Salad
Fiesta Hot Three Bean Salad
Indian-Style Coleslaw with Orange Mayonnaise
Mandarin Beef with Sesame-Mustard Dressing
Thai Beef Salad
Mexican Fiesta Chicken Salad
Mexican Emperor French Dressing

Soups

▲ Calalou
Caribbean Red Bean and Lentil Soup
Creme Senegalaise
Mexican Gazpacho
Tortilla Soup Monterey
Green Chile Beef Stew
Philadelphia Pepper Pot Soup
Southwestern Herbed Meatball Soup
Cajun Chicken Jambalaya
Pistol Pete's Green Chicken Chili

Seafood

- ▲ Curried Scallops with Spiced Apple Relish
  Spiced Apple Relish
  Broiled Shrimp with Chinese-Style Basting Sauce
  Glazed Shrimp with Chilies and Sesame
  Louisiana Shrimp Pilau
  Shrimp Creole
  Broiled Cod with Jalapeño Onion Marmalade
  Szechuan Broiled Flounder
  Baked Haddock with Herbs and Chablis
  Baked Haddock with Indonesian Curry Sauce
  Red Snapper Veracruz

Poultry

- ▲ Austin Chicken Burritos
  Blue Mountain Barbecued Chicken
  Braised Chicken, Mexican Style
  Chicken Chili with Tortilla "Pasta"
  Szechuan Velvet Chicken
  Tandoori-Style Roasted Chicken Breasts
  Thai-Style Chicken Legs

Meats

- ▲ Jamaican-Style Marinated Flank Steak
  Roast Lamb with Ginger Baste
  Chinese Firecracker Pork Loin
  Grilled Pork Loin Santa Fe
  Szechuan Pork with Peanuts

Pasta

- ▲ Stir-Fried Noodles with Ginger and Scallions
  Chilled Linguine with Ginger and Peanuts
  Chinese Shrimp Shells with Broccoli Florets

Pasta Salad Mexicana

Szechuan Noodles with Bean Sauce and Chicken

Vermicelli with Chili Oil and Cashews

Starches

▲ Grilled Potatoes O'Brien

Jamaican Curried Yams

Baked Chile-Cheese Rice

Fried Rice Espagnole

Baked Jamaican Pepper-Herb Grits

Creole White Hominy

Red Pepper Couscous

Vegetables

▲ Cajun Barbecued Green Beans

Chinese Green Beans with Sesame Oil and Almonds

Oriental Cucumbers with Shredded Carrots

Szechuan Barbecued Eggplant

Caribbean Sautéed Mushrooms

Mexican Squash Succotash

Black-Eyed Peas with Spiced Sausage

Egyptian Red Lentil Puree

Breads

▲ Mexican Jalapeño Biscuits

Pepper-Cheese Boarding House Biscuits

Corn Muffins with Jalapeño and Bacon

Brunch

▲ Huevos Rancheros

Southwestern Rarebit

Peppered Roast Beef Hash

Philadelphia Scrapple

PART TWO

Recipes

Appetizers. 211

Soups 245

Salads and Salad Dressings. 271

Seafood 311

Meats 343

Poultry. 371

Pasta and Noodles 399

Potatoes and Grains 421

Vegetables and Legumes. 453

Breads, Muffins, and Biscuits 481

Desserts. 501

Breakfast and Brunch 537

Appetizers

APPETIZERS WITH MEAT

▲ Argentine Spiced Beef Empanadas

These savory turnovers are traditional throughout South America, Mexico, and Spain.

Menu Category:	Appetizer, Entrée, Beef, Ethnic, South American
Cooking Method:	Sauté/Simmer/Bake
Preparation Time:	30 minutes
Oven Temperature:	350°F
Cooking Time:	2 hours
Variations:	Substitute chopped chicken, pork, or even seafood.
	Add almonds or pine nuts.
Yield:	50 portions (6 oz)

Ingredient	U.S.	Metric	Method
Olive oil, hot	2 c	480 ml	Sauté in large pot or brazier just until
Onion, minced	1 qt	950 ml	vegetables are tender, about 5 minutes.
Green bell pepper, minced	2 c	480 ml	
Chili powder	1 c	240 ml	Add to vegetables. Stir constantly over high heat for 1 minute.
Roast beef, minced	5 lb	2.3 kg	Add to mixture. Heat to a boil. Reduce
Tomatoes, peeled, chopped	3 lb	1.4 kg	heat to a simmer. Simmer until mixture is
Garlic, minced	½ c	120 ml	very thick, about 45 minutes. Remove from
Raisins	1 lb	454 g	heat. Cool to room temperature. Cover.
Olives, ripe, chopped	2 c	480 ml	Chill well.
Pie dough, 6-inch circles	50	50	Arrange on work surface. Portion 4 ounces filling in mound on side of each circle.
Egg white, slightly beaten	4 each	4 each	Combine. Brush edge of each circle with
Water	2 c	480 ml	eggwash. Fold into half-moon shapes. Press edges. Place on oiled or paper-lined sheet pans. Brush tops with eggwash. Cut slit in each. Bake in preheated 350°F oven about 30 minutes until golden brown and juices bubble slightly through hole. Transfer to wire racks to cool slightly. Serve warm.
Chimichurri Sauce, recipe follows	3¼ qt	3.1 L	Serve in 2-ounce ramekins on the side.

Nutrient Analysis	Calories	500	Protein	16 gm
Per Serving	Fat	35.4 gm	Carbohydrate	34 gm
	Cholesterol	42 mg	Calcium	37 mg
	Sodium	512 mg	Fiber	1 gm

Companion Recipe

▲ **Chimichurri Sauce**

Serve with empanadas, Mexican Stuffed Beef Nachos Campeche, and grilled pork or chicken entrées.

Menu Category:	Appetizer, Entrée, Ethnic, Mexican
Cooking Method:	Blanch
Preparation Time:	1 hour
Marination Time:	24 hours
Cooking Time:	5–10 minutes
Yield:	1 gallon

Ingredient	U.S.	Metric	Method
Water, boiling	2 gal	7.6 L	Blanch onions and jalapeños for 3 minutes.
Red onion, thinly sliced	2 qt	1.9 L	Drain well. Transfer to a large bowl.
White onion, thinly sliced	2 qt	1.9 L	
Jalapeño, seeded, minced	1 c	240 ml	
Cider vinegar	1 qt	950 ml	Add to onions. Stir well. Cover. Chill for
Orange juice	1 qt	950 ml	24 hours. Remove bay leaf. Drain.
Allspice, ground	2 T	30 ml	
Oregano, dried	2 T	30 ml	
Bay leaf	8 each	8 each	
Salt	2 t	10 ml	

Nutrient Analysis	Calories	12	Protein	.3 gm
Per Ounce	Fat	0 gm	Carbohydrate	3.1 gm
	Cholesterol	0 mg	Calcium	7 mg
	Sodium	34 mg	Fiber	0.1 gm

▲ Greek-Style Herbed Cocktail Meatballs

Serve skewered as appetizers or as filling for Greek pita sandwiches.

Menu Category:	Appetizer, Entrée, Sandwich, Ethnic, Greek
Cooking Method:	Sauté/Roast
Preparation Time:	30 minutes
Marination Time:	Overnight
Oven Temperature:	450°F
Cooking Time:	15–20 minutes
Variations:	Substitute herbs and spices (e.g., cumin, curry powder) in beef mixture.
Yield:	50 portions (2 oz)

Ingredient	U.S.	Metric	Method
Ground beef	5 lb	2.5 kg	Combine in large bowl. Mix well. Form into ¾-inch-diameter meatballs. Place on sheet pans and bake at 450°F for about 15 minutes. Drain on paper towels. Transfer to shallow roasting pans.
Bread crumbs, dry	2 c	480 ml	
Eggs, beaten	4	4	
Onion, minced	2 c	480 ml	
Ice water	1 c	240 ml	
Worcestershire sauce	1 T	15 ml	
Mustard, dried	1 T	15 ml	
Parsley, fresh	¼ c	60 ml	
Oregano, dried	1 t	5 ml	
Mint, dried	1 T	15 ml	
Allspice, ground	¼ t	1.3 ml	
Cinnamon, ground	¼ t	1.3 ml	
Cloves, ground	¼ t	1.3 ml	
Garlic powder	1 t	5 ml	
Salt	1 t	5 ml	
Black pepper	1 t	5 ml	
Commercial tomato sauce	2 c	480 ml	Combine in heavy saucepan. Heat just to a boil. Pour over meatballs. Cool to room temperature. Cover and chill overnight. Heat at 250°F just until heated through, stirring gently and occasionally.
White wine	½ c	120 ml	
Water	½ c	120 ml	

Nutrient Analysis	Calories	120	Protein	9.8 gm
Per Serving	Fat	6.1 gm	Carbohydrate	4.5 gm
	Cholesterol	45.2 mg	Calcium	15.2 mg
	Sodium	168 mg	Fiber	0.1 gm

▲ Mexican Stuffed Beef Nachos Campeche

Serve as appetizers or a unique Mexican entrée.

Menu Category:	Appetizer, Entrée, Ethnic, Mexican
Cooking Method:	Deep-fry
Preparation Time:	1 hour
Cooking Time:	5–10 minutes
Variations:	These versions of the empanada can be filled with virtually anything savory.
Yield:	50 portions (4 oz)

Ingredient	U.S.	Metric	Method
Mexican Carne Picadillo, cold, recipe follows	6 lb	2.7 kg	Place in large bowl. Mix well. Stir well to combine.
Refried beans, cold	2 lb	908 g	
Wheat tortillas, 6-inch	100	100	Portion 2 T mixture on lower part of each tortilla.
Egg wash	as needed	as needed	Brush edges of tortillas. Fold top half over bottom. Press firmly to seal. Cut with 4½-inch cutter. Press edges again as needed.
Frying oil, 375°F	as needed	as needed	Deep fry until golden brown. Drain.
Chimichurri Sauce, p. 214	3¼ qt.	3.1 L	Serve in 2-ounce ramekins on the side.

Nutrient Analysis Per Serving	Calories	451	Protein	14.7 gm
	Fat	26.4 gm	Carbohydrate	40 gm
	Cholesterol	41.2 mg	Calcium	110 mg
	Sodium	284 mg	Fiber	0.7 gm

Companion Recipe

▲ **Mexican Carne Picadillo**

Use this spicy shredded meat filling for Mexican or American Southwest tortillas.

Menu Category:	Appetizer, Entrée, Ethnic, Mexican, American Regional
Cooking Method:	Sauté/Simmer
Preparation Time:	30 minutes
Cooking Time:	1 hour
Variations:	This process works well with chicken, too.
Yield:	15 pounds

Ingredient	U.S.	Metric	Method
Cooking oil, hot	3 c	720 ml	Sauté in large pot or brazier until meat is well browned. Stir occasionally.
Beef, cubed	4 lb	1.8 kg	
Pork, cubed	4 lb	1.8 kg	
Chili powder	½ c	120 ml	Add to meat. Stir well to coat meat. Cook for about one minute. Do not scorch.
Cinnamon, ground	1 T	15 ml	
Cumin, ground	1 T	15 ml	
Commercial picante sauce	3 qt	2.8 L	Add to mixture. Stir well. Adjust heat to a simmer. Cover. Simmer 30 minutes. Remove from heat and let mixture cool. Pass in batches through food processor, food chopper, or vertical cutter mixer. Transfer to storage containers. Cover and chill for use.
Red wine vinegar	2 c	480 ml	

Nutrient Analysis Per Ounce				
Calories	84	Protein	4.3 gm
Fat	7.1 gm	Carbohydrate	1.1 gm
Cholesterol	14.8 mg	Calcium	4.2 mg
Sodium	106 mg	Fiber	0.1 gm

▲ Quesadillas Con Carne (Tortillas with Spiced Meat)

Serve as a Mexican or American Southwest appetizer or entrée.

Menu Category:	Appetizer, Entrée, Ethnic, Mexican, American Regional
Cooking Method:	Bake
Preparation Time:	10 minutes
Marination Time:	Several hours
Oven Temperature:	350°F
Cooking Time:	20 minutes
Variations:	Serve as a sandwich on toasted buns or in warmed pita pockets.
Yield:	50 portions (4 oz)

Ingredient	U.S.	Metric	Method
Mexican Carne Picadillo meat mixture, p. 217	4 lb	1.8 kg	Place in large bowl.
Monterey jack cheese, grated	4 lb	1.8 kg	Add to meat mixture. Mix well.
Green onions, chopped	1 qt	950 ml	
Flour tortillas, 6-inch	100	100	Place on work surface. Spoon ⅓ cup of picadillo mixture over one half of each tortilla, spreading to within ½ inch of edge. Fold other half over top of filling. Place on full-size sheet pan. Bake at 350°F for 10 minutes. Remove from oven.
Guacamole	2 qt	1.9 L	Portion over quesadillas. Cut in wedges.
Tomato, chopped	1 qt	950 ml	
Black olives, chopped	2 c	480 ml	

Nutrient Analysis Per Serving				
	Calories	523	Protein	21.1 gm
	Fat	31 gm	Carbohydrate	42.2 gm
	Cholesterol	57.2 mg	Calcium	377 mg
	Sodium	747 mg	Fiber	0.3 gm

▲ Oriental Flank Steak Spirals

A great way to turn an economical cut into creative Chinese fare.

Menu Category:	Appetizer, Meat, Ethnic, Oriental
Cooking Method:	Broil/Grill
Preparation Time:	30 minutes
Marination Time:	Several hours
Cooking Time:	20 minutes
Variations:	Substitute thinly sliced and pounded chicken breast.
Yield:	50 portions (4 oz)

Ingredient	U.S.	Metric	Method
Flank steak	10 lb	4.5 kg	Slice crosswise at an angle into 100 ¼-inch thick strips. Roll strips tightly and secure each roll with two toothpicks. Place rolls in shallow roasting pans.
Soy sauce	1 qt	950 ml	Combine in sauce pot. Heat to a simmer.
Sherry, dry	2 c	480 ml	Pour over steak swirls. Cool to room
Gingerroot, minced	1 c	240 ml	temperature. Cover and chill. Let marinate
Scallion, minced	1 c	240 ml	for several hours. Remove swirls from
Garlic, minced	1 T	15 ml	marinade. Cook at medium-high heat on
Sugar	½ c	120 ml	preheated grill for approximately 3 minutes on each side.

Nutrient Analysis Per Serving				
	Calories	249	Protein	19.3 gm
	Fat	15.3 gm	Carbohydrate	5.2 gm
	Cholesterol	61 mg	Calcium	15.4 mg
	Sodium	1359 mg	Fiber	0.1 gm

▲ Skewered Swedish Meatballs

This version takes meatballs from the chafing dish to the bamboo skewer. Great for catered events!

Menu Category:	Appetizer, Beef, Ethnic, Scandinavian
Cooking Method:	Roast/Braise
Preparation Time:	30 minutes
Oven Temperature:	450°F/325°F
Cooking Time:	45 minutes to 1 hour
Variations:	As many as there are spices and herbs: Substitute freely!
Yield:	50 portions (4 oz)

Ingredient	U.S.	Metric	Method
Olive oil, hot	¼ c	60 ml	Sauté in large pot or brazier kettle just until vegetables are tender. Remove from heat. Reserve.
Onion, minced	1 c	240 ml	
Green bell pepper, minced	1 c	240 ml	
Garlic, minced	2 T	30 ml	
Beef, lean, medium-ground	5 lb	2.3 kg	Combine in mixer bowl with paddle attachment. Add reserved onion mixture. Mix at low speed just until mixture is well blended. Portion into 2-ounce balls. Place in two shallow 12″ × 20″ roasting pans. Roast in preheated 450°F oven. Roast just until well browned, about 10 minutes. Reduce oven temperature to 325°F.
Bread crumbs, dry	1½ qt	1.4 L	
Milk, cold	2 c	480 ml	
Caraway seed	1 T	15 ml	
Parsley, chopped	1 c	240 ml	
Eggs, beaten	6 each	6 each	
Salt	1 T	15 ml	
Black pepper	1 T	15 ml	
Brown gravy	2 qt	1.9 L	Add to roasting pans. Cover. Braise until meatballs are firm and done, about 20 to 30 minutes. Divide among bamboo skewers. Serve with extra gravy.

Nutrient Analysis Per Serving				
	Calories	274	Protein	13.2 gm
	Fat	18.6 gm	Carbohydrate	12.9 gm
	Cholesterol	68.3 mg	Calcium	50 mg
	Sodium	447 mg	Fiber	0.1 gm

▲ Grilled Pork Toasts with Mango Chutney

Serve as a Polynesian or Pacific Rim appetizer.

Menu Category:	Appetizer, Pork, Ethnic, Polynesian
Cooking Method:	Broil/Grill
Preparation Time:	30 minutes
Marination Time:	1 hour
Cooking Time:	5 minutes
Variations:	Substitute peeled shrimp or thickly sliced chicken, lamb, or beef.
Yield:	50 portions (4 oz)

Ingredient	U.S.	Metric	Method
Commercial mango chutney	1 qt	950 ml	Combine in food processor with metal blade. Process until pureed. Reserve.
Apricot preserves	1 qt	950 ml	
Pork tenderloin, trimmed	8 lb	3.6 kg	Slice crosswise into ¼-inch thick rounds. Place in large bowl.
Lemon juice, fresh	2 c	480 ml	Combine. Pour over pork slices. Stir well to combine and coat slices. Cover and chill for at least one hour. Drain off all marinade. Cook pork at medium high heat on preheated grill for approximately 2 or 3 minutes on each side.
Mustard, Dijon style	2 c	480 ml	
Soy sauce	1 c	240 ml	
Black pepper	2 T	30 ml	
Salt	1 T	15 ml	
French bread slices, ½-inch	100	100	Toast lightly on both sides. Place a slice of grilled pork on each slice. Portion chutney mixture on top of each slice. Serve hot.

Nutrient Analysis Per Serving				
	Calories	328	Protein	20.3 gm
	Fat	4.7 gm	Carbohydrate	50 gm
	Cholesterol	51.6 mg	Calcium	56.3 mg
	Sodium	925 mg	Fiber	0.4 gm

▲ Polynesian *Pu Pu* Appetizer Pork

Serve as an appetizer or entrée on Polynesian and other Oriental menus.

Menu Category:	Appetizer, Entrée, Pork, Ethnic, Polynesian
Cooking Method:	Grill/Broil
Preparation Time:	30 minutes
Marination Time.:	1 hour
Cooking Time:	10 minutes
Variations:	Substitute shrimp, chicken, or tender beef strips.
Yield:	50 portions (4 oz)

Ingredient	U.S.	Metric	Method
Pork loin, trimmed	8 lb	3.6 kg	Slice into 1″ × 6″ × ¼ ″ strips. Place in plastic storage container.
Sherry, dry	2 c	480 ml	Combine. Add to pork strips. Cover. Chill
Commercial hoisin sauce	2 c	480 ml	for 1 hour. Remove strips from marinade.
Soy sauce	2 c	480 ml	Reserve marinade. Thread strips onto
Gingerroot, grated	¼ c	60 ml	soaked bamboo skewers. Broil/grill at
Garlic, minced	1 T	15 ml	medium-high heat until crisp on both sides, approximately 5 to 10 minutes total. Baste occasionally with marinade.

Nutrient Analysis				
Per Serving	Calories	148	Protein	12 gm
	Fat	9.2 gm	Carbohydrate	1.9 gm
	Cholesterol	38.5 mg	Calcium	5.7 mg
	Sodium	1071 mg	Fiber	0.1 gm

▲ Spicy Indonesian Pork Sates

Serve these kebabs as an Indonesian or Polynesian appetizer.

Menu Category:	Appetizer, Pork, Ethnic, Indonesian
Cooking Method:	Broil/Grill
Preparation Time:	30 minutes
Marination Time:	Several hours
Cooking Time:	10 minutes
Variations:	Substitute peeled shrimp or thickly sliced chicken, lamb, or beef.
Yield:	50 portions (4 oz)

Ingredient	U.S.	Metric	Method
Peanut butter	2 c	480 ml	Combine in sauce pot. Heat to a simmer, mixing well. Remove from heat. Cool to room temperature.
Soy sauce	2 c	480 ml	
Sherry, dry	1 c	240 ml	
Lime juice, fresh	1 c	240 ml	
Commercial coconut puree	1 c	240 ml	
Garlic, minced	¼ c	60 ml	
Gingerroot, minced	¼ c	60 ml	
Crushed red pepper	2 T	30 ml	
Pork loin, ¼″ × 1″ × 6″ strips	8 lb	3.6 kg	Place in bowl or shallow roasting pans with reserved marinade. Cover and chill for several hours. Remove pork strips from marinade and place on soaked bamboo skewers. Heat marinade to a simmer. Simmer for 5 minutes. Cook pork strips on hot grill for 5 minutes on each side. Serve with hot marinade.

Nutrient Analysis	Calories	211	Protein	14.1 gm
Per Serving	Fat	15 gm	Carbohydrate	4.7 gm
	Cholesterol	38.5 mg	Calcium	11.4 mg
	Sodium	735 mg	Fiber	0.4 gm

Appetizers with Poultry

▲ Chicken Drumsticks with Jalapeño Jelly

Even easier than Buffalo wings!

Menu Category:	Appetizer, Entrée, Poultry, Ethnic, Mexican
Cooking Method:	Deep-fry/Simmer
Preparation Time:	30 minutes
Cooking Time:	15 minutes
Variations:	Substitute skinless chicken, using the jalapeño jelly as a marinade before grilling and a sauce afterward.
Yield:	50 portions (8 oz)

Ingredient	U.S.	Metric	Method
Chicken drumsticks, IQF, breaded	25 lb	11.4 kg	Deep-fry in 350°F oil until done, approximately 6 to 8 minutes. Drain well. Do not salt.
Chili powder	2 c	480 ml	Sprinkle over drumsticks. Toss well.
Commercial jalapeño jelly	3 qt	1.9 L	Combine in sauce pot. Heat to a simmer. Simmer 5 minutes. Portion into 2-ounce ramekins. Serve with drumsticks.
Red wine vinegar	2 c	240 ml	
Butter	1 lb	454 g	

Nutrient Analysis Per Serving				
	Calories	848	Protein	62 gm
	Fat	39.3 gm	Carbohydrate	61 gm
	Cholesterol	224 mg	Calcium	59 mg
	Sodium	337 mg	Fiber	2 gm

▲ Grilled Chicken Strips with Red Chile Marinade

These do double duty as a fajita or burrito filling.

Menu Category:	Appetizer, Entrée, Poultry, Ethnic, Mexican
Cooking Method:	Grill/Broil
Preparation Time:	30 minutes
Marination Time:	1 hour
Cooking Time:	10 minutes
Variations:	Substitute shrimp, pork strips, or thinly sliced tender beef.
Yield:	50 portions (3 oz)

Ingredient	U.S.	Metric	Method
Chicken breast, boneless, skinless	8 lb	3.6 kg	Slice into 1″ × 6″ × ¼″ strips. Place in plastic storage container.
Lime juice, fresh	1 c	240 ml	Combine. Add to chicken strips.
Lemon juice, fresh	1 c	240 ml	
Tequila, golden	1 c	240 ml	
Red wine vinegar	1 c	240 ml	
Olive oil, hot	1 c	240 ml	Combine in small saucepan. Heat until pepper darkens. Cool to room temperature. Strain oil into chicken mixture. Toss well. Cover. Chill at least 1 hour. Remove chicken from marinade. Cook at high heat on preheated grill or broiler until crisp on both sides, about 5 to 10 minutes total. Baste occasionally with marinade.
Crushed red pepper	1 c	240 ml	

Nutrient Analysis Per Serving				
	Calories	196	Protein	24.5 gm
	Fat	8 gm	Carbohydrate	2.5 gm
	Cholesterol	66 mg	Calcium	15.3 mg
	Sodium	58 mg	Fiber	0.4 gm

▲ Shanghai Chicken Wings

Serve as appetizers or double the portion for entrée menus.

Menu Category:	Appetizer, Entrée, Poultry, Ethnic, Chinese
Cooking Method:	Braise
Preparation Time:	30 minutes
Cooking Time:	15–20 minutes
Variations:	For an Indian curry version, add curry powder and substitute mango chutney for the bean sauce.
Yield:	50 portions (8 oz)

Ingredient	U.S.	Metric	Method
Chicken wings, split, tips off	25 lb	11.4 kg	Combine in large bowl. Mix well to combine ingredients and coat chicken. Transfer to heavy pot or brazier kettle.
Soy sauce	1 c	240 ml	
Sugar	½ c	120 ml	
Commercial bean sauce	½ c	120 ml	
Sherry, dry	½ c	120 ml	
Gingerroot, minced	½ c	120 ml	
Garlic, minced	¼ c	60 ml	
Commercial chili paste	¼ c	60 ml	
Chicken stock	to cover	to cover	Pour over chicken wings just to cover. Heat to a boil over high heat. Reduce heat to a simmer. Simmer just until chicken is tender, approximately 35 to 40 minutes. Baste with sauce occasionally. Remove wings and reduce sauce over high heat just until it is thick and takes on a glaze consistency. Pour sauce over wings.

Nutrient Analysis Per Serving	Calories	272	Protein	24 gm
	Fat	17 gm	Carbohydrate	4.4 gm
	Cholesterol	73 mg	Calcium	20 mg
	Sodium	418 mg	Fiber	0.3 gm

▲ Two-Alarm Chinese Chicken Wings

Serve as an informal appetizer for fans of the Oriental red-hot.

Menu Category:	Appetizer, Entrée, Poultry, Ethnic, Chinese
Cooking Method:	Broil/Grill
Preparation Time:	30 minutes
Marination Time:	1 hour
Cooking Time:	15–20 minutes
Variations:	Substitute chicken breasts and serve as a plated entrée or sandwich.
Yield:	50 portions (8 oz)

Ingredient	U.S.	Metric	Method
Chicken wings, split, tips off	25 lb	11.4 kg	Dry wing parts and place in shallow roasting pans.
Soy sauce	3 c	720 ml	Combine and mix well. Pour over chicken and rub well into all pieces. Cover and chill. Marinate at least one hour. Remove chicken from marinade. Reserve marinade. Cook at medium high heat on preheated grill or broiler until crisp on both sides. Wrap wings and reserved marinade in aluminum foil. Return packets to grill. Cook, turning occasionally, for about 10 minutes.
Sherry, dry	1 c	240 ml	
Peanut oil	1 c	240 ml	
Commercial chili paste	1 c	240 ml	
Cayenne pepper	1 T	15 ml	
Sugar	2 T	30 ml	

Nutrient Analysis Per Serving				
	Calories	292	Protein	25 gm
	Fat	19 gm	Carbohydrate	4.2 gm
	Cholesterol	73 mg	Calcium	24 mg
	Sodium	1084 mg	Fiber	0.7 gm

▲ Yakitori

Serve this Japanese skewered chicken as an appetizer or as a carry-out entrée on Oriental menus.

Menu Category:	Appetizer, Entrée, Poultry, Ethnic, Japanese
Cooking Method:	Grill/Broil
Preparation Time:	30 minutes
Marination Time:	1 hour
Cooking Time:	10 minutes
Variations:	Substitute shrimp, pork strips, or thinly sliced tender beef. Serve with extra soy sauce for dipping.
Yield:	50 portions (3 oz)

Ingredient	U.S.	Metric	Method
Chicken breast, boneless, skinless	8 lb	3.6 kg	Slice into 1″ × 6″ × ¼″ strips. Place in plastic storage container.
Sake	2 c	480 ml	Combine. Add to chicken strips. Cover. Chill at least 1 hour. Remove strips from marinade. Reserve marinade. Thread strips onto soaked bamboo skewers. Cook at high heat on preheated grill or broiler until crisp on both sides, approximately 5 to 10 minutes total. Baste occasionally with marinade.
Sugar, granulated	1 c	240 ml	
Soy sauce	2 c	480 ml	
Rice wine vinegar	2 c	480 ml	
Peanut oil	1 c	240 ml	
Scallions, minced	2 c	480 ml	
Gingerroot, grated	¼ c	60 ml	

Nutrient Analysis Per Serving				
	Calories	184	Protein	26 gm
	Fat	5 gm	Carbohydrate	6.8 gm
	Cholesterol	66 mg	Calcium	22 mg
	Sodium	717 mg	Fiber	0.1 gm

Appetizers with Seafood

▲ Crabmeat Norfolk

This is a mid-Atlantic American regional shellfish appetizer.

Menu Category:	Appetizer, Entrée, Seafood, American Regional
Cooking Method:	Bake
Preparation Time:	10 minutes
Oven Temperature:	350°F
Cooking Time:	15 minutes
Variations:	Substitute tiny peeled shrimp or bay scallops.
Yield:	50 portions (3 oz)

Ingredient	U.S.	Metric	Method
Lump crabmeat, picked	7 lb	3.2 kg	Combine in bowl. Toss gently to mix well.
Tabasco sauce	1 T	15 ml	Portion into buttered 6-ounce casseroles.
Worcestershire sauce	1 T	15 ml	Bake at 350°F for 15 minutes.
Red wine vinegar	1 T	15 ml	
Salt	2 t	10 ml	
Black pepper	1 t	5 ml	
Parmesan cheese, grated	1 c	240 ml	Sprinkle over each portion.

Nutrient Analysis	Calories	73	Protein	12.1 gm
Per Serving	Fat	2.1 gm	Carbohydrate	.7 gm
	Cholesterol	65 mg	Calcium	57.4 mg
	Sodium	444 mg	Fiber	0 gm

▲ Crabmeat Remick with Chile Mayonnaise

Serve as a special appetizer, a light entrée, or a fancy open-face sandwich.

Menu Category:	Appetizer, Sandwich, Entrée, American Regional
Cooking Method:	Bake/Broil
Preparation Time:	30 minutes
Cooking Time:	20 minutes
Variations:	Substitute cooked, chopped shrimp or tuna.
	Change flavors by adding curry powder and chopped chutney.
Yield:	50 portions (3 oz)

Ingredient	U.S.	Metric	Method
Crabmeat, shredded or lump	6 lb	2.7 kg	Combine in large bowl. Mix gently but well. Transfer to standard 2-inch insert pans prepped with nonstick spray.
Mayonnaise, reduced-fat	1½ qt	1.5 L	
Ketchup	3 c	720 ml	
Red wine vinegar	2 T	30 ml	
Bacon, cooked, drained, minced	2 c	480 ml	
Mustard, dry	2 T	30 ml	
Paprika	1 T	15 ml	
Tarragon, dried	1 t	5 ml	
Cayenne pepper, ground	2 t	10 ml	
Celery salt	1 T	15 ml	
Parmesan cheese, grated	2 c	480 ml	Sprinkle over top. Cover and chill until ready to bake. Bake in preheated 350°F oven for 20 minutes, or until bubbly and golden brown. Portion into service dishes or onto toasted croissants or English muffins.

Nutrient Analysis Per Serving	Calories	284	Protein	12.1 gm
	Fat	24 gm	Carbohydrate	5.5 gm
	Cholesterol	74 mg	Calcium	90 mg
	Sodium	787 mg	Fiber	0.2 gm

▲ Ceviche of Scallops Veracruz

Serve as an appetizer or on a Caribbean/Mexican buffet.

Menu Category:	Appetizer, Salad, Seafood, Ethnic, Mexican
Cooking Method:	None required
Preparation Time:	30 minutes
Marination Time:	4 hours
Variations:	Substitute shrimp or firm, white-fleshed lean fish.
Yield:	50 portions (5 oz)

Ingredient	U.S.	Metric	Method
Bay scallops, rinsed	8 lb	3.6 kg	Combine in large bowl. Stir well. Cover
Orange juice	1 qt	950 ml	and chill for 4 hours, or until scallops are
Lemon juice, fresh	3 c	720 ml	white and firm. Drain well. Transfer
Lime juice, fresh	1 c	240 ml	scallops to another bowl.
Red wine vinegar	½ c	120 ml	
Jalapeño peppers, minced	1 c	240 ml	
Red onion, minced	1 lb	454 g	
Tomatoes, seeded, minced	5 lb	2.3 kg	Add to scallops. Stir to combine well.
Avocado, peeled, diced	5 lb	2.3 kg	Portion into lettuce-lined service bowls or
Cilantro, fresh, chopped	1 qt	950 ml	individual service pieces.
Jalapeño peppers, minced	½ c	240 ml	

Nutrient Analysis	Calories	173	Protein	14 gm
Per Serving	Fat	8.6 gm	Carbohydrate	12 gm
	Cholesterol	24 mg	Calcium	47.3 mg
	Sodium	279 mg	Fiber	1.5 gm

▲ Baked Shrimp Italiano

Serve as an antipasto course or an entrée with a simple pasta side.

Menu Category:	Appetizer, Entrée, Seafood, Ethnic, Italian
Cooking Method:	Sauté/Bake
Preparation Time:	30 minutes
Oven Temperature:	400°F
Cooking Time:	5 minutes sauté plus 10 minutes baking
Variations:	Substitute lobster, scallops, or sliced monkfish.
Yield:	50 portions (4 oz)

Ingredient	U.S.	Metric	Method
Shrimp (15 to 20 per lb), peeled	8 lb	3.6 kg	Toss shrimp with flour. Shake off all excess.
Flour	as needed	as needed	
Olive oil, hot	1 c	240 ml	Heat in 350°F brazier or flattop grill. Add dredged shrimp. Sauté quickly, just until shrimp are golden. Transfer to roasting pan.
Tomatoes, seeded, chopped	4 lb	1.8 kg	Add to shrimp. Stir well.
Parsley, chopped, squeezed dry	1 qt	950 ml	
Oregano, dried	1 T	15 ml	
White wine, dry	1 qt	950 ml	Heat to a simmer in sauce pot. Pour over shrimp mixture. Cover. Bake in 400°F oven for 10 minutes or just until firm.
Brandy	1 c	240 ml	

Nutrient Analysis Per Serving				
	Calories	149	Protein	15.2 gm
	Fat	5.7 gm	Carbohydrate	2.8 gm
	Cholesterol	112 mg	Calcium	58.2 mg
	Sodium	171 mg	Fiber	0.2 gm

▲ Louisiana-Style Barbecued Shrimp

Serve with sliced lemon, saltine crackers, and Tabasco sauce.

Menu Category:	Appetizer, Entrée, Seafood, American Regional
Cooking Method:	Roast
Preparation Time:	30 minutes
Marination Time:	1 hour
Oven Temperature:	450°F
Cooking Time:	15–20 minutes
Variations:	Substitute sliced boneless chicken breasts.
Yield:	50 portions (4 oz)

Ingredient	U.S.	Metric	Method
Shrimp (15 to 20 per lb), unpeeled	10 lb	4.5 kg	Combine in large bowl. Stir to mix well and coat shrimp uniformly. Cover and chill for one hour. Portion into shallow roasting pans so that shrimp are in one layer. Divide marinade over shrimp.
Black pepper	1 c	240 ml	
Salt	¼ c	60 ml	
Worcestershire sauce	2 c	480 ml	
Lemon juice	1 c	240 ml	
Tabasco sauce	½ c	120 ml	
Butter, melted	2 c	480 ml	Divide over shrimp. Bake uncovered in preheated 450°F oven for 15 minutes or until shrimp are firm. Stir shrimp once during baking.

Nutrient Analysis	Calories	176	Protein	19 gm
Per Serving	Fat	9 gm	Carbohydrate	4.2 gm
	Cholesterol	160 mg	Calcium	73 mg
	Sodium	830 mg	Fiber	0.3 gm

▲ Phoenix-Style Chinese Fried Shrimp

Serve as an appetizer or entrée on Cantonese menus.

Menu Category:	Appetizer, Entrée, Seafood, Ethnic, Chinese
Cooking Method:	Fry
Preparation Time:	30 minutes
Marination Time:	1 hour
Cooking Time:	10 minutes
Variations:	Substitute scallops or small pieces of monkfish.
Yield:	50 portions (4 oz)

Ingredient	U.S.	Metric	Method
Sherry, dry	2 c	480 ml	Combine in mixer bowl with whip
Commercial hoisin sauce	1 qt	950 ml	attachment. Blend well. Cover. Chill well.
Soy sauce	1 c	240 ml	
Honey	1 c	240 ml	
Gingerroot, grated	¼ c	60 ml	
Garlic, minced	1 T	15 ml	
Crushed red pepper	1 T	15 ml	
Shrimp (10 to 15 per lb), peeled, tails on	10 lb	4.5 kg	Combine in large bowl. Mix well. Cover and chill for one hour. Drain shrimp and
Sherry, dry	1 qt	950 ml	dry well.
Gingerroot, peeled minced	½ c	120 ml	
Egg white	1 qt	950 ml	Beat in mixer with whip attachment until
Cornstarch	1 c	240 ml	peaks form, but mixture is not dry. Dip
Flour	½ c	120 ml	shrimp quickly into batter and deep-fry at 350°F until golden brown, about 5 minutes. Serve with reserved sauce.

Nutrient Analysis Per Serving				
	Calories	194	Protein	21.3 gm
	Fat	1.7 gm	Carbohydrate	15 gm
	Cholesterol	140 mg	Calcium	64 mg
	Sodium	880 mg	Fiber	0.1 gm

APPETIZERS WITH VEGETABLES

▲ Cheese Calzone

We've provided a dough recipe for this stuffed pizza, but you can use any pizza dough you want.

Menu Category:	Appetizer, Entrée, Ethnic, Italian
Cooking Method:	Bake
Preparation Time:	20 minutes
Oven Temperature:	450°F
Baking Time:	30 minutes
Variations:	Use anything you can imagine, but remember: The key is do not overfill the shells; the filling can swell and break the crust seal.
Yield:	50 portions (6 oz)

Ingredient	U.S.	Metric	Method
Cornmeal	2 c	480 ml	Sprinkle over four oiled or paper-lined half-sized sheet pans.
Italian Pizza Crust Dough, recipe follows	6 lb	2.7 kg	Divide into fifty 2-ounce portions. Roll dough into 6-inch circles. Chill until ready to use.
Eggs, beaten	12	12	Combine in large bowl. Mix well to combine. Portion 3 ounces onto each dough circle.
Ricotta cheese	4½ lb	2 kg	
Parmesan cheese, grated	1 lb	454 g	
Mozzarella cheese, diced	3 lb	1.4 kg	
Egg white, slightly beaten	4 each	4 each	Combine. Brush edge of each circle. Fold into half-moon shapes. Press edges. Place on oiled or paper-lined sheet pans. Brush tops with eggwash. Cut slit in each. Bake in preheated 450°F until golden brown, about 25 to 30 minutes. Transfer to wire racks.
Water	2 c	480 ml	

Nutrient Analysis Per Serving				
	Calories	385	Protein	23 gm
	Fat	16 gm	Carbohydrate	40 gm
	Cholesterol	100 mg	Calcium	374 mg
	Sodium	458 mg	Fiber	1 gm

Companion Recipe

▲ # Italian Pizza Crust Dough

Use for a variety of pizza and calzone preparations.

Menu Category:	Appetizer, Entrée, Ethnic, Italian
Cooking Method:	None required
Preparation Time:	20 minutes
Rising Time:	1 to 2 hours
Variations:	Add a variety of herbs and spices to the basic crust.
Yield:	6 lb, sufficient for four half-sized sheet pans.

Ingredient	U.S.	Metric	Method
Yeast, dry	2 oz	56 g	Combine in mixer bowl. Let rest until frothy.
Water, warm	2 qt	1.9 L	
Sugar	2 T	30 ml	
Flour, all purpose	5 lb	2.3 kg	Combine. Add to yeast mixture. Attach dough hook. Mix at low speed until dough is elastic, smooth, and leaves side of bowl, about 12 to 15 minutes. Add flour as needed to prevent dough from sticking to sides of bowl and climbing the dough hook. Transfer dough to large oiled bowl. Cover. Let rest until double in volume, about 1 to 2 hours. Divide dough as needed.
Salt	1 T	15 ml	

Nutrient Analysis Per Ounce				
	Calories	53	Protein	2.2 gm
	Fat	0.3 gm	Carbohydrate	11.3 gm
	Cholesterol	0 mg	Calcium	5.8 mg
	Sodium	44 mg	Fiber	0.3 gm

▲ Grilled Crostini with Caponata

Serve as an Italian appetizer or as a vegetarian entrée.

Menu Category:	Appetizer, Entrée, Ethnic, Italian	
Cooking Method:	Simmer	
Preparation Time:	30 minutes	
Cooking Time:	45 minutes	
Variations:	Add chopped shrimp or tuna after mixture is cooked and chilled.	
Yield:	50 portions (4 oz)	

Ingredient	U.S.	Metric	Method
Tomatoes, peeled, seeded, diced	1 qt	950 ml	Combine in large bowl. Mix well. Reserve.
Ripe olives, pitted, diced	2 c	480 ml	
Green olives, pitted, diced	2 c	480 ml	
Red wine vinegar	1 c	240 ml	
Capers, small	1 c	240 ml	
Currants	1 c	240 ml	
Olive oil, hot	1 c	240 ml	Sauté until golden brown. Drain oil. Add eggplant to tomato mixture.
Eggplant, ½-inch dice	1 qt	950 ml	
Olive oil, hot	1 c	240 ml	Sauté until tender. Drain oil. Add to eggplant and tomato mixture. Combine well. Transfer to a heavy pot or brazier skillet. Cook over low heat until mixture is thick and glossy, about 45 minutes.
Onions, yellow, minced	1 qt	950 ml	
Celery, minced	1 qt	950 ml	
Pine nuts, toasted	1 c	240 ml	Add. Stir well. Cool. Cover. Chill.
Salt	to taste	to taste	Adjust seasoning.
Black pepper	to taste	to taste	
French bread slices	100	100	Brush rounds with oil. Place on sheet pans. Broil just until barely golden but crisp. Portion vegetable mixture onto grilled bread slices. Serve warm, cold, or at room temperature.
Olive oil	2 c	480 ml	

Nutrient Analysis Per Serving				
	Calories	325	Protein	7.8 gm
	Fat	15 gm	Carbohydrate	41 gm
	Cholesterol	0 mg	Calcium	110 mg
	Sodium	576 mg	Fiber	0.6 gm

▲ Guacamole Pancho Villa

Serve with tortilla chips or as a topping/side for Mexican entrées.

Menu Category:	Appetizer, Ethnic, Mexican, American Regional
Cooking Method:	None required
Preparation Time:	30 minutes
Variations:	Add sliced mandarin orange sections and thinly sliced radishes.
Yield:	50 portions (3 oz)

Ingredient	U.S.	Metric	Method
Onion, minced	3 c	720 ml	Combine in large bowl. Mix gently but well. Transfer to service bowls.
Tomato, seeded, chopped	1 qt	950 ml	
Avocado, peeled, diced	1 gal	3.8 L	
Mayonnaise	2 c	480 ml	
Lime juice, fresh	1 c	240 ml	
Crushed red pepper	1 T	15 ml	
Cilantro, chopped	1 c	240 ml	
Salt	2 T	30 ml	
Lime juice, fresh	¼ c	60 ml	Sprinkle over top of guacamole. Cover. Chill well.

Nutrient Analysis Per Serving				
	Calories	202	Protein	2 gm
	Fat	20 gm	Carbohydrate	7.6 gm
	Cholesterol	5.1 mg	Calcium	20.3 mg
	Sodium	347 mg	Fiber	1.7 gm

▲ Pita Wedges with Red Lentil Hummus

Serve as a Mediterranean appetizer or as a vegetarian entrée.

Menu Category:	Appetizer, Entrée, Ethnic, Mediterranean
Cooking Method:	Simmer
Preparation Time:	30 minutes
Cooking Time:	15 minutes
Variations:	Add chopped shrimp or tuna after mixture is cooked and chilled.
Yield:	50 portions (4 oz)

Ingredient	U.S.	Metric	Method
Lentils, red	2 qt	1.9 L	Combine in large pot or steam kettle. Heat
Water, cold	1½ gal	5.7 L	to a boil. Reduce heat to a simmer. Simmer just until lentils are tender, about 15 minutes. Drain off all cooking liquid. Transfer lentils to a large bowl.
Garlic, minced	1 T	15 ml	Add to lentils. Puree mixture in food
Lemon juice	1 c	240 ml	processor with metal blade. Mix well.
Tahini paste	2 c	480 ml	Cover. Chill well.
White wine, dry	2 c	480 ml	
Chick-peas, drained	1 qt	950 ml	
Olive oil, fruity	½ c	120 ml	
Cumin, ground	¼ c	60 ml	
Paprika	2 T	30 ml	
Salt	1 T	15 ml	
Black pepper	2 t	10 ml	
Pita breads, cut in 6 wedges	20	20	Arrange wedges on service trays. Portion hummus mixture onto each wedge. Garnish as desired.

Nutrient Analysis	Calories	238	Protein	20.3 gm
Per Serving	Fat	8.8 gm	Carbohydrate	18.5 gm
	Cholesterol	45 mg	Calcium	43 mg
	Sodium	528 mg	Fiber	0.4 gm

▲ Spiced Cocktail Pecans

An old Southern appetizer.

Menu Category:	Appetizer, American Regional
Cooking Method:	Roast
Preparation Time:	10 minutes
Marination Time:	1 hour
Oven Temperature:	300°F
Cooking Time:	15 minutes
Variations:	Substitute shelled walnuts or fresh peanuts.
Yield:	50 portions (2 oz)

Ingredient	U.S.	Metric	Method
Pecan halves	5 lb	2.3 kg	Combine in large bowl. Let rest for 1 hour.
Butter, melted	1 c	240 ml	Spread pecans on sheet pans. Bake in
Worcestershire sauce	2 c	480 ml	preheated 300°F oven for about 15 minutes
Tabasco sauce	2 T	30 ml	or until golden brown and dry.
Chili powder	1 T	15 ml	
Black pepper	1 t	5 ml	
Salt	1 t	5 ml	
Cayenne pepper	1 T	15 ml	Sprinkle over pecans. Toss well. Serve hot, warm, or at room temperature.

Nutrient Analysis Per Serving	Calories	343	Protein	3.8 gm
	Fat	34.4 gm	Carbohydrate	10.2 gm
	Cholesterol	10 mg	Calcium	28 mg
	Sodium	179 mg	Fiber	0.8 gm

▲ Spicy Marinated Mushrooms

Serve with Mexican and southwestern American menus.

Menu Category:	Appetizer, Salad, Ethnic, Mexican, American Regional
Cooking Method:	Simmer
Preparation Time:	10 minutes
Marination Time:	Several hours
Cooking Time:	20 minutes
Variations:	Substitute sliced zucchini for mushrooms.
Yield:	50 portions (4 oz)

Ingredient	U.S.	Metric	Method
Commercial picante sauce	1 qt	950 ml	Combine in sauce pot. Heat to a simmer.
Lemon juice	1 c	240 ml	Simmer for 10 minutes. Remove from heat.
White wine, dry	1 c	240 ml	Cool completely.
Garlic powder	½ c	120 ml	
Button mushrooms	Two #10 cans	6 kg	Drain well and add to picante mixture. Cover and chill for several hours, stirring occasionally.
Parsley, chopped	1 c	240 ml	Add to mushrooms. Stir well. Use slotted
Ripe olives, sliced	2 c	480 ml	spoon to portion into service pieces.

Nutrient Analysis	Calories	47	Protein	2.2 gm
Per Serving	Fat	1.6 gm	Carbohydrate	7.7 gm
	Cholesterol	0 mg	Calcium	24.2 mg
	Sodium	606 mg	Fiber	0.7 gm

▲ Sicilian Vegetarian Pizza

The dough recipe is provided, but you can use any pizza dough you want.

Menu Category:	Appetizer, Entrée, Ethnic, Italian, Vegetarian
Cooking Method:	Bake
Preparation Time:	20 minutes
Oven Temperature:	375°F
Baking Time:	30 minutes
Variations:	The method is more important than what goes on top, and that can be just about anything you can imagine!
Yield:	50 portions (4 oz)

Ingredient	U.S.	Metric	Method
Cornmeal	2 c	480 ml	Sprinkle over four oiled or paper-lined half-sized sheet pans.
Italian Pizza Crust Dough, p. 236	6 lb	2.7 kg	Divide into four portions. Spread over prepared sheet pans.
Commercial pizza sauce	2 qt	1.9 L	Spread over crusts.
Capers	1 qt	950 ml	Divide over sauce.
Olives, ripe, chopped	1 qt	950 ml	
Mozzarella cheese, grated	2 lb	908 g	
Bread crumbs, coarse	1 qt	950 ml	Sprinkle over the top. Bake in preheated 375°F oven until golden brown and bubbly, about 30 minutes. Transfer to wire racks. Let rest 15 minutes before slicing.

Nutrient Analysis Per Serving	Calories	354	Protein	17.7 gm
	Fat	11.7 gm	Carbohydrate	50 gm
	Cholesterol	134 mg	Calcium	209 mg
	Sodium	936 mg	Fiber	1.4 gm

▲ Take-a-Break Mushroom Pizza Snacks

Serve as an appetizer or lunch entrée or as a midday snack.

Menu Category:	Snack, Appetizer, Entrée, Ethnic, Italian
Cooking Method:	Sauté/Bake
Preparation Time:	30 minutes
Oven Temperature:	450°F
Cooking Time:	5 minutes
Variations:	Substitute a variety of toppings.
	Season tomato sauce with fennel and oregano.
	For a Mexican version, add cumin to tomato sauce and use grated Monterey Jack cheese with jalapeños.
Yield:	50 portions (5 oz)

Ingredient	U.S.	Metric	Method
French loaf, split	5 lb	2.3 kg	Slice bread into 50 portions. Place on sheet pans. Brown cut surface under broiler just until golden. Remove from oven.
Mushrooms, sliced	5 lb	2.3 kg	Heat griddle or tilt brazier and spray with cooking spray. Add mushrooms and seasoning. Sauté until tender. Remove.
Italian seasoning	¼ c	60 ml	
Olive oil nonstick cooking spray	as needed	as needed	
Commercial tomato sauce	3 c	720 ml	Spread over toasted bread slices.
Mozzarella cheese, grated	4 lb	1.8 kg	Distribute over slices. Top with reserved mushrooms. Bake at 450°F just until cheese melts, about 4 or 5 minutes.

Nutrient Analysis Per Serving				
	Calories	251	Protein	12.5 gm
	Fat	10.3 gm	Carbohydrate	27 gm
	Cholesterol	28.1 mg	Calcium	240 mg
	Sodium	401 mg	Fiber	0.5 gm

▲ Vegetable Fritatta

This sauté-and-broil version of the classic Italian flat omelet holds well for service.

Menu Category:	Appetizer, Breakfast, Brunch, Ethnic, Italian
Cooking Method:	Sauté/Broil
Preparation Time:	20 minutes
Cooking Time:	20 minutes
Variations:	Just as with omelets and crepes: If you have it, put it in! This version is really tasty when served with a light tomato sauce.
Yield:	50 portions (3 oz)

Ingredient	U.S.	Metric	Method
Olive oil, hot	1 c	240 ml	Divide among four 12-inch skillets. Sauté over high heat just until vegetables are tender. Remove from heat.
Onion, minced	1 c	240 ml	
Green bell pepper, minced	1 c	240 ml	
Garlic, minced	2 T	30 ml	
Zucchini, minced	1 qt	950 ml	
Egg yolks	3 lb	1.4 kg	Combine in medium bowl. Whip well to combine.
Flour, all purpose	2 c	480 ml	
Milk	2 c	480 ml	Add to yolk mixture. Mix well.
Egg whites, beaten stiff	3 lb	1.4 kg	Fold into yolk mixture. Reheat 12-inch skillets over medium-high heat until vegetables begin to sizzle. Divide egg mixture among pans. Sauté until golden on the bottom, shaking pans often. Transfer to preheated medium broiler. Broil until mixture is firm and tops are golden, about 10 minutes. Transfer to sheet pans. Cut into wedges for serving.

Nutrient Analysis Per Serving				
	Calories	177	Protein	8.7 gm
	Fat	13 gm	Carbohydrate	6.3 gm
	Cholesterol	350 mg	Calcium	56.3 mg
	Sodium	78 mg	Fiber	0.2 gm

Soups

MEAT SOUPS

▲ Autumn Beef Ragout

This French beef stew can be served with pasta.

Menu Category:	Soup, Appetizer, Ethnic, French
Cooking Method:	Sauté/Simmer
Preparation Time:	45 minutes
Marination Time:	Overnight
Cooking Time:	3 hours
Variations:	Substitute pork, chicken, or rabbit and use white wine and appropriate stock. If using chicken, reduce cooking time by half.
Yield:	50 portions (6 oz)

Ingredient	U.S.	Metric	Method
Stew beef, 1-inch cubes	8 lb	3.6 kg	Combine in plastic storage container.
Red wine	2 qt	1.9 L	Cover. Chill overnight. Remove beef cubes
Red wine vinegar	1 c	240 ml	and dry with paper towels. Strain off and
Carrots, sliced	2 qt	1.9 L	reserve liquid. Reserve vegetables.
Onion, sliced	1 qt	950 ml	
Celery, sliced	1 qt	950 ml	
Garlic, minced	1 T	15 ml	
Bay leaves	4	4	
Oregano, dried	2 t	10 ml	
Thyme, dried	1 t	5 ml	
Bacon, diced	2 c	480 ml	Heat in heavy pot or brazier. Add drained
Olive oil	1 c	240 ml	beef cubes. Sauté over medium-high heat until lightly browned. Add vegetables from marinade. Sauté for 5 minutes. Add reserved marinade.
Beef stock	2 qt	1.9 L	Add to beef mixture. Heat to a boil.
Salt	as needed	as needed	Reduce heat to a simmer. Simmer until
Black pepper	as needed	as needed	meat is fork-tender, about 2 hours. Remove bay leaves. Adjust seasoning with salt and pepper. Ladle off all fat.

Nutrient Analysis Per Serving				
	Calories	275	Protein	19.8 gm
	Fat	16.9 gm	Carbohydrate	4.4 gm
	Cholesterol	61.5 mg	Calcium	26.5 mg
	Sodium	315 mg	Fiber	0.3 gm

▲ Green Chile Beef Stew

A Santa Fe version of the all-American classic.

Menu Category:	Soup, Appetizer, American Regional
Cooking Method:	Simmer
Preparation Time:	30 minutes
Cooking Time:	2 hours
Variations:	Substitute pork or chicken for beef and reduce cooking time.

Yield: 50 portions (6 oz)

Ingredient	U.S.	Metric	Method
Beef stew meat, 1-inch cubes	2 lb	908 g	Combine in large bowl. Toss to coat well.
Flour	1 c	240 ml	
Cooking oil	1 c	240 ml	Heat in steam kettle or brazier. Add beef. Sauté over medium-high heat until browned.
Beef broth	1 gal	3.8 L	Add to beef. Simmer, covered, until beef is tender, about 1½ hours, stirring frequently.
Cooking oil, hot	1 c	240 ml	Sauté until vegetables begin to brown. Add to simmering beef.
Carrots, diced	2 c	480 ml	
Celery, diced	2 c	480 ml	
Onion, chopped	2 c	480 ml	
Garlic, minced	1 T	15 ml	
Potatoes, diced	1½ qt	1.4 L	Add with other vegetables. Simmer until potatoes are tender, about 20 minutes.
Green chilies, mild, canned	2 c	480 ml	
Commercial picante sauce, mild	1 qt	950 ml	
Oregano, dried	1 T	15 ml	
Chili powder	1 T	15 ml	

Nutrient Analysis Per Serving				
	Calories	110	Protein	6.8 gm
	Fat	12 gm	Carbohydrate	10.4 gm
	Cholesterol	13.4 mg	Calcium	19 mg
	Sodium	441 mg	Fiber	0.3 gm

▲ Hungarian Goulash Stew

A thick, hearty version of the eastern European classic. Use Hungarian paprika if you can.

Menu Category:	Soup, Appetizer, Ethnic, Hungarian
Cooking Method:	Sauté/Simmer
Preparation Time:	30 minutes
Cooking Time:	2 hours
Variations:	Substitute pork or chicken and use appropriate stock.
Yield:	50 portions (6 oz)

Ingredient	U.S.	Metric	Method
Olive oil	1 c	240 ml	Sauté in large pot or steam kettle just until
Beef, 1-inch cubes	3 lb	1.4 kg	beef cubes are lightly browned.
Onions, diced	1 qt	950 ml	
Celery, diced	1 qt	950 ml	
Paprika	¼ c	60 ml	Add to beef. Stir well to coat.
Flour	1 c	240 ml	
Tomato puree	½ c	120 ml	Add to mixture. Heat to a boil. Reduce
Beef stock	1½ gal	5.7 L	heat to a simmer. Simmer 30 minutes.
Red wine, hearty, dry	1 qt	950 ml	
Caraway seeds	1 T	15 ml	
Potatoes, diced	1 qt	950 ml	Add to mixture. Continue to simmer until
Carrots, diced	1 qt	950 ml	beef and vegetables are tender, about 1 hour.
Salt	1 T	15 ml	Adjust seasoning.
Black pepper	2 t	10 ml	

Nutrient Analysis				
Per Serving	Calories	158	Protein	9.4 gm
	Fat	8.1 gm	Carbohydrate	8.9 gm
	Cholesterol	20.2 mg	Calcium	22.4 mg
	Sodium	393 mg	Fiber	0.5 gm

▲ Philadelphia Pepper Pot Soup

A spicy soup that's popular at lunch or before dinner.

Menu Category:	Soup, Appetizer, American Regional
Cooking Method:	Sauté/Simmer
Preparation Time:	30 minutes
Cooking Time:	1 hour
Variations:	Eliminate tripe.
	Substitute chicken stock for beef.
Yield:	50 portions (6 oz)

Ingredient	U.S.	Metric	Method
Bacon, diced	2 c	480 ml	Sauté in large pot or steam kettle just until golden.
Onion, minced	3 c	720 ml	Add to bacon. Sauté until vegetables are tender, about 5 minutes.
Celery, minced	2 c	480 ml	
Green bell pepper, minced	2 c	480 ml	
Flour	½ c	120 ml	Add to vegetables. Stir well for about 5 minutes.
Tripe, parboiled, minced	1 qt	950 ml	Add to vegetables. Stir until mixture thickens and is smooth. Heat to a boil. Reduce to a simmer. Simmer for 30 minutes.
Beef stock	1½ gal	5.7 L	
Black pepper, coarse grind	1 T	15 ml	
Potatoes, diced	2 qt	1.9 L	Add to mixture. Simmer until potatoes are tender, about 20 minutes. Adjust seasoning. Serve hot.
Tomatoes, seeded, diced	1 qt	950 ml	
Thyme, dried	1 t	5 ml	
Tabasco sauce	1 T	15 ml	

Nutrient Analysis Per Serving				
	Calories	121	Protein	6.5 gm
	Fat	5.3 gm	Carbohydrate	12.1 gm
	Cholesterol	7.7 mg	Calcium	19.5 mg
	Sodium	584 mg	Fiber	0.4 gm

▲ Southwestern Herbed Meatball Soup (*Sopa Albondiga*)

A creative use for popular meatballs.

Menu Category:	Soup, Appetizer, Ethnic, Mexican
Cooking Method:	Sauté/Simmer
Preparation Time:	30 minutes
Cooking Time:	1 hour
Variations:	Try pita bread instead of tortillas.
	Garnish with lime wedges.
Yield:	50 portions (6 oz)

Ingredient	U.S.	Metric	Method
Olive oil	1 c	240 ml	Sauté in large pot or steam kettle just until
Onion, minced	1 qt	950 ml	vegetables are tender, about 5 minutes.
Garlic, minced	1 T	15 ml	
Canned green chilies, mild,			
chopped, drained	2 c	480 ml	
Cumin, ground	1 T	15 ml	Add. Stir for about 1 minute.
Chili powder	2 T	30 ml	
Tomatoes, chopped,			Add to vegetables. Heat to a boil. Reduce
drained	2 qt	1.9 L	heat to a simmer. Simmer 30 minutes.
Beef stock	1 gal	3.8 L	
Cilantro, chopped	1 c	240 ml	
Salt	1 T	15 ml	
Black pepper	2 t	10 ml	
Ground beef, lean	5 lb	2.3 kg	Combine in large bowl. Mix gently but
Egg, beaten	6	6	well. Portion with 1-ounce scoop. Form
Garlic, minced	1 T	15 ml	into small meatballs. Drop meatballs in
Cumin, ground	2 t	10 ml	simmering soup. Simmer until meatballs
Corn tortillas, minced	2 c	480 ml	rise to the surface, about 30 minutes.

Nutrient Analysis	Calories	185	Protein	11.7 gm
Per Serving	Fat	11.9 gm	Carbohydrate	7.9 gm
	Cholesterol	53.5 mg	Calcium	43.4 mg
	Sodium	530 mg	Fiber	0.5 gm

Poultry Soups

▲ Cajun Chicken Jambalaya

A hearty version that features chicken instead of seafood.

Menu Category:	Soup, Appetizer, American Regional
Cooking Method:	Simmer
Preparation Time:	30 minutes
Cooking Time:	1 hour
Variations:	Substitute freely: pork, beef, shrimp, oysters—any meat or shellfish.
Yield:	50 portions (6 oz)

Ingredient	U.S.	Metric	Method
Bacon, chopped	½ lb	227 g	Sauté in large pot or steam kettle. Cook just until bacon begins to turn crisp.
Onion, minced	3 c	720 ml	Add. Sauté for 5 minutes.
Celery, minced	3 c	720 ml	
Green bell pepper, minced	3 c	720 ml	
Rice	3 c	720 ml	Add. Stir for 1 minute.
Chili powder	1 T	15 ml	
Crushed red pepper	2 t	10 ml	
Tomato sauce	3 qt	2.8 L	Add. Heat to a boil. Reduce heat to a simmer. Cover. Simmer for 15 minutes.
Chicken stock	1 qt	950 ml	
Chicken breast, skinned, diced	5 lb	2.3 kg	Add. Stir in gently. Simmer until rice and chicken are cooked, about 15 minutes.

Nutrient Analysis Per Serving	Calories	163	Protein	18.6 gm
	Fat	4.8 gm	Carbohydrate	11.6 gm
	Cholesterol	45 mg	Calcium	24.8 mg
	Sodium	576 mg	Fiber	0.7 gm

▲ Chinese Eggdrop Soup

This classic is as simple to prepare as it is delicious.

Menu Category:	Soup, Ethnic, Chinese
Cooking Method:	Sauté, Simmer
Preparation Time:	20 minutes
Cooking Time:	20 minutes
Variations:	Add julienne or sliced cooked chicken, pork, or shrimp. Garnish with minced scallions.
Yield:	50 portions (5 oz)

Ingredient	U.S.	Metric	Method
Chicken stock or broth	1½ gal	5.7 L	Heat to a rolling boil.
Cornstarch	¾ c	180 ml	Combine in small bowl. Mix well. Add to boiling broth. Reduce heat to a simmer.
Water	2 c	480 ml	
Soy sauce	½ c	120 ml	
Sugar	2 t	10 ml	
Egg, beaten	4	4	Drizzle into simmering soup. Simmer 1 minute, stirring constantly.
Water	1 c	240 ml	
Sesame oil	1 T	15 ml	

Nutrient Analysis Per Serving				
	Calories	38	Protein	3.1 gm
	Fat	1.4 gm	Carbohydrate	2.9 gm
	Cholesterol	17 mg	Calcium	9.8 mg
	Sodium	543 mg	Fiber	0.1 gm

▲ Pistol Pete's Green Chicken Chili

A Santa Fe style favorite with chicken instead of beef.

Menu Category:	Soup, Appetizer, American Regional
Cooking Method:	Simmer
Preparation Time:	30 minutes
Cooking Time:	1 hour
Variations:	Substitute pork, turkey, or beef for chicken. Garnish with lime wedges.
Yield:	50 portions (6 oz)

Ingredient	U.S.	Metric	Method
Chicken breast, skinned	3 lb	1.4 kg	Combine in large pot or steam kettle. Heat to a boil. Reduce to a simmer. Simmer until chicken is cooked, about 15 minutes. Remove chicken breasts. Cool completely. Dice and reserve.
Chicken stock	1½ gal	5.7 L	
Dried ancho chilies, sliced	6	6	Add to chicken broth. Simmer 15 minutes. Discard chilies.
Rice, cooked	1 qt	950 ml	Add to chicken broth with reserved chicken. Simmer 5 minutes.
Cumin, ground	2 T	30 ml	
Zucchini, diced	1 qt	950 ml	Add. Simmer 3 minutes.
Scallions, minced	2 c	480 ml	Add. Simmer 2 minutes.
Mild green chilies, sliced	2 c	480 ml	
Tomato, seeded, diced	3 c	720 ml	Divide among service bowls. Add hot soup.
Cilantro, chopped	1 c	240 ml	

Nutrient Analysis Per Serving	Calories	101	Protein	12.5 gm
	Fat	2.1 gm	Carbohydrate	7.2 gm
	Cholesterol	24.7 mg	Calcium	27.5 mg
	Sodium	458 mg	Fiber	0.3 gm

SeaFood Soups

▲ Manhattan Clam Chowder with Dry Sherry

Sherry and tarragon add a novel flavor to this classic.

Menu Category:	Soup, Appetizer, American Regional
Cooking Method:	Simmer
Preparation Time:	30 minutes
Cooking Time:	1 hour
Variations:	Substitute other shellfish such as mussels or crabmeat.
Yield:	50 portions (4 oz)

Ingredient	U.S.	Metric	Method
Tomatoes, chopped, canned	2 qt	1.9 L	Combine in large pot or steam kettle.
Potatoes, diced	1 qt	950 ml	Simmer until vegetables are barely tender,
Carrot, diced	2 c	480 ml	about 20 minutes.
Green bell pepper, diced	2 c	480 ml	
Onion, diced	2 c	480 ml	
Celery, diced	2 c	480 ml	
Clams, chopped	1 qt	950 ml	Add to vegetables. Simmer 10 minutes.
Clam broth	2 qt	1.9 L	
Parsley, chopped	1 c	240 ml	
Tarragon, dried	2 t	10 ml	
Garlic powder	1 T	15 ml	
Salt	1 T	15 ml	
Black pepper	2 t	10 ml	
Sherry, dry	1 c	240 ml	Add. Simmer 5 minutes. Serve hot.
Worcestershire sauce	2 T	30 ml	

Nutrient Analysis	Calories	68	Protein	4.3 gm
Per Serving	Fat	0.6 gm	Carbohydrate	9.4 gm
	Cholesterol	6.2 mg	Calcium	31.2 mg
	Sodium	366 mg	Fiber	0.4 gm

▲ San Francisco Bayside Cioppino

This fisherman's favorite originated on 19th century sailing ships.

Menu Category:	Soup, Appetizer, American Regional
Cooking Method:	Sauté/Simmer
Preparation Time:	30 minutes
Cooking Time:	1 hour
Variations:	Substitute fresh fish and other shellfish.
Yield:	50 portions (5 oz)

Ingredient	U.S.	Metric	Method
Olive oil, hot	½ c	120 ml	Sauté in heavy pot or steam kettle until
Onion, chopped	2 c	480 ml	vegetables are tender, about 5 minutes.
Celery, chopped	2 c	480 ml	
Garlic, minced	1 T	15 ml	
Roma tomatoes, canned, chopped, drained	2 qt	1.9 L	Add to vegetables. Heat to a boil. Reduce heat to a simmer. Simmer 20 minutes.
Clam juice	1 qt	950 ml	
White wine, dry	1 qt	950 ml	
Parsley, chopped	1 c	240 ml	
Bay leaf	2	2	
Fennel seeds, crushed	2 t	10 ml	
Thyme, dried	1 t	5 ml	
Salt	2 t	10 ml	
Black pepper	1 t	5 ml	
Shrimp, peeled	3 lb	1.4 kg	Add to mixture. Simmer just until shrimp and lobster are firm, about 5 minutes. Remove bay leaves. Serve hot.
Lobster meat, sliced	1 lb	454 g	
Scallops	2 lb	908 g	

Nutrient Analysis	Calories	101	Protein	11.4 gm
Per Serving	Fat	3.1 gm	Carbohydrate	3.6 gm
	Cholesterol	54.5 mg	Calcium	45.1 mg
	Sodium	317 mg	Fiber	0.3 gm

Vegetable Soups

▲ Calalou

This vegetable stew is popular throughout the Caribbean.

Menu Category:	Soup, Appetizer, Ethnic, Caribbean
Cooking Method:	Simmer
Preparation Time:	30 minutes
Cooking Time:	1 hour
Variations:	Substitute shrimp or crab for the ham.
Yield:	50 portions (6 oz)

Ingredient	U.S.	Metric	Method
Okra, IQF, sliced	4 lb	1.8 kg	Combine in a large pot or steam kettle.
Spinach, fresh, chopped	4 lb	1.8 kg	Heat to a boil. Reduce to a simmer.
Onion, chopped	1 qt	950 ml	Simmer for 30 minutes. Strain. Puree
Scallions, chopped	2 c	480 ml	solids. Return puree and liquid to pot.
Thyme, dried	1 t	5 ml	
Chicken stock	1½ gal	5.7 L	
Ham, diced	2 lb	908 g	Add to mixture. Heat to a simmer. Simmer
Garlic, minced	1 T	15 ml	for 15 minutes. Do not boil. Serve hot.
Lime juice	1 c	240 ml	

Nutrient Analysis				
Per Serving	Calories	90	Protein	7.3 gm
	Fat	4.3 gm	Carbohydrate	6.4 gm
	Cholesterol	9 mg	Calcium	74 mg
	Sodium	653 mg	Fiber	0.7 gm

▲ Caribbean Red Bean and Lentil Soup

Hearty and spicy—just the soup for a chilly day.

Menu Category:	Soup, Appetizer, Ethnic, Caribbean
Cooking Method:	Simmer
Soaking Time:	Overnight
Preparation Time:	30 minutes
Cooking Time:	1 hour
Variations:	Substitute different beans or eliminate the lentils entirely.
Yield:	50 portions (8 oz)

Ingredient	U.S.	Metric	Method
Red beans, dried	3 lb	1.4 kg	Combine in pot. Let rest overnight. Drain well. Place beans in large pot or steam kettle.
Water	to cover	to cover	
Ham hocks, smoked	8	8	Add to beans. Heat to a boil. Reduce heat to a simmer. Simmer for 30 minutes.
Beef stock	1 gal	3.8 L	
Onion, diced	2 c	480 ml	Add to beans. Continue to simmer until beans are tender, about 30 to 45 minutes. Strain soup, reserving liquid in pot or steam kettle. Remove ham hocks from solids and trim hocks of all fat. Dice meat and add to the liquid. Puree solids and return to liquid.
Carrots, diced	2 c	480 ml	
Celery, diced	2 c	480 ml	
Garlic, minced	1 T	15 ml	
Thyme, dried	1 t	5 ml	
Curry powder	1 T	15 ml	
Cinnamon, ground	1 t	5 ml	
Parsley, chopped	2 c	480 ml	
Jalapeño pepper, seeded, minced	1 T	15 ml	
Lentils, green, dried	1 lb	454 g	
Red wine vinegar	½ c	120 ml	Add to soup. Simmer 10 minutes. If you prefer a thinner soup, add additional beef stock.
Sherry, dry	1 c	240 ml	

Nutrient Analysis Per Serving				
	Calories	185	Protein	15.4 gm
	Fat	3 gm	Carbohydrate	23.4 gm
	Cholesterol	13.2 mg	Calcium	39.4 mg
	Sodium	592 mg	Fiber	2.9 gm

▲ **Chilled and Spiced Melon Soup**

Serve this chilled soup as a "dog days" summer special.

Menu Category:	Soup, Appetizer
Cooking Method:	Simmer
Preparation Time:	30 minutes
Cooking Time:	1 hour
Variations:	Substitute peaches, strawberries, or other fruit.
Yield:	50 portions (6 oz)

Ingredient	U.S.	Metric	Method
Cantaloupe, diced	2 qt	1.9 L	Combine in large pot or steam kettle. Heat to a simmer. Simmer until melon is soft. Remove from heat. Cool. Puree in batches. Chill well.
Peach nectar	1 qt	950 ml	
Pear nectar	1 qt	950 ml	
Papaya juice	2 c	480 ml	
Orange juice	2 c	480 ml	
Ginger, ground	½ t	3 ml	
Allspice, ground	½ t	3 ml	
Cinnamon, ground	½ t	3 ml	
Heavy cream	1 qt	950 ml	Add to chilled puree. Mix well. Serve cold.

Nutrient Analysis Per Serving	Calories	67	Protein	1 gm
	Fat	2.3 gm	Carbohydrate	11.4 gm
	Cholesterol	7.1 mg	Calcium	27.4 mg
	Sodium	13.1 mg	Fiber	0.2 gm

▲ Creamy Corn Chowder with Grilled Pepper

Serve this robust chowder on southwestern and American Regional menus.

Menu Category:	Soup, Appetizer, American Regional
Cooking Method:	Simmer
Preparation Time:	15 minutes
Cooking Time:	30 minutes
Variations:	Add crumbled bacon and minced, seeded jalapeño peppers.
Yield:	50 portions (4 oz)

Ingredient	U.S.	Metric	Method
Butter, melted	2 c	480 ml	Sauté in stockpot, steam kettle, or brazier.
Onion, finely chopped	2 c	480 ml	Cook just until vegetables are tender.
Celery, finely chopped	2 c	480 ml	
Green bell pepper, finely chopped	2 c	480 ml	
Thyme, dried	1 t	5 ml	
Marjoram, dried	1 t	5 ml	
Whole kernel corn	2 qt	1.9 L	Add to vegetables. Heat to a simmer.
Flour	2 c	480 ml	Add to vegetables. Stir gently, but well. Cook over medium heat for 5 minutes.
Chicken stock	1½ gal	5.7 L	Add to mixture. Stir well. Simmer over medium-low heat for 15 minutes. Stir frequently.
Red bell pepper, seeded, grilled and diced	1 qt	950 ml	Add to soup. Simmer for 5 minutes.
Milk, lowfat	1 qt	950 ml	
Salt	1 T	15 ml	Adjust seasoning. Serve soup hot.
Black pepper	1 T	15 ml	
Lemon juice	¼ c	60 ml	

Nutrient Analysis	Calories	202	Protein	4.6 gm
Per Serving	Fat	9.3 gm	Carbohydrate	26.3 gm
	Cholesterol	21.4 mg	Calcium	36.2 mg
	Sodium	320 mg	Fiber	0.9 gm

▲ Creme Senegalaise (Chilled Curry Soup)

Serve this British-Indian classic on your hot-weather lunch menus.

Menu Category:	Soup, Appetizer, Ethnic, Anglo-Indian
Cooking Method:	Sauté/Simmer
Preparation Time:	30 minutes
Cooking Time:	1 hour
Variations:	Garnish each portion with snipped chives or scallion greens.
Yield:	50 portions (4 oz)

Ingredient	U.S.	Metric	Method
Olive oil, hot	1 c	240 ml	Sauté in preheated brazier just until vegetables are soft, about 5 minutes.
Onion, diced	1 c	240 ml	
Scallions, chopped	1 c	240 ml	
Celery, diced	1 c	240 ml	
Gingerroot, minced	2 t	10 ml	
Flour	1½ c	360 ml	Add to vegetables. Stir over medium heat for about 5 minutes. Do not brown flour.
Curry powder	½ c	120 ml	Add. Stir for 2 minutes.
Tomatoes, chopped	1 qt	950 ml	Add. Heat to a boil. Stir until mixture is smooth and begins to thicken. Reduce heat to a simmer. Simmer for 30 minutes. Remove from heat. Strain through very fine sieve. Cool to room temperature. Cover. Chill well.
Chicken stock	1 gal	3.8 L	
Cinnamon stick, small	2	2	
Milk, cold	1 qt	950 ml	Add to chilled mixture.

Nutrient Analysis Per Serving				
	Calories	83	Protein	3.2 gm
	Fat	5.4 gm	Carbohydrate	6 gm
	Cholesterol	1.4 mg	Calcium	45.6 mg
	Sodium	290 mg	Fiber	0.6 gm

▲ Fresh Mushroom Cream Bisque

Serve as an appetizer, soup course, or soup-and-sandwich combo.

Menu Category:	Soup, Appetizer
Cooking Method:	Sauté/Simmer
Preparation Time:	30 minutes
Cooking Time:	1 hour
Variations:	Sauté minced bacon with onions and celery.
	Serve with lightly toasted herbed garlic toasts.
Yield:	50 portions (5 oz)

Ingredient	U.S.	Metric	Method
Water, boiling	2 c	480 ml	Combine in small bowl. Let rest until
Dried mushrooms, chopped	4 oz	114 g	mushrooms soften, about 30 minutes.
Butter, melted	1 c	240 ml	Combine in large pot or steam kettle. Cook
Onion, minced	2 c	480 ml	over medium heat for 15 minutes.
Red bell pepper, minced	2 c	480 ml	
Celery, minced	2 c	480 ml	
Mushrooms, fresh, diced	4 lb	1.8 kg	
Flour	1 c	240 ml	Add to vegetables. Stir over medium heat for 5 minutes.
Chicken stock	2 qt	1.9 L	Add to mixture with reserved soaked
Bay leaves	2	2	mushrooms and their liquid. Stir well until
Salt	1 T	15 ml	mixture is thickened and smooth. Simmer
Black pepper	2 t	10 ml	for 30 minutes. Remove bay leaves.
Milk	2 qt	1.9 L	Add to mixture. Simmer just until well
Sherry, dry	1 c	240 ml	heated.

Nutrient Analysis				
Per Serving	Calories	99	Protein	3.8 gm
	Fat	5 gm	Carbohydrate	9.9 gm
	Cholesterol	12.8 mg	Calcium	58.7 mg
	Sodium	343 mg	Fiber	0.7 gm

▲ **Harvest Peach Chilled Bisque with Brandy**

Serve this delightful fruit soup with croissant sandwiches.

Menu Category:	Soup, Appetizer, American Regional
Cooking Method:	None required
Preparation Time:	20 minutes
Variations:	Substitute ripe melon for peaches and add some melon liqueur.
Yield:	50 portions (4 oz)

Ingredient	U.S.	Metric	Method
Peaches sliced, peeled	6 lb	2.7 kg	Combine in food processor with metal
Sugar, granulated	2 c	480 ml	blade. Puree completely. Transfer to mixer
Honey	1 c	240 ml	bowl with whip attachment.
Brandy or cognac	1 c	240 ml	
Lemon juice	1 c	240 ml	
Cinnamon, ground	1 t	5 ml	
Ginger, ground	½ t	3 ml	
Sour cream, light	3 c	720 ml	Add to peach mixture. Mix to blend well.
White wine, medium dry	2 qt	1.9 L	Transfer to storage containers. Cover. Chill
Orange juice	1 c	240 ml	well.
Water	2 c	480 ml	

Nutrient Analysis	Calories	132	Protein	0.9 gm
Per Serving	Fat	1.8 gm	Carbohydrate	20.9 gm
	Cholesterol	5.8 mg	Calcium	23.5 mg
	Sodium	9.5 mg	Fiber	0.4 gm

▲ Light Fresh Mushroom Soup with Vermouth

Serve as an appetizer, soup course, or soup-and-sandwich combo.

Menu Category:	Soup, Appetizer
Cooking Method:	Simmer
Preparation Time:	30 minutes
Cooking Time:	1 hour
Variations:	Sauté minced bacon with onions and celery.
	Finish with a dash of dry sherry.
	Serve with lightly toasted herbed garlic toasts.

Yield: 50 portions (5 oz)

Ingredient	U.S.	Metric	Method
Butter, melted	1½ c	360 ml	Sauté over medium-high heat in large pot
Onions, minced	2 qt	1.9 L	or steam kettle just until onions begin to
Sugar	1 T	15 ml	turn golden.
Mushrooms, sliced	4 lb	1.8 kg	Add to onions. Sauté 5 minutes.
Flour	1 c	240 ml	Add to mixture. Stir well for 3 minutes.
Chicken stock	2 qt	1.9 L	Add slowly to mixture. Stir well until
Water	1 qt	950 ml	mixture is thickened and smooth. Simmer
Vermouth, dry	1 qt	950 ml	for 10 minutes. Serve hot.
Salt	1 T	15 ml	
Black pepper	1 t	5 ml	

Nutrient Analysis	Calories	102	Protein	2.2 gm
Per Serving	Fat	6 gm	Carbohydrate	6.2 gm
	Cholesterol	14.9 mg	Calcium	13.7 mg
	Sodium	312 mg	Fiber	0.5 gm

▲ Mexican-Style Gazpacho

This refreshing, chilled soup is ideal for southwestern, Mexican, and Spanish menus.

Menu Category:	Soup, Appetizer, Ethnic, Mexican
Cooking Method:	Simmer
Preparation Time:	15 minutes
Cooking Time:	30 minutes
Variations:	For a zestier version, add Tabasco sauce or red pepper flakes.
Yield:	50 portions (6 oz)

Ingredient	U.S.	Metric	Method
Commercial picante sauce	2 gal	7.6 L	Combine in large pot. Heat to a simmer.
Sugar	1 c	240 ml	Stir well to dissolve sugar.
Olive oil, hot	2 c	480 ml	Cook onions over moderate heat. Do not
Onions, sliced	10 lb	4.54 kg	stir often. Cook until onions are brown. Scrape onions into picante sauce mixture. Remove from heat. Cool.
Green bell pepper, diced	2 lb	908 gm	Add to picante sauce mixture. Puree in
Cucumber, diced	2 lb	908 gm	food processor with metal blade. Pass
Parsley, chopped	1 c	240 ml	through fine strainer. Press well to get all
Red wine vinegar	2 c	480 ml	liquid. Cover and chill well.
Garlic powder	2 T	30 ml	
Chili powder	2 T	30 ml	
Green bell pepper, minced	1 c	240 ml	Use to garnish each portion. Serve very
Red bell pepper, minced	1 c	240 ml	cold.
Cucumber, minced	1 c	240 ml	
Tomato, minced	1 c	240 ml	
Parsley, chopped	1 c	240 ml	

Nutrient Analysis				
Per Serving	Calories	200	Protein	3.5 gm
	Fat	11.6 gm	Carbohydrate	28.3 gm
	Cholesterol	0 mg	Calcium	4.8 mg
	Sodium	1226 mg	Fiber	0.9 gm

▲ Minestrone

This version of the Italian vegetable soup hails from Calabria, a region that forms the foot of Italy's boot.

Menu Category:	Soup, Appetizer, Ethnic, Italian
Cooking Method:	Sauté/Simmer
Preparation Time:	30 minutes
Cooking Time:	1½ hours
Variations:	Substitute a variety of fresh vegetables.
	Add cooked navy or fava beans.
Yield:	50 portions (6 oz)

Ingredient	U.S.	Metric	Method
Olive oil	1 c	240 ml	Combine in food processor with metal
Bacon, diced	1 c	240 ml	blade. Process until completely pureed.
Celery, minced	1 c	240 ml	Transfer to a heavy pot or steam kettle.
Parsley, chopped	1 c	240 ml	Sauté over medium high heat until the
Garlic, chopped	1 T	15 ml	mixture begins to turn golden.
Basil, fresh, chopped	½ c	120 ml	
Chicken stock	1½ gal	5.7 L	Add to pot. Heat to a boil. Reduce heat to
Carrots, diced	1 lb	454 g	a simmer. Simmer until potatoes and
Potatoes, diced	1 lb	454 g	carrots are barely tender.
Green bell pepper, julienne	2 c	480 ml	Add. Simmer 5 minutes.
Green beans, sliced	1 lb	454 g	Add to mixture. Simmer until all
Zucchini, diced	1 lb	454 g	vegetables are tender, about 20 minutes.
Parmesan cheese, grated	2 c	480 ml	Sprinkle over each serving.

Nutrient Analysis	Calories	126	Protein	6.2 gm
Per Serving	Fat	8.6 gm	Carbohydrate	6.3 gm
	Cholesterol	7 mg	Calcium	85 mg
	Sodium	579 mg	Fiber	0.5 gm

▲ Pistou Provençale

This is a French version of the Italian minestrone.

Menu Category:	Soup, Appetizer, Ethnic, French
Cooking Method:	Sauté/Simmer
Preparation Time:	30 minutes
Soaking Time:	Overnight
Cooking Time:	1½ hours
Variations:	Substitute different beans and vegetables.
	Serve over a slice of toasted French bread.
Yield:	50 portions (6 oz)

Ingredient	U.S.	Metric	Method
Navy beans	2 lb	908 g	Combine in pot. Let rest overnight. Place
Beef stock	1½ gal	5.7 L	beans in large pot or steam kettle. Heat to
Red beans, dried	3 lb	1.4 kg	a boil. Reduce heat to a simmer. Simmer
Water	to cover	to cover	for 1 hour.
Olive oil	1 c	240 ml	Combine in food processor with metal
Parmesan cheese, grated	2 c	480 ml	blade. Process until completely pureed.
Garlic, chopped	1 T	15 ml	Reserve.
Parsley, chopped	1 c	240 ml	
Basil, fresh, chopped	1 c	240 ml	
Onion, diced	2 c	480 ml	Add to beans. Continue to simmer until
Carrots, diced	2 c	480 ml	beans are tender, about 30 to 45 minutes.
Celery, diced	2 c	480 ml	
Potatoes, diced	1 qt	950 ml	
Tomatoes, seeded, diced	1 qt	950 ml	
Green beans, sliced	1 lb	454 g	Add to mixture. Simmer until all
Zucchini, diced	1 lb	454 g	vegetables are tender, and macaroni is
Macaroni	1 lb	454 g	cooked, about 20 minutes. Add reserved
			herb-cheese mixture. Stir well. Serve hot.

Nutrient Analysis				
Per Serving	Calories	160	Protein	7.8 gm
	Fat	6.7 gm	Carbohydrate	17.6 gm
	Cholesterol	11 mg	Calcium	116 mg
	Sodium	508 mg	Fiber	0.9 gm

▲ Squash Bisque with Ginger

Serve this southern American soup with bread sticks.

Menu Category:	Soup, Appetizer, American Regional
Cooking Method:	Sauté/Simmer
Preparation Time:	20 minutes
Cooking Time:	30 minutes
Variations:	Substitute zucchini, pumpkin, or other squash.
Yield:	50 portions (5 oz)

Ingredient	U.S.	Metric	Method
Butter, melted	1 c	240 ml	Sauté in heavy pot or steam kettle until onions just begin to turn golden.
Onion, chopped	1 qt	950 ml	
Gingerroot, minced	½ c	120 ml	
Chicken stock	3 qt	2.8 L	Add to onions. Heat to boiling. Reduce heat to a simmer. Simmer, covered, until vegetables are tender. Puree in batches. Return puree to pot.
Potatoes, sliced	3 c	720 ml	
Carrots, sliced	2 c	480 ml	
Yellow squash, sliced	2 qt	1.9 L	
Cayenne pepper	1 t	5 ml	
Salt	2 T	30 ml	
White pepper	2 t	10 ml	
Heavy cream	3 c	720 ml	Add to soup. Heat just to a simmer. Simmer for 5 minutes.

Nutrient Analysis Per Serving				
	Calories	117	Protein	2.2 gm
	Fat	9.5 gm	Carbohydrate	6.4 gm
	Cholesterol	30 mg	Calcium	27.4 mg
	Sodium	488 mg	Fiber	0.4 gm

▲ Tortilla Soup Monterey

This version uses chicken stock instead of the more traditional beef stock.

Menu Category:	Soup, Appetizer, Ethnic, Mexican
Cooking Method:	Sauté/Simmer
Preparation Time:	30 minutes
Cooking Time:	1½ hours
Variations:	Add diced chicken, pork, turkey, or beef and use appropriate stock. Garnish each portion with lime wedges.
Yield:	50 portions (4 oz)

Ingredient	U.S.	Metric	Method
Olive oil	1 c	240 ml	Sauté in large pot or steam kettle until
Onion, minced	1 qt	950 ml	vegetables are just tender, about 5
Garlic, minced	1 T	15 ml	minutes.
Green chilies, chopped, drained	2 c	480 ml	
Cumin, ground	1 T	15 ml	
Chili powder	2 T	30 ml	
Tomatoes, chopped, drained	1 qt	950 ml	Add to vegetables. Heat to a boil. Reduce heat to a simmer. Simmer for about 1 hour.
Chicken stock	3 qt	2.8 L	
Worcestershire sauce	¼ c	60 ml	
Salt	1 T	15 ml	
Black pepper	2 t	10 ml	
Corn tortillas, thinly sliced	1 qt	950 ml	Add. Simmer 10 more minutes.
Cheddar cheese, grated	2 c	480 ml	

Nutrient Analysis	Calories	119	Protein	4.1 gm
Per Serving	Fat	7 gm	Carbohydrate	10.9 gm
	Cholesterol	4.8 mg	Calcium	74.7 mg
	Sodium	460 mg	Fiber	0.5 gm

▲ Wisconsin Cheese Soup

Serve this satisfying soup with melba toasts or grilled bratwurst sandwiches.

Menu Category:	Soup, Appetizer, American Regional
Cooking Method:	Simmer
Preparation Time:	15 minutes
Cooking Time:	1 hour
Variations:	Experiment with varieties of cheese.
	Substitute dry white wine for the beer. Garnish with popcorn.
Yield:	50 portions (4 oz)

Ingredient	U.S.	Metric	Method
Butter, melted	4 oz	114 g	Sauté in stockpot, steam kettle, or brazier.
Onion, finely chopped	2 c	480 ml	Cook just until vegetables are tender,
Celery, finely chopped	1 c	240 ml	about 15 to 20 minutes.
Carrots, finely chopped	1 c	240 ml	
Scallions, finely chopped	1 c	240 ml	
Thyme, dried	1 t	240 ml	
		5 ml	
Flour	1 c	240 ml	Add to vegetables. Stir gently over medium heat until roux darkens slightly, about 5 minutes.
Chicken stock	3 qt	2.8 L	Add to vegetable mixture. Stir well. Simmer gently for 15 minutes, stirring frequently.
Cheddar Cheese, grated	2 lb	908 g	Add to soup. Simmer gently 30 minutes.
Beer, gently heated	1 qt	950 ml	
Cayenne pepper	2 t	10 ml	

Nutrient Analysis	Calories	120	Protein	6.3 gm
Per Serving	Fat	8.3 gm	Carbohydrate	4 gm
	Cholesterol	24.1 mg	Calcium	142 mg
	Sodium	321 mg	Fiber	0.2 gm

Salads and Salad Dressings

Vegetable and Legume Salads

▲ Spiced Black Bean Salad

Serve this salad with Mexican or Caribbean dishes.

Menu Category:	Salad, Ethnic
Cooking Method:	None required
Preparation Time:	30 minutes
Variations:	Substitute other beans, lentils, or black-eyed peas.
Yield:	50 servings (4 oz)

Ingredient	U.S.	Metric	Method
Black beans, canned	1 gal	3.8 L	Drain beans in colander. Rinse and drain well. Transfer to large bowl.
Commercial picante sauce, hot	1 qt	950 ml	Add to beans. Toss well to combine.
Sweet onion, minced	2 c	480 ml	
Tomato, seeded, minced	2 c	480 ml	
Green pepper, minced	2 c	480 ml	
Celery, minced	2 c	480 ml	
Jalapeño pepper, minced	½ c	120 ml	
Lime juice	½ c	120 ml	
Commercial vinaigrette dressing	1 qt	950 ml	Combine in mixer bowl with whip attachment. Whip well. Transfer to bean mixture. Toss gently but completely. Transfer to storage container. Cover. Chill well.
Garlic, minced	1 T	15 ml	
Cilantro, chopped	½ c	120 ml	
Cumin, ground	1 T	15 ml	

Nutrient Analysis	Calories	126	Protein	55 gm
Per Serving	Fat	4.4 gm	Carbohydrate	17.5 gm
	Cholesterol	0 mg	Calcium	27.8 mg
	Sodium	228 mg	Fiber	1.3 gm

▲ Fiesta Hot Three Bean Salad

This is a zesty variation of a universally popular salad.

Menu Category:	Salad, Ethnic
Cooking Method:	Steam
Preparation Time:	10 minutes
Cooking Time:	5 minutes
Variations:	For an Oriental version, substitute soy sauce and ginger for the cumin, chili powder, and cilantro. Omit tortilla chips.
Yield:	50 portions (4 oz)

Ingredient	U.S.	Metric	Method
Commercial picante sauce	2 gal	7.6 L	Combine in mixer bowl with whip attachment. Whip at high speed to mix well.
Garlic powder	2 T	30 ml	
Parsley, chopped	2 c	480 ml	
Cilantro, chopped	1 T	15 ml	
Cumin, ground	1 T	15 ml	
Chili powder	2 T	30 ml	
Red wine vinegar	2 c	480 ml	Add to mixture. Mix well.
Olive oil	1 qt	950 ml	Add gradually. Reserve at room temperature.
Green beans, drained	4 lb	1.8 kg	Combine in large bowl. Mix well. Place in steamer tray. Steam just until well heated. Pour into large bowl. Add the picante mixture. Toss well. Serve with slotted spoon. Serve hot.
Yellow beans, drained	4 lb	1.8 kg	
Kidney beans, drained	4 lb	1.8 kg	
Tortilla chips	3 c	720 ml	Crumble chips and sprinkle on each serving.

Nutrient Analysis	Calories	224	Protein	6.9 gm
Per Serving	Fat	13.7 gm	Carbohydrate	23.3 gm
	Cholesterol	0 mg	Calcium	58 mg
	Sodium	859 mg	Fiber	0.1 gm

▲ Green Beans with Dill and Garlic Vinaigrette

Serve this salad any time of year, with almost any menu.

Menu Category:	Salad
Cooking Method:	None required
Preparation Time:	30 minutes
Marination Time:	Several hours
Variations:	Substitute raw sliced zucchini or steamed broccoli florets.
Yield:	50 servings (4 oz)

Ingredient	U.S.	Metric	Method
Green beans, canned, drained	1½ gal	5.7 L	Combine in large bowl. Toss well.
Dill seed	1 T	15 ml	
Sugar	1 c	480 ml	
Commercial vinaigrette dressing	1 qt	950 ml	Combine in mixer bowl with whip attachment. Whip well. Add to bean mixture. Toss gently but completely. Transfer to storage container. Cover. Chill well.
Garlic, minced	1 T	15 ml	
Parsley, chopped	½ c	120 ml	
Pimentos, minced	2 c	480 ml	

Nutrient Analysis Per Serving	Calories	65	Protein	1 gm
	Fat	4 gm	Carbohydrate	7.7 gm
	Cholesterol	0 mg	Calcium	21 mg
	Sodium	183 mg	Fiber	0.6 gm

▲ Herbed Broccoli with Mixed Peppers

Serve as an appetizer, on the salad bar, or as an antipasto offering.

Menu Category:	Salad, Appetizer, Ethnic, Italian
Cooking Method:	None required
Preparation Time:	30 minutes
Variations:	Substitute cauliflower or green beans.
	Add toasted pine nuts.
Yield:	50 portions (4 oz)

Ingredient	U.S.	Metric	Method
Broccoli florets	1 gal	3.8 L	Combine in large bowl.
Zucchini, diced	1 qt	950 ml	
Red bell pepper, diced	1 qt	950 ml	
Green bell pepper, diced	1 qt	950 ml	
Sweet onion, minced	2 c	480 ml	
Carrot, julienne	2 c	480 ml	
Light Vinaigrette Dressing, p. 304	1½ qt	1.4 L	Add to vegetables. Toss gently but completely. Transfer to storage containers. Cover. Chill well.

Nutrient Analysis Per Serving	Calories	88	Protein	6.5 gm
	Fat	2.8 gm	Carbohydrate	10.6 gm
	Cholesterol	12.8 mg	Calcium	23 mg
	Sodium	252 mg	Fiber	0.7 gm

▲ Indian-Style Coleslaw with Orange Mayonnaise

This version features sweet curried orange mayonnaise and golden raisins.

Menu Category:	Salad, Appetizer, Ethnic, Indian
Cooking Method:	None required
Preparation Time:	30 minutes
Variations:	Substitute plain yogurt for mayonnaise.
Yield:	50 portions (4 oz)

Ingredient	U.S.	Metric	Method
Cabbage, shredded	10 lb	4.5 kg	Combine in a large bowl.
Carrots, julienne	1 qt	950 ml	
Golden raisins	1 qt	950 ml	
Mayonnaise, cholesterol-free	3 qt	2.8 L	Combine in medium bowl. Whip well. Add to cabbage mixture. Stir well. Transfer to storage containers. Cover. Chill well.
Orange juice	2 c	480 ml	
Curry powder	½ c	120 ml	
Sugar	3 c	720 ml	

Nutrient Analysis Per Serving				
	Calories	296	Protein	1.8 gm
	Fat	20.4 gm	Carbohydrate	29.3 gm
	Cholesterol	0 mg	Calcium	57.6 mg
	Sodium	172 mg	Fiber	1.2 gm

▲ Catalanian Tomato Salad with Lentils and Olives

Serve as a salad, a Spanish tapas appetizer, or a vegetarian entrée.

Menu Category:	Salad, Appetizer, Entrée, Ethnic, Spanish
Cooking Method:	Simmer
Preparation Time:	30 minutes
Cooking Time:	15 minutes
Variations:	Add chopped grilled shrimp to chilled salad.
	Substitute chopped fresh mint for parsley.
	Serve in lettuce cups or in endive spears.
Yield:	50 portions (4 oz)

Ingredient	U.S.	Metric	Method
Lentils, red	2 qt	1.9 L	Combine in large pot or steam kettle. Heat
Water, cold	1½ gal	5.7 L	to a boil. Reduce heat to a simmer. Simmer just until lentils are tender, about 15 minutes. Drain off all cooking liquid. Transfer lentils to a large bowl.
Tomatoes, minced	1 qt	950 ml	Add to lentils. Cover. Chill well.
Pimentos, minced	2 c	480 ml	
Egg, hard-cooked, chopped	2 c	480 ml	
Black olives, sliced	2 c	480 ml	
Parsley, chopped	1 c	240 ml	
Scallions, minced	2 c	480 ml	
Cilantro, chopped	1 c	240 ml	
Red wine vinegar	½ c	120 ml	Whip together until well blended.
Dry mustard	2 T	30 ml	
Olive oil	2 c	480 ml	Add to vinegar. Mix. Pour over lentil and tomato mixture. Toss gently but well.

Nutrient Analysis	Calories	149	Protein	5 gm
Per Serving	Fat	11 gm	Carbohydrate	9.4 gm
	Cholesterol	39 mg	Calcium	38 mg
	Sodium	126 mg	Fiber	1.1 gm

▲ Green Lentil Salad with Red Wine Vinaigrette

This Mediterranean salad is great with grilled chicken or pork

Menu Category:	Salad, Appetizer, Ethnic, Mediterranean
Cooking Method:	Simmer
Preparation Time:	30 minutes
Cooking Time:	15 minutes
Variations:	Try this with black beans, adding a bit more "bite" with minced jalapeños.
Yield:	50 portions (4 oz)

Ingredient	U.S.	Metric	Method
Green lentils	4 lb	1.8 kg	Combine in large pot or steam kettle. Heat
Water	2 gal	7.6 L	to a boil. Reduce heat to a simmer. Simmer
Bay leaves	3	3	just until lentils are tender, about 15
Cloves, ground	½ t	3 ml	minutes. Drain off all cooking liquid.
Cinnamon, ground	1 t	5 ml	Transfer lentils to a large bowl. Discard
Crushed red pepper	2 t	10 ml	bay leaves.
Green bell pepper, minced	3 c	720 ml	Add to lentils. Mix gently but completely.
Red bell pepper, minced	3 c	720 ml	Adjust seasoning. Transfer to storage
Sweet onion, minced	2 c	480 ml	container. Cover. Chill well.
Celery, minced	2 c	480 ml	
Tomatoes, seeded, diced	1 qt	950 ml	
Parsley, chopped	2 c	480 ml	
Cilantro, chopped	1 c	240 ml	
Red Wine Vinaigrette Salad Dressing, p. 307	2 qt	1.9 L	

Nutrient Analysis Per Serving					
	Calories	134	Protein	4.3 gm
	Fat	8 gm	Carbohydrate	15 gm
	Cholesterol	0 mg	Calcium	29 mg
	Sodium	177 mg	Fiber	1.5 gm

▲ Mediterranean Lentil Salad with Grilled Peppers

Serve as a vegetarian entrée or as a side dish with grilled meat or poultry.

Menu Category:	Salad, Appetizer, Side, Vegetarian Entrée, Ethnic, Mediterranean
Cooking Method:	Simmer
Preparation Time:	15 minutes
Cooking Time:	30 minutes
Variations:	Substitute cooked and drained black-eyed peas for lentils.
Yield:	50 portions (4 oz)

Ingredient	U.S.	Metric	Method
Lentils, brown	1 qt	950 ml	Combine in large pot or steam kettle. Heat to a boil. Reduce heat to a simmer. Simmer just until lentils are tender, about 15 minutes. Drain off all cooking liquid. Transfer lentils to a large bowl.
Chicken stock	3 qt	2.8 L	
Green bell peppers	3 lb	1.4 kg	Roast peppers under boiler or over grill just until skin is well charred. Cool. Remove skin. Cut peppers into small dice. Add to lentils.
Tomatoes, seeded, diced	3 lb	1.4 kg	Add to lentils. Mix well.
Cucumber, seeded, diced	1 lb	454 gm	
Jalapeño pepper, minced	2 T	30 ml	
Yogurt Vinaigrette with Cumin and Cilantro, p. 310	1 qt	950 ml	Add to lentils. Mix well. Cover. Chill well.
Parsley, chopped	½ c	120 ml	Add just before service. Mix well.
Cilantro, chopped	½ c	120 ml	

Nutrient Analysis Per Serving				
	Calories	187	Protein	14.2 gm
	Fat	10 gm	Carbohydrate	10.9 gm
	Cholesterol	34 mg	Calcium	33.6 mg
	Sodium	372 mg	Fiber	0.9 gm

▲ Mediterranean New Potato Salad

Serve this zesty salad as an antipasto appetizer or on your daily salad bar.

Menu Category:	Salad, Appetizer, Ethnic, Italian
Cooking Method:	Simmer
Preparation Time:	30 minutes
Cooking Time:	20 minutes
Variations:	Add shrimp, chicken, turkey, or pork.
	Substitute curry for cumin.
Yield:	50 portions (4 oz)

Ingredient	U.S.	Metric	Method
New potatoes, halved	12 lb	5.5 kg	Cook over medium-high heat in a large pot
Water, boiling	as needed	as needed	or steam kettle just until tender, about 20
Salt	2 T	30 ml	minutes. Drain well. Cool. Transfer to a
			large bowl.
Yogurt, lowfat, plain	1 qt	950 ml	Combine in mixer with whip attachment.
Olive oil	½ c	120 ml	Mix at low speed just to blend. Add to
Lemon juice	1 c	240 ml	potatoes. Toss gently but well. Transfer to
Cayenne pepper	2 t	10 ml	storage containers. Cover. Chill well.
Cumin, ground	½ c	120 ml	
Parsley, chopped	2 c	480 ml	

Nutrient Analysis	Calories	130	Protein	3.1 gm
Per Serving	Fat	2.8 gm	Carbohydrate	24 gm
	Cholesterol	1.4 mg	Calcium	56 mg
	Sodium	22.9 mg	Fiber	0.6 gm

▲ Signature Potato Salad

Use this delightful version as a starting point for your own signature salad.

Menu Category:	Salad, Appetizer, American
Cooking Method:	None required
Preparation Time:	30 minutes
Variations:	The sky's the limit: Substitute freely with vegetables, salad dressing, herbs, and spices.
Yield:	50 portions (4 oz)

Ingredient	U.S.	Metric	Method
White potatoes, boiled, drained, peeled	8 lb	3.6 kg	Combine in large bowl. Mix gently but completely. Transfer to storage containers. Cover. Chill well.
Eggs, hard-cooked, chopped	8	8	
Celery, diced	2 qt	1.9 L	
Scallions, minced	2 c	480 ml	
Cucumbers, seeded, diced	1 qt	950 ml	
Mustard, Dijon style	2 T	30 ml	
Mayonnaise	1 qt	950 ml	
Green Goddess salad dressing	1 qt	950 ml	
Salt	2 T	30 ml	
White pepper	1 T	15 ml	

Nutrient Analysis Per Serving				
	Calories	234	Protein	2.9 gm
	Fat	17.9 gm	Carbohydrate	17 gm
	Cholesterol	44.3 mg	Calcium	31 mg
	Sodium	407 mg	Fiber	0.5 gm

▲ Sweet Potato Salad with Pineapple and Ginger

This salad has a definite tropical/Oriental flavor.

Menu Category:	Salad, Appetizer, Ethnic, Polynesian
Cooking Method:	Simmer
Preparation Time:	30 minutes
Cooking Time:	30 minutes
Variations:	Substitute an herbal vinaigrette for the Orange Yogurt Sauce.
Yield:	50 portions (4 oz)

Ingredient	U.S.	Metric	Method
Sweet potatoes, peeled, ½-inch dice	9 lb	4.1 kg	Cook at a rapid boil for 15 minutes or until tender. Drain potatoes and transfer to large bowl.
Water, boiling	as needed	as needed	
Salt	2 T	30 ml	
Orange Yogurt Sauce, p. 306	1 qt	950 ml	Combine in mixer with whip attachment. Mix at low speed just to blend. Add to potatoes. Mix gently but completely. Transfer to storage containers. Cover. Chill well.
Crystalized ginger, minced	1 c	240 ml	
Celery, minced	1 qt	950 ml	
Sweet onion, minced	2 c	480 ml	
Pecans, chopped	2 c	480 ml	
Golden raisins	2 c	480 ml	
Pineapple, crushed, drained	2 qt	1.9 L	

Nutrient Analysis	Calories	134	Protein	2.6 gm
Per Serving	Fat	4.2 gm	Carbohydrate	23.8 gm
	Cholesterol	0.2 gm	Calcium	48 mg
	Sodium	283 mg	Fiber	1.0 gm

MEAT Salads

▲ Mandarin Beef with Sesame-Mustard Dressing

Serve as an appetizer or entrée salad or as a sandwich filling.

Menu Category:	Salad, Appetizer, Entrée, Beef, Ethnic, Chinese
Cooking Method:	Grill/Broil
Preparation Time:	30 minutes
Marination Time:	Several hours
Cooking Time:	15 minutes
Variations:	Serve sliced grilled steak as an entrée, without the dressing.
Yield:	50 portions (6 oz)

Ingredient	U.S.	Metric	Method
Soy sauce	2 c	480 ml	Combine in small bowl. Mix well.
Brown sugar	2 c	480 ml	
Pineapple juice	2 c	480 ml	
Garlic, minced	¼ c	60 ml	
Gingerroot, minced	¼ c	60 ml	
Scallions, minced	1 c	240 ml	
Flank steak, lean	10 lb	4.5 kg	Place in shallow roasting pans. Cover with marinade. Cover and chill several hours, turning frequently. Remove from marinade. Grill/broil at medium-high heat for 6 minutes per side. Cool. Slice thinly on the bias.
Red onion, julienne	2 lb	908 g	Blanch onions for 1 minute. Drain well. Cool. Reserve.
Water, boiling	1 gal	3.8 L	
Cloves, whole	1 t	5 ml	
Cinnamon stick	1	1	
Leaf lettuce cups	50	50	Portion steak slices on lettuce leaves. Portion blanched onions on side.
Sesame-Mustard Salad Dressing, p. 309	3 qt	2.8 L	Portion over steak slices.

Nutrient Analysis Per Serving	Calories	391	Protein	29 gm
	Fat	23 gm	Carbohydrate	19 gm
	Cholesterol	60 mg	Calcium	43 mg
	Sodium	795 mg	Fiber	0.8 gm

▲ Thai Beef Salad

Serve as an appetizer or entrée salad or on grilled hamburger buns.

Menu Category:	Salad, Appetizer, Entrée, Meat, Ethnic, Oriental
Cooking Method:	None required
Preparation Time:	30 minutes
Variations:	Substitute sliced cooked chicken, shrimp, or pork.
Yield:	50 portions (4 oz)

Ingredient	U.S.	Metric	Method
Roast beef, 1″ × 4″ × ½″			Combine in large bowl.
slices	8 lb	3.6 kg	
Green beans, cooked	4 lb	1.8 kg	
Bean sprouts, drained	2 lb	908 g	
Soy sauce	2 c	480 ml	Combine in small bowl. Whip well. Add to
Lime juice	1 qt	950 ml	beef mixture. Toss well. Transfer to storage
Sugar	1 c	240 ml	containers. Cover. Chill well.
Salt	1 T	15 ml	
Garlic, minced	2 T	30 ml	
Jalapeño pepper, minced	1 c	240 ml	
Mint, chopped	2 c	480 ml	

Nutrient Analysis	Calories	211	Protein	21.2 gm
Per Serving	Fat	10.2 gm	Carbohydrate	8.8 gm
	Cholesterol	58.8 mg	Calcium	29.2 mg
	Sodium	983 mg	Fiber	0.5 gm

▲ Venetian Pork Salad with Walnuts

Serve as a salad or light entrée.

Menu Category:	Salad, Appetizer, Entrée, Ethnic, Italian
Cooking Method:	None required
Preparation Time:	30 minutes
Variations:	Substitute cooked shrimp, chicken, or turkey.

Yield:	50 portions (4 oz)

Ingredient	U.S.	Metric	Method
Golden raisins	1 qt	950 ml	Combine in large bowl. Let rest until
Water, hot	1 gal	3.8 L	raisins soften and swell, about 1 hour. Drain well. Reserve raisins.
Red onion, julienne	3 lb	1.4 kg	Blanch onions for 1 minute. Drain well.
Water, boiling	1 gal	3.9 L	Cool. Add to reserved raisins.
Pork loin, cooked, julienne	7 lb	3.2 kg	Add to raisins and onions. Toss gently but
Celery, julienne	2 qt	1.9 L	well. Cover. Chill well.
Walnut pieces	1 qt	950 ml	
Commercial Italian salad dressing	3 qt	2.8 L	
Bibb lettuce cups	50	50	Arrange on service plates. Portion salad in center of each lettuce cup.

Nutrient Analysis Per Serving	Calories	333	Protein	13.3 gm
	Fat	24.8 gm	Carbohydrate	16.1 gm
	Cholesterol	33.6 mg	Calcium	43.3 mg
	Sodium	95 mg	Fiber	1.4 gm

Poultry Salads

▲ Arabian Nights Chicken Salad

Serve as a light entrée, sandwich filling, or hors d'oeuvre spread.

Menu Category:	Salad, Appetizer, Entrée, Sandwich
Cooking Method:	None required
Preparation Time:	30 minutes
Variations:	Substitute cooked turkey, pork, or shrimp.
	Grill chicken breasts and cut into 1″ × ½″ × 4″ strips.
Yield:	50 portions (4 oz)

Ingredient	U.S.	Metric	Method
Commercial IQF chicken fajita strips, fully cooked, thawed, diced	7 lb	3.2 kg	Combine in large bowl. Reserve.
Green bell pepper, minced	1 qt	950 ml	
Red onion, minced	2 c	480 ml	
Lime juice	½ c	120 ml	
Parsley, chopped	1 c	240 ml	
Cilantro, chopped	1 c	240 ml	
Garlic, minced	1 t	15 ml	
Light Vinaigrette Dressing, p. 304	1 qt	950 ml	Combine in food processor with metal blade. Process until well blended. Add to chicken mixture. Stir well. Cover. Chill well.
Paprika	2 T	30 ml	
Cumin, ground	1 T	15 ml	
Cayenne pepper, ground	1 T	15 ml	
Lettuce cups	50	50	Portion salad. Serve cold.

Nutrient Analysis Per Serving				
	Calories	177	Protein	22 gm
	Fat	6.6 gm	Carbohydrate	6.5 gm
	Cholesterol	65 mg	Calcium	30.9 mg
	Sodium	200 mg	Fiber	0.6 gm

▲ Chicken Salad Bali Hai with Mango Chutney Dressing

Serve as an appetizer or entrée salad, as a sandwich filling, or as a topping for unique tortillas.

Menu Category:	Salad, Appetizer, Entrée, Sandwich, Poultry, Ethnic, Polynesian
Cooking Method:	None required
Preparation Time:	30 minutes
Variations:	Substitute diced cooked shrimp, turkey, or roast pork.
	Garnish with lime slices or wedges.
Yield:	50 portions (6 oz)

Ingredient	U.S.	Metric	Method
Yogurt, lowfat, plain	3 qt	2.8 L	Combine in mixer bowl with whip attachment. Mix well. Cover. Chill well.
Mango chutney, chopped finely	2 c	480 ml	
Brown sugar	1 c	240 ml	
Lemon juice	¼ c	60 ml	
Orange juice	1 c	240 ml	
Ginger, ground	1 T	15 ml	
Cinnamon, ground	1 t	5 ml	
Chicken, cooked, diced	10 lb	4.5 kg	Combine in large bowl. Add reserved dressing. Toss gently but well.
Green grapes, split	1 qt	950 ml	
Mandarin orange sections	1 qt	950 ml	
Spinach, fresh, chopped	5 lb	2.3 kg	Arrange on service plates. Portion salad on top of spinach.
Slivered almonds, toasted	1 qt	950 ml	Sprinkle over each portion.

Nutrient Analysis Per Serving				
	Calories	243	Protein	27 gm
	Fat	7.6 gm	Carbohydrate	16.5 gm
	Cholesterol	64 mg	Calcium	147 mg
	Sodium	113 mg	Fiber	0.6 gm

▲ Chicken Salad Bombay with Curry and White Grapes

Serve as an appetizer or entrée salad or as a pita sandwich filling.

Menu Category:	Salad, Appetizer, Entrée, Sandwich, Poultry, Ethnic, Indian
Cooking Method:	None required
Preparation Time:	30 minutes
Variations:	Substitute diced cooked turkey, pork, or shrimp.
Yield:	50 portions (5 oz)

Ingredient	U.S.	Metric	Method
Chicken, diced	10 lb	4.5 kg	Combine in large bowl. Toss gently but well.
Celery, minced	1 qt	950 ml	
Red onion, minced	½ c	120 ml	
White grapes, split, seeded	2 qt	1.9 L	
Sour cream	3 c	720 ml	Combine in mixer bowl with whip attachment. Mix well. Add to chicken mixture. Toss gently but completely. Cover. Chill well.
Mayonnaise	3 c	720 ml	
Cider vinegar	1 c	240 ml	
Curry powder	3 T	45 ml	
White pepper	2 t	10 ml	
Salt	2 t	10 ml	

Nutrient Analysis per Serving				
	Calories	307	Protein	31 gm
	Fat	18 gm	Carbohydrate	5 gm
	Cholesterol	96 mg	Calcium	43 mg
	Sodium	241 mg	Fiber	0.2 gm

▲ Grilled Chicken Salad with Chopped Pecans

Serve as an appetizer or entrée salad or as a sandwich filling.

Menu Category:	Salad, Appetizer, Entrée, Sandwich, Poultry, Ethnic, Mexican
Cooking Method:	None required
Preparation Time:	30 minutes
Variations:	Substitute diced cooked turkey, pork, or shrimp.
	Garnish with lime slices and a sprinkle of chili powder.
Yield:	50 portions (5 oz)

Ingredient	U.S.	Metric	Method
Chicken, grilled, cold, diced	10 lb	4.5 kg	Combine in large bowl. Toss gently but
Celery, minced	1 qt	950 ml	well.
Scallion greens, minced	2 c	480 ml	
Pecans, toasted, chopped	1 qt	950 ml	
Sour cream	1 qt	950 ml	Combine in mixer bowl with whip
Mayonnaise	1 qt	950 ml	attachment. Mix well. Add to chicken
Cider vinegar	1 c	240 ml	mixture. Toss gently but completely. Cover
Chili powder	2 T	30 ml	and chill completely.
White pepper	1 t	5 ml	
Salt	2 t	10 ml	
Leaf lettuce cups	50	50	Portion chicken mixture into lettuce cups.

Nutrient Analysis	Calories	398	Protein	32 gm
Per Serving	Fat	28 gm	Carbohydrate	4.6 gm
	Cholesterol	101 mg	Calcium	54 mg
	Sodium	271 mg	Fiber	0.3 gm

▲ Mexican Fiesta Chicken Salad

Serve as an appetizer or entrée salad, a sandwich filling, or an unusual tortilla topping.

Menu Category:	Salad, Appetizer, Entrée, Sandwich, Poultry, Ethnic, Mexican
Cooking Method:	None required
Preparation Time:	30 minutes
Variations:	Substitute diced cooked shrimp.
Yield:	50 portions (5 oz)

Ingredient	U.S.	Metric	Method
Chicken, cooked, diced	10 lb	4.5 kg	Combine in large bowl. Toss gently but well.
Chick-peas, drained	1 qt	950 ml	
Green bell pepper, julienne	1 qt	950 ml	
Celery, julienne	1 qt	950 ml	
Jicama, julienne	1 qt	950 ml	
Red onion, julienne	1 c	240 ml	
Sour cream	1 qt	950 ml	Combine in mixer bowl with whip attachment. Whip well. Pour over chicken mixture. Toss well to combine. Cover. Chill well.
Chili powder	1 c	240 ml	
Cumin, ground	2 T	30 ml	
Jalapeño pepper, minced	2 T	30 ml	
Red wine vinegar	½ c	120 ml	
Salt	1 T	15 ml	
Black pepper	2 t	10 ml	
Leaf lettuce cups	50	50	Portion chicken mixture into lettuce.

Nutrient Analysis	Calories	245	Protein	32.5 gm
Per Serving	Fat	8.8 gm	Carbohydrate	8.6 gm
	Cholesterol	90.4 mg	Calcium	55 mg
	Sodium	176 mg	Fiber	1.1 gm

▲ Southwestern Duck Salad with Melon and Pecans

Serve as an entrée or appetizer salad in Bibb lettuce cups.

Menu Category:	Salad, Appetizer, Entrée, Poultry, American Regional	
Cooking Method:	None required	
Preparation Time:	30 minutes	
Variations:	Substitute diced cooked chicken, turkey, pork, or shrimp.	
Yield:	50 portions (5 oz)	

Ingredient	U.S.	Metric	Method
Duck breast, cooked, skinned, diced	8 lb	3.6 kg	Combine in large bowl. Toss well to combine.
Honeydew melon, diced	2 qt	1.9 L	
Cantaloupe, diced	2 qt	1.9 L	
Lime juice	2 c	480 ml	
Avocado puree	1½ qt	1.4 L	Combine in mixer bowl with whip attachment. Blend well. Pour over duck mixture.
Sour cream	1½ qt	1.4 L	
Mayonnaise	3 c	720 ml	
Garlic, minced	1 T	15 ml	
Chili powder	½ c	120 ml	
Cayenne pepper	1 T	15 ml	
Salt	1 T	15 ml	
Pecans, toasted, chopped	1 qt	950 ml	Add to mixture. Fold gently but completely.
Bibb lettuce cups	50	50	Portion duck mixture into lettuce cups.

Nutrient Analysis Per Serving				
	Calories	374	Protein	17.3 gm
	Fat	30.3 gm	Carbohydrate	11.2 gm
	Cholesterol	20 mg	Calcium	53.4 mg
	Sodium	283 mg	Fiber	1.3 gm

▲ Granny Smith's Turkey Salad

Serve as an entrée salad or as a topping for toasted English muffins.

Menu Category:	Salad, Appetizer, Entrée, Poultry, American Regional
Cooking Method:	None required
Preparation Time:	30 minutes
Variations:	Substitute diced cooked chicken, pork, or shrimp.
	Any sweet, firm apple can be used, but then change the menu name.
Yield:	50 portions (6 oz)

Ingredient	U.S.	Metric	Method
Turkey, cooked and diced	10 lb	4.5 kg	Combine in large bowl. Toss gently but well.
Celery, minced	1 qt	950 ml	
Granny Smith apples, cored, peeled, diced	1 gal	3.8 L	
Walnuts, chopped	2 c	480 ml	
Dates, chopped	2 c	480 ml	
Yogurt, lowfat, plain	2 qt	1.9 L	Combine in mixer bowl with whip attachment. Mix well. Add to turkey mixture. Toss gently but completely. Cover. Chill well.
Mayonnaise	1 qt	950 ml	
Honey	1 c	240 ml	
Cinnamon, ground	1 t	5 ml	
White pepper	2 t	10 ml	
Salt	2 t	10 ml	

Nutrient Analysis Per Serving				
	Calories	289	Protein	22.8 gm
	Fat	14.3 gm	Carbohydrate	18.4 gm
	Cholesterol	68 mg	Calcium	53.7 mg
	Sodium	188 mg	Fiber	0.7 gm

▲ Moroccan-Style Turkey Salad

Serve as an appetizer or entrée salad or as a pita-pocket sandwich filling.

Menu Category:	Salad, Appetizer, Entrée, Sandwich, Poultry, Ethnic, Mediterranean
Cooking Method:	None required
Preparation Time:	30 minutes
Variations:	Substitute julienne cooked chicken, shrimp, or pork.
Yield:	50 portions (5 oz)

Ingredient	U.S.	Metric	Method
Red onion, julienne	1 qt	950 ml	Blanch onions for 1 minute. Drain well.
Water, boiling	1 gal	3.8 L	Cool. Place in large bowl.
Turkey, cooked, julienne	10 lb	4.5 kg	Add to onions. Mix well.
Bell pepper, julienne	1 qt	950 ml	
Parsley, chopped	¼ c	60 ml	
Red wine vinegar	1 c	240 ml	Combine in mixer bowl with whip
Lemon juice	1 c	240 ml	attachment. Mix at high speed to blend
Paprika	2 T	30 ml	well.
Cayenne pepper	2 t	10 ml	
Cumin, ground	2 T	30 ml	
Salt	2 t	10 ml	
Black pepper	2 t	10 ml	
Olive oil	1½ qt	1.4 L	Add gradually to vinegar mixture. Whip until thickened. Add to turkey mixture. Toss well to combine. Cover. Chill well.
Leaf lettuce cups	50	50	Arrange on service plates. Portion salad in center.
Black olives, sliced	1 qt	950 ml	Garnish center of each salad.

Nutrient Analysis Per Serving				
	Calories	394	Protein	28.1 gm
	Fat	28.8 gm	Carbohydrate	6.4 gm
	Cholesterol	75.3 mg	Calcium	35 mg
	Sodium	270 mg	Fiber	0.3 gm

▲ Smoked Turkey Salad Calypso

Serve as a Caribbean appetizer or entrée salad.

Menu Category:	Salad, Appetizer, Entrée, Poultry, Ethnic, Caribbean
Cooking Method:	None required
Preparation Time:	30 minutes
Variations:	Substitute sliced cooked chicken, shrimp, or pork.
Yield:	50 portions (5 oz)

Ingredient	U.S.	Metric	Method
Brown sugar	2 c	480 ml	Combine in mixer bowl with whip
Curry powder	½ c	120 ml	attachment. Mix well to blend. Cover.
Yogurt, lowfat, plain	2 qt	1.9 L	Chill well.
Lemon juice	½ c	120 ml	
White grapes, sliced	1 qt	950 ml	
Smoked turkey slices, thin	100	100	Wrap turkey slice around papaya slice.
Papaya slices, thin	100	100	Secure with frilly toothpicks. Place two rolls on each service plate.
Pineapple slices	50	50	Arrange on service plates around turkey
Pear slices	50	50	rolls. Spoon curry dressing over each
Strawberries	50	50	turkey roll.
Lime juice	1 c	240 ml	Sprinkle over fruit slices.

Nutrient Analysis	Calories	162	Protein	7.6 gm
Per Serving	Fat	4.1 gm	Carbohydrate	26.1 gm
	Cholesterol	2.2 mg	Calcium	135 mg
	Sodium	313 mg	Fiber	1.1 gm

▲ Smoked Turkey Salad with Honey and Soy Sauce

Serve as a lowfat entrée or appetizer salad or as filling for sandwiches.

Menu Category:	Salad, Appetizer, Entrée, Sandwich, Poultry
Cooking Method:	None required
Preparation Time:	30 minutes
Variations:	Substitute diced cooked chicken, pork, or shrimp.
Yield:	50 portions (6 oz)

Ingredient	U.S.	Metric	Method
Turkey, cooked and diced	8 lb	3.6 kg	Combine in large bowl. Toss gently but well.
Celery, julienne	2 qt	1.9 L	
Carrot, julienne	2 qt	1.9 L	
Green pepper, julienne	1 qt	950 ml	
Orange zest, blanched	1 c	240 ml	
Orange juice	3 qt	2.8 L	Combine in mixer bowl with whip attachment. Whip to combine well. Add to turkey mixture. Toss well. Chill well.
Rice wine vinegar	1 qt	950 ml	
Soy sauce	1 c	240 ml	
Honey	2 c	480 ml	
Cayenne pepper	2 t	10 ml	

Nutrient Analysis Per Serving				
	Calories	193	Protein	23.3 gm
	Fat	0.8 gm	Carbohydrate	24.2 gm
	Cholesterol	60.2 mg	Calcium	33.5 mg
	Sodium	440 mg	Fiber	0.5 gm

▲ Turkey Salad with Wild Rice and Mandarin Orange

Serve as an appetizer or entrée salad.

Menu Category:	Salad, Appetizer, Entrée, Poultry, American Regional
Cooking Method:	None required
Preparation Time:	30 minutes
Variations:	Substitute smoked chicken or pork.
Yield:	50 portions (6 oz)

Ingredient	U.S.	Metric	Method
Turkey, cooked, diced	8 lb	3.6 kg	Combine in a large bowl.
Wild rice, cooked, cold	2 qt	1.9 L	
Green bell pepper, minced	2 c	480 ml	
Red bell pepper, minced	2 c	480 ml	
Scallions, minced	2 c	480 ml	
Mandarin orange sections	1 qt	950 ml	
Water chestnuts, diced	2 c	480 ml	
Pine nuts, toasted	2 c	480 ml	
Commercial Italian salad dressing	2 qt	1.9 L	Add to mixture. Toss gently but completely. Cover. Chill well.

Nutrient Analysis				
Nutrient Analysis	Calories	283	Protein	24.8 gm
Per Serving	Fat	11 gm	Carbohydrate	20.8 gm
	Cholesterol	60.2 mg	Calcium	31 mg
	Sodium	143 mg	Fiber	0.5 gm

Seafood Salads

▲ Chilled Shrimp with Rotini and Olives

Serve with breadsticks.

Menu Category:	Salad, Appetizer, Entrée, Ethnic, French
Cooking Method:	None required
Preparation Time:	30 minutes
Variations:	Substitute cooked chicken, turkey, or pork.
Yield:	50 portions (5 oz)

Ingredient	U.S.	Metric	Method
Shrimp, cooked, peeled, diced	10 lb	4.5 kg	Combine in large bowl. Mix well.
Lowfat yogurt, plain	3 qt	2.8 L	
Tri-color pasta swirls, cooked	2 gal	7.6 L	
Red onion, minced	1½ c	360 ml	
Celery, minced	1 qt	950 ml	
Sugar	1½ c	360 ml	Combine in bowl. Mix well. Add to shrimp mixture. Toss well. Cover. Chill completely.
Water	1 c	240 ml	
Commercial Italian dressing	2 qt	1.9 L	
Lemon juice	½ c	120 ml	
Dill, dried	2 T	30 ml	
Salt	1 T	15 ml	
Black pepper	1 T	15 ml	
Red leaf lettuce cups	50	50	Portion salad into lettuce cups.
Pine nuts, toasted	1 c	240 ml	Sprinkle on top.

Nutrient Analysis Per Serving	Calories	466	Protein	23 gm
	Fat	22 gm	Carbohydrate	43 gm
	Cholesterol	152 mg	Calcium	170 mg
	Sodium	1183 mg	Fiber	0.4 gm

▲ "Light Lunch" Warm Caribbean Shrimp Salad

Serve as a salad, a Caribbean appetizer, or a light seafood entrée.

Menu Category:	Salad, Appetizer, Entrée, Ethnic, Caribbean		
Cooking Method:	Sauté		
Preparation Time:	30 minutes		
Cooking Time:	15 minutes		
Variations:	Substitute grilled scallops for shrimp.		
	Add chopped cilantro or fresh mint.		
Yield:	50 portions (5 oz)		

Ingredient	U.S.	Metric	Method
Shrimp (10 to 15 per lb)	15 lb	6.8 kg	Peel, devein, and butterfly. Press flat.
Olive oil, hot	8 oz	227 g	Sauté shrimp in preheated brazier kettle until golden.
Green pepper, julienne	3 c	720 ml	Add to shrimp. Sauté just until tender.
Onion, julienne	3 c	720 ml	
Garlic, minced	¼ c	60 ml	
Curry powder	½ c	120 ml	Add. Stir well for one minute.
Cinnamon, ground	1 T	15 ml	
Clove, ground	½ t	3 ml	
Tequila, golden	6 oz	170 g	Add. Deglaze. Flambé until flames die.
Lime juice	½ c	120 ml	Add. Use spatula to mix well.
Curly endive	6	6	Portion leaf on one half of each plate. Arrange 3 shrimp at inside edge of endive. Portion julienne vegetables on top of endive.
Yogurt, tropical fruit flavor	2 qt	1.9 L	Portion 1½ oz. on side of shrimp.
Coconut, toasted	1 qt	950 ml	Sprinkle over each portion. Serve warm.

Nutrient Analysis Per Serving	Calories	305	Protein	30.4 gm
	Fat	4.6 gm	Carbohydrate	17.2 gm
	Cholesterol	212 mg	Calcium	144 mg
	Sodium	296 mg	Fiber	0.8 gm

▲ Paella Salad

Serve as an entrée or appetizer salad or as a filling for pita sandwiches.

Menu Category:	Salad, Appetizer, Entrée, Sandwich, Seafood, Ethnic, Mediterranean
Cooking Method:	None required
Preparation Time:	30 minutes
Variations:	Substitute shellfish varieties and/or add smoked turkey or pork.
Yield:	50 portions (5 oz)

Ingredient	U.S.	Metric	Method
Shrimp, small, peeled, cooked	3 lb	1.4 kg	Combine in a large bowl. Mix gently but well.
Scallops, cooked	3 lb	1.4 kg	
Chicken, cooked, diced	3 lb	1.4 kg	
Italian sausage, cooked, diced	1 lb	454 g	
Green peas, IQF, thawed	2 lb	908 g	
Rice, cooked	1 gal	3.8 L	
Olive oil	1 qt	950 ml	Combine in mixer bowl with whip attachment. Mix to blend well. Pour over salad ingredients. Toss gently but completely. Cover. Chill well.
Mustard, Dijon style	¼ c	60 ml	
Lemon juice	3 c	720 ml	
Garlic, minced	2 T	30 ml	
Crushed red pepper	2 t	10 ml	
Turmeric	2 t	10 ml	
Cinnamon, ground	1 t	5 ml	
Salt	1 T	15 ml	
White pepper	1 T	15 ml	

Nutrient Analysis Per Serving				
	Calories	400	Protein	25 gm
	Fat	23 gm	Carbohydrate	23 gm
	Cholesterol	89 mg	Calcium	69 gm
	Sodium	452 mg	Fiber	5 gm

▲ Warm Shrimp Salad with Sesame Vinaigrette

Serve as a salad or a light Oriental seafood entrée.

Menu Category:	Salad, Appetizer, Entrée, Ethnic, Oriental
Cooking Method:	Sauté
Preparation Time:	30 minutes
Cooking Time:	15 minutes
Variations:	Substitute diced grilled chicken.
	Add chopped cilantro or fresh mint.
Yield:	50 portions (5 oz)

Ingredient	U.S.	Metric	Method
Bean sprouts, rinsed	2 qt	1.9 L	Blanch for 1 minute. Drain. Reserve.
Water, boiling	1 gal	3.8 L	
Shrimp (10 to 15 per lb)	15 lb	6.8 kg	Peel, devein, and butterfly. Press flat.
Peanut oil, hot	8 oz	227 g	Sauté shrimp in preheated brazier kettle until golden. Remove shrimp with slotted spoon. Keep warm.
Scallions, shredded	1 qt	950 ml	Add to brazier. Stir-fry for 2 minutes. Add reserved bean sprouts. Stir-fry 1 minute.
Garlic, minced	½ c	120 ml	
Ginger, minced	½ c	120 ml	
Sherry, dry	1 c	240 ml	Combine. Mix well. Add scallion mixture and reserved shrimp. Toss well to heat.
Rice wine vinegar	2 c	480 ml	
Sesame oil	1 c	240 ml	
Hot pepper oil	¼ c	60 ml	
Leaf lettuce cups	50	50	Line service plates. Portion shrimp salad in center. Serve warm.

Nutrient Analysis	Calories	234	Protein	29.4 gm
Per Serving	Fat	9.4 gm	Carbohydrate	5.8 gm
	Cholesterol	210 mg	Calcium	93.4 mg
	Sodium	221 mg	Fiber	0.6 gm

▲ Provençale-Style Salade Nicoise

Serve as a salad or light seafood entrée.

Menu Category:	Salad, Appetizer, Entrée, Ethnic, French		
Cooking Method:	Blanching		
Preparation Time:	30 minutes		
Variations:	Substitute cooked shrimp, chicken, turkey, or pork.		
Yield:	50 portions (6 oz)		

Ingredient	U.S.	Metric	Method
Red onion, julienne	5 lb	2.3 kg	Blanch onions for 1 minute. Drain well.
Water, boiling	2 gal	7.6 L	Cool. Reserve.
Leaf lettuce cups	50	50	Arrange on service plates.
Tuna, chunk, waterpack, drained	6 lb	2.7 kg	Portion in sections on lettuce base, along with portion of blanched onions.
Red potatoes, cooked, sliced	6 lb	2.7 kg	
Green beans	6 lb	2.7 kg	
Eggs, hard-boiled, quartered	25	25	
Commercial French dressing	3 qt	2.8 L	Portion over all ingredients.
Capers, drained	2 c	480 ml	Sprinkle over salads.

Nutrient Analysis Per Serving	Calories	315	Protein	22.6 gm
	Fat	14.4 gm	Carbohydrate	23 gm
	Cholesterol	193 mg	Calcium	46 mg
	Sodium	662 mg	Fiber	1 gm

Salad Dressings

▲ Apple-Walnut Vinaigrette Dressing

Serve as tangy dressing on salads and sandwiches or use as a marinade for poultry and seafood.

Menu Category:	Salad Dressing, Marinade
Cooking Method:	None required
Preparation Time:	30 minutes
Yield:	1 gallon

Ingredient	U.S.	Metric	Method
Apple cider	1 c	240 ml	Combine in mixer bowl with whip attachment. Mix well.
Cider vinegar	1 qt	950 ml	
Mustard, Dijon style	1 c	240 ml	
Walnut oil	3 c	720 ml	Add slowly to vinegar mixture. Whip until well combined and thickened.
Olive oil	1½ qt	1.4 L	
Walnuts, toasted, chopped	2 c	480 ml	Add to dressing. Mix well. Cover and chill well.

Approximate	Calories	140	Protein	1.1 gm
Nutrient Analysis	Fat	15.4 gm	Carbohydrate	2.5 gm
Per Ounce	Cholesterol	0 mg	Calcium	4.4 mg
	Sodium	43 mg	Fiber	0.2 gm

▲ Light Vinaigrette Dressing

Serve as a healthful alternative to traditional dressings.

Menu Category:	Salad Dressing, Sauce, Marinade
Cooking Method:	None required
Preparation Time:	10 minutes
Variations:	Substitute fruit-flavored vinegar for balsamic.
	Substitute beef broth for chicken stock.
Yield:	1 gallon

Ingredient	U.S.	Metric	Method
Chicken broth	3 qt	2.8 L	Combine in food processor with metal
Balsamic vinegar	2 c	480 ml	blade. Process until well blended. Cover.
Olive oil	½ c	120 ml	Chill well. Mix well before serving.
Lemon juice	½ c	120 ml	
Orange juice	½ c	120 ml	
Garlic, minced	¼ c	60 ml	
Mustard, Dijon style	½ c	120 ml	

Approximate	Calories	49	Protein	4.8 gm
Nutrient Analysis	Fat	2.6 gm	Carbohydrate	1.2 gm
Per Ounce	Cholesterol	13.5 mg	Calcium	4.2 mg
	Sodium	122 mg	Fiber	0 gm

▲ Mexican Emperor French Dressing

Use as a dressing for Mexican or southwestern American salads and sandwiches.

Menu Category:	Salad Dressing, Ethnic, Mexican, American Regional
Cooking Method:	None required
Preparation Time:	10 minutes
Variations:	Add oregano and fennel seeds for an Italian version.
Yield:	1 gallon

Ingredient	U.S.	Metric	Method
Commercial picante sauce	2 qt	1.9 L	Combine in mixer bowl with whip attachment. Whip at high speed until well blended.
Red wine vinegar	2 c	480 ml	
Mustard, dry	¼ c	60 ml	
Parsley, chopped	1 c	240 ml	
Olive oil	1 qt	950 ml	Add gradually while mixer operates at high speed. Continue to add all the oil and whip until dressing thickens. Cover. Chill well. Mix well before serving.

Approximate	Calories	113	Protein	0.4 gm
Nutrient Analysis	Fat	12 gm	Carbohydrate	2.2 gm
Per Ounce	Cholesterol	0 mg	Calcium	7.1 mg
	Sodium	186 mg	Fiber	0.1 gm

▲ Orange Yogurt Sauce

Serve as a salad dressing or as a topping for grilled seafood and sandwiches.

Menu Category:	Salad Dressing, Marinade
Cooking Method:	None required
Preparation Time:	10 minutes
Variations:	Substitute lemon or lime yogurt.
	Serve with fruit salads.
Yield:	1 gallon

Ingredient	U.S.	Metric	Method
Yogurt, lowfat, plain	2½ qt	2.4 L	Combine in mixer bowl with whip
Orange juice	3 c	720 ml	attachment. Whip at high speed for 2
Orange marmalade	2 c	480 ml	minutes. Transfer to storage containers.
Lowfat oil	1 c	240 ml	Cover. Chill well.
Orange zest, blanched	1 c	240 ml	

Approximate				
Nutrient Analysis	Calories	35	Protein	0.9 gm
Per Ounce	Fat	1.5 gm	Carbohydrate	4.8 gm
	Cholesterol	0.3 mg	Calcium	32.5 mg
	Sodium	12.1 mg	Fiber	0.1 gm

▲ Red Wine Vinaigrette Salad Dressing

This dressing is good on chilled roast and barbecued chicken or pork.

Menu Category:	Salad Dressing
Preparation Time:	30 minutes
Cooking Method:	None required
Variations:	This works well with white wine vinegar and with other herbs.
Yield:	1 gallon

Ingredient	U.S.	Metric	Method
Red wine vinegar	3 c	720 ml	Combine in mixer bowl with whip
Scallion, minced	2 c	480 ml	attachment. Mix well to blend all
Mustard, dry	¼ c	60 ml	ingredients.
Garlic, minced	1 T	15 ml	
Oregano, dried	1 t	5 ml	
Thyme, dried	½ t	3 ml	
Salt	1 T	15 ml	
Black pepper	1 t	15 ml	
Olive oil	1 qt	950 ml	Add gradually to mixer bowl at low speed.
Vegetable oil	1½ qt	1.4 L	Increase speed and continue to add remaining oil. Transfer to storage container. Chill well.

Approximate				
Approximate	Calories	163	Protein	0.2 gm
Nutrient Analysis	Fat	18 gm	Carbohydrate	0.7 gm
Per Ounce	Cholesterol	0 mg	Calcium	4.9 mg
	Sodium	54 mg	Fiber	0.1 gm

▲ Russian Salad Dressing

Serve as a salad dressing or as a topping for seafood or roast beef sandwiches.

Menu Category:	Salad Dressing, Marinade
Cooking Method:	None required
Preparation Time:	10 minutes
Variations:	Add chopped parsley and chopped egg yolks for a quick remoulade sauce.
Yield:	1 gallon

Ingredient	U.S.	Metric	Method
Mayonnaise	3 qt	2.8 L	Combine in mixer with whip attachment.
Pimento, drained, minced	1 c	240 ml	Mix at high speed for 2 minutes. Transfer
Green bell pepper, minced	1½ c	360 ml	to storage containers. Cover. Chill well.
Celery, minced	1½ c	360 ml	
Tomato paste	½ c	120 ml	
Worcestershire sauce	½ c	120 ml	
Cayenne pepper, ground	2 t	10 ml	

Approximate	Calories	186	Protein	0.6 gm
Nutrient Analysis	Fat	20.2 gm	Carbohydrate	2 gm
Per Ounce	Cholesterol	14.6 mg	Calcium	6.6 mg
	Sodium	184 mg	Fiber	0.1 gm

▲ Sesame-Mustard Salad Dressing

Serve as a salad dressing or with chilled cooked meats, poultry, or shrimp.

Menu Category:	Salad Dressing
Cooking Method:	None required
Preparation Time:	30 minutes
Variations:	This is a great marinade for chicken and pork.
Yield:	1 gallon

Ingredient	U.S.	Metric	Method
Sesame oil	½ c	120 ml	Combine in mixer bowl with whip
Peanut oil	3 qt	2.8 L	attachment. Mix at low speed for 1 minute.
Mustard, Dijon style	1 c	240 ml	Increase speed gradually to high. Mix at
White wine vinegar	3 c	720 ml	high speed until well blended and
Brown sugar	1 T	15 ml	thickened. Transfer to storage containers.
Garlic powder	1 T	15 ml	Cover. Chill well.
White pepper	2 t	10 ml	

Approximate	Calories	91	Protein	3.8 gm
Nutrient Analysis	Fat	7.9 gm	Carbohydrate	2.8 gm
Per Ounce	Cholesterol	0 mg	Calcium	7.9 mg
	Sodium	46 mg	Fiber	0.3 gm

▲ Yogurt Vinaigrette with Cumin and Cilantro

Serve as a dressing for Mediterranean vegetable and seafood salads.

Menu Category:	Salad Dressing, Ethnic, Mediterranean
Cooking Method:	None required
Preparation Time:	30 minutes
Variations:	Substitute fresh mint for cilantro.
Yield:	1 gallon

Ingredient	U.S.	Metric	Method
Lemon juice	1 qt	950 ml	Combine in mixer bowl with whip
Cumin, ground	½ c	120 ml	attachment.
Garlic, minced	½ c	120 ml	
Cilantro, chopped	1 c	240 ml	
Olive oil	1 qt	950 ml	Add gradually to mixer bowl at low speed. Increase speed and continue to add remaining oil.
Yogurt, plain	2 qt	1.9 L	Whip in. Mix well. Chill.

Approximate	Calories	72	Protein	0.6 gm
Nutrient Analysis	Fat	7.3 gm	Carbohydrate	1.5 gm
Per Ounce	Cholesterol	1.8 mg	Calcium	23.2 mg
	Sodium	9.1 mg	Fiber	0.1 gm

Seafood

Shellfish

▲ Low Country White Corn Crab Cakes

A Carolina-Georgia version of zesty crab patties.

Menu Category:	Appetizer, Entrée, Seafood, American Regional		
Cooking Method:	Sauté		
Preparation Time:	30 minutes		
Cooking Time:	15 minutes		
Variations:	Substitute cooked, chopped lobster, clams, or scallops.		
Yield:	50 portions (4 oz)		

Ingredient	U.S.	Metric	Method
White corn bread crumbs, dry	2 qt	1.9 L	Combine in a large bowl. Mix gently but well.
Lump crabmeat, picked	7 lb	3.2 kg	
Onion, minced	1 c	240 ml	
Celery, minced	1 c	240 ml	
Green bell pepper, minced	2 c	480 ml	
Mayonnaise	1 c	240 ml	Combine in medium bowl. Whip to combine. Add to crab mixture. Toss gently but well. Portion into balls. Press flat.
Mustard, Dijon style	½ c	120 ml	
Tabasco sauce	1 T	15 ml	
Egg, beaten	8	8	
Parsley, chopped	1 c	240 ml	
Salt	2 t	10 ml	
White pepper	2 t	10 ml	
Butter, melted	2 c	480 ml	Heat on preheated 325°F flattop grill. Sauté crab cakes until fully cooked and golden brown on both sides, about 6 minutes per side.

Nutrient Analysis Per Serving	Calories	156	Protein	13.4 gm
	Fat	7 gm	Carbohydrate	9.5 gm
	Cholesterol	100 mg	Calcium	38 mg
	Sodium	675 mg	Fiber	0.1 gm

▲ Broiled Scallops with Spiced Orange Sauce

These tender scallops have just the right touch of exotic Caribbean spices.

Menu Category:	Appetizer, Entrée, Seafood, Ethnic, Caribbean
Cooking Method:	Broil/Grill
Preparation Time:	30 minutes
Marination Time:	1 hour
Cooking Time:	10 minutes
Variations:	Substitute shrimp, chicken, or pork.
Yield:	50 portions (4 oz)

Ingredient	U.S.	Metric	Method
Scallops, small	12 lb	5.5 kg	Combine in large bowl. Stir well to coat
Ginger, ground	1 T	15 ml	scallops. Transfer to storage containers.
Cinnamon, ground	2 t	10 ml	Cover. Chill for 1 hour. Remove from
Allspice, ground	1 t	5 ml	container and portion onto soaked bamboo
Cayenne pepper, ground	1 t	5 ml	skewers. Grill/broil at medium-high heat just until scallops are firm, about 5 to 10 minutes.
Spiced Orange Sauce, recipe follows	2 qt	1.9 L	Portion over scallops or serve on the side.

Nutrient Analysis Per Serving	Calories	156	Protein	18 gm
	Fat	0.8 gm	Carbohydrate	25 gm
	Cholesterol	36 mg	Calcium	36 mg
	Sodium	371 mg	Fiber	0.4 gm

Companion Recipe

▲ ## Spiced Orange Sauce

Serve this with broiled scallops or other grilled seafood, chicken, or pork.

Menu Category:	Sauce, Ethnic, Caribbean
Cooking Method:	Simmer
Preparation Time:	10 minutes
Cooking Time:	15 minutes
Variations:	Substitute other jams or preserves, such as apricot or peach.
Yield:	1 gallon

Ingredient	U.S.	Metric	Method
Orange marmalade	2 qt	1.9 L	Combine in nonreactive pot. Heat to a boil,
Cider vinegar	1½ c	720 ml	stirring constantly. Reduce heat to a
Ketchup	1½ qt	1.4 L	simmer. Simmer for 10 minutes.
Gingerroot, minced	2 T	30 ml	
Cayenne pepper, ground	1 t	5 ml	
Salt	2 t	10 ml	

Nutrient Analysis Per Ounce				
	Calories	60	Protein	0 gm
	Fat	0 gm	Carbohydrate	15.5 gm
	Cholesterol	0 mg	Calcium	6 mg
	Sodium	137 mg	Fiber	0.2 gm

▲ Curried Scallops with Spiced Apple Relish

Serve this mild version of the Indian dish with white rice.

Menu Category:	Appetizer, Entrée, Seafood, Ethnic, Indian
Cooking Method:	Sauté
Preparation Time:	30 minutes
Cooking Time:	30 minutes
Variations:	Substitute shrimp, veal, pork, or chicken.
Yield:	50 portions (5 oz)

Ingredient	U.S.	Metric	Method
Clarified butter	2 c	480 ml	Sauté in preheated brazier until vegetables
Onions, minced	1 qt	950 ml	are lightly golden.
Garlic, minced	1 T	15 ml	
Gingerroot, minced	½ c	120 ml	
Curry powder, mild	½ c	120 ml	Add to vegetables. Stir for 1 minute.
Turmeric, ground	1 T	15 ml	
Salt	1 T	15 ml	
Black pepper	2 t	10 ml	
Scallops, small	12 lb	5.5 kg	Add to mixture. Sauté just until scallops are firm, about 3 minutes.
White wine, dry	3 c	720 ml	Add to mixture. Stir well. Simmer 1 minute. Remove from heat.
Scallion greens, minced	2 c	480 ml	Sprinkle over each portion.
Spiced Apple Relish, recipe follows	1 qt	950 ml	Serve on the side of scallops.

Nutrient Analysis Per Serving				
	Calories	216	Protein	19 gm
	Fat	8.5 gm	Carbohydrate	14.2 gm
	Cholesterol	56 mg	Calcium	45 mg
	Sodium	381 mg	Fiber	0.4 gm

Companion Recipe

▲ **Spiced Apple Relish**

Serve this with curried scallops or anytime as a chutney alternative.

Menu Category:	Sauce, Ethnic, Indian
Cooking Method:	Simmer
Preparation Time:	30 minutes
Cooking Time:	3 hours
Variations:	Substitute pears.
Yield:	1 gallon

Ingredient	U.S.	Metric	Method
Cooking apples, peeled, chopped	12 lb	5.5 kg	Combine in heavy nonreactive pot or steam kettle. Cook over medium heat until sugar dissolves. Increase heat to a boil. Stir carefully for 5 minutes. Reduce heat to a simmer. Cook until very thick, about 3 hours. Transfer to storage containers. Cover. Chill well.
Ginger, ground	⅓ c	80 ml	
Sugar	6 lb	2.3 kg	

Nutrient Analysis Per Ounce	Calories	53	Protein	0.1 gm
	Fat	0.1 gm	Carbohydrate	14 gm
	Cholesterol	0 mg	Calcium	1 mg
	Sodium	0.1 mg	Fiber	0.1 gm

▲ Beer-Batter Coconut Shrimp with Orange Sauce

Serve this Polynesian dish as a festive entrée or appetizer.

Menu Category:	Appetizer, Entrée, Seafood, American Regional
Cooking Method:	Deep-fry
Preparation Time:	30 minutes
Cooking Time:	15 minutes
Variations:	Substitute scallops or boneless chicken strips.
Yield:	50 portions (5 oz)

Ingredient	U.S.	Metric	Method
Shrimp (15 to 20 per pound)	12 lb	5.5 kg	Peel and devein, leaving tail fanshell intact. Butterfly if desired.
Beer	2 qt	1.9 L	Combine in large bowl. Dip shrimp in mixture. Shake off excess batter.
Flour	2 qt	1.9 L	
Salt	2 T	30 ml	
Pepper, white	1 T	15 ml	
Cayenne pepper, ground	2 t	10 ml	
Coconut, shredded	3 qt	2.4 L	Dip battered shrimp in coconut. Shake off excess. Deep-fry in preheated 350°F fryer until lightly browned. Drain well.
Orange Sauce, recipe follows	3½ qt	3.3 L	Serve 2-ounce ramekins on the side for dipping.

Nutrient Analysis Per Serving	Calories	306	Protein	25.5 gm
	Fat	13 gm	Carbohydrate	19.4 gm
	Cholesterol	168 mg	Calcium	17.6 mg
	Sodium	426 mg	Fiber	1.2 gm

Companion Recipe

▲ **Orange Sauce**

This zesty sauce is great on sandwiches and as a base for salad dressings.

Menu Category:	Sauce
Cooking Method:	None required
Preparation Time:	5 minutes
Variations:	Substitute chopped chutney for marmalade.
Yield:	1 gallon

Ingredient	U.S.	Metric	Method
Orange marmalade	1½ qt	1.4 L	Combine in large bowl. Whip well to
Sherry, semisweet	2 c	480 ml	combine. Transfer to storage containers.
Orange juice	1½ qt	1.4 L	Cover. Chill well.
Mustard, Dijon style	2 c	480 ml	
Cloves, ground	½ t	3 ml	

Nutrient Analysis Per Ounce				
	Calories	56	Protein	0.3 gm
	Fat	0.2 gm	Carbohydrate	12.2 gm
	Cholesterol	0 mg	Calcium	5.3 mg
	Sodium	91 mg	Fiber	0.2 gm

▲ Broiled Shrimp with Chinese-Style Basting Sauce

Serve as an appetizer or entrée.

Menu Category:	Appetizer, Entrée, Seafood, Ethnic, Oriental
Cooking Method:	Grill/Broil
Preparation Time:	30 minutes
Marination Time:	1 hour
Cooking Time:	15 minutes
Variations:	Substitute scallops, pork nuggets, or chicken strips.
Yield:	50 portions (5 oz)

Ingredient	U.S.	Metric	Method
Shrimp (15 to 20 per pound), peeled and deveined	12 lb	5.5 kg	Place in shallow roasting pans.
Sherry, dry	1 qt	950 ml	Combine. Pour over shrimp. Cover. Chill for 1 hour. Remove from marinade. Grill/broil at medium high heat, basting with reserved marinade. Turn frequently just until firm, about 10 to 15 minutes.
Soy sauce	2 c	480 ml	
Gingerroot, minced	1 c	240 ml	
Garlic, minced	1 T	15 ml	
Chili paste	¼ c	60 ml	
Lime juice	½ c	120 ml	
Molasses, light	½ c	120 ml	

Nutrient Analysis Per Serving				
	Calories	160	Protein	23 gm
	Fat	1.9 gm	Carbohydrate	6.5 gm
	Cholesterol	168 mg	Calcium	69 mg
	Sodium	839 mg	Fiber	0.1 gm

▲ Glazed Shrimp with Chilies and Sesame

This stir-fry version features traditional Oriental seasonings.

Menu Category:	Appetizer, Entrée, Seafood, Ethnic, Oriental
Cooking Method:	Stir-fry/Sauté
Preparation Time:	30 minutes
Marination Time:	1 hour
Cooking Time:	10 minutes
Variations:	Substitute chicken wings and oven broil.

Yield: 50 portions (5 oz)

Ingredient	U.S.	Metric	Method
Shrimp (15 to 20 per pound), peeled and deveined	12 lb	5.5 kg	Combine in large bowl. Mix well. Cover. Chill for 1 hour.
Egg white, lightly beaten	2 c	480 ml	
Sesame oil	2 T	30 ml	
Cornstarch	¾ c	180 ml	
Baking soda	½ t	3 ml	
Dry sherry	¾ c	180 ml	
Soy sauce	1 c	240 ml	
Gingerroot, minced	½ c	120 ml	
Garlic, minced	1 T	15 ml	
Cooking oil	2 c	480 ml	Heat in 350°F brazier. Add shrimp mixture. Stir-fry for 1 minute. Reduce heat to 300°F. Simmer 5 minutes.
Scallions, minced	1 qt	950 ml	Add. Cover. Simmer 1 minute or until shrimp are nicely glazed.

Nutrient Analysis Per Serving	Calories	230	Protein	24 gm
	Fat	11.2 gm	Carbohydrate	6.2 gm
	Cholesterol	168 mg	Calcium	72 mg
	Sodium	517 mg	Fiber	0.2 gm

▲ Louisiana Shrimp Pilau

This is an American regional version of Italian shellfish pilaf.

Menu Category:	Appetizer, Entrée, Seafood, American Regional
Cooking Method:	Sauté/Simmer
Preparation Time:	30 minutes
Cooking Time:	30 minutes
Variations:	Substitute cooked chicken, crab, crayfish, or shucked oysters.
Yield:	50 portions (5 oz)

Ingredient	U.S.	Metric	Method
Shrimp (15 to 20 per pound), peeled and deveined.	12 lb	5.5 kg	Combine in large bowl. Toss shrimp well.
Worcestershire sauce	1 c	240 ml	
Tabasco sauce	½ c	120 ml	
Flour	1 qt	950 ml	Add to shrimp. Toss well. Shake off all excess flour. Reserve shrimp.
Bacon, diced	1 lb	454 g	Sauté in large heavy pot or brazier just until slightly crisp.
Onion, minced	2 c	480 ml	Add to bacon. Sauté 5 minutes. Add reserved shrimp. Sauté 1 minute. Reduce heat and simmer until shrimp is firm, about 5 minutes.
Celery, minced	2 c	480 ml	
Green bell pepper, minced	2 c	480 ml	
Rice, cooked	3 qt	2.8 L	Add to mixture. Stir well. Cook just until well heated.

Nutrient Analysis Per Serving				
	Calories	225	Protein	26 gm
	Fat	3.5 gm	Carbohydrate	22 gm
	Cholesterol	170 mg	Calcium	78 mg
	Sodium	299 mg	Fiber	0.4 gm

▲ Shrimp Americaine

A shrimp version of the lobster classic. Prepare sauce in advance for quick service.

Menu Category:	Appetizer, Entrée, Seafood, American Regional
Cooking Method:	Sauté/Simmer
Preparation Time:	30 minutes
Cooking Time:	1 hour
Variations:	Substitute lobster, crab, scallops, or shucked oysters. Serve with steamed or boiled white or flavored rice.
Yield:	50 portions (6 oz)

Ingredient	U.S.	Metric	Method
Shrimp (15 to 20 per pound)	12 lb	5.5 kg	Peel and devein. Reserve shells. Cover and chill shrimp.
Olive oil	1½ c	360 ml	Sauté in large pot or brazier for 2 minutes. Remove and reserve shells.
Shrimp shells	from above	from above	
Onion, chopped	2 qt	1.9 L	Add to heated shrimp oil. Sauté 5 minutes.
Carrots, chopped	1 qt	950 ml	
Garlic, chopped	¼ c	60 ml	
Brandy	2 c	480 ml	Add. Flame if possible.
Flour	1½ c	360 ml	Add. Stir well for 1 minute.
White wine, dry	2 qt	1.9 L	Add. Stir until smooth. Simmer 10 minutes. Add reserved shrimp shells.
Tomatoes, chopped	2 qt	1.9 L	Add. Simmer 30 minutes. Strain through a fine sieve, pressing hard to extract all liquid. Return sauce to heavy pot. Add reserved shrimp. Simmer about 8 minutes.
Tomato paste	1 c	240 ml	
Lemon juice	½ c	120 ml	
Parsley, chopped	2 c	480 ml	
Tarragon, dried	2 T	30 ml	
Cayenne pepper, ground	2 t	10 ml	
Heavy cream	2 c	480 ml	Add. Simmer another 5 minutes or until shrimp are firm.

Nutrient Analysis Per Serving				
	Calories	276	Protein	24 gm
	Fat	9.8 gm	Carbohydrate	11 gm
	Cholesterol	172 mg	Calcium	92.1 mg
	Sodium	181 mg	Fiber	0.7 gm

▲ Shrimp Creole

A favorite throughout the American Southeast.

Menu Category:	Appetizer, Entrée, Seafood, American Regional
Cooking Method:	Sauté/Simmer
Preparation Time:	30 minutes
Cooking Time:	45 minutes
Variations:	Substitute scallops, crab, or lobster.
	Serve with white rice.
Yield:	50 portions (5 oz)

Ingredient	U.S.	Metric	Method
Bacon, diced	1 lb	454 g	Sauté in heavy pot or brazier just until lightly browned.
Onions, diced	2 qt	1.9 L	Add to bacon. Sauté 5 minutes.
Celery, diced	1 qt	950 ml	
Green pepper, diced	1 qt	950 ml	
Tomatoes, chopped	1 gal	3.8 L	Add to vegetable mixture. Heat to a boil. Reduce heat to a simmer. Simmer 45 minutes or until mixture thickens.
Tomato paste	2 c	480 ml	
Brown sugar	½ c	120 ml	
Shrimp (15 to 20 per pound), cooked, peeled, and deveined	12 lb	5.5 kg	Add. Simmer 10 minutes. Adjust seasoning with salt, pepper, and hot pepper sauce.

Nutrient Analysis Per Serving	Calories	194	Protein	25 gm
	Fat	4.4 gm	Carbohydrate	12.6 gm
	Cholesterol	170 mg	Calcium	77.4 mg
	Sodium	353 mg	Fiber	0.8 gm

▲ Shrimp and Vegetable Teriyaki

The term teriyaki *means broiled with a glaze. Here, we have added stir-fried vegetables.*

Menu Category:	Appetizer, Entrée, Seafood, Ethnic, Japanese
Cooking Method:	Grill/Sauté
Preparation Time:	30 minutes
Marination Time:	1 hour
Cooking Time:	15 minutes
Variations:	Substitute chicken, scallops, or sliced pork.
Yield:	50 portions (6 oz)

Ingredient	U.S.	Metric	Method
Shrimp (15 to 20 per pound), peeled and deveined	12 lb	5.5 kg	Place in shallow roasting pans.
Sherry, dry	2 c	480 ml	Combine. Pour over shrimp. Cover. Chill for 1 hour. Remove from marinade. Grill/ broil at medium high heat, basting with reserved marinade. Turn frequently just until firm, about 10 minutes.
Soy sauce	3 c	720 ml	
Sake	3 c	720 ml	
Sugar	2 c	480 ml	
Peanut oil, hot	1 c	240 ml	Sauté in preheated 350°F brazier. Cook just until vegetables are tender, about 5 minutes. Add reserved shrimp. Toss well.
Carrots, julienne	1 qt	950 ml	
Onion julienne	1 qt	950 ml	
Celery, julienne	1 qt	950 ml	

Nutrient Analysis Per Serving	Calories	205	Protein	24.2 gm
	Fat	3.4 gm	Carbohydrate	13.9 gm
	Cholesterol	168 mg	Calcium	7.3 mg
	Sodium	1164 mg	Fiber	0.3 gm

▲ Mixed Seafood Paella

This Spanish classic takes its name from the traditional round pan used to cook it.

Menu Category:	Entrée, Seafood, Ethnic, Spanish
Cooking Method:	Simmer
Preparation Time:	30 minutes
Cooking Time:	60 minutes
Variations:	Add nonseafood items such as chicken and smoked pork.
	Substitute turmeric for very expensive saffron.
Yield:	50 portions (8 oz)

Ingredient	U.S.	Metric	Method
Olive oil, hot	2 c	480 ml	Sauté in large pot for 3 minutes. Remove
Lobster tails, thinly sliced	12	12	with slotted spoon.
Shrimp (10 to 15 per pound), unpeeled	50	50	
Sausage, links, 2 oz	50	50	Add to same pot. Sauté 3 minutes. Remove with slotted spoon.
Onions, minced	1 qt	950 ml	Add to same pot. Sauté 5 minutes.
Garlic, minced	2 T	30 ml	
Tomatoes, chopped	2 qt	1.9 L	Add to onions. Simmer 10 minutes or until
Saffron threads	1 t	5 ml	moisture evaporates.
Rice	3 qt	2.8 L	Add to tomatoes. Stir well.
Crushed red pepper	1 T	15 ml	
Fish stock	3 qt	2.8 L	Add with reserved shrimp, lobster, and
Scallops, large	50	50	sausage. Stir well. Heat to a simmer.
Clams, scrubbed	50	50	Cover. Simmer 25 minutes or until rice is
Mussels, scrubbed	50	50	cooked and shellfish are open. Divide among service plates.

Nutrient Analysis Per Serving				
	Calories	350	Protein	31 gm
	Fat	15.5 gm	Carbohydrate	20.5 gm
	Cholesterol	103 mg	Calcium	134 mg
	Sodium	568 mg	Fiber	0.3 gm

Finfish

▲ Broiled Cod with Jalapeño Onion Marmalade

This exotic Mexican preparation is a variation of a Yucatán peninsula specialty.

Menu Category:	Entrée, Seafood, Ethnic, Mexican
Cooking Method:	Broil/Grill
Preparation Time:	20 minutes
Cooking Time:	20 minutes
Variations:	Substitute shrimp, scallops, or skinless, boneless chicken.
Yield:	50 portions (6 oz)

Ingredient	U.S.	Metric	Method
Olive oil, hot	1 c	240 ml	Sauté over high heat until golden. Do not
Red onions, minced	1 qt	950 ml	stir often.
Jalapeño peppers, seeded, minced	¼ c	60 ml	
Orange marmalade	1 qt	950 ml	Add to onions. Heat to a simmer. Simmer
Cider vinegar	1 c	240 ml	10 minutes. Remove from heat. Reserve.
Cod fillets, boneless, 1-inch thick	16 lb	7.3 kg	Season and reserve in shallow roasting pans. When ready to cook, grill/broil over/
Olive oil	1 c	240 ml	under medium-high heat until cod is firm
Salt	1 T	15 ml	and flakes easily, about 10 minutes. Serve
White pepper	1 t	5 ml	with 1 ounce of reserved marmalade mixture on top.

Nutrient Analysis				
Per Serving	Calories	272	Protein	26 gm
	Fat	9.6 gm	Carbohydrate	19.5 gm
	Cholesterol	63.2 mg	Calcium	31.3 mg
	Sodium	209 mg	Fiber	0.4 gm

▲ Szechuan Broiled Flounder

An easy Oriental seafood classic.

Menu Category:	Entrée, Seafood, Ethnic, Chinese
Cooking Method:	Broil
Preparation Time:	30 minutes
Marination Time:	1 hour
Cooking Time:	15 minutes
Variations:	Substitute other lean fish, shrimp, or skinless, boneless chicken.
Yield:	50 portions (5 oz)

Ingredient	U.S.	Metric	Method
Flounder fillets, ½-inch thick	16 lb	7.3 kg	Arrange in one layer on sheet pans.
Peanut oil, hot	2 c	480 ml	Cook over medium heat until pepper is very dark. Strain off all pepper flakes and discard. Transfer oil to small bowl and cool to room temperature.
Crushed red pepper	1 T	15 ml	
Soy sauce	2 c	480 ml	Add to cooled oil. Mix well. Pour over fish fillets. Cover. Chill for 1 hour. Place sheet pans in preheated 400°F broiler. Cook until fish is firm and flakes easily, about 10 minutes. Remove with slotted spatula. Spoon juices over fillets.
Five-spice powder	2 t	10 ml	
Sherry, dry	2 c	480 ml	
Gingerroot, minced	½ c	120 ml	

Nutrient Analysis Per Serving	Calories	223	Protein	37.3 gm
	Fat	5.2 gm	Carbohydrate	2.9 gm
	Cholesterol	98.3 mg	Calcium	33 mg
	Sodium	813 mg	Fiber	0.2 gm

▲ Baked Haddock with Herbs and Chablis

A light and lean way to prepare a variety of fish.

Menu Category:	Entrée, Seafood, Ethnic, French
Cooking Method:	Bake
Preparation Time:	30 minutes
Marination Time:	30 minutes
Oven Temperature:	450°F
Cooking Time:	10 minutes
Variations:	Substitute other lean fish, shrimp, or skinless, boneless chicken.
Yield:	50 portions (5 oz)

Ingredient	U.S.	Metric	Method
Haddock fillets, 5 oz	15 lb	6.8 kg	Sprinkle fillets with salt and arrange in shallow roasting pans.
Salt	⅓ c	80 ml	
Chablis	3 c	720 ml	Combine in large bowl. Mix well. Pour over haddock fillets. Marinate for 30 minutes. Remove fillets from marinade. Place in oiled sheet pans. Brush with extra marinade. Bake in preheated 450°F oven until fillets are firm and flake easily, about 7 to 10 minutes.
Olive oil	2 c	480 ml	
Mustard, Dijon style	¾ c	180 ml	
Tarragon, dried	2 T	30 ml	
Parsley, chopped	1 c	240 ml	
Black pepper	2 t	10 ml	

Nutrient Analysis Per Serving	Calories	266	Protein	21.5 gm
	Fat	15.1 gm	Carbohydrate	6.8 gm
	Cholesterol	52.3 mg	Calcium	52.9 mg
	Sodium	949 mg	Fiber	0.1 gm

▲ Baked Haddock with Indonesian Curry Sauce

A creative, exotic Indonesian specialty.

Menu Category:	Entrée, Seafood, Ethnic, Indonesian
Cooking Method:	Bake/Simmer
Preparation Time:	30 minutes
Oven Temperature:	450°F
Cooking Time:	45 minutes
Variations:	Substitute other lean fish, shrimp, or skinless, boneless chicken.
Yield:	50 portions (5 oz)

Ingredient	U.S.	Metric	Method
Haddock fillets, 5 oz	15 lb	6.8 kg	Sprinkle fillets with salt and arrange in shallow roasting pans.
Salt	⅓ c	80 ml	
Clarified butter	2 c	480 ml	Sauté in preheated brazier until vegetables are lightly golden.
Onions, minced	1 qt	950 ml	
Garlic, minced	1 T	15 ml	
Gingerroot, minced	½ c	120 ml	
Curry powder, mild	½ c	120 ml	Add to vegetables. Stir for 1 minute.
Turmeric, ground	1 T	15 ml	
Black pepper	2 t	10 ml	
Soy sauce	1 c	240 ml	Add to curry mixture. Simmer for 5 minutes. Remove from heat. Portion mixture over fillets. Bake in preheated 450°F oven until fillets are firm and flake easily, about 7 minutes. Serve fillets topped with sauce.
Sesame oil	2 T	30 ml	
Sherry, dry	1 c	240 ml	
Peanuts, unsalted	1 qt	950 ml	

Nutrient Analysis	Calories	339	Protein	25 gm
Per Serving	Fat	21.2 gm	Carbohydrate	11 gm
	Cholesterol	74.6 mg	Calcium	65.4 mg
	Sodium	1278 mg	Fiber	0.5 gm

▲ Oriental Barbecued Haddock

This Oriental preparation is a pleasing alternative for your barbecue menu.

Menu Category:	Entrée, Seafood, Ethnic, Oriental
Cooking Method:	Broil/Grill
Preparation Time:	20 minutes
Cooking Time:	15 minutes
Variations:	Substitute other lean fish, shrimp, or skinless, boneless chicken.
Yield:	50 portions (5 oz)

Ingredient	U.S.	Metric	Method
Haddock, 1-inch thick	16 lb	7.3 kg	Arrange in one layer in shallow roasting pans.
Peanut oil	1 c	240 ml	Combine. Pour over haddock. Marinate 30
Soy sauce	1½ c	360 ml	minutes. Turn portions occasionally.
Salt	2 t	10 ml	Remove haddock from marinade. Grill/broil
Five-spice powder	2 t	10 ml	over/under medium-high heat until fish is
Sherry, dry	1½ c	360 ml	firm and flakes easily, about 10 minutes.
Ginger, ground	1 T	15 ml	Baste with excess marinade.

Nutrient Analysis Per Serving				
	Calories	158	Protein	28.8 gm
	Fat	2.5 gm	Carbohydrate	1.9 gm
	Cholesterol	83.7 mg	Calcium	52.6 mg
	Sodium	679 mg	Fiber	0.1 gm

▲ Polynesian Baked Monkfish with Sweet 'n' Sour Sauce

This Pacific isles variation is simple and superb.

Menu Category:	Entrée, Seafood, Ethnic, Polynesian
Cooking Method:	Sauté/Simmer
Preparation Time:	20 minutes
Cooking Time:	20 minutes
Variations:	Substitute shrimp, scallops, or skinless, boneless chicken.
Yield:	50 portions (5 oz)

Ingredient	U.S.	Metric	Method
Monkfish	16 lb	7.3 kg	Slice monkfish into 1-inch pieces. Season
Salt	2 T	30 ml	and reserve.
Tomato puree	1 qt	950 ml	Combine. Reserve.
Pineapple juice, unsweetened	2 c	480 ml	
Water	2 c	480 ml	
Brown sugar	1½ c	360 ml	
Gingerroot, grated	½ c	120 ml	
Scallion, minced	1 c	240 ml	
Cornstarch	½ c	120 ml	
Peanut oil	2 c	480 ml	Heat in tilt kettle or large shallow pot(s). Add reserved monkfish. Sauté 6 or 7 minutes, stirring constantly. Add reserved sauce mixture. Heat to a boil. Reduce to a simmer until monkfish is firm, about 5 minutes.

Nutrient Analysis Per Serving				
	Calories	188	Protein	23 gm
	Fat	5.2 gm	Carbohydrate	12.3 gm
	Cholesterol	35.9 mg	Calcium	28.5 mg
	Sodium	34.5 mg	Fiber	0.4 gm

▲ Red Snapper Veracruz

This classic from Mexico has many variations.

Menu Category:	Entrée, Seafood, Ethnic, Mexican
Cooking Method:	Sauté/Bake
Preparation Time:	20 minutes
Oven Temperature:	350°F
Cooking Time:	30 minutes
Variations:	Substitute shrimp, scallops, or skinless, boneless chicken.
Yield:	50 portions (6 oz)

Ingredient	U.S.	Metric	Method
Red snapper fillets, 1-inch thick	16 lb	7.3 kg	Season and reserve in shallow roasting pans.
Lime juice	2 c	480 ml	
Salt	1 T	15 ml	
Black pepper	1 t	5 ml	
Olive oil, hot	2 c	480 ml	Sauté in heavy pot just until golden.
Onion, minced	1 qt	950 ml	
Garlic, minced	¼ c	60 ml	
Commercial picante sauce, mild	1 gal	3.8 L	Add to onions. Heat to a boil. Reduce to a simmer. Simmer 10 minutes. Pour over fish just to cover. Place in preheated 350°F oven. Bake until snapper is firm and flakes easily, about 10 minutes. Remove fish with slotted spatula. Transfer sauce to heavy pot. Heat to a boil. Boil until sauce thickens. Spoon over snapper.
Olives, stuffed, chopped	3 c	720 ml	
Capers, drained	1 c	240 ml	
Almonds, slivered	2 c	480 ml	
Cilantro, minced	2 c	480 ml	

Nutrient Analysis Per Serving				
	Calories	302	Protein	32.2 gm
	Fat	15.8 gm	Carbohydrate	10.2 gm
	Cholesterol	53.3 mg	Calcium	96.8 mg
	Sodium	918 mg	Fiber	0.3 gm

▲ Baked Sole with Mixed Peppers and Fruit

A colorful crowd pleaser that's a breeze to prepare.

Menu Category:	Entrée, Seafood
Cooking Method:	Bake
Preparation Time:	30 minutes
Oven Temperature:	450°F
Cooking Time:	15 minutes
Variations:	Substitute other lean fish, shrimp, or skinless, boneless chicken.
Yield:	50 portions (6 oz)

Ingredient	U.S.	Metric	Method
Sole fillets, ½-inch thick	16 lb	7.3 kg	Arrange in one layer on oiled sheet pans. Reserve.
Olive oil	1½ c	360 ml	Heat in large pot or brazier.
Onions, diced	1 qt	950 ml	Add to hot oil. Sauté over medium high heat until vegetables are just tender, about 5 minutes.
Celery, diced	2 c	480 ml	
Gingerroot, minced	¼ c	60 ml	
Garlic, minced	2 T	30 ml	
Green bell pepper, diced	2 c	480 ml	
Red bell pepper, diced	2 c	480 ml	
Jalapeño pepper, seeded, minced	¼ c	60 ml	
Raisins, golden	2 c	480 ml	Add to vegetable mixture. Mix well. Portion this mixture over sole fillets. Place sheet pans in preheated 450°F oven. Cook until fish is firm and flakes easily, about 10 minutes. Remove with spatula.
Pineapple, chopped	2 c	480 ml	
Yogurt, plain	1 qt	950 ml	Portion as quantity dictates over each serving.
Almonds, sliced, toasted	2 c	480 ml	

Nutrient Analysis Per Serving	Calories	256	Protein	26.6 gm
	Fat	11.2 gm	Carbohydrate	12.6 gm
	Cholesterol	70.4 mg	Calcium	62.8 mg
	Sodium	193 mg	Fiber	0.5 gm

▲ Baked Turban of Sole Florentine

A delicate spinach filling highlights this appealing seafood winner.

Menu Category:	Entrée, Seafood, Ethnic, Italian
Cooking Method:	Bake
Preparation Time:	45 minutes
Oven Temperature:	350°F
Cooking Time:	30 minutes
Variations:	Substitute other lean fish, shrimp, or skinless, boneless chicken.
Yield:	50 portions (6 oz)

Ingredient	U.S.	Metric	Method
Sole fillets, ½-inch thick	16 lb	7.3 kg	Arrange rough-side down in one layer on oiled sheet pans. Reserve.
Olive oil	1½ c	360 ml	Heat in large pot.
Onion, sliced	2 c	480 ml	Add to olive oil. Sauté until golden.
Garlic, minced	1 T	15 ml	
Spinach, cooked, drained	3 qt	2.8 L	Add to onion mixture. Cook over medium heat until all liquid is removed. Remove from heat. Cool to room temperature. Spread ¼ cup mixture over sole fillets. Roll pinwheel-style and secure with toothpicks. Place on oiled sheet pans and bake in preheated 350°F oven until fish is firm and flakes easily, about 10 minutes. Spoon any excess juices over each portion.
Basil, dried	1 T	15 ml	
Salt	2 t	10 ml	
Black pepper	1 t	5 ml	

Nutrient Analysis Per Serving				
	Calories	188	Protein	25.6 gm
	Fat	8.1 gm	Carbohydrate	2.4 gm
	Cholesterol	68.1 mg	Calcium	81.3 mg
	Sodium	221 mg	Fiber	0.5 gm

▲ Broiled Roughy with Orange Sauce and Pecans

This increasingly popular fish is perfect with a light touch of orange and toasted nuts.

Menu Category:	Appetizer, Entrée, Seafood, American Regional
Cooking Method:	Broil
Preparation Time:	30 minutes
Cooking Time:	45 minutes
Variations:	Substitute boneless chicken breast, shrimp, or other varieties of lean fish.
Yield:	50 portions (5 oz)

Ingredient	U.S.	Metric	Method
Orange marmalade	1 qt	950 ml	Combine in nonreactive pot. Heat to a boil, stirring constantly. Reduce heat to a simmer. Simmer for 10 minutes. Reserve.
Cider vinegar	¾ c	180 ml	
Ketchup	2 c	480 ml	
Orange brandy	¼ c	60 ml	
Lemon juice	¼ c	60 ml	
Pecans, chopped, toasted	2 c	480 ml	
Salt	1 t	5 ml	
Black pepper	1 t	5 ml	
Orange roughy fillets, 5 oz	16 lb	7.3 kg	Arrange on oiled sheet pans. Place sheet pans in preheated 400°F broiler. Cook until fish is firm and flakes easily, about 10 minutes. Serve with reserved sauce.

Nutrient Analysis	Calories	297	Protein	22 gm
Per Serving	Fat	13.3 gm	Carbohydrate	22 gm
	Cholesterol	29 mg	Calcium	9.3 mg
	Sodium	237 mg	Fiber	0.4 gm

▲ Poached Salmon with Aromatic Vegetables

A heart-healthy way to serve salmon.

Menu Category:	Entrée, Seafood
Cooking Method:	Poach
Preparation Time:	20 minutes
Cooking Time:	20 minutes
Variations:	Substitute tuna steaks, orange roughy, scallops, or monkfish.
Yield:	50 portions (5 oz)

Ingredient	U.S.	Metric	Method
Carrots, julienne	1 qt	950 ml	Divide among four 12″ × 20″ × 2½″ insert pans rubbed with olive oil, butter or non-stick spray.
Celery, julienne	1 qt	950 ml	
Leeks, white part, julienne	1 qt	950 ml	
Salmon steaks or fillets, 1-inch thick	16 lb	7.3 kg	Season and place over aromatic vegetables.
Salt	1 T	15 ml	
White pepper	2 t	10 ml	
Fish stock, cold	1 gal	3.8 L	Divide among pans. Heat just to a boil. Reduce to a simmer. Cover. Poach just until salmon is firm and flakes easily, about 10 to 12 minutes. Remove salmon with slotted spatula. Divide vegetables over the top of each portion.

Nutrient Analysis Per Serving				
	Calories	150	Protein	21.2 gm
	Fat	5 gm	Carbohydrate	4.1 gm
	Cholesterol	26 mg	Calcium	36.1 mg
	Sodium	1421 mg	Fiber	0.5 gm

▲ Baked Trout Romano

An Italian specialty that is simplicity itself!

Menu Category:	Entrée, Seafood, Ethic, Italian
Cooking Method:	Bake
Preparation Time:	30 minutes
Oven Temperature:	450°F
Cooking Time:	15 minutes
Variations:	Substitute other lean fish, shrimp, or skinless, boneless chicken.
Yield:	50 portions (5 oz)

Ingredient	U.S.	Metric	Method
Trout fillets, ½-inch thick	16 lb	7.3 kg	Arrange in one layer on oiled sheet pans. Reserve.
Olive oil	¾ c	180 ml	Combine in large bowl. Mix well. Portion this mixture over trout fillets. Place sheet pans in preheated 450°F oven. Cook just until fish is firm and flakes easily, about 10 minutes. Remove with spatula.
Bread crumbs, stale	2 qt	1.9 L	
Lemon zest	½ c	120 ml	
Garlic, minced	1 T	15 ml	
Scallion greens, minced	½ c	120 ml	
Parsley, chopped	1 c	240 ml	
Romano cheese, grated	2 c	480 ml	

Nutrient Analysis Per Serving				
	Calories	280	Protein	13.1 gm
	Fat	10 gm	Carbohydrate	12.2 gm
	Cholesterol	85.4 mg	Calcium	145 mg
	Sodium	192 mg	Fiber	0.1 gm

▲ Cantonese Sweet and Sour Trout

This is the traditional popular Cantonese style.

Menu Category:	Entrée, Seafood, Ethnic, Chinese
Cooking Method:	Sauté/Simmer
Preparation Time:	30 minutes
Cooking Time:	45 minutes
Variations:	Substitute other lean fish, shrimp, or skinless, boneless chicken.
Yield:	50 portions (6 oz)

Ingredient	U.S.	Metric	Method
Pineapple juice	1 qt	950 ml	Combine in heavy nonreactive pot. Heat to
Rice wine vinegar	1½ c	360 ml	a boil, stirring constantly. Reduce heat to a
Sesame oil	2 T	30 ml	simmer. Simmer 3 minutes. Remove from
Soy sauce	¾ c	180 ml	heat. Reserve.
Ketchup	¼ c	60 ml	
Brown sugar	1½ c	360 ml	
Gingerroot, minced	½ c	120 ml	
Cornstarch	¼ c	60 ml	
Trout fillets, 5 oz	16 lb	7.3 kg	Season fillets. Arrange on oiled sheet pans.
Salt	2 T	30 ml	Cook in preheated 450°F broiler until fillets
Black pepper	1 T	15 ml	are firm and flake easily, about 8 minutes. Remove fillets with spatula. Portion reserved sauce like a glaze over the top of fillets.

Nutrient Analysis				
Per Serving	Calories	263	Protein	30.5 gm
	Fat	10.2 gm	Carbohydrate	10.9 gm
	Cholesterol	83.7 mg	Calcium	71.6 mg
	Sodium	337 mg	Fiber	0.1 gm

▲ Italian-Style Baked Trout

An ethnic variation on this ever-popular fish.

Menu Category:	Entrée, Seafood, Ethnic, Italian
Cooking Method:	Bake
Preparation Time:	20 minutes
Oven Temperature:	350°F
Cooking Time:	30 minutes
Variations:	Substitute other lean fish, shrimp, or skinless, boneless chicken.
Yield:	50 portions (6 oz)

Ingredient	U.S.	Metric	Method
Trout fillets, ½-inch thick	16 lb	7.3 kg	Arrange in one layer on oiled sheet pans. Reserve.
Olive oil	1½ c	360 ml	Heat in large pot.
Garlic, chopped	1 T	15 ml	Add. Sauté just until golden.
Tomatoes, canned	8 lb	3.6 kg	Add to garlic. Simmer until slightly thickened, about 15 minutes. Spoon over trout. Bake in preheated 350°F oven for 15 minutes or until fish is firm and flakes easily. Portion sauce over each fillet.
Black pepper	1 T	15 ml	
Parsley, chopped	2 c	480 ml	

Nutrient Analysis Per Serving	Calories	289	Protein	31 gm
	Fat	16.3 gm	Carbohydrate	35 gm
	Cholesterol	83.7 mg	Calcium	85 mg
	Sodium	194 mg	Fiber	0.4 gm

▲ Sweet and Sour Whitefish Fillets

This Oriental cooking style works with a variety of lean fish.

Menu Category:	Entrée, Seafood, Ethnic, Chinese		
Cooking Method:	Sauté		
Preparation Time:	30 minutes		
Cooking Time:	45 minutes		
Variations:	Substitute other lean fish, shrimp, or skinless, boneless chicken.		
Yield:	50 portions (6 oz)		

Ingredient	U.S.	Metric	Method
Whitefish fillets, ½-inch			Season fillets.
thick	16 lb	7.3 kg	
Salt	2 T	30 ml	
Black pepper	1 T	15 ml	
Cornstarch	2 lb	908 g	Dredge fillets in cornstarch. Shake off excess.
Peanut oil	2 c	480 ml	Heat in 350°F brazier or flattop. Sauté fillets until golden on both sides, about 10 minutes.
Sweet and Sour Sauce, recipe follows	3 qt	2.8 L	Portion over fillets.

Nutrient Analysis Per Serving	Calories	336	Protein	29.5
	Fat	11.5 gm	Carbohydrate	26.5
	Cholesterol	87 mg	Calcium	9.6
	Sodium	260	Fiber	0.2

Companion Recipe

▲ **Sweet and Sour Sauce**

This sauce is perfect for seafood, pork, and chicken.

Menu Category:	Sauce, Ethnic, Chinese
Cooking Method:	Simmer
Preparation Time:	20 minutes
Cooking Time:	30 minutes
Variations:	Serve with lean fish, shrimp, chicken, or pork.
Yield:	1½ gallon

Ingredient	U.S.	Metric	Method
Scallion, minced	1 qt	950 ml	Combine in large pot. Heat to a boil, stirring constantly. Reduce heat to a simmer.
Gingerroot, minced	½ c	120 ml	
Soy sauce	½ c	120 ml	
Cider vinegar	3 c	720 ml	
Sugar	3 c	720 ml	
Cornstarch	1 c	240 ml	
Dry sherry	2 c	480 ml	
Water	1½ qt	1.4 L	
Tomato, seeded, quartered	1 qt	950 ml	Add to mixture. Simmer 5 minutes. Remove from heat. Serve hot.

Nutrient Analysis Per Ounce				
	Calories	20	Protein	0.1 gm
	Fat	0 gm	Carbohydrate	4.7 gm
	Cholesterol	0 mg	Calcium	2.8 mg
	Sodium	52 mg	Fiber	0.1 gm

Meats

Beef

▲ **Baked Meat Loaf with Creole Tomato Sauce**

This version originated in the kitchens of southern Louisiana.

Menu Category:	Entrée, Beef, Ethnic, American Regional
Cooking Method:	Roast
Preparation Time:	30 minutes
Cooking Time:	45 minutes to 1 hour
Oven Temperature:	375°F
Variations:	As many as you'd like to try. Just substitute herbs and spices of virtually any country in the culinary world!

Yield:	50 portions (4 oz)

Ingredient	U.S.	Metric	Method
Olive oil, hot	½ c	120 ml	Sauté in large pot or brazier just until
Onion, minced	2 c	480 ml	vegetables are tender. Remove from heat.
Green bell pepper, minced	2 c	480 ml	Cool to room temperature. Cover. Chill
Garlic, minced	¼ c	60 ml	well. Reserve.
Beef, lean, medium-ground	10 lb	4.5 kg	Combine in mixer bowl with paddle
Bread crumbs, dry	3 qt	2.8 L	attachment. Add reserved onion mixture.
Milk, cold	3 c	720 ml	Mix at low speed just until mixture is well
Crushed red pepper	1 t	5 ml	blended. Form mixture into six loaves. Put
Parsley, chopped	2 c	480 ml	loaves in oiled or paper-lined 9″ × 5″ × 3″
Eggs, beaten	12	12	loaf pans. Place loaf pans on sheet pans.
Salt	2 T	30 ml	Place in preheated 375°F oven. Roast until
Black pepper	1 T	15 ml	done, about 45 minutes. Transfer to wire racks. Let rest 15 minutes before slicing.
Creole Tomato Sauce, recipe follows	1 gal	3.8 L	Portion 2½ ounces over each slice.

Nutrient Analysis	Calories	478	Protein	27 gm
Per Serving	Fat	29 gm	Carbohydrate	27 gm
	Cholesterol	127 mg	Calcium	92 mg
	Sodium	662 mg	Fiber	0.7 gm

Companion Recipe

▲ **Creole Tomato Sauce**

A spicy variation of traditional tomato sauce to serve with meatballs, pasta, meat loaf, and any of a variety of sautéed or panfried meats, poultry, and seafood.

Menu Category:	Sauce, Ethnic, Caribbean
Cooking Method:	Simmer
Preparation Time:	30 minutes
Cooking Time:	1 hour
Variations:	Add fennel seeds for an Italian flavor.
Yield:	1 gallon

Ingredient	U.S.	Metric	Method
Olive oil, hot	½ c	120 ml	Sauté in large pot or steam kettle just until
Onion, minced	2 c	480 ml	vegetables are tender.
Green bell pepper, minced	2 c	480 ml	
Garlic, minced	¼ c	60 ml	
Gingerroot, minced	2 T	30 ml	
Crushed red pepper	2 t	10 ml	
Tomatoes, canned, chopped	3 qt	2.8 L	Add to vegetables. Heat to a boil. Reduce
Bay leaf	3	3	heat to a simmer. Simmer about 1 hour.
Cinnamon, ground	1 T	15 ml	Remove from heat. Remove bay leaves. Cool to room temperature. Cover. Chill well.

Nutrient Analysis	Calories	17	Protein	0.4 gm
Per Ounce	Fat	19 gm	Carbohydrate	2.1 gm
	Cholesterol	0 mg	Calcium	8.2 mg
	Sodium	49 mg	Fiber	0.2 gm

▲ Bavarian Meat Loaf with Ginger Glaze

This unique version features a beef-pork mixture and the tang of ginger.

Menu Category:	Entrée, Beef, Pork, Ethnic, German
Cooking Method:	Roast
Preparation Time:	30 minutes
Oven Temperature:	375°F
Cooking Time:	45 minutes to 1 hour
Variations:	Use mixture to make savory hamburgers or meatballs.
Yield:	50 portions (4 oz)

Ingredient	U.S.	Metric	Method
Onion, minced	2 lb	908 g	Sauté just until onions are tender. Remove
Olive oil, hot	½ c	120 ml	from heat. Reserve.
Pork, lean, medium-ground	4 lb	1.8 kg	Combine in mixer bowl with paddle
Beef, lean, medium-ground	6 lb	3.8 kg	attachment. Add reserved onion mixture.
Garlic, minced	1 T	15 ml	Mix at low speed just until mixture is well
Fennel seed	2 t	10 ml	blended. Form mixture into six loaves. Put
Bread crumbs, rye	3 qt	2.8 L	loaves in oiled or paper-lined 9″ × 5″ × 3″
Milk, cold	3 c	720 ml	loaf pans. Place loaf pans on sheet pans.
Parsley, chopped	2 c	480 ml	Place in preheated 375°F oven. Roast until
Eggs, beaten	12	12	done, about 45 minutes. Baste with Ginger
Salt	2 T	30 ml	Glaze Basting Sauce during last 15
Black pepper	1 T	15 ml	minutes. Transfer to wire racks. Let rest 15
			minutes before slicing.
Ginger Glaze Basting Sauce, recipe follows	1 qt	950 ml	

Nutrient Analysis	Calories	422	Protein	25 gm
Per Serving	Fat	22 gm	Carbohydrate	29.4 gm
	Cholesterol	124 mg	Calcium	77.4 mg
	Sodium	529 mg	Fiber	0.3 gm

Companion Recipe

▲ **Ginger Glaze Basting Sauce**

Use to baste roasted or grilled meats toward the end of cooking.

Menu Category:	Sauce
Cooking Method:	Simmer
Preparation Time:	10 minutes
Cooking Time:	15 minutes
Yield:	1 gallon

Ingredient	U.S.	Metric	Method
Butter, soft	1 c	240 ml	Combine ingredients in large pot. Heat to
Mustard, Dijon style	½ c	120 ml	a boil, stirring frequently. Reduce heat to a
Orange marmalade	1 qt	950 ml	simmer. Simmer 10 minutes. Remove from
Brown sugar	2 lb	908 g	heat. Cool to room temperature. Cover.
Ginger, ground	¼ c	60 ml	Chill well. Warm for use.
White wine, dry	2 qt	1.9 L	

Nutrient Analysis Per Ounce				
	Calories	78	Protein	0.1 gm
	Fat	1.5 gm	Carbohydrate	14.1 gm
	Cholesterol	3.9 mg	Calcium	10.1 mg
	Sodium	41 mg	Fiber	0.1 gm

▲ Bracciole (Italian Braised Beef Rolls)

A classic Italian dish that yields the best of the braising procedure.

Menu Category:	Entrée, Beef, Ethnic, Italian
Cooking Method:	Braise
Preparation Time:	30 minutes
Cooking Time:	1½ to 2 hours
Variations:	This recipe works equally well with thinly pounded veal, pork, or chicken. You can also use the filling with thin strips of lean white fish.
Yield:	50 portions (5 oz)

Ingredient	U.S.	Metric	Method
Beef round, 4-ounce slices	15 lb	6.8 kg	Pound thinly. Reserve.
Spinach, chopped,	2 qt	1.9 L	Combine in food processor or food
Garlic, minced	¼ c	60 ml	chopper. Process until well pureed.
Basil, dried	1 T	15 ml	Reserve. Portion filling over beef slices.
Pine nuts, chopped	2 c	480 ml	Roll each slice tightly. Secure each roll
Parmesan cheese, grated	1 lb	454 g	with toothpicks.
Bread crumbs, fine, dried	1 qt	950 ml	
Olive oil	2 c	480 ml	
Black pepper	1 T	15 ml	
Olive oil, hot	1½ c	360 ml	Sauté beef rolls in brazier or tilt kettle.
Beef stock	1½ gal	5.7 L	Add to beef rolls. Heat to a boil. Reduce to a simmer. Cover. Simmer until beef is tender, about 1½ to 2 hours. Remove beef. Keep warm. Heat liquid to a boil.
Sherry, dry	1 qt	950 ml	Add to liquid. Boil to reduce by half. Portion 2 ounces sauce over each beef roll.

Nutrient Analysis	Calories	570	Protein	50 gm
Per Serving	Fat	33 gm	Carbohydrate	11.3 gm
	Cholesterol	122 mg	Calcium	207 mg
	Sodium	715 mg	Fiber	0.5 gm

▲ Bul-Kogi (Korean Grilled Beef)

This Korean classic, pronounced BULL go-KEE, is a labor-saving winner.

Menu Category:	Entrée, Beef, Ethnic, Korean
Cooking Method:	Grill/Broil
Preparation Time:	30 minutes
Marination Time:	Several hours
Cooking Time:	10 minutes
Variations:	Although this is classically a beef dish, the marinade and cooking procedure work equally well with pork, game, or seafood.
Yield:	50 portions (3½ oz)

Ingredient	U.S.	Metric	Method
Beef rump roast	15 lb	6.8 kg	Slice into ½-inch slices. Place slices in plastic storage containers. Reserve.
Onion, sliced	1 qt	950 ml	Combine in large bowl. Mix well. Pour
Scallions, minced	1 qt	950 ml	over beef slices. Rub slices well. Cover.
Garlic, minced	½ c	120 ml	Chill several hours. Remove from
Gingerroot, minced	1 c	240 ml	marinade. Grill or broil over/under
Brown sugar	½ c	120 ml	medium-high heat, turning only once.
Soy sauce	1 c	240 ml	Cook for about 3 to 5 minutes on each
Peanut oil	1 c	240 ml	side. Serve slices fanned on plate.
Sesame oil	½ c	120 ml	
Burgundy wine	2 c	480 ml	
Sesame seeds, toasted	1 c	240 ml	Sprinkle as quantity dictates over each portion.

Nutrient Analysis				
Per Serving	Calories	336	Protein	32 gm
	Fat	19.6 gm	Carbohydrate	5.4 gm
	Cholesterol	97.3 mg	Calcium	55.4 mg
	Sodium	301 mg	Fiber	0.5 gm

▲ Jamaican Marinated Flank Steak

A touch of the Caribbean for any festive island menu. Great for sandwiches!

Menu Category:	Entrée, Beef, Ethnic, Caribbean
Cooking Method:	Grill/Broil
Preparation Time:	30 minutes
Cooking Time:	40 minutes
Variations:	The black pepper and chile pepper give this a traditional bite that can be reduced by varying the quantities of either or both.
	Try this with pork, chicken, and shrimp too.
Yield:	50 portions (3½ oz)

Ingredient	U.S.	Metric	Method
Peanut oil, hot	1 c	240 ml	Sauté just until garlic is golden.
Garlic, minced	¼ c	60 ml	
Gingerroot, minced	¼ c	60 ml	
Green pepper, julienne	1 qt	950 ml	Add. Continue to sauté just until
Onion, julienne	1 qt	950 ml	vegetables are tender, about 5 minutes.
Chile peppers, red	2 T	30 ml	
Dark rum	1 c	240 ml	Add. Flame if possible. Remove from heat. Reserve.
Beef flank steak, trimmed	18 lb	6.8 kg	Rub flank steak with oil and pepper. Cook
Olive oil	2 c	480 ml	at medium-high heat, turning only once.
Black pepper, coarsely ground	1 c	240 ml	When cooked as desired, let rest a few minutes. Slice on the bias. Portion reserved vegetables over slices.

Nutrient Analysis Per Serving	Calories	455	Protein	27 gm
	Fat	35 gm	Carbohydrate	5 gm
	Cholesterol	93.7 mg	Calcium	22 mg
	Sodium	109 mg	Fiber	0.4 gm

▲ Oriental Smoke-Roasted Beef Tenderloin

Serve slices of this full-flavored beef dish either hot or cold.

Menu Category:	Entrée, Beef, Ethnic, Oriental
Cooking Method:	Roast
Preparation Time:	30 minutes
Marination Time:	Several hours
Oven Temperature:	400°F
Cooking Time:	35 minutes
Variations:	Substitute chicken breast, pork, or even peeled jumbo shrimp.
Yield:	50 portions (3½ oz)

Ingredient	U.S.	Metric	Method
Beef tenderloin, trimmed	15 lb	6.8 kg	Combine in plastic storage containers. Mix
Scallions, chopped	1 qt	950 ml	well. Cover. Chill several hours. Remove
Soy sauce	1 c	240 ml	tenderloin from marinade. Roast tenderloin
Pineapple juice	1 c	240 ml	in preheated 400°F oven to internal
Brown sugar	1 c	240 ml	temperature of 135°F, about 25 minutes.
Hot pepper oil	¼ c	60 ml	Baste frequently with marinade. Remove
Gingerroot, minced	½ c	120 ml	beef from oven. Cover and let rest for 15
Garlic, minced	¼ c	60 ml	minutes. Slice. Serve with any
Peanut oil	1 c	240 ml	accumulated juices.
Beef broth	2 c	480 ml	
Liquid smoke	1 T	15 ml	

Nutrient Analysis	Calories	200	Protein	21.7 gm
Per Serving	Fat	8.9 gm	Carbohydrate	7.6 gm
	Cholesterol	58 mg	Calcium	24.6 mg
	Sodium	315 mg	Fiber	0.2 gm

▲ Roestbraten

Serve this German style marinated roast beef with red cabbage and steamed gnocchi.

Menu Category:	Entrée, Beef, Ethnic, German
Cooking Method:	Roast
Preparation Time:	30 minutes
Marination Time:	Several days
Oven Temperature:	325°F
Cooking Time:	2½ to 3 hours
Variations:	Serve with pan gravy made with crumbled gingersnaps mixed in.
Yield:	50 portions (4 oz)

Ingredient	U.S.	Metric	Method
Beef top round roast, trimmed	18 lb	8.2 kg	Combine in plastic storage containers. Mix well. Cover. Chill several days. Turn beef frequently. Drain off marinade. Roast beef in preheated 325°F oven to internal temperature of 135°F, about 2½ to 3 hours. Baste frequently with marinade. Remove beef from oven. Cover and let rest for 30 minutes. Slice. Serve with any accumulated juices or with a sauce derived from roasting juices.
Red wine, dry	1 qt	950 ml	
Water	2 qt	1.9 L	
Onion, thinly sliced	1 qt	950 ml	
Peppercorns, crushed	1 c	240 ml	
Bay leaves, whole	¼ c	60 ml	
Pickling spice	½ c	120 ml	
Salt	½ c	120 ml	

Nutrient Analysis Per Serving				
	Calories	294	Protein	32 gm
	Fat	16 gm	Carbohydrate	2.3 gm
	Cholesterol	101 mg	Calcium	24.2 mg
	Sodium	722 mg	Fiber	0.4 gm

▲ Sukiyaki (Japanese Grilled Meat in Broth)

Japanese grilled meat in broth is light and tempting.

Menu Category:	Entrée, Beef, Ethnic, Japanese
Cooking Method:	Sauté/Simmer
Preparation Time:	30 minutes
Cooking Time:	1 hour
Variations:	This procedure can be used with any meat, poultry, or seafood.
Yield:	50 portions (6 oz)

Ingredient	U.S.	Metric	Method
Beef flank steak, trimmed	15 lb	5.5 kg	Slice thinly against the grain. Reserve.
Peanut oil, hot	1½ c	360 ml	Heat in large pot, tilt kettle, or steam kettle. Add reserved beef. Sauté just until lightly colored.
Potatoes, red, peeled, sliced	5 lb	2.3 kg	Add to beef. Sauté 5 minutes.
Carrots, peeled, sliced	5 lb	2.3 kg	
Onions, peeled, sliced	3 lb	1.4 kg	
Beef broth	1 gal	3.8 L	Add to mixture. Heat to a simmer. Cover. Simmer just until beef is tender, about 45 minutes to one hour. Portion into shallow bowls.
Japanese sake	2 c	480 ml	
Sugar	1 c	240 ml	
Soy sauce	2 c	480 ml	
Scallion greens, minced	2 c	480 ml	Garnish each portion.

Nutrient Analysis Per Serving	Calories	215	Protein	22.8 gm
	Fat	5.8 gm	Carbohydrate	16.6 gm
	Cholesterol	52 mg	Calcium	31.1 mg
	Sodium	734 mg	Fiber	0.7 gm

Lamb

▲ Roast Lamb with Ginger Baste

Tender boneless leg of lamb with an Oriental flavor.

Menu Category:	Entrée, Lamb, Ethnic, Oriental
Cooking Method:	Roast
Preparation Time:	30 minutes
Oven Temperature:	350°F
Cooking Time:	45 minutes for medium rare
Variations:	This procedure works equally well with chicken breast and pork.
Yield:	50 portions (3½ oz)

Ingredient	U.S.	Metric	Method
Leg of lamb, boneless	18 lb	8.2 kg	Trim. Lay out flat. Secure with long metal skewers to maintain shape during roasting.
Gingerroot, minced	½ c	120 ml	Combine. Rub over all surfaces of lamb.
Garlic, minced	¼ c	60 ml	Place lamb on racks on sheet pans. Roast
Soy sauce	2 c	480 ml	at 350°F to desired doneness. Turn lamb
Rice wine vinegar	1 c	240 ml	once during roasting. Baste often. Remove
Brown sugar	1 c	240 ml	from oven. Cover. Let rest 10 minutes.
Salt	2 T	30 ml	Slice thinly. Serve with any accumulated
Black pepper	1 T	15 ml	juices.

Nutrient Analysis	Calories	136	Protein	17.5 gm
Per Serving	Fat	4.7 gm	Carbohydrate	3.9 gm
	Cholesterol	53.7 mg	Calcium	11.4 mg
	Sodium	637 mg	Fiber	0.1 gm

▲ Skewered Lamb with Cinnamon-Pepper Marinade

Serve these Moroccan kebabs with chilled cucumber-mint salad with yogurt dressing.

Menu Category:	Entrée, Lamb, Ethnic, Moroccan
Cooking Method:	Grill/Broil
Preparation Time:	30 minutes
Marination Time:	1 hour
Cooking Time:	30 minutes
Variations:	To reduce piquancy, adjust amounts of cayenne and black peppers.
Yield:	50 portions (3½ oz)

Ingredient	U.S.	Metric	Method
Leg of lamb, boneless	18 lb	6.8 kg	Trim. Cut into 1-inch cubes. Place in plastic storage containers.
Gingerroot, minced	½ c	120 ml	Combine. Rub over lamb cubes. Cover.
Garlic, minced	¼ c	60 ml	Chill for one hour. Portion lamb onto
Chili powder	¼ c	60 ml	metal skewers. Cook at medium-high heat
Cinnamon, ground	1 T	15 ml	to desired doneness. Turn lamb as needed
Cayenne pepper, ground	1 T	15 ml	to brown all surfaces. Serve on skewers.
Lime juice	1 c	240 ml	
Olive oil	2 c	240 ml	
Salt	1 T	15 ml	
Black pepper	2 t	10 ml	

Nutrient Analysis Per Serving				
	Calories	192	Protein	13.9 gm
	Fat	14.6 gm	Carbohydrate	0.9 gm
	Cholesterol	50 mg	Calcium	10.6 mg
	Sodium	123 mg	Fiber	0.2 gm

PORK

▲ **Barbecued Pork with Apricots**

A grilled entrée with a Spanish touch.

Menu Category:	Entrée, Pork, Ethnic, Spanish
Cooking Method:	Grill/Broil
Preparation Time:	30 minutes
Marination Time:	Several hours
Cooking Time:	35 minutes
Variations:	This procedure works equally well with chicken breast or haddock fillets.
Yield:	50 portions (3½ oz)

Ingredient	U.S.	Metric	Method
Pork tenderloin	18 lb	6.8 kg	Rub to coat pork well. Place in plastic
Olive oil	1 c	240 ml	storage containers. Reserve.
Kosher salt	¼ c	60 ml	
Tawny port	1 qt	950 ml	Combine in large pot. Heat to a simmer.
Orange juice	1 qt	950 ml	Simmer for 10 minutes. Remove from heat.
Orange liqueur	1 c	240 ml	Cool. Pour over pork. Cover. Chill several
Cider vinegar	½ c	120 ml	hours. Remove pork. Reserve marinade.
Scallions, minced	1 c	240 ml	Broil pork under/over medium-high heat to
Dried apricots, diced	1 lb	454 g	internal temperature of 150°F, about 35
Rosemary, dried	1 T	15 ml	minutes. Baste frequently with marinade. Remove pork. Cover. Keep warm and let rest for 15 minutes. Reserve all juices. Heat reserved marinade to a boil. Add pork juices. Simmer 5 minutes. Slice pork loin. Serve with warm sauce over slices.

Nutrient Analysis	Calories	208	Protein	23.4 gm
Per Serving	Fat	7.8 gm	Carbohydrate	9.1 gm
	Cholesterol	72.7 mg	Calcium	29.6 mg
	Sodium	444 mg	Fiber	0.3 gm

▲ Chinese Firecracker Pork Loin

Serve as a traditional Chinese entrée or as an appetizer in wonton skins or eggroll wrappers.

Menu Category:	Entrée, Pork, Ethnic, Chinese
Cooking Method:	Stir-fry/Sauté
Preparation Time:	20 minutes
Marination Time:	1 hour
Cooking Time:	10 minutes
Variations:	Substitute chicken for pork.
	For a Korean twist, add peanut butter and sesame seeds to final sauce mixture.
Yield:	50 portions (3½ oz)

Ingredient	U.S.	Metric	Method
Pork loin, trimmed	12 lb	4.5 kg	Trim any surface fat. Cut into julienne strips. Place in large bowl. Reserve.
Egg white, beaten	3 c	720 ml	Combine in small bowl. Mix well. Add to reserved pork. Stir well. Chill for 1 hour.
Cornstarch	2 c	480 ml	
Water, boiling	to cover	to cover	Add pork mixture. Stir well. Cook for 1 minute. Remove with "spider" sieve or strainer. Reserve.
Cooking spray	as needed	as needed	Spray in preheated tilt skillet/brazier.
Celery, julienne	1 qt	950 ml	Add to skillet. Stir and cook over high heat just until vegetables soften. Add reserved pork. Continue to cook until pork is golden, about 2 minutes.
Scallions, julienne	2 c	480 ml	
Ginger, shredded	½ c	120 ml	
Red pepper flakes	1 T	15 ml	
Chicken broth	1 qt	950 ml	Add to pork mixture. Cook over high heat until mixture boils. Turn off heat immediately. Serve hot.
Dry sherry	1 c	240 ml	
Sesame oil	¼ c	60 ml	
Soy sauce	½ c	120 ml	

Nutrient Analysis	Calories	209	Protein	17 gm
Per Serving	Fat	11.8 gm	Carbohydrate	6.8 gm
	Cholesterol	49.7 mg	Calcium	18 mg
	Sodium	307 mg	Fiber	0.2 gm

▲ Grilled Pork Loin Santa Fe

Serve as a Mexican or American regional entrée.

Menu Category:	Entrée, Pork, American Regional
Cooking Method:	Grill/Broil
Preparation Time:	30 minutes
Marination Time:	Several hours
Cooking Time:	30 minutes
Variations:	Substitute chicken, turkey, veal, or shrimp for pork.
Yield:	50 portions (3½ oz)

Ingredient	U.S.	Metric	Method
Butter	2 lb	908 g	Combine in food processor with metal blade. Puree well. Spread mixture over plastic wrap. Roll into a cylinder. Chill at least 1 hour. Cut chilled cylinder into 50 slices. Reserve.
Commercial picante sauce	2 c	480 ml	
Jalapeño peppers, seeded	¼ c	60 ml	
Lime juice	¼ c	60 ml	
Chili powder	2 T	30 ml	
Pork loin chops, boneless	15 lb	6.8 kg	Butterfly pork with sharp knife. Press flat. Place in shallow pans.
Lime juice	1 qt	950 ml	Add to pork. Cover. Marinate at least 1 hour. Remove pork from marinade. Drain well. Grill/broil over/under medium-high heat for 3 to 5 minutes on each side. Serve each portion with seasoned butter slice.
Olive oil	2 c	480 ml	
Scallion greens, minced	1 c	240 ml	Garnish each portion.
Parsley, chopped	2 c	480 ml	
Lime slices	50	50	

Nutrient Analysis Per Serving	Calories	301	Protein	13.5 gm
	Fat	26.6 gm	Carbohydrate	2.9 gm
	Cholesterol	72.8 mg	Calcium	16.4 mg
	Sodium	188 mg	Fiber	0.2 gm

▲ Grilled Pork with Ginger and Burgundy

A delightful entrée in which East meets West.

Menu Category:	Entrée, Pork, Ethnic, European
Cooking Method:	Grill/Broil
Preparation Time:	30 minutes
Marination Time:	Several hours
Cooking Time:	10 minutes
Variations:	Use the marinade/rub with chicken pieces or shrimp.
Yield:	50 portions (3½ oz)

Ingredient	U.S.	Metric	Method
Pork loin, trimmed	15 lb	6.8 kg	Slice pork loin into ½-inch slices. Place slices in plastic storage containers. Reserve.
Onion, sliced	2 qt	1.9 L	Combine in large bowl. Mix well. Pour over pork slices. Rub slices well. Cover. Chill several hours. Remove from marinade. Grill or broil over/under medium-high heat, turning only once. Cook for about 3 to 5 minutes on each side.
Scallions, minced	1 c	240 ml	
Garlic, minced	1 T	15 ml	
Parsley, chopped	1 c	240 ml	
Gingerroot, minced	1 c	240 ml	
Sugar	½ c	120 ml	
Burgundy wine	2 c	480 ml	
Soy sauce	1 c	240 ml	
Olive oil	1 c	240 ml	
Sesame oil	½ c	120 ml	

Nutrient Analysis Per Serving				
	Calories	230	Protein	14.7 gm
	Fat	16.7 gm	Carbohydrate	3.9 gm
	Cholesterol	50.5 mg	Calcium	11.6 mg
	Sodium	267 mg	Fiber	0.2 gm

▲ Pork Medallions Barcelona

Serve as a Spanish or Mediterranean entrée or as a light tapas appetizer.

Menu Category:	Entrée, Pork, Ethnic, Spanish
Cooking Method:	Sauté
Preparation Time:	20 minutes
Cooking Time:	30 minutes
Variations:	Substitute chicken or skewered butterflied jumbo shrimp.
	Garnish with orange slices or wedges.
Yield:	50 portions (3½ oz)

Ingredient	U.S.	Metric	Method
Pork tenderloin, sliced	15 lb	6.8 kg	Combine in bowl. Rub to coat pork well.
Olive oil	1 c	240 ml	Chill for several hours. Remove pork.
Sherry, semisweet	1 c	240 ml	Reserve marinade.
Cointreau	1 c	240 ml	
Orange juice	3 c	720 ml	
Orange marmalade	1½ qt	1.4 L	Combine in sauce pan. Heat to a boil.
Raisins	1 qt	950 ml	Reduce heat to a simmer. Cover pan.
Orange juice	2 c	480 ml	Simmer for 10 minutes.
White wine, dry	2 c	480 ml	
Walnut pieces	1 qt	950 ml	Add. Simmer 5 minutes more.
Flour	1 qt	950 ml	Dip pork slices. Shake off all excess.
Olive oil	1 c	240 ml	Heat. Sauté pork slices just until golden on both sides.
Orange zest	1 c	240 ml	Add to pork just at the end of cooking. Remove pork and orange zest from the pan and pour out all oil. Add reserved marinade to the pan. Heat to a boil and add to prepared sauce. Arrange pork medallions on plates. Spoon sauce over slices.

Nutrient Analysis	Calories	359	Protein	24.8 gm
Per Serving	Fat	14.6 gm	Carbohydrate	31.5 gm
	Cholesterol	17.6 mg	Calcium	26.6 mg
	Sodium	57.5 mg	Fiber	0.9 gm

▲ Pork Tenderloin with Orange and Ginger

Tenderloin of pork highlighted with two traditional flavoring ingredients.

Menu Category:	Entrée, Pork, Ethnic, Tropical
Cooking Method:	Grill/Broil
Preparation Time:	30 minutes
Marination Time:	Several hours
Cooking Time:	25 minutes
Variations:	Use with other boneless pork cuts, as well as chicken, veal, or lean white fish.
Yield:	50 portions (3½ oz)

Ingredient	U.S.	Metric	Method
Pork tenderloin	15 lb	6.8 kg	Combine in plastic storage container. Mix well. Cover. Chill several hours. Remove pork from marinade. Broil or grill at medium-high heat to internal temperature of 150°F, about 25 minutes. Baste frequently with marinade. Remove pork. Cover and keep warm and let rest for 15 minutes. Reserve all juices. Heat reserved marinade to a boil. Add pork juices. Simmer 5 minutes. Slice pork loin. Strain warm sauce over slices.
Olive oil	2 c	480 ml	
Cointreau	2 c	480 ml	
Ginger, minced	1½ c	640 ml	
Soy sauce	1 c	240 ml	
Garlic, minced	¼ c	60 ml	
Scallions, minced	1 c	240 ml	
Lime juice	½ c	120 ml	
Red pepper flakes	2 T	30 ml	
Beef or pork stock	2 qt	1.9 L	

Nutrient Analysis Per Serving				
	Calories	201	Protein	23.4 gm
	Fat	10.5 gm	Carbohydrate	2.4 gm
	Cholesterol	73 mg	Calcium	15.1 mg
	Sodium	395 mg	Fiber	0.2 gm

▲ Roast Pork Loin Florentine

This procedure originated in Florence, Italy, proving that "florentine" doesn't always mean spinach!

Menu Category:	Entrée, Pork, Ethnic, Italian
Cooking Method:	Roast
Preparation Time:	30 minutes
Marination Time:	Several hours
Oven Temperature:	350°F
Cooking Time:	1 to 1½ hours
Variations:	For a quick shift to Mexican pork roast, follow the same procedure but add chili powder or cumin to the marinade and eliminate the capers.
Yield:	50 portions (3½ oz)

Ingredient	U.S.	Metric	Method
Pork loin, boneless, trimmed	15 lb	6.8 kg	Combine in plastic storage containers. Mix well. Cover. Chill several hours. Remove pork loin from marinade. Roast in preheated 350°F oven to internal temperature of 150°F, about 1 hour. Baste frequently with marinade. Remove pork loin from oven. Cover and let rest for 15 minutes.
Garlic powder	2 T	30 ml	
Olive oil	2 c	480 ml	
White wine, dry	1 qt	950 ml	
Lemon juice	1 c	240 ml	
Capers, drained	1 c	240 ml	
Parsley, chopped	1 c	240 ml	
Lemon juice	½ c	120 ml	Slice pork loin. Ladle with any juices and sprinkle with lemon juice, capers, and parsley.
Capers, tiny	2 c	480 ml	
Parsley, chopped	2 c	480 ml	

Nutrient Analysis Per Serving	Calories	243	Protein	15.1 gm
	Fat	19 gm	Carbohydrate	1 gm
	Cholesterol	72 mg	Calcium	19 mg
	Sodium	115 mg	Fiber	0.1 gm

▲ Sautéed Pork with Bourbon and Mustard

This dish combines the distinct flavors of French mustard and American bourbon.

Menu Category:	Entrée, Pork, Ethnic, American Regional
Cooking Method:	Sauté
Preparation Time:	30 minutes
Marination Time:	Several hours
Cooking Time:	10 minutes
Variations:	Substitute another liquor (e.g., scotch) or eliminate entirely from the marinade.
Yield:	50 portions (3½ oz)

Ingredient	U.S.	Metric	Method
Pork loin	15 lb	6.8 kg	Slice pork loin into ¼-inch slices. Place slices in plastic storage containers. Reserve.
Brown sugar	1 lb	454 g	Combine in small bowl. Add to pork. Mix well. Chill several hours. When ready to cook, remove pork slices from marinade. Reserve marinade. Heat oil in skillet, flattop grill or brazier. Sauté pork until well browned on both sides. Remove from heat and keep warm. Heat marinade to a boil. Reduce heat and simmer a few minutes.
Mustard, Dijon style	2 c	480 ml	
Bourbon	2 c	480 ml	
Chicken or pork stock	2 qt	1.9 L	
Scallions, minced	1 c	240 ml	
Garlic, minced	1 T	15 ml	
Worcestershire sauce	½ c	120 ml	
Cooking oil	2 c	480 ml	
Butter, chopped	½ c	120 ml	Add to sauce, swirling pan to melt butter. Season to taste. Strain sauce over the pork slices.

Nutrient Analysis Per Serving				
	Calories	304	Protein	16.3 gm
	Fat	21 gm	Carbohydrate	7.7 gm
	Cholesterol	56 mg	Calcium	16 mg
	Sodium	329 mg	Fiber	0.1 gm

▲ Szechuan Pork with Peanuts

Serve as a hot and spicy entrée on Chinese or Oriental menus.

Menu Category:	Entrée, Pork, Ethnic, Chinese
Cooking Method:	Sauté
Preparation Time:	30 minutes
Cooking Time:	20 minutes
Variations:	Substitute shrimp or chicken.
	Serve each portion in a ring of cellophane noodles.
Yield:	50 portions (3½ oz)

Ingredient	U.S.	Metric	Method
Peanut oil, hot	1 c	240 ml	Sauté in heavy pans or brazier kettle until
Garlic, minced	¼ c	60 ml	garlic is golden and peppers are dark.
Gingerroot, minced	¼ c	60 ml	
Chile peppers, red	2 T	30 ml	
Pork loin, 1-inch strips	15 lb	6.8 kg	Add. Stir-fry over high heat until golden.
Green bell pepper, julienne	1 qt	950 ml	Add. Continue to sauté just until
Onion, julienne	1 qt	950 ml	vegetables are tender.
Sesame oil	¾ c	180 ml	Add. Toss mixture vigorously for one minute.
Sherry, dry	1½ c	360 ml	Add. Mix well. Remove from heat.
Peanuts, roasted	1 qt	950 ml	Divide over each portion.

Nutrient Analysis Per Serving				
	Calories	289	Protein	18.7 gm
	Fat	21 gm	Carbohydrate	6 gm
	Cholesterol	54 mg	Calcium	18.1 mg
	Sodium	124 mg	Fiber	0.7 gm

▲ Tuscan-Style Pork with Herbed Lentils

Serve as an entrée for Italian or Mediterranean menus.

Menu Category:	Entrée, Pork, Ethnic, Italian
Cooking Method:	Sauté
Preparation Time:	30 minutes
Cooking Time:	40 minutes
Variations:	Substitute veal, shrimp, or chicken.
Yield:	50 portions (4 oz)

Ingredient	U.S.	Metric	Method
Lentils, brown	4 lb	1.8 kg	Rinse well. Place in large pot.
Water, cold	2 gal	7.6 L	Pour over lentils. Heat to a simmer. Check
Oregano, dried	2 T	30 ml	in 10 minutes. Do not overcook. Strain off
Thyme, dried	2 t	10 ml	liquid. Place lentils in large bowl.
Olive oil, hot	1 c	240 ml	Sauté just until golden in heavy pans or
Italian pancetta, minced	2 lb	908 g	brazier kettle.
Pork medallions (4 oz)	15 lb	6.8 kg	Add to hot oil and pancetta. Sauté until pork is golden. Transfer pork to sheet pans. Cover. Keep warm. Drain and reserve hot oil but discard pancetta.
Red onion, julienne	1 qt	950 ml	Using reserved oil, sauté until very tender. Add the reserved lentils. Heat just until warmed through.
Parsley, chopped	1 c	240 ml	Add to mixture. Stir gently but well.
Oregano, dried	2 t	10 ml	Portion onto serving plates. Top with
Basil, dried	2 t	10 ml	portion of sautéed pork loin.
Black pepper, cracked	2 t	10 ml	

Nutrient Analysis	Calories	197	Protein	18 gm
Per Serving	Fat	10 gm	Carbohydrate	8.3 gm
	Cholesterol	46 mg	Calcium	17.4 mg
	Sodium	37 mg	Fiber	1.1 gm

▲ Velvet Pork Ribbons with Spinach

The "velveting" procedure yields a succulent, tender pork dish.

Menu Category:	Entrée, Pork, Ethnic, Chinese
Cooking Method:	Sauté/Stir-fry
Preparation Time:	30 minutes
Marination Time:	1 hour
Cooking Time:	20 minutes
Variations:	Substitute shrimp, chicken, or turkey.
	Change flavors by adding curry powder to cornstarch mixture.
Yield:	50 portions (4 oz)

Ingredient	U.S.	Metric	Method
Pork loin, julienne	12 lb	5.5 kg	Combine in large bowl. Mix well to coat
Sherry	1 c	240 ml	pork strips. Cover. Chill for at least 1 hour.
Egg white, lightly beaten	1 qt	950 ml	
Sesame oil	½ c	120 ml	
Cornstarch	2 c	480 ml	
Salt	2 T	30 ml	
Water, boiling	3 gal	11.4 L	Add pork mixture. Turn heat high. Cook until water boils. Lower heat to a simmer. Simmer 1 minute. Remove from water. Drain well.
Peanut oil	1 c	240 ml	Heat in preheated 350°F brazier kettle.
Scallions, shredded	3 c	720 ml	Sauté in brazier kettle just until peppers are soft. Add reserved pork mixture. Stir-fry for 3 to 5 minutes, or until heated through. Drain and reserve any oil. Transfer mixture to large bowl. Keep warm.
Gingerroot, shredded	½ c	120 ml	
Green bell pepper, shredded	1 qt	950 ml	
Spinach, fresh, washed, ½-inch slices	5 lb	2.3 kg	Sauté in reserved oil. Add to pork mixture. Toss well to combine. Serve hot.

Nutrient Analysis	Calories	262	Protein	11.2 gm
Per Serving	Fat	15.5 gm	Carbohydrate	12 gm
	Cholesterol	48.1 mg	Calcium	62.7 mg
	Sodium	420 mg	Fiber	0.8 gm

VEAL

▲ Braised Veal Saltimbocca

Serve this fork-tender, delicately flavored veal with buttered gnocchi and sautéed fresh spinach.

Menu Category:	Entrée, Veal, Ethnic, Italian
Cooking Method:	Braise
Preparation Time:	30 minutes
Cooking Time:	45 minutes to 1 hour
Variations:	Substitute beef, pork, or lamb for veal.
	Substitute slices of cheese for ham.
Yield:	50 portions (4 oz)

Ingredient	U.S.	Metric	Method
Veal round, 4-ounce slices	15 lb	6.8 kg	Pound thinly. Reserve.
Prosciutto ham, ½-ounce slices	2 lb	908 g	Arrange a slice of ham on top of each veal slice.
Sage, dried	¼ c	60 ml	Sprinkle over ham. Roll slices tightly. Secure with toothpicks.
Flour, all purpose	1 lb	454 g	Dredge veal rolls. Shake off excess.
Salt	1 T	15 ml	
Black pepper	1 T	15 ml	
Olive oil, hot	1½ c	360 ml	Sauté veal rolls in brazier or tilt kettle.
Beef stock	1 gal	3.8 L	Add to veal rolls. Heat to a boil. Reduce to a simmer. Cover. Simmer until veal is tender, about 45 minutes. Remove veal. Keep warm. Heat liquid to a boil. Boil to reduce by half. Portion 2 ounces sauce over each veal roll.

Nutrient Analysis Per Serving	Calories	316	Protein	41.4 gm
	Fat	13.2 gm	Carbohydrate	5.7 gm
	Cholesterol	145 mg	Calcium	16.8 mg
	Sodium	530 mg	Fiber	0.2 gm

▲ Veal Piccata Milanese

This procedure takes the classic panfrying procedure to flavorful heights.

Menu Category:	Entrée, Veal, Ethnic, Italian
Cooking Method:	Panfry
Preparation Time:	30 minutes
Cooking Time:	15 minutes
Variations:	Substitute virtually any thinly sliced meat or poultry.
	This dish is especially good with Madeira-laced mushroom sauce.

Yield:	50 portions (4 oz)

Ingredient	U.S.	Metric	Method
Veal round, 1-ounce slices	15 lb	6.8 kg	Pound thinly. Reserve.
Flour	1 lb	454 g	Dredge veal. Shake off excess.
Salt	1 T	15 ml	
Black pepper	1 T	15 ml	
Eggs, beaten	4	4	Combine. Dip floured veal slices.
Milk	1 qt	950 ml	
Breadcrumbs, dried	2 qt	1.9 L	Dredge veal slices. Shake off excess. If
Parmesan, finely grated	2 c	480 ml	desired, veal can now be covered and
Parsley, chopped	2 c	480 ml	chilled for later cooking.
Cooking oil, hot	3 c	720 ml	Panfry veal in brazier or tilt kettle until golden on first side. Turn over and panfry until done.

Nutrient Analysis	Calories	397	Protein	41.5 gm
Per Serving	Fat	18.4 gm	Carbohydrate	14.7 gm
	Cholesterol	153 mg	Calcium	89.3 mg
	Sodium	321 mg	Fiber	0.2 gm

Poultry

Chicken

▲ Austin-Style Chicken Burritos

The essence of Tex-Mex cooking.

Menu Category:	Entrée, Poultry, American Regional
Cooking Method:	Bake
Preparation Time:	10 minutes
Oven Temperature:	375°F
Cooking Time:	30 minutes
Variations:	Substitute virtually any meat or poultry.
Yield:	50 portions (4 oz)

Ingredient	U.S.	Metric	Method
Chicken breast, skinless, diced	8 lb	3.6 kg	Sauté in large pot or steam kettle just until golden.
Olive oil, hot	1 c	240 ml	
Green bell pepper, julienne	1 qt	950 ml	Add to chicken. Sauté 2 minutes.
Red onion, julienne	2 c	480 ml	
Commercial picante sauce	1 qt	950 ml	Add. Adjust heat to a simmer. Cover and cook 5 minutes. Transfer to a food processor or food chopper. Process until chicken is shredded. Cool to room temperature. Cover. Chill.
Cumin, ground	½ c	120 ml	
Chili powder	¼ c	60 ml	
Cinnamon, ground	1 T	15 ml	
Cloves, ground	1 t	5 ml	
Wheat tortillas, 10-inch	50	50	Arrange on work surface. Portion filling in middle. Fold sides of tortillas 1 inch over filling. Roll tightly from bottom to top. Transfer to oiled or paper-lined sheet pans. Bake at 375°F for 20 minutes.
Sour cream	2 qt	1.9 L	Combine in small bowl. Portion 1½ ounce on top of each burrito.
Lime juice	1 c	240 ml	
Commercial picante sauce	1 c	240 ml	
Chili powder	¼ c	60 ml	
Cumin, ground	1 T	15 ml	
Jalapeño pepper, minced	1 T	15 ml	

Nutrient Analysis	Calories	381	Protein	29 gm
Per Serving	Fat	18.3 gm	Carbohydrate	26.3 gm
	Cholesterol	82 mg	Calcium	122 mg
	Sodium	333 mg	Fiber	0.6 gm

▲ Blue Mountain Barbecued Chicken

Serve this grilled chicken as a Caribbean entrée or appetizer.

Menu Category:	Appetizer, Entrée, Poultry, Ethnic, Caribbean
Cooking Method:	Grill
Preparation Time:	10 minutes
Marination Time:	12 hours
Cooking Time:	30 minutes
Variations:	Substitute pork loin or jumbo shrimp for chicken breasts.
Yield:	50 portions (5 oz)

Ingredient	U.S.	Metric	Method
Chicken breasts, 4 oz, boneless, skinless	50	50	Place in single layer in shallow pans.
Ketchup	2 qt	1.9 L	Combine in mixer bowl with whip
Brown sugar	2 c	480 ml	attachment. Mix at medium speed until
Cider vinegar	2 c	480 ml	well blended. Pour over chicken breasts.
Black coffee, cold	1 qt	950 ml	Cover. Refrigerate at least 12 hours.
Worcestershire sauce	1 c	240 ml	Remove from marinade. Reserve marinade.
Dark rum	1 c	240 ml	Cook at high heat on preheated grill for
Red pepper flakes	1 T	15 ml	approximately 5 to 7 minutes on each side.
Black pepper	1 T	15 ml	Baste frequently with reserved marinade. Serve hot.

Nutrient Analysis	Calories	311	Protein	34 gm
Per Serving	Fat	8.8 gm	Carbohydrate	20.4 gm
	Cholesterol	96 mg	Calcium	38 mg
	Sodium	531 mg	Fiber	0.2 gm

▲ Braised Chicken, Mexican Style

Serve as a light Mexican or Southwest American entrée.

Menu Category:	Entrée, Poultry, Ethnic, Mexican, American Regional
Cooking Method:	Braise
Preparation Time:	10 minutes
Oven Temperature:	350°F
Cooking Time:	30 minutes
Variations:	Substitute pork chops or Cornish hens for chicken breasts.
Yield:	50 portions (5 oz)

Ingredient	U.S.	Metric	Method
Commercial picante sauce	1 gal	3.8 L	Combine in large pot. Simmer for 10 minutes. Remove from heat.
Carrot, thinly sliced	2 lb	980 g	
White wine, dry	1 qt	950 ml	
Olive oil, hot	2 c	480 ml	Sauté in large pot or brazier until chicken is brown on both sides. Transfer chicken to roasting pans. Reserve oil.
Chicken breasts, boneless, 4 oz	50	50	
Green bell pepper, sliced	1 lb	454 g	Add to reserved oil. Sauté for 2 minutes. Distribute over chicken breasts with enough reserved sauce to almost cover chicken. Cover roasting pan. Place in preheated 350°F oven for about 30 minutes or until chicken is fork tender. Serve chicken with peppers and sauce ladled on top.
Red bell pepper, sliced	1 lb	454 g	

Nutrient Analysis Per Serving				
	Calories	357	Protein	35.2 gm
	Fat	19 gm	Carbohydrate	10.2 gm
	Cholesterol	96 mg	Calcium	34.2 mg
	Sodium	714 mg	Fiber	0.4 gm

▲ Chicken Chili with Tortilla "Pasta"

Thinly sliced tortillas look and taste like pasta.

Menu Category:	Soup, Entrée, Poultry, Ethnic, Mexican
Cooking Method:	Simmer
Preparation Time:	30 minutes
Cooking Time:	60 minutes
Variations:	Substitute diced turkey or pork for chicken.
Yield:	50 portions (8 oz)

Ingredient	U.S.	Metric	Method
Chicken breast, skinless, diced	5 lb	2.3 kg	Dredge chicken pieces and shake off all excess flour.
Flour	1 qt	950 ml	
Salt	1 T	15 ml	
Pepper	1 T	15 ml	
Corn oil	1 c	480 ml	Heat in heavy pot or steam kettle. Sauté chicken just until golden brown.
Cumin, ground	¼ c	60 ml	Add to chicken. Sauté for 1 minute. Drain off any excess oil.
Chili powder	1 c	240 ml	
Chicken broth	1 gal	3.8 L	Add to chicken. Heat to a simmer. Simmer for 10 minutes.
Mild green chilies, canned	2 c	480 ml	
Tomatoes, canned, chopped	2 qt	1.9 L	
Corn oil	1 c	240 ml	Sauté just until onion is tender. Add to chicken mixture. Simmer for 30 minutes or just until potatoes are tender.
Onion, diced	1 qt	950 ml	
Potatoes, peeled, diced	1 qt	950 ml	
Carrot, diced	2 c	480 ml	
Celery, diced	2 c	480 ml	
Garlic, minced	¼ c	60 ml	
Corn tortillas, cut into julienne strips	2 qt	1.9 L	Add to mixture. Simmer 5 more minutes.

Nutrient Analysis Per Serving				
	Calories	227	Protein	11.7 gm
	Fat	12.4 gm	Carbohydrate	18.7 gm
	Cholesterol	20.8 mg	Calcium	69.7 mg
	Sodium	473 mg	Fiber	1.3 gm

▲ Chicken Tetrazzini Milano

A savory version of the basic noodle dish, rich with peppers and sherry.

Menu Category:	Entrée, Poultry, Pasta, Ethnic, Italian
Cooking Method:	Boil/Simmer/Bake
Preparation Time:	30 minutes
Oven Temperature:	350°F
Cooking Time:	1 hour
Variations:	Add crumbled bacon or minced smoked ham.
Yield:	50 portions (8 oz)

Ingredient	U.S.	Metric	Method
Vermicelli pasta, dried Water, boiling	6 lb as needed	2.7 kg as needed	Add vermicelli to boiling water. Stir occasionally until just *al dente*, about 5 to 7 minutes. Drain, rinse, and reserve.
Butter, melted Flour Salt Nutmeg, grated	1½ c 1½ c 2 T 1 t	360 ml 360 ml 30 ml 5 ml	Combine in large pot or steam kettle. Stir until mixture is smooth and barely yellow. Remove from heat.
Chicken stock Sherry, dry Milk Parmesan cheese, grated	3 qt 1½ c 1½ c 2 c	2.9 L 360 ml 360 ml 480 ml	Add to flour mixture. Blend well until smooth. Heat to a simmer. Simmer 20 minutes, stirring occasionally.
Egg yolks, beaten well	6	6	Add to 2 cups of heated cream sauce. Stir. Add this mixture back to cream sauce.
Chicken, cooked, diced Green bell pepper, minced Mushrooms, diced Scallions, minced	6 lb 2 c 2 lb 1 c	2.7 kg 480 ml 908 g 240 ml	Add to cream sauce with reserved pasta. Mix well. Transfer to four oiled or sprayed 12″ × 20″ × 2½″ insert pans. Bake uncovered in preheated 350°F oven until golden brown and bubbly, about 30 minutes. Let rest 10 minutes before serving.

Nutrient Analysis Per Serving	Calories	412	Protein	30.6 gm
	Fat	12.1 gm	Carbohydrate	42.5 gm
	Cholesterol	141 mg	Calcium	95.6 mg
	Sodium	669 mg	Fiber	0.5 gm

▲ Chicken with Orange Sauce Orlando

Tender chicken is enhanced with delicate orange cream sauce and toasted almonds.

Menu Category:	Entrée, Poultry, American regional
Cooking Method:	Sauté/Simmer
Preparation Time:	30 minutes
Cooking Time:	20 minutes
Variations:	This procedure is also wonderful with lean white fish fillets.
Yield:	50 portions (6 oz)

Ingredient	U.S.	Metric	Method
Chicken breasts, boneless	18 lb	8.2 kg	Pound chicken breasts to flatten slightly.
Flour	1 qt	950 ml	Dredge chicken in seasoned flour.
Salt	2 T	30 ml	
White pepper	1 T	15 ml	
Olive oil	1½ c	360 ml	Heat in heavy skillets or brazier. Sauté chicken until golden brown on both sides.
Orange Sauce Orlando, recipe follows	3 qt	2.8 L	Add to chicken. Simmer over gentle heat for about five minutes. Place chicken on plates. Spoon sauce over top.
Slivered almonds, toasted	3 c	720 ml	

Nutrient Analysis	Calories	458	Protein	30 gm
Per Serving	Fat	25.8 gm	Carbohydrate	27.9 gm
	Cholesterol	94.5 mg	Calcium	61.1 mg
	Sodium	373 mg	Fiber	0.6 gm

Companion Recipe

▲ **Orange Sauce Orlando**

Serve with a variety of sautéed and/or panfried poultry, veal, and seafood entrées.

Menu Category:	Sauce
Cooking Method:	Sauté/Simmer
Preparation Time:	30 minutes
Cooking Time:	20 minutes
Variations:	Substitute lemon for orange.
	Add orange marmalade.

Yield:	1 gallon

Ingredient	U.S.	Metric	Method
Olive oil, hot	1 c	240 ml	Cook slowly in large covered pot or steam
Scallion, white only, minced	1 qt	950 ml	kettle until vegetables are tender, about 15
Celery, minced	1 qt	950 ml	minutes.
Honey	1 qt	950 ml	Add to vegetables. Cook, uncovered, until
Orange zest, blanched	½ c	120 ml	mixture is golden and glazed, about 5 minutes.
Orange juice	1 qt	950 ml	Add. Simmer 15 minutes. Remove from
Chicken stock	1 qt	950 ml	heat. Puree in blender or food processor.
Heavy cream	1 qt	950 ml	Strain through very fine sieve.
Saffron threads	½ t	3 ml	Add to sauce. Stir well.

Nutrient Analysis	Calories	78	Protein	0.5 gm
Per Ounce	Fat	4.5 gm	Carbohydrate	10 gm
	Cholesterol	10.2 mg	Calcium	12.9 mg
	Sodium	28.2 mg	Fiber	0.1 gm

▲ Country Captain Chicken Breasts

Serve this southern dish with steamed white rice.

Menu Category:	Entrée, Poultry, American Regional
Cooking Method:	Sauté/Roast
Preparation Time:	30 minutes
Oven Temperature:	350°F
Cooking Time:	20 minutes
Variations:	Substitute shrimp or boneless pork loin.
Yield:	50 portions (6 oz)

Ingredient	U.S.	Metric	Method
Olive oil, hot	8 oz	227 g	Sauté in preheated brazier until golden.
Chicken breasts, boneless,			Transfer to sheet pans. Roast in 350°F oven
4 oz	50	50	until done, about 20 minutes. Remove from oven. Cover and keep warm.
Green bell pepper, julienne	1 qt	950 ml	Add to brazier. Sauté just until tender.
Onion, julienne	1 qt	950 ml	
Garlic, minced	¼ c	60 ml	
Curry powder	½ c	120 ml	Add. Stir well for one minute.
Dry sherry	8 oz	227 g	Add. Deglaze pan. Flame if necessary.
Tomato, seeded, chopped	6 lb	2.7 kg	Add. Reduce heat. Simmer just until well
Currants, dried	3 c	720 ml	combined. Portion over chicken breasts as
Thyme, dried	1 T	15 ml	quantity dictates for service.
Almonds, toasted	1 qt	950 ml	Sprinkle over each portion.
Parsley, chopped	3 c	720 ml	

Nutrient Analysis	Calories	552	Protein	62.2 gm
Per Serving	Fat	25.6 gm	Carbohydrate	17.1 gm
	Cholesterol	166 mg	Calcium	83 mg
	Sodium	211 mg	Fiber	25.6 gm

▲ Grilled Chicken with Apricot Glaze

Serve as part of a western American Regional menu.

Menu Category:	Entrée, Poultry, American Regional
Cooking Method:	Grill/Broil
Preparation Time:	30 minutes
Marination Time:	12 hours
Cooking Time:	30 minutes
Variations:	Serve sliced on sesame buns.
	Add commercial barbecue sauce to glaze ingredients.
Yield:	50 portions (5 oz)

Ingredient	U.S.	Metric	Method
Chicken breasts, 4 oz, boneless, skinless	50	50	Place in single layer in shallow pans.
Peanut oil	1 c	240 ml	Combine in mixer bowl with whip
Apricot preserves	1 qt	950 ml	attachment. Mix at medium speed until
Soy sauce	1 c	240 ml	blended. Pour over chicken breasts. Cover.
Cider vinegar	1 c	240 ml	Refrigerate for at least 12 hours. Remove
Gingerroot, minced	¼ c	60 ml	from marinade. Reserve marinade. Cook at
Garlic powder	1 T	15 ml	high heat on preheated grill for
Red pepper flakes	1 T	15 ml	approximately 5 to 7 minutes on each side. Baste frequently with reserved marinade. Serve hot.

Nutrient Analysis Per Serving				
	Calories	213	Protein	19.4 gm
	Fat	6.3 gm	Carbohydrate	19.5 gm
	Cholesterol	52 mg	Calcium	17.3 mg
	Sodium	377 mg	Fiber	0.4 gm

▲ Grilled Chicken Breast with Lemon and Capers

Serve as a light Mediterranean or Italian entrée.

Menu Category:	Entrée, Poultry, Ethnic, Italian, Mediterranean
Cooking Method:	Grill/Broil
Preparation Time:	10 minutes
Marination Time:	Several hours
Cooking Time:	20 minutes
Variations:	Serve as a sandwich on toasted buns or in warmed pita pockets.
Yield:	50 portions (5 oz)

Ingredient	U.S.	Metric	Method
Chicken breasts, skinless,			Season chicken and place in shallow pans.
4 oz	50	50	
Salt	1 T	15 ml	
Black pepper	1 T	15 ml	
White wine, dry	1 qt	950 ml	Combine and add to chicken. Cover. Chill several hours. Remove chicken. Reserve marinade. Cook over medium heat for about 5 to 7 minutes per side, basting often with marinade. Transfer to sheet pans. Cover. Keep warm.
Rosemary, dried	1 T	15 ml	
Garlic, minced	1 c	240 ml	
Butter, melted	1 lb	454 g	Combine in sauce pot. Cook over high heat just until butter begins to brown.
Lemon juice	1 c	240 ml	
Capers, tiny, drained	2 c	480 ml	Add to lemon butter with any juices from grilled chicken breasts. Mix well. Portion over chicken breasts.
Chicken stock	1 qt	950 ml	
Parsley, chopped	2 c	248 ml	

Nutrient Analysis	Calories	215	Protein	19.6 gm
Per Serving	Fat	12.5 gm	Carbohydrate	2.5 gm
	Cholesterol	72.2 mg	Calcium	29.1 mg
	Sodium	377 mg	Fiber	0.2 gm

▲ Lime-Marinated Grilled Chicken

Serve this simple, tangy chicken entrée on your festive summer menus.

Menu Category:	Entrée, Poultry, American Regional
Cooking Method:	Grill/Broil
Preparation Time:	30 minutes
Marination Time:	12 hours
Cooking Time:	30 minutes
Variations:	Substitute firm white-fleshed fish and reduce marination time to no more than one hour.
	Add fruit, juice, and spices to commercial vinaigrette dressing.
Yield:	50 portions (5 oz)

Ingredient	U.S.	Metric	Method
Chicken breasts, 4 oz, boneless, skinless	50	50	Place in single layer in shallow pans.
Olive oil	2 c	480 ml	Combine in small bowl. Mix well. Pour over chicken breasts. Cover. Refrigerate for at least 12 hours. Remove from marinade. Reserve marinade. Cook at high heat on preheated grill for approximately 5 to 7 minutes on each side, basting frequently with reserved marinade. Serve hot.
Lemon, chopped	1 c	240 ml	
Lime, chopped	1 c	240 ml	
Lime juice	2 c	480 ml	
Garlic, minced	¼ c	60 ml	
Black pepper, coarse	1 T	15 ml	
Salt	1 T	15 ml	

Nutrient Analysis Per Serving				
	Calories	204	Protein	18.5 gm
	Fat	13.5 gm	Carbohydrate	2 gm
	Cholesterol	52 mg	Calcium	16.1 mg
	Sodium	173 mg	Fiber	0.1 gm

▲ Peach-Basted Broiled Chicken Breasts

From the Georgia orchards, here's a peach of an entrée.

Menu Category:	Entrée, Poultry, American Regional
Cooking Method:	Grill/Broil
Preparation Time:	30 minutes
Marination Time:	1 hour
Cooking Time:	20 minutes
Variations:	Substitute boneless pork chops or jumbo butterflied shrimp.

Yield: 50 portions (5 oz)

Ingredient	U.S.	Metric	Method
Peach preserves	2 qt	1.9 ml	Combine in sauce pot. Heat to a simmer.
White wine, dry	2 c	480 ml	Simmer 10 minutes. Remove from heat.
Orange juice	2 c	480 ml	Cool to room temperature.
Ginger, ground	1 T	15 ml	
Chicken breasts, bone-in	20 lb	9.1 kg	Grill/broil over/under medium-high heat for about 6 to 10 minutes on each side. Baste frequently with peach sauce. Spoon 1 ounce warm peach sauce over each breast before service.
Coconut, toasted	2 c	480 ml	Sprinkle over breasts just before service.

Nutrient Analysis	Calories	399	Protein	29.9 gm
Per Serving	Fat	12 gm	Carbohydrate	41.3 gm
	Cholesterol	83.2 mg	Calcium	27.6 mg
	Sodium	96 mg	Fiber	0.9 gm

▲ Sesame Chicken with Mild Chilies

Serve as an Oriental entrée or appetizer.

Menu Category:	Appetizer, Entrée, Poultry, Ethnic, Chinese
Cooking Method:	Braise
Preparation Time:	10 minutes
Marination Time:	Several hours
Cooking Time:	30 minutes
Variations:	Substitute pork loin or Cornish hens for chicken breasts.
	Use as an Oriental omelette filling.
Yield:	50 portions (5 oz)

Ingredient	U.S.	Metric	Method
Chicken, skinless, diced	12 lb	5.5 kg	Combine in large bowl. Mix well. Cover.
Scallions, chopped	1 qt	950 ml	Chill for several hours.
Mild green chilies, sliced	1 qt	950 ml	
Cornstarch	1 c	240 ml	
Soy sauce	2 c	480 ml	
Wine vinegar	1 c	240 ml	
Sugar	1 c	240 ml	
Pepper oil	2 T	30 ml	
Gingerroot, minced	½ c	120 ml	
Garlic, minced	½ c	120 ml	
Black pepper	2 T	30 ml	
Peanut oil	2 c	480 ml	Heat in preheated 350°F brazier kettle. Add chicken mixture. Stir-fry for 7 to 10 minutes.
Chicken broth	2 qt	1.9 L	Add to mixture. Stir until mixture simmers. Simmer for about 1 minute. Serve hot.

Nutrient Analysis Per Serving				
	Calories	297	Protein	33 gm
	Fat	13 gm	Carbohydrate	11.3 gm
	Cholesterol	102 mg	Calcium	38.5 mg
	Sodium	962 mg	Fiber	0.5 gm

▲ Szechuan Velvet Chicken

This can be served as an entrée or as part of an Oriental buffet.

Menu Category:	Entrée, Poultry, Ethnic, Chinese
Cooking Method:	Stir-fry/Sauté
Preparation Time:	30 minutes
Marination Time:	1 hour
Cooking Time:	20 minutes
Variations:	Substitute pork, turkey, or shrimp.
Yield:	50 portions (6 oz)

Ingredient	U.S.	Metric	Method
Chicken, skinned, julienne	12 lb	5.5 kg	Combine in large bowl. Mix well. Chill for
Egg white, beaten lightly	2 c	480 ml	one hour.
Cornstarch	2 c	480 ml	
Peanut oil	2 c	480 ml	Heat in preheated 350°F brazier. Add chicken mixture. Sauté just until chicken turns white, about 3 or 4 minutes. Remove chicken with slotted spoon or spatula. Reserve.
Celery, shredded	2 qt	1.9 L	Add to remaining oil. Stir-fry just until
Scallions, shredded	1 qt	950 ml	vegetables soften, about 4 or 5 minutes.
Gingerroot, minced	1 c	240 ml	
Hot pepper, shredded	½ c	120 ml	
Chicken broth	3 c	720 ml	Add with reserved chicken. Cook 5
Sherry, dry	1 c	240 ml	minutes. Serve hot.
Sesame oil	¼ c	60 ml	
Soy sauce	½ c	120 ml	

Nutrient Analysis Per Serving				
	Calories	297	Protein	33 gm
	Fat	13.4 gm	Carbohydrate	8.5 gm
	Cholesterol	102 mg	Calcium	41.2 mg
	Sodium	338 mg	Fiber	0.6 gm

▲ Tandoori-Style Roasted Chicken Breasts

Serve as a part of an Indian menu.

Menu Category:	Entrée, Poultry, Ethnic, Indian
Cooking Method:	Roast
Preparation Time:	30 minutes
Marination Time:	Several hours
Oven Temperature:	350°F
Cooking Time:	30 minutes
Variations:	Substitute turkey, pork, veal, or shrimp for chicken.
Yield:	50 portions (5 oz)

Ingredient	U.S.	Metric	Method
Chicken breasts, 4 oz, boneless, skinless	50	50	Place in single layer in shallow roasting pans. Cut shallow diagonal slashes across each breast.
Yogurt, plain	2 qt	1.9 L	Combine in mixer bowl with whip attachment. Mix at medium speed until blended. Pour over chicken breasts. Cover. Refrigerate for at least 12 hours. Remove from marinade. Place on sheet pans. Roast in preheated 350°F oven for about 30 minutes. Serve hot.
Lemon juice	1 qt	950 ml	
Garlic, minced	½ c	120 ml	
Gingerroot, minced	½ c	120 ml	
Curry powder, mild	1 c	240 ml	
Cumin, ground	¼ c	60 ml	
Cayenne pepper, ground	1 T	15 ml	

Nutrient Analysis Per Serving				
	Calories	158	Protein	20 gm
	Fat	6.4 gm	Carbohydrate	4.9 gm
	Cholesterol	56.6 mg	Calcium	71.6 mg
	Sodium	66.3 mg	Fiber	0.4 gm

▲ Thai-Style Chicken Legs

Slightly hot and very aromatic.

Menu Category:	Entrée, Poultry, Thai
Cooking Method:	Grill/Broil
Preparation Time:	30 minutes
Marination Time:	1 hour
Cooking Time:	20 minutes
Variations:	Substitute shrimp, scallops, or pressed tofu.
	Serve with a cucumber salad dressed with light vinaigrette and chopped peanuts.
Yield:	50 portions (5 oz)

Ingredient	U.S.	Metric	Method
Chicken leg, bone-in	20 lb	9.1 kg	Combine. Mix well. Chill for 1 hour. Cook
Commercial chili-garlic			at medium heat on preheated grill until
paste	2 c	480 ml	firm and golden brown, about 15 to 20
Lime juice	1 c	240 ml	minutes. Serve hot.
Soy sauce	2 c	480 ml	
Sugar	1 c	240 ml	
Coriander, ground	1 T	15 ml	
Cilantro, chopped	1 c	240 ml	

Nutrient Analysis				
Per Serving	Calories	246	Protein	24.5 gm
	Fat	13 gm	Carbohydrate	8 gm
	Cholesterol	82.5 mg	Calcium	29 mg
	Sodium	788 mg	Fiber	1.1 gm

Turkey

▲ Broiled Turkey Breast with Black Currant Sauce

Tiny currants offer a subtle balance to glistening broiled turkey breast.

Menu Category:	Entrée, Poultry, American Regional	
Cooking Method:	Broil	
Preparation Time:	30 minutes	
Cooking Time:	30 to 40 minutes	
Variations:	Substitute chicken breast, ham steaks, or butterflied pork chops.	
Yield:	50 portions (5 oz)	

Ingredient	U.S.	Metric	Method
Turkey breast, whole, boneless	16 lb	7.3 kg	Rub turkey with olive oil. Place on sheet pans. Broil under medium heat with rack position 7 to 8 inches below heater elements. Broil to internal temperature of 165°F. Remove from heat. Cover. Let rest 15 minutes before carving.
Olive oil	1 c	240 ml	
Black Currant Sauce, recipe follows	1 gal	3.8 L	Portion 2½ ounces over each turkey serving.

Nutrient Analysis Per Serving	Calories	365	Protein	45.6 gm
	Fat	6.6 gm	Carbohydrate	18.1 gm
	Cholesterol	122 mg	Calcium	38.3 mg
	Sodium	403 mg	Fiber	0.6 gm

Companion Recipe

▲ **Black Currant Sauce**

This condiment sauce highlights the flavors of roasted and broiled meats, poultry, and game.

Menu Category:	Sauce
Cooking Method:	Simmer
Preparation Time:	10 minutes
Cooking Time:	20 to 30 minutes
Variations:	Substitute golden raisins or diced prunes.
Yield:	1 gallon

Ingredient	U.S.	Metric	Method
Currants	2 lb	908 g	Combine in small bowl. Let rest 30 minutes.
Brandy	1 qt	950 ml	
Brown sugar	3 c	720 ml	Combine in sauce pot or steam kettle. Heat to a simmer. Simmer 10 minutes. Add reserved currant mixture. Simmer 10 more minutes.
Mustard, Dijon style	1 c	240 ml	
Red wine vinegar	3 c	720 ml	
Beef gravy, thin	2 qt	1.9 L	
Cinnamon, ground	1 t	5 ml	

Nutrient Analysis Per Ounce				
Calories	51	Protein	0.8 gm
Fat	0.5 gm	Carbohydrate	7.1 gm
Cholesterol	0.4 mg	Calcium	8.2 mg
Sodium	128 mg	Fiber	0.2 gm

▲ Chinese-Style Roasted Turkey Breast

The soy sauce and rice vinegar give the turkey a subtle Oriental aroma and flavor. This is great sliced warm or diced for use in salads.

Menu Category:	Entrée, Poultry, Oriental
Cooking Method:	Roast
Preparation Time:	30 minutes
Marination Time:	Several hours
Oven Temperature:	350°F
Cooking Time:	2 to 3 hours
Yield:	50 portions (5 oz)

Ingredient	U.S.	Metric	Method
Turkey breast, whole, boneless	16 lb	7.3 kg	Combine in large plastic container. Cover. Chill several hours. Remove turkey breast.
Soy sauce	1 qt	950 ml	Place on rack in shallow roasting pan.
Rice wine vinegar	1 qt	950 ml	Roast at 350°F to internal temperature of
Brown sugar	2 c	480 ml	165°F. Remove from oven. Cover. Let rest 30 minutes before carving.

Nutrient Analysis	Calories	243	Protein	45 gm
Per Serving	Fat	1.1 gm	Carbohydrate	11.4 gm
	Cholesterol	120 mg	Calcium	28.8 mg
	Sodium	1395 mg	Fiber	0 gm

▲ Grilled Turkey for Fajitas

Serve with traditional fajita accompaniments: guacamole, sour cream, picante sauce.

Menu Category:	Entrée, Poultry, American Regional
Cooking Method:	Grill/Sauté
Preparation Time:	30 minutes
Marination Time:	Several hours
Cooking Time:	2 to 3 hours
Yield:	50 portions (5 oz)

Ingredient	U.S.	Metric	Method
Turkey breast, skinless, boneless	16 lb	7.3 kg	Combine in large plastic container. Cover. Chill several hours. Remove turkey breast. Drain turkey well. Discard marinade. Slice turkey breast into ½ ″ × ½ ″ × 4″ slices.
Commercial teriyaki sauce	2 qt	1.9 L	
Commercial barbecue sauce	2 qt	1.9 ml	
Brown sugar	2 c	480 ml	
Liquid smoke	¼ c	60 ml	
Olive oil	2 c	480 ml	Heat in preheated 350°F brazier. Add turkey strips. Stir occasionally until strips are firm, about 10 minutes.

Nutrient Analysis Per Serving				
	Calories	374	Protein	47.1 gm
	Fat	10.4 gm	Carbohydrate	20.9 gm
	Cholesterol	120 mg	Calcium	44.1 mg
	Sodium	2170 mg	Fiber	0.3 gm

▲ Medallions of Turkey in Mustard Sauce

Piquant mustard adds a perfect touch to delicate turkey slices.

Menu Category:	Entrée, Poultry, American Regional
Cooking Method:	Sauté
Preparation Time:	30 minutes
Marination Time:	Overnight
Cooking Time:	30 minutes
Variations:	Substitute chicken, pork, veal, or shrimp for turkey.
Yield:	50 portions (5 oz)

Ingredient	U.S.	Metric	Method
Turkey breast, 1-ounce slices	12 lb	5.5 kg	Combine. Toss well to coat all slices. Cover and refrigerate overnight. Remove from marinade. Reserve marinade.
Brown sugar	2 c	480 ml	
Mustard, Dijon style	1 c	240 ml	
Chicken stock	2 qt	1.9 L	
Scallions, minced	½ c	120 ml	
Garlic, minced	2 T	30 ml	
White pepper	1 T	15 ml	
Cooking oil	1 c	240 ml	Heat in preheated 350°F brazier, flattop grill, or sauté pans. Sauté turkey until well browned on both sides. Transfer turkey slices to sheet pans. Keep warm.
Heavy cream	1 qt	950 ml	Place in large pot with reserved marinade. Heat to boiling. Reduce heat and simmer a few minutes. Season to taste. Strain sauce. Portion turkey on plates. Ladle 2 ounces sauce over turkey slices.

Nutrient Analysis Per Serving				
	Calories	217	Protein	34 gm
	Fat	5.9 gm	Carbohydrate	10 gm
	Cholesterol	90.4 mg	Calcium	29.1 mg
	Sodium	321 mg	Fiber	0.1 gm

▲ Oven-Smoked Barbecued Turkey Breast

A taste of the great Southwest permeates tender sliced turkey breast.

Menu Category:	Entrée, Poultry, American Regional
Cooking Method:	Roast
Preparation Time:	30 minutes
Marination Time:	Several hours
Cooking Time:	2 to 3 hours
Variations:	This works equally well with chicken and pork, even shrimp and lean fish.
Yield:	50 portions (5 oz)

Ingredient	U.S.	Metric	Method
Turkey breast, skinless, boneless	16 lb	7.3 kg	Combine in large plastic container. Cover. Chill several hours. Remove turkey breast.
Beer	1 qt	950 ml	Place on rack in shallow roasting pan.
Commercial barbecue sauce	1 qt	950 ml	Roast at 350°F to internal temperature of 165°F. Remove from oven. Cover. Let rest
Commercial steak sauce	2 c	480 ml	30 minutes before carving. Serve with extra
Worcestershire sauce	1 c	240 ml	barbecue sauce if desired.
Liquid smoke	¼ c	60 ml	

Nutrient Analysis Per Serving				
	Calories	232	Protein	44.4 gm
	Fat	1.6 gm	Carbohydrate	5.9 gm
	Cholesterol	120 mg	Calcium	27 mg
	Sodium	456 mg	Fiber	0.1 gm

▲ Roast Turkey with Spiced Cranberry Sauce

For your traditional holiday menus.

Menu Category:	Entrée, Poultry, American Regional	
Cooking Method:	Roast	
Preparation Time:	30 minutes	
Oven Temperature:	350°F	
Cooking Time:	2 to 3 hours	
Variations:	Try this procedure with other poultry as well as with pork and game.	
Yield:	50 portions (6 oz)	

Ingredient	U.S.	Metric	Method
Turkey breast, skinless, boneless	16 lb	7.3 kg	Place on rack in shallow roasting pan. Roast at 350°F to internal temperature of 165°F. Remove from oven. Cover. Let rest 30 minutes before carving.
Spiced Cranberry Sauce, recipe follows	1 gal	3.8 L	Portion 2½ ounces over turkey slices.

Nutrient Analysis Per Serving	Calories	379	Protein	43.6 gm
	Fat	4.8 gm	Carbohydrate	32.3 gm
	Cholesterol	101 mg	Calcium	53.9 mg
	Sodium	96 mg	Fiber	0.5 gm

Companion Recipe

▲ Spiced Cranberry Sauce

Zesty, fruity, and semisweet: Just the touch for poultry, pork, and game.

Menu Category:	Sauce, American Regional
Cooking Method:	Simmer
Preparation Time:	30 minutes
Cooking Time:	2 to 3 hours
Variations:	Try this sauce with roasted chicken, Cornish hens, pork, and veal.
Yield:	1 gallon

Ingredient	U.S.	Metric	Method
Cranberries, whole, rinsed	5 lb	2.3 kg	Combine in sauce pot or steam kettle. Heat
White wine, dry	2 c	480 ml	to a boil. Reduce heat to a simmer. Simmer
Molasses	2 c	480 ml	until berries pop open, about 5 to 10
Sugar	2 lb	908 g	minutes, stirring frequently.
Dark rum	2 c	480 ml	
Water	1 qt	950 ml	
Cloves, ground	1 t	5 ml	

Nutrient Analysis Per Ounce				
	Calories	59	Protein	0.1 gm
	Fat	0 gm	Carbohydrate	12.6 gm
	Cholesterol	0 mg	Calcium	10.1 mg
	Sodium	1.5 mg	Fiber	0.2 gm

▲ Turkey Marsala with Mushrooms

A variation of the traditional Italian veal entrée.

Menu Category:	Entrée, Poultry, Ethnic, Italian
Cooking Method:	Sauté
Preparation Time:	30 minutes
Marination Time:	Several hours
Cooking Time:	30 minutes
Variations:	Substitute chicken, pork, veal, or shrimp for turkey.
Yield:	50 portions (5 oz)

Ingredient	U.S.	Metric	Method
Turkey breast, 1 ounce slices	12 lb	5.5 kg	Dredge slices in seasoned flour. Shake off all excess flour.
Flour	1 qt	950 ml	
Salt	1 T	15 ml	
White pepper	1 T	15 ml	
Cooking oil	1 c	240 ml	Heat in preheated 350°F brazier, flattop grill, or sauté pans. Sauté turkey until well browned on both sides. Transfer turkey slices to sheet pans. Keep warm.
Mushrooms, sliced	5 lb	2.3 kg	Add to hot brazier. Sauté just until mushrooms begin to release their liquid, about 5 minutes.
Marsala wine, dry	2 c	480 ml	Add to mushrooms. Flame if possible. Simmer for 1 minute.
Chicken or turkey stock	1 qt	950 ml	Add to mushrooms. Simmer 1 or 2 minutes. Put turkey on plates. Divide sauce over turkey slices.
Parsley, chopped	2 c	480 ml	
Lemon juice	¼ c	60 ml	

Nutrient Analysis Per Serving	Calories	178	Protein	34.2 gm
	Fat	5.7 gm	Carbohydrate	2.6 gm
	Cholesterol	90.4 mg	Calcium	20.1 mg
	Sodium	122 mg	Fiber	0.4 gm

Pasta and Noodles

Hot Pastas

▲ Cheese Tortellini with Roma Tomato Sauce

Serve this light southern Italian pasta as a side dish or vegetarian entrée.

Menu Category:	Pasta, Entrée, Side, Ethnic, Italian
Cooking Method:	Boil/Sauté
Preparation Time:	10 minutes
Cooking Time:	45 minutes
Variations:	Substitute ravioli or cheese-stuffed manicotti pasta.
Yield:	50 portions (8 oz)

Ingredient	U.S.	Metric	Method
Commercial cheese tortellini, IQF	8 lb	3.6 kg	Add tortellini to boiling water. Stir occasionally until just *al dente*, following package directions. Drain, rinse, and reserve.
Water, boiling	20 gal	76 L	
Salt	½ c	120 ml	
Italian-style tomatoes, canned, chopped	1 gal	3.8 L	Place in large pot or steam kettle. Cook over medium heat until juices thicken. Stir often. Reduce heat to a simmer.
Anchovy paste	½ c	120 ml	
Heavy cream	2 qt	1.9 L	Add gradually to tomato sauce. Simmer for five minutes. Portion sauce over pasta.
Crushed red pepper	2 t	10 ml	
Black pepper, coarse	1 t	5 ml	
Oregano, dried	1 T	15 ml	

Nutrient Analysis Per Serving	Calories	400	Protein	12 gm
	Fat	17 gm	Carbohydrate	51.8 gm
	Cholesterol	117 mg	Calcium	62.3 mg
	Sodium	235 mg	Fiber	0.6 gm

▲ Creamy Fettuccine with Smoked Chicken

Serve as a hearty pasta entrée with crusty bread and green salad.

Menu Category:	Pasta, Entrée, Poultry, Ethnic, Italian
Cooking Method:	Boil, Sauté
Preparation Time:	10 minutes
Cooking Time:	20 minutes
Variations:	Substitute smoked shrimp, mussels, oysters, or crisply cooked thickly diced bacon.
	Add sautéed mushrooms, sliced ripe olives, or drained capers.
	Substitute ⅓ c dried basil.
Yield:	50 portions (8 oz)

Ingredient	U.S.	Metric	Method
Fettuccine pasta, dried	6 lb	2.7 kg	Add fettuccine to boiling water. Stir occasionally just until *al dente*, about 8 to 10 minutes. Drain, rinse, and reserve.
Water, salted, boiling	20 gal	76 L	
Salt	½ c	120 ml	
Butter, melted	1 c	240 ml	Sauté just until garlic begins to brown.
Garlic	¼ c	60 ml	
Heavy cream	2 qt	1.9 L	Add to garlic. Increase heat to a boil. Reduce heat and simmer just until cream yellows slightly and begins to thicken.
Black pepper, coarse grind	1 T	15 ml	
Smoked chicken, ½-inch dice	4 lb	1.8 kg	Add to cream mixture. Simmer gently for 5 minutes. Add reserved fettuccine. Toss gently. Hold in covered insert pans or serve immediately.
Basil, fresh, thinly sliced	2 c	480 ml	

Nutrient Analysis Per Serving				
	Calories	437	Protein	15 gm
	Fat	25 gm	Carbohydrate	39.9 gm
	Cholesterol	109 mg	Calcium	94.5 mg
	Sodium	62 mg	Fiber	0.7 gm

▲ Fettuccine Pasta with Tomato and Capers

A seaside favorite for true Mediterranean-style pasta menus.

Menu Category:	Pasta, Entrée, Ethnic, Italian
Cooking Method:	Boil, Sauté
Preparation Time:	10 minutes
Cooking Time:	30 minutes
Variations:	Substitute linguini, spaghettini, or other flat pasta.
	Serve with bread rounds toasted with olive oil and grated Parmesan cheese.
Yield:	50 portions (6 oz)

Ingredient	U.S.	Metric	Method
Fettuccine pasta, dried	6 lb	2.7 kg	Add fettuccine to boiling water. Stir
Water, boiling	20 gal	76 L	occasionally just until *al dente*, about 8 to
Salt	½ c	120 ml	10 minutes. Drain, rinse, and reserve.
Olive oil	1 c	240 ml	Heat in large pot.
Scallions, minced	2 c	480 ml	Add to oil. Sauté just until garlic is
Garlic, minced	2 T	30 ml	softened, about 5 minutes.
Capers, small, drained	¾ c	180 ml	Add to scallion mixture. Cook over
Pimentos, drained, minced	1 qt	950 ml	medium heat just until warmed
Anchovy filets, rinsed,			thoroughly. Add reserved fettuccine and
minced	½ c	120 ml	toss well to coat.
Parsley, chopped	2 c	480 ml	Add to pasta. Toss gently. Hold in covered
Lemon rind, grated	1 T	15 ml	insert pans or serve immediately.

Nutrient Analysis	Calories	238	Protein	8.4 gm
Per Serving	Fat	6.1 gm	Carbohydrate	37.2 gm
	Cholesterol	49 mg	Calcium	26 mg
	Sodium	144 mg	Fiber	0.5 gm

▲ Fusilli with Meatless Marinara Sauce

Vary the pasta for a variety of classic southern Italian specialties.

Menu Category:	Pasta, Entrée, Ethnic, Italian
Cooking Method:	Boil, Sauté
Preparation Time:	10 minutes
Cooking Time:	45 minutes
Variations:	Substitute ziti or other tubular pasta.
	Substitute shell pasta and add sliced shrimp or chopped clams.
	Serve with grated Parmesan or Romano cheese.
Yield:	50 portions (8 oz)

Ingredient	U.S.	Metric	Method
Fusilli pasta, dried	6 lb	2.7 kg	Add fusilli to boiling water. Stir
Water, boiling	20 gal	76 L	occasionally just until *al dente*, about 8 to
Salt	½ c	120 ml	10 minutes. Drain, rinse, and reserve.
Olive oil	1 c	240 ml	Heat oil in large pot. Add onion to oil.
Onion, sliced thinly	1 qt	950 ml	Sauté just until tender, about 5 minutes.
Garlic, minced	2 T	30 ml	Add to onions. Cook over medium heat for
Oregano, dried	1 T	15 ml	one or two minutes.
Tomatoes, Italian-style, chopped	13 lb	5.9 kg	Add to garlic mixture. Heat to boiling. Reduce to a simmer. Stir frequently to
Basil, dried	1 T	15 ml	break up tomatoes. Simmer gently,
Crushed red pepper	2 t	10 ml	uncovered, until sauce thickens, about 30 minutes. Add reserved fusilli and toss well to coat. Hold in covered insert pans or serve immediately.

Nutrient Analysis Per Serving				
	Calories	255	Protein	8.7 gm
	Fat	6.2 gm	Carbohydrate	42 gm
	Cholesterol	47 mg	Calcium	46.2 mg
	Sodium	201 mg	Fiber	0.9 gm

▲ Linguine with White Clam Sauce

Serve this classic favorite as a seafood pasta entrée.

Menu Category:	Pasta, Entrée, Ethnic, Italian
Cooking Method:	Boil, Sauté
Preparation Time:	30 minutes
Cooking Time:	30 minutes
Variations:	Substitute shrimp, monkfish, or chopped mussels.
Yield:	50 portions (8 oz)

Ingredient	U.S.	Metric	Method
Linguine pasta, dried	6 lb	2.7 kg	Add linguine to boiling water. Stir
Water, boiling	20 gal	76 L	occasionally just until *al dente*, about 8 to
Salt	½ c	120 ml	10 minutes. Drain, rinse, and reserve.
Olive oil	2 c	480 ml	Heat in large pot.
Garlic, chopped	2 c	480 ml	Add to hot oil. Cook over medium heat
Crushed red pepper	1 T	15 ml	just until garlic begins to brown.
Clams, water pack	13 lb	5.9 kg	Drain, rinse, and chop clams. Add to garlic. Simmer over medium heat for 5 minutes.
Clam broth or stock	2 qt	1.9 L	Add to clam mixture. Simmer for 5 minutes.
Parsley, finely chopped	3 c	720 ml	Add with reserved linguine. Toss well to
Scallion greens, minced	1 c	240 ml	combine. Hold in covered insert pans or
Lemon juice	½ c	120 ml	serve immediately.

Nutrient Analysis	Calories	323	Protein	15.6 gm
Per Serving	Fat	11.4 gm	Carbohydrate	4.3 gm
	Cholesterol	98 mg	Calcium	79.7 mg
	Sodium	179 mg	Fiber	0.4 gm

▲ Manicotti Pasta Rolls with Cheese and Spinach

These stuffed pasta rolls add a splash of color to Italian menus.

Menu Category:	Pasta, Entrée, Side, Ethnic, Italian
Cooking Method:	Boil/Sauté/Bake
Preparation Time:	45 minutes
Oven Temperature:	350°F
Cooking Time:	45 minutes
Variations:	Substitute reduced-labor ravioli or cheese-stuffed tortellini pasta and serve with sauce.
Yield:	50 portions (8 oz)

Ingredient	U.S.	Metric	Method
Manicotti shells, dried	50	50	Add manicotti to boiling water. Stir occasionally just until *al dente*, about 8 to 10 minutes. Drain, rinse, and reserve.
Water, boiling	5 gal	19 L	
Salt	½ c	120 ml	
Spinach, IQF, chopped	8 lb	3.6 kg	Thaw completely and press out all possible liquid. Transfer to large bowl.
Olive oil, hot	2 c	480 ml	Sauté in brazier just until garlic begins to brown. Add reserved spinach. Cook over low heat to cook off all liquid. Drain all oil. Transfer to a large bowl. Cool.
Garlic, minced	½ c	120 ml	
Onion, minced	1 qt	950 ml	
Mozzarella cheese, grated	2 lb	908 g	Add to spinach mixture. Mix well. Use a piping bag with large star tip to fill manicotti shells. Place in standard 2-inch insert pans prepared with cooking spray.
Parmesan cheese, grated	2 c	480 ml	
Ricotta cheese	5 lb	2.3 kg	
Egg, beaten	6	6	
Commercial tomato sauce	1 gal	3.8 L	Pour over manicotti shells. Cover and bake in preheated 350°F oven for 30 minutes. Remove cover and bake 20 more minutes. Let rest 15 minutes before service.

Nutrient Analysis				
Per Serving	Calories	459	Protein	21.6 gm
	Fat	22 gm	Carbohydrate	45 gm
	Cholesterol	113 mg	Calcium	372 mg
	Sodium	270 mg	Fiber	1.1 gm

▲ Mixed Cheese Manicotti with Pimento Cream Sauce

Serve these stuffed pasta rolls with light tomato sauce.

Menu Category:	Pasta, Entrée, Side, Ethnic, Italian
Cooking Method:	Boil/Sauté/Bake
Preparation Time:	45 minutes
Oven Temperature:	350°F
Cooking Time:	45 minutes
Variations:	Substitute ravioli or cheese-stuffed tortellini pasta.
Yield:	50 portions (8 oz)

Ingredient	U.S.	Metric	Method
Manicotti shells, dried	50	50	Add manicotti to boiling water. Stir
Water, boiling	5 gal	19 L	occasionally just until *al dente*, about 8 to
Salt	½ c	120 ml	10 minutes. Drain, rinse, and reserve.
Bacon, sliced	½ lb	227 g	Sauté just until lightly crisp. Drain. Discard fat. Transfer bacon to a large bowl.
Mozzarella cheese, grated	2 lb	908 g	Add to sautéed bacon. Mix well. Use a
Parmesan cheese, grated	2 c	480 ml	piping bag with large star tip to fill
Ricotta cheese	5 lb	2.3 kg	manicotti shells. Place in standard 2-inch
Egg, beaten	6	6	insert pans prepared with cooking spray.
Pimentos, drained, chopped	2 c	480 ml	
Parsley, minced	2 c	480 ml	
Nutmeg, ground	½ t	3 ml	
Pimento Cream Sauce, recipe follows	1 gal	3.8 L	Pour over manicotti shells. Cover and bake in preheated 350°F oven for 30 minutes. Remove cover and bake 20 more minutes. Let rest at least 15 minutes before service.

Nutrient Analysis	Calories	480	Protein	21 gm
Per Serving	Fat	24.7 gm	Carbohydrate	44 gm
	Cholesterol	143 mg	Calcium	294 mg
	Sodium	436 mg	Fiber	0.7 gm

Companion Recipe

▲ **Pimento Cream Sauce**

Serve with stuffed manicotti pasta rolls or with panfried chicken or veal.

Menu Category:	Sauce, Ethnic, Italian
Cooking Method:	Simmer
Preparation Time:	10 minutes
Cooking Time:	45 minutes
Yield:	1 gallon

Ingredient	U.S.	Metric	Method
Olive oil, hot	½ c	120 ml	Sauté in large pot or steam kettle just until vegetables are tender.
Onion, minced	2 c	480 ml	
Green bell pepper, minced	2 c	480 ml	
Tomatoes, canned, chopped	3 qt	2.8 L	Add to vegetables. Heat to a boil. Reduce heat to a simmer. Simmer 1 hour. Remove from heat. Remove bay leaves. Cool to room temperature. Puree in food processor with metal blade. Strain through fine sieve into large pot.
Bay leaf	3	3	
Heavy cream	1 qt	950 ml	Add to strained sauce. Heat to a simmer. Simmer 5 minutes.
Pimentos, minced	2 c	480 ml	

Nutrient Analysis Per Ounce				
	Calories	42	Protein	0.5 gm
	Fat	3.6 gm	Carbohydrate	2.3 gm
	Cholesterol	10.2 mg	Calcium	13.7 mg
	Sodium	64.2 mg	Fiber	0.2 gm

▲ Oriental Noodles with Beef Broth

Serve this Oriental pasta as a side dish or light entrée.

Menu Category:	Pasta, Entrée, Side, Ethnic, Oriental
Cooking Method:	Boil/Sauté
Preparation Time:	10 minutes
Cooking Time:	45 minutes
Variations:	Substitute linguine or other flat pasta.
	Add thinly sliced stir-fried shrimp or pork.
	Garnish with additional minced scallions.
Yield:	50 portions (8 oz)

Ingredient	U.S.	Metric	Method
Spaghetti pasta, dried	6 lb	2.7 kg	Add spaghetti to boiling water. Stir
Water, boiling	20 gal	76 L	occasionally just until *al dente*, about 8 to
Salt	½ c	120 ml	10 minutes. Drain and rinse. Transfer to large bowl.
Garlic powder	1 T	15 ml	Combine. Add to pasta. Toss well.
Soy sauce	1 c	240 ml	Reserve.
Gingerroot, minced	½ c	120 ml	
Sesame oil	½ c	120	
Peanut oil	1½ c	360 ml	Heat in brazier just until smoking. Add pasta. Toss briskly to coat and heat.
Scallions, sliced	2 qt	1.9 L	Add to noodles. Toss briskly. Remove from heat. Portion into serving bowls.
Beef broth	1½ gal	5.7 L	Pour over noodles as quantity dictates.

Nutrient Analysis	Calories	245	Protein	11.9 gm
Per Serving	Fat	4.5 gm	Carbohydrate	39.4 gm
	Cholesterol	47 mg	Calcium	38.8 mg
	Sodium	728 mg	Fiber	0.6 gm

▲ Spaghettini Porcini with Garlic and Herbs

Serve as a vegetarian pasta entrée or as a side dish with roasted or grilled chicken.

Menu Category:	Pasta, Entrée, Side, Ethnic, Italian
Cooking Method:	Boil/Sauté
Preparation Time:	30 minutes
Cooking Time:	30 minutes
Variations:	Substitute other mushrooms and herbs.
	Add cooked and diced chicken or shrimp for entrée alternative.
Yield:	50 portions (6 oz)

Ingredient	U.S.	Metric	Method
Porcini mushrooms, dried	4 oz	114 g	Combine in sauce pan. Heat to a boil. Remove from heat. Let rest 30 minutes. Drain and reserve liquid. Dice and reserve porcini.
Water	2 c	480 ml	
Spaghettini pasta, dried	6 lb	2.7 kg	Add spaghettini to boiling water. Stir occasionally until just *al dente*, about 8 to 10 minutes. Drain, rinse, and reserve.
Water, boiling	20 gal	76 L	
Salt	½ c	120 ml	
Olive oil	2 c	480 ml	Heat in large pot.
Garlic, chopped	½ c	120 ml	Add to hot oil. Cook over medium heat just until garlic begins to color. Add reserved porcini and liquid. Stir well.
Crushed red pepper	1 T	15 ml	
Parsley, finely chopped	3 c	720 ml	Add to pasta. Toss well to combine. Hold in covered insert pans or serve immediately.
Scallion greens, minced	1 c	240 ml	
Oregano, dried	1 T	30 ml	
Lemon juice	½ c	120 ml	

Nutrient Analysis	Calories	271	Protein	7.7 gm
Per Serving	Fat	10.2 gm	Carbohydrate	37.1 gm
	Cholesterol	47 mg	Calcium	22.6 mg
	Sodium	11.5 mg	Fiber	0.3 gm

▲ Spaghetti with Mixed Herbs

Vary the pasta for a variety of classic southern Italian specialties.

Menu Category:	Pasta, Entrée, Ethnic, Italian
Cooking Method:	Boil/Sauté
Preparation Time:	10 minutes
Cooking Time:	45 minutes
Variations:	Substitute linguine or other flat pasta. Add chopped clams or other cooked shellfish.
	Substitute margarine, olive oil, or other oil.
Yield:	50 portions (6 oz)

Ingredient	U.S.	Metric	Method
Spaghetti pasta, dried	6 lb	2.7 kg	Add spaghetti to boiling water. Stir
Water, boiling	20 gal	76 L	occasionally just until *al dente*, about 8 to
Salt	½ c	120 ml	10 minutes. Drain, rinse, and reserve.
Butter, melted	2 c	480 ml	Heat in preheated brazier just until foam subsides. Do not brown.
Garlic, minced	2 T	30 ml	Add to butter. Cook just until garlic begins
Oregano, dried	1 T	15 ml	to turn brown. Add reserved pasta. Toss
Tarragon, dried	1 t	5 ml	well to coat.
Crushed red pepper	1 t	5 ml	
Parsley, chopped	1 c	240 ml	Add to pasta. Toss well. Serve immediately
Scallion, minced	2 c	480 ml	or hold warm in covered insert pans.

Nutrient Analysis Per Serving				
	Calories	256	Protein	7.7 gm
	Fat	8.9 gm	Carbohydrate	36.4 gm
	Cholesterol	67 mg	Calcium	20.7 mg
	Sodium	85 mg	Fiber	0.3 gm

▲ Stir-Fried Noodles with Ginger and Scallions

Serve this Oriental pasta as a side dish or light vegetarian entrée.

Menu Category:	Pasta, Entrée, Side, Ethnic, Oriental
Cooking Method:	Boil/Sauté
Preparation Time:	10 minutes
Cooking Time:	45 minutes
Variations:	Substitute linguine or other flat pasta.
	Add thinly sliced stir-fried shrimp or pork.
	Garnish with additional minced scallions.
Yield:	50 portions (6 oz)

Ingredient	U.S.	Metric	Method
Spaghetti pasta, dried	6 lb	2.7 kg	Add spaghetti to boiling water. Stir
Water, boiling	20 gal	76 L	occasionally just until *al dente*, about 8 to
Salt	½ c	120 ml	10 minutes. Drain and rinse. Transfer to large bowl.
Garlic powder	1 T	15 ml	Combine. Add to pasta. Toss well.
Soy sauce	1 c	240 ml	Reserve.
Gingerroot, minced	½ c	120 ml	
Sesame oil	½ c	120 ml	
Crushed red pepper	¼ c	60 ml	
Peanut oil	1½ c	360 ml	Heat in brazier just until smoking. Add pasta. Toss briskly to coat and heat.
Scallions, sliced	2 qt	1.9 L	Add to noodles. Toss briskly. Transfer to service pieces. Serve warm.

Nutrient Analysis	Calories	225	Protein	9.5 gm
Per Serving	Fat	3.8 gm	Carbohydrate	39 gm
	Cholesterol	47 mg	Calcium	34 mg
	Sodium	340 mg	Fiber	0.6 gm

Chilled Pastas

▲ Chilled Linguine with Ginger and Peanuts

An Oriental salad.

Menu Category:	Appetizer, Salad, Ethnic, Italian/Oriental	
Cooking Method:	Simmer/Sauté	
Preparation Time:	30 minutes	
Cooking Time:	30 minutes	
Variations:	Add grilled chicken, shrimp, or pork.	
Yield:	50 portions (5 oz)	

Ingredient	U.S.	Metric	Method
Linguine pasta, dried	6 lb	2.7 kg	Add linguine to boiling water. Stir occasionally just until *al dente*, about 8 to 10 minutes. Drain and rinse. Transfer to large bowl.
Water, boiling	20 gal	76 L	
Salt	½ c	120 ml	
Peanut oil	1½ c	360 ml	Sauté in preheated brazier just until ginger and garlic are barely golden.
Gingerroot, minced	½ c	120 ml	
Garlic, minced	1 T	15 ml	
Crushed red pepper	1 T	15 ml	
Peanuts, unsalted	2 qt	1.9 L	Add to ginger mixture. Sauté for 2 minutes. Add to reserved pasta.
Commercial vinaigrette dressing	1 qt	950 ml	Add to pasta. Mix well. Cover. Chill well.
Soy sauce	1 c	240 ml	
Sesame oil	1 T	15 ml	

Nutrient Analysis Per Serving					
	Calories	386	Protein	15 gm	
	Fat	19 gm	Carbohydrate	46 gm	
	Cholesterol	0 mg	Calcium	34 mg	
	Sodium	380 mg	Fiber	1 gm	

▲ Chilled Rainbow Pasta Primavera

Vary the pasta style and vegetables in this classic pasta favorite.

Menu Category:	Pasta, Entrée, Ethnic, Italian
Cooking Method:	Boil/Steam
Preparation Time:	20 minutes
Cooking Time:	30 minutes
Variations:	Add drained, rinsed tuna, sliced pimentos, and cherry tomatoes.
Yield:	50 portions (8 oz)

Ingredient	U.S.	Metric	Method
Tri-color pasta swirls, dried	6 lb	2.7 kg	Add pasta to boiling water. Stir
Water, boiling	20 gal	76 L	occasionally just until *al dente*, about 8 to
Salt	½ c	120 ml	10 minutes. Drain, rinse, and reserve.
Broccoli florets	1 qt	950 ml	Arrange in steamer trays. Steam just until
Carrots, diced	1 qt	950 ml	each vegetable is tender, about 5 minutes
Asparagus, fresh or IQF, sliced	1 qt	950 ml	each. Remove from steamer. Drain. Cool.
Green beans, fresh or IQF, sliced	1 qt	950 ml	Cover and chill.
Green peas, fresh or IQF	1 qt	950 ml	
Yogurt, plain	2 qt	1.9 L	Combine in large bowl. Whip well.
Milk	2 c	480 ml	
Red wine vinegar	1 c	240 ml	
Parmesan cheese	2 c	480 ml	
Garlic, crushed	1 T	15 ml	
Oregano, dried	1 T	15 ml	
Scallion greens, minced	2 c	480 ml	Add to dressing with reserved pasta and
Parsley, chopped	2 c	480 ml	vegetables. Mix gently but completely.
Pine nuts, toasted	2 c	480 ml	Serve slightly chilled.

Nutrient Analysis Per Serving	Calories	301	Protein	13.9 gm
	Fat	7.2 gm	Carbohydrate	46.2 gm
	Cholesterol	56.1 mg	Calcium	158 mg
	Sodium	116 mg	Fiber	1.3 gm

▲ Chinese Shrimp Shells with Broccoli Florets

Serve these tiny pasta shells as an appetizer or light, cold entrée.

Menu Category:	Pasta, Appetizer, Entrée, Ethnic, Oriental
Cooking Method:	Boil/Sauté
Preparation Time:	30 minutes
Marination Time:	Several hours
Cooking Time:	30 minutes
Variations:	Substitute bowties or linguine.
	Substitute crabmeat or sliced lobster.
	Substitute diced chicken.
Yield:	50 portions (6 oz)

Ingredient	U.S.	Metric	Method
Pasta shells, small, dried	6 lb	2.7 kg	Add shells to boiling water. Stir
Water, boiling	20 gal	76 L	occasionally just until *al dente*, about 8 to
Salt	½ c	120 ml	10 minutes. Drain, rinse, and reserve.
Shrimp, peeled, sliced	5 lb	2.3 kg	Combine in large bowl. Cover. Chill for
Olive oil	½ c	120 ml	several hours. Preheat brazier to 350°F.
Lime juice	½ c	120 ml	Add chilled shrimp mixture. Sauté just
Soy sauce	1 c	240 ml	until shrimp turns pink and becomes
Cilantro, chopped	½ c	120 ml	slightly firm.
Garlic, minced	¼ c	60 ml	
Gingerroot, minced	¼ c	60 ml	
Crushed red pepper	1 T	15 ml	
Broccoli florets, blanched	4 lb	1.8 kg	Add to shrimp mixture. Sauté for 2 or 3 minutes. Transfer to large bowl.
Olive oil	2 c	480 ml	Add to shrimp mixture with reserved pasta
Sesame oil	2 T	30 ml	shells. Toss well. Cool to room
Scallion greens, minced	2 c	480 ml	temperature. Cover. Chill well.

Nutrient Analysis	Calories	354	Protein	18.2 gm
Per Serving	Fat	13.7 gm	Carbohydrate	39.6 gm
	Cholesterol	117 mg	Calcium	61.2 mg
	Sodium	416 mg	Fiber	0.7 gm

▲ Cold Cheese Tortellini with Mustard Yogurt Sauce

Serve as a salad, antipasto appetizer, or light entrée.

Menu Category:	Salad, Appetizer, Entrée, Ethnic, Italian
Cooking Method:	Boil
Preparation Time:	30 minutes
Variations:	Add steamed or grilled shrimp.
Yield:	50 portions (5 oz)

Ingredient	U.S.	Metric	Method
Commercial cheese tortellini, IQF	8 lb	3.6 kg	Add tortellini to boiling water. Stir occasionally just until *al dente*, following package directions. Drain, rinse, and transfer to a large bowl.
Water, boiling	20 gal	76 L	
Salt	½ c	120 ml	
Broccoli florets, steamed, chilled	3 lb	1.4 kg	Add to pasta. Toss gently.
Yogurt, plain	2 qt	1.9 L	Combine in large bowl. Whip well. Add to pasta and broccoli. Fold gently but completely. Transfer to storage containers. Cover. Chill well.
Mayonnaise	2 c	480 ml	
Mustard, Dijon style	½ c	120 ml	

Nutrient Analysis Per Serving				
	Calories	314	Protein	11 gm
	Fat	10 gm	Carbohydrate	45 gm
	Cholesterol	65 mg	Calcium	68 mg
	Sodium	141 mg	Fiber	0.5 gm

▲ Cold Noodles with Shredded Vegetables

Serve this flavorful chilled pasta as an appetizer, salad, or light entrée.

Menu Category:	Pasta, Salad, Appetizer, Entrée, Ethnic, Oriental
Cooking Method:	Boil
Preparation Time:	30 minutes
Marination Time:	Several hours
Cooking Time:	30 minutes
Variations:	Add cooked shrimp, crab, or diced chicken.
Yield:	50 portions (8 oz)

Ingredient	U.S.	Metric	Method
Vermicelli pasta, dried	6 lb	2.7 kg	Add vermicelli to boiling water. Stir
Water, boiling	20 gal	76 L	occasionally just until *al dente*, about 8 to
Salt	½ c	120 ml	10 minutes. Drain, rinse, and reserve.
Soy sauce	2 c	240 ml	Combine in large bowl. Whip to blend
Sesame oil	½ c	120 ml	well. Cover and chill.
Peanut oil	½ c	120 ml	
Rice wine vinegar	½ c	120 ml	
Red wine vinegar	¼ c	60 ml	
Sugar	¼ c	60 ml	
Gingerroot, minced	¼ c	60 ml	
Garlic, minced	2 T	30 ml	
Crushed red pepper	1 T	15 ml	
Carrot, julienne	1 qt	950 ml	Combine well in large bowl. Add reserved
Cucumber, julienne	1 qt	950 ml	pasta and chilled dressing. Toss gently but
Radishes, julienne	1 qt	950 ml	completely. Serve cold.
Cilantro, chopped	1 c	240 ml	

Nutrient Analysis				
Nutrient Analysis	Calories	234	Protein	8.7 gm
Per Serving	Fat	4.6 gm	Carbohydrate	40 gm
	Cholesterol	47 mg	Calcium	21.6 mg
	Sodium	676 mg	Fiber	0.5 gm

▲ Pasta Salad Mexicana

Mexico meets Italy in this full-flavored pasta dish.

Menu Category:	Salad, Appetizer, Ethnic, Mexican, Italian
Cooking Method:	Boil
Preparation Time:	30 minutes
Cooking Time:	15 minutes
Variations:	Add toasted pine nuts or sesame seeds.
	Substitute curry powder for chili powder and relabel as Indian Pasta Salad.
Yield:	50 portions (5 oz)

Ingredient	U.S.	Metric	Method
Linguine pasta, dried	6 lb	2.7 kg	Add linguine to boiling water. Stir
Water, boiling	20 gal	76 L	occasionally just until *al dente*, about 8 to
Salt	½ c	120 ml	10 minutes. Drain and rinse. Transfer to large bowl.
Lemon juice	2 c	480 ml	Combine in mixer bowl with whip
Lime juice	2 c	480 ml	attachment. Mix at high speed to blend
Chili powder	¼ c	60 ml	well.
Cumin, ground	¼ c	60 ml	
Garlic, minced	¼ c	60 ml	
Cilantro, chopped	2 c	480 ml	
Olive oil	1 qt	950 ml	Add gradually to dressing. Whip until thickened.
Yogurt, plain	2 qt	1.9 L	Add gradually to dressing. Add to linguine. Mix well. Transfer to storage containers. Cover. Chill well.

Nutrient Analysis				
Per Serving	Calories	372	Protein	9 gm
	Fat	20.3 gm	Carbohydrate	40 gm
	Cholesterol	52 mg	Calcium	68.2 mg
	Sodium	293 mg	Fiber	0.4 gm

▲ Szechuan Noodles with Bean Sauce and Chicken

Serve this rich, nut-brown Chinese pasta as an entrée or appetizer.

Menu Category:	Pasta, Salad, Appetizer, Entrée, Ethnic, Oriental
Cooking Method:	Boil
Preparation Time:	10 minutes
Cooking Time:	30 minutes
Variations:	Substitute sautéed pork loin or shrimp.
Yield:	50 portions (8 oz)

Ingredient	U.S.	Metric	Method
Linguine pasta, dried	6 lb	2.7 kg	Add linguine to boiling water. Stir
Water, boiling	20 gal	76 L	occasionally just until *al dente*, about 8 to
Salt	½ c	120 ml	10 minutes. Drain and rinse. Transfer to a large bowl.
Chicken, cooked, julienne	3 lb	1.4 kg	Add to pasta. Toss gently but well.
Green bell pepper, julienne	1 qt	950 ml	
Cucumbers, julienne	1 qt	950 ml	
Hot red pepper oil	½ c	120 ml	Combine in small bowl. Mix well. Add to
Commercial bean paste, sweet	2 c	480 ml	pasta mixture. Toss gently but completely. Cover. Chill completely for service.
Sesame oil	¼ c	60 ml	
Peanut oil	1 c	240 ml	
Gingerroot, grated	½ c	120 ml	
Rice wine vinegar	¾ c	180 ml	
Red wine vinegar	½ c	120 ml	
Soy sauce	1 c	240 ml	

Nutrient Analysis Per Serving				
	Calories	312	Protein	17.6 gm
	Fat	8.5 gm	Carbohydrate	42 gm
	Cholesterol	70 mg	Calcium	20 mg
	Sodium	467 mg	Fiber	0.5 gm

▲ Vermicelli with Chili Oil and Cashews

Serve this Oriental pasta dish hot or cold.

Menu Category:	Pasta, Side, Ethnic, Oriental
Cooking Method:	Boil
Preparation Time:	10 minutes
Cooking Time:	30 minutes
Variations:	Substitute toasted almonds or sesame seeds.
	Add crisp-fried strips of batter-dipped cooked chicken or pork.
Yield:	50 portions (6 oz)

Ingredient	U.S.	Metric	Method
Vermicelli pasta, dried	6 lb	2.7 kg	Add vermicelli to boiling water. Stir
Water, boiling	20 gal	76 L	occasionally just until *al dente*, about 8 to
Salt	½ c	120 ml	10 minutes. Drain, rinse, and reserve.
Oriental chili paste, prepared	1 c	240 ml	Add to pasta. Toss well to combine. Hold in covered insert pans or serve
Soy sauce	1 c	240 ml	immediately. To serve chilled, cool to room
Cashews, toasted, chopped	1 qt	950 ml	temperature, cover, and chill several
Scallion greens, minced	3 c	720 ml	hours.

Nutrient Analysis Per Serving	Calories	264	Protein	9.9 gm
	Fat	7.1 gm	Carbohydrate	41.7 gm
	Cholesterol	47 mg	Calcium	29.4 mg
	Sodium	365 mg	Fiber	0.9 gm

Potatoes and Grains

POTATOES

▲ **Cantonese Braised Potatoes**

An alternative to rice on Oriental menus.

Menu Category:	Side, Starch, Ethnic, Oriental
Cooking Method:	Braise
Preparation Time:	30 minutes
Cooking Time:	25 minutes
Variations:	This method works well with celery, carrots, and root vegetables.
Yield:	50 portions (3 oz)

Ingredient	U.S.	Metric	Method
Peanut oil, hot	2 c	480 ml	In a large pot or tilt kettle, sauté potatoes just until golden, about 5 minutes.
Potatoes, baking, peeled, ½-inch sliced	12 lb	5.5 kg	
Soy sauce	2 c	480 ml	Add to potatoes. Sauté and stir 1 minute.
Sugar	½ c	120 ml	
Chicken broth, hot	2 qt	1.9 L	Add to potatoes. Heat to a boil. Reduce heat to a simmer. Cover. Simmer until potatoes are tender, about 15 minutes.

Nutrient Analysis Per Serving				
	Calories	147	Protein	4.8 gm
	Fat	3.3 gm	Carbohydrate	25.8 gm
	Cholesterol	0 mg	Calcium	15.2 mg
	Sodium	789 mg	Fiber	0.5 gm

▲ Cheese 'n' Bacon Mashed Potatoes

A sure-fire hit with grilled or roasted meats and poultry.

Menu Category:	Side, Starch
Cooking Method:	Boil
Preparation Time:	30 minutes
Cooking Time:	30 minutes
Variations:	Add a touch of chili powder or dry mustard.
Yield:	50 portions (4 oz)

Ingredient	U.S.	Metric	Method
Potatoes, baking, peeled	12 lb	5.5 kg	Combine in large pot or steam kettle. Heat
Water	as needed	as needed	to a boil. Reduce heat to medium simmer.
Salt	2 T	30 ml	Cook until potatoes are fork tender, about 30 minutes. Drain off all liquid. Dry potatoes by stirring over heat for a few minutes. Transfer to mixer bowl with whip attachment.
Bacon, fried crisp, crumbled	1 lb	454 g	Add to potatoes. Mix at low speed to break up potatoes. Increase speed gradually to
Cheddar cheese, grated	1 lb	454 g	high. Whip until creamy and fluffy.
Milk	2 qt	1.9 L	Transfer to two 12″ × 20″ × 2½″ insert pans. Cover loosely until service.

Nutrient Analysis				
Per Serving	Calories	202	Protein	8.2 gm
	Fat	8.3 gm	Carbohydrate	23.8 gm
	Cholesterol	20.2 mg	Calcium	124 mg
	Sodium	483 mg	Fiber	0.4 gm

▲ Grilled Potatoes O'Brien

A favorite side dish any time of the day.

Menu Category:	Side, Starch, American Regional
Cooking Method:	Grill/Sauté
Preparation Time:	30 minutes
Cooking Time:	20 minutes
Variations:	For a unique twist, substitute sweet potatoes.
Yield:	50 portions (3 oz)

Ingredient	U.S.	Metric	Method
Olive oil, hot	½ c	120 ml	Sauté in heavy pot or griddle just until
Bacon, diced	2 c	480 ml	onions and peppers are tender and bacon
Onion, minced	2 c	480 ml	is barely crisp.
Red bell peppers, minced	1 qt	950 ml	
Green bell peppers, minced	1 qt	950 ml	
Garlic, minced	2 T	30 ml	
Potatoes, baking, cooked, peeled, diced	1½ gal	5.7 L	Add to onion mixture. Sauté over medium heat until potatoes are golden brown.
Hot pepper sauce	1 T	15 ml	
Black pepper, coarsely ground	1 T	15 ml	

Nutrient Analysis Per Serving	Calories	157	Protein	3.5 gm
	Fat	3.6 gm	Carbohydrate	29.3 gm
	Cholesterol	1.9 mg	Calcium	13.7 mg
	Sodium	168 mg	Fiber	0.7 gm

▲ Gnocchi

Serve these versatile potato dumplings with roast or braised beef.

Menu Category:	Side, Starch, Ethnic, Italian
Cooking Method:	Boil/Poach
Preparation Time:	30 minutes
Cooking Time:	40 minutes
Variations:	Add a touch of curry powder or even a hint of mint.
Yield:	50 portions (4 oz)

Ingredient	U.S.	Metric	Method
Potatoes, boiling, peeled	12 lb	5.5 kg	Combine in large pot or steam kettle. Heat to a boil. Reduce heat to medium simmer. Cook until potatoes are fork tender, about 30 minutes. Drain off all liquid. Dry potatoes by stirring over heat for a few minutes. Transfer to mixer bowl with whip attachment. Whip until fluffy and light.
Water	as needed	as needed	
Salt	2 T	30 ml	
Flour	2 qt	1.9 L	Add gradually to potatoes. Mix at low speed and then gradually increase speed to high. Transfer to large bowl. Cool to room temperature. Cover and chill. When cold, form into small (¾-inch) balls.
Parmesan cheese, grated	2 c	480 ml	
Parsley, chopped, squeezed	2 c	480 ml	
Flour	1 qt	950 ml	Dust balls with flour. Press balls against the back of a dinner fork to flatten. Chill until ready to finish.
Water, boiling	as needed	as needed	Drop gnocchi in batches into water. Boil for about 10 seconds after each dumpling floats to the surface. Drain and hold warm for service.

Nutrient Analysis Per Serving	Calories	178	Protein	6.2 gm
	Fat	1.7 gm	Carbohydrate	36 gm
	Cholesterol	3.2 mg	Calcium	74.5 mg
	Sodium	210 mg	Fiber	0.8 gm

▲ Potato Croquettes with Garlic and Cheese

Soft and creamy on the inside, crisp and golden on the outside.

Menu Category:	Side, Starch
Cooking Method:	Boil/Deep-fry
Preparation Time:	30 minutes
Cooking Time:	40 minutes
Variations:	Substitute minced ham or smoked chicken for the bacon.
Yield:	50 portions (4 oz)

Ingredient	U.S.	Metric	Method
Potatoes, baking, peeled	12 lb	5.5 kg	Combine in large pot or steam kettle. Heat to a boil. Reduce heat to medium simmer. Cook until potatoes are fork tender, about 30 minutes. Drain off all liquid. Dry potatoes by stirring over heat for a few minutes. Transfer to mixer bowl with whip attachment.
Water	as needed	as needed	
Salt	2 T	30 ml	
Bacon, fried crisp, crumbled	2 c	480 ml	Add to potatoes. Mix at low speed to break up potatoes. Increase speed gradually to high. Whip until creamy and fluffy. Transfer to large bowl. Cool to room temperature. Cover and chill. When cold, portion 2 ounces and form into balls. Reserve.
Monterey Jack cheese, grated	2 c	480 ml	
Milk	2 qt	1.9 L	
Nutmeg	1 t	5 ml	
Flour	1 qt	950 ml	Dredge each ball in flour.
Eggs, beaten	6	6	Dip floured balls in egg.
Bread crumbs, fine, dry	2 qt	1.9 L	Dip balls into breadcrumbs. Deep-fry at 350°F until puffed and golden, about 5 minutes.

Nutrient Analysis Per Serving	Calories	125	Protein	3.9 gm
	Fat	1.8 gm	Carbohydrate	23.7 gm
	Cholesterol	5.3 mg	Calcium	75 mg
	Sodium	301 mg	Fiber	0.4 gm

▲ Potato Kugel with Golden Raisins

Of Jewish origin, this slightly sweet version is wonderful with grilled beef, poultry, and seafood.

Menu Category:	Side, Starch, Ethnic, Jewish
Cooking Method:	Bake
Preparation Time:	10 minutes
Oven Temperature:	400°F then 350°F
Cooking Time:	1 hour
Variations:	Substitute other dried fruits, such as diced apples or apricots.
Yield:	50 portions (3 oz)

Ingredient	U.S.	Metric	Method
Potatoes, baking, peeled	8 lb	3.6 kg	Grate with food processor or hand grater. Place in large bowl.
Water, ice cold	as needed	as needed	Pour over potatoes until ready to finish. Then drain potatoes in colander and squeeze out all excess moisture with back of large spoon. Place in mixer bowl with whip attachment.
Onion, minced	1 qt	950 ml	Add to potatoes in mixer bowl. Mix at medium speed just until well blended. Transfer to two oiled 12″ × 20″ × 2″ insert pans. Bake at 400°F for 20 minutes. Reduce temperature to 350°F. Bake until puffed, golden, and firm, about 45 minutes. Let rest 20 minutes before portioning.
Golden raisins	1 lb	454 g	
Eggs, beaten	12	12	
Sour cream	1½ qt	1.4 L	
Half-and-half	2 c	480 ml	
Cinnamon, ground	2 t	10 ml	
Salt	1 T	15 ml	

Nutrient Analysis				
Per Serving	Calories	185	Protein	4.4 gm
	Fat	8.2 gm	Carbohydrate	24.6 gm
	Cholesterol	67 mg	Calcium	63.4 mg
	Sodium	167 mg	Fiber	0.5 gm

▲ Potato Pancakes *Roesti*

An alternative potato side dish for sautéed chicken and pork entrées.

Menu Category:	Side, Starch, Ethnic, Austrian/Swiss
Cooking Method:	Sauté
Preparation Time:	10 minutes
Cooking Time:	20 minutes
Variations:	Add various chopped fresh herbs: parsley, oregano, dill.
Yield:	50 portions (3 oz)

Ingredient	U.S.	Metric	Method
Potatoes, baking, boiled, peeled	12 lb	5.5 kg	Grate potatoes with medium blade into large bowl. Toss with salt and pepper.
Salt	2 T	30 ml	
Pepper	1 T	15 ml	
Olive oil	2 c	480 ml	Heat in preheated 350°F brazier or griddle. Portion potatoes with 2-ounce scoop into hot oil. Press flat with spatula. Sauté until golden. Flip over. Sauté until second side is golden. Total cooking time is about 10 minutes. These should be served as soon as possible after cooking.

Nutrient Analysis Per Serving	Calories	170	Protein	1.9 gm
	Fat	8.8 gm	Carbohydrate	21.8 gm
	Cholesterol	0 mg	Calcium	10.9 mg
	Sodium	261 mg	Fiber	0.4 gm

▲ Roasted Potatoes with Garlic and Herbs

Ideal to prepare and serve with roasted meats and poultry.

Menu Category:	Side, Starch, Ethnic, Italian
Cooking Method:	Roast
Preparation Time:	30 minutes
Oven Temperature:	425°F
Cooking Time:	30 minutes
Variations:	Vary the herb blend with spices such as curry powder, chili powder, and cinnamon to change the ethnic flavor completely.

Yield: 50 portions (3½ oz)

Ingredient	U.S.	Metric	Method
Olive oil, hot	2 c	480 ml	Combine in large bowl. Toss well to coat potatoes. Transfer to sheet pans or shallow roasting pans. Bake at 425°F until golden brown and tender, about 20 minutes. Serve as soon as possible after cooking.
Potatoes, baking, peeled,			
½-inch wedges	12 lb	5.5 kg	
Garlic, minced	½ c	120 ml	
Oregano, dried	1 T	15 ml	
Basil, dried	1 T	15 ml	
Salt	1 T	15 ml	
Black pepper, coarsely			
ground	2 t	10 ml	

Nutrient Analysis				
Per Serving	Calories	174	Protein	2 gm
	Fat	8.8 gm	Carbohydrate	22.7 gm
	Cholesterol	0 mg	Calcium	17.3 mg
	Sodium	134 mg	Fiber	0.5 gm

▲ Saratoga Potato Crisps

These are the original potato chips and are great with broiled meats.

Menu Category:	Side, Starch, American Regional
Cooking Method:	Deep-fry
Preparation Time:	30 minutes
Cooking Time:	5 minutes
Variations:	To vary the flavor, sprinkle with herb or spice blends just before service.
Yield:	50 portions (2 oz)

Ingredient	U.S.	Metric	Method
Potatoes, baking, peeled, ⅛-inch slices	6 lb	2.7 kg	Combine in storage containers. Chill several hours. Drain well and dry by spreading over towels. When ready to cook, plunge in batches into 375°F oil. Deep-fry until golden, about 4 to 5 minutes. Serve as soon as possible after cooking. *Do not salt before service.*
Ice water	to cover	to cover	

Nutrient Analysis Per Serving				
	Calories	315	Protein	3.4 gm
	Fat	22 gm	Carbohydrate	29 gm
	Cholesterol	0 mg	Calcium	14 mg
	Sodium	371 mg	Fiber	0.8 gm

▲ Swiss-Style Mashed Potatoes with Pear

A hint of delicate pear and nutmeg make this variation special.

Menu Category:	Side, Starch
Cooking Method:	Boil
Preparation Time:	30 minutes
Cooking Time:	30 minutes
Variations:	Substitute applesauce for pears and add a touch of cinnamon.
Yield:	50 portions (4 oz)

Ingredient	U.S.	Metric	Method
Potatoes, baking, peeled	12 lb	5.5 kg	Combine in large pot or steam kettle. Heat to a boil. Reduce heat to medium simmer. Cook until potatoes are fork tender, about 30 minutes. Drain off all liquid. Dry potatoes by stirring over heat for a few minutes. Transfer to mixer bowl with whip attachment.
Water	as needed	as needed	
Salt	2 T	30 ml	
Pears, water pack, drained	2 lb	908 g	Puree and add to potatoes. Mix at low speed to break up potatoes. Increase speed gradually to high. Whip until creamy and fluffy. Transfer to two 12″ × 20″ × 2½″ insert pans. Cover loosely until service.
Milk	1 qt	950 ml	
Butter, soft	8 oz	227 g	
White pepper, ground	1 T	15 ml	

Nutrient Analysis Per Serving	Calories	142	Protein	2.6 gm
	Fat	4.2 gm	Carbohydrate	24.4 gm
	Cholesterol	11.4 mg	Calcium	36.5 mg
	Sodium	309 mg	Fiber	0.4 gm

▲ Jamaican Curried Yams

An exotic departure from traditional yams, these are wonderful with roasted pork or lamb.

Menu Category:	Side, Starch, Caribbean
Cooking Method:	Simmer
Preparation Time:	10 minutes
Cooking Time:	30 minutes
Variations:	Add toasted slivered almonds and plumped currants.
Yield:	50 portions (4 oz)

Ingredient	U.S.	Metric	Method
Butter, melted	1 lb	454 g	Sauté in large pot or brazier just until
Onion, minced	1 qt	950 ml	onions are almost golden.
Curry powder, mild	¼ c	60 ml	Add to onions. Sauté 1 minute.
Sweet potatoes, cooked, peeled, diced	12 lb	5.5 kg	Add to onions. Heat to a simmer. Mix well. Simmer for 10 minutes.
Chicken stock	1½ qt	1.4 L	
Lemon juice	¼ c	60 ml	
Hot pepper sauce	1 T	15 ml	
Black pepper, ground	1 T	15 ml	

Nutrient Analysis Per Serving	Calories	179	Protein	7.4 gm
	Fat	9.7 gm	Carbohydrate	15.8 gm
	Cholesterol	36.8 mg	Calcium	27 mg
	Sodium	240 mg	Fiber	0.9 gm

▲ Kentucky Sweet Potatoes

Just a hint of Kentucky whiskey.

Menu Category:	Side, Starch, American Regional
Cooking Method:	Bake
Preparation Time:	10 minutes
Oven Temperature:	350°F
Cooking Time:	30 minutes
Variations:	Eliminate bourbon or substitute extract.
Yield:	50 portions (4 oz)

Ingredient	U.S.	Metric	Method
Sweet potatoes, canned, sliced, drained	12 lb	5.5 kg	Divide the slices between two oiled 12″ × 20″ × 2″ insert pans.
Brown sugar, light	1 lb	454 g	Combine in small bowl. Sprinkle over the two pans. Bake at 350°F until browned, about 30 minutes.
Butter, soft	2 c	480 ml	
Bourbon	1½ c	360 ml	
Orange juice	1½ c	360 ml	
Pumpkin pie spice	1 T	15 ml	

Nutrient Analysis Per Serving				
	Calories	181	Protein	1.3 gm
	Fat	7.4 gm	Carbohydrate	23.7 gm
	Cholesterol	19.9 mg	Calcium	26.5 mg
	Sodium	101 mg	Fiber	0.8 gm

▲ Praline Yams

A low-labor side dish that features yams and pecans.

Menu Category:	Side, Starch, American Regional
Cooking Method:	Bake
Preparation Time:	10 minutes
Oven Temperature:	350°F
Cooking Time:	45 minutes
Variations:	Add a touch of orange zest and/or liqueur.
Yield:	50 portions (4 oz)

Ingredient	U.S.	Metric	Method
Sweet potatoes, canned, drained, mashed	1 gal	3.8 L	Combine in mixer bowl with whip attachment. Mix at medium speed until well blended. Transfer mixture to two oiled 12″ × 20″ × 2½″ insert pans.
Granulated sugar	2 c	480 ml	
Eggs, beaten	8	8	
Milk	2 c	480 ml	
Salt	2 t	10 ml	
Brown sugar	2 lb	910 g	Combine in small bowl. Mix well. Spread over yam mixture. Bake uncovered at 350°F until firm, about 30 to 45 minutes. Let rest 20 minutes before portioning.
Pecans, chopped	1 qt	950 ml	
Flour	2 c	480 ml	
Butter, soft	1 c	240 ml	

Nutrient Analysis Per Serving				
	Calories	261	Protein	3.5 gm
	Fat	10.6 gm	Carbohydrate	40.2 gm
	Cholesterol	44.8 mg	Calcium	47.9 mg
	Sodium	159 mg	Fiber	0.8 gm

▲ Sweet Potatoes with Orange and Pecans

A classic combination of fruit, nuts, coconut, and sweet potatoes.

Menu Category:	Side, Starch, American Regional
Cooking Method:	Bake/Simmer
Preparation Time:	10 minutes
Oven Temperature:	350°F
Cooking Time:	45 minutes
Variations:	Substitute chopped walnuts.
Yield:	50 portions (4 oz)

Ingredient	U.S.	Metric	Method
Sweet potatoes, canned, sliced, drained	12 lb	5.5 kg	Divide the slices between two oiled 12″ × 20″ × 2″ insert pans.
Brown sugar	2 lb	908 g	Combine in sauce pan. Heat to a boil. Reduce heat to simmer. Simmer 10 minutes, stirring frequently. Remove from heat. Pour over pans of sweet potatoes. Bake at 350°F for 30 minutes.
Orange juice	2 qt	1.9 L	
Orange rind, grated	½ c	120 ml	
Butter	8 oz	227 g	
Pecans, chopped	2 c	480 ml	
Coconut, shredded	2 c	480 ml	

Nutrient Analysis Per Serving				
	Calories	218	Protein	1.9 gm
	Fat	7.7 gm	Carbohydrate	37.1 gm
	Cholesterol	10 mg	Calcium	38.6 mg
	Sodium	67.5 mg	Fiber	1 gm

Rice

▲ Baked Chile-Cheese Rice

A variation on Southern grits.

Menu Category:	Side, Starch, American Regional		
Cooking Method:	Bake		
Preparation Time:	10 minutes		
Oven Temperature:	350°F		
Cooking Time:	1 hour		
Variations:	Heat it up with hot pepper sauce and/or cayenne pepper.		
Yield:	50 portions (4 oz)		

Ingredient	U.S.	Metric	Method
Olive oil, hot	1 c	240 ml	Sauté in heavy pot or steam kettle just
Onion, minced	2 c	480 ml	until onions are tender. Transfer to a large bowl.
Rice, cooked	1½ gal	5.7 L	Add to onion mixture. Mix well. Transfer
Monterey Jack cheese,			to two oiled 12″ × 20″ × 2″ insert pans.
grated	1 lb	454 g	Bake uncovered in 350°F oven until firm,
Tabasco sauce	¼ c	60 ml	about 1 hour. Cool for 20 minutes before
Eggs, beaten	8	8	portioning.
Mild chilies, sliced	2 c	480 ml	
Salt	2 t	10 ml	
White pepper, ground	2 t	10 ml	

Nutrient Analysis				
Per Serving	Calories	184	Protein	5.3 gm
	Fat	8.1 gm	Carbohydrate	21.9 gm
	Cholesterol	42.1 mg	Calcium	90.2 mg
	Sodium	216 mg	Fiber	0.3 gm

▲ Down South White Rice with Raisins

Easy to prepare.

Menu Category:	Side, Starch, American Regional
Cooking Method:	Steam
Preparation Time:	10 minutes
Cooking Time:	30 minutes
Variations:	Add chopped pecans and a touch of chili powder.
Yield:	50 portions (4 oz)

Ingredient	U.S.	Metric	Method
Raisins	2 c	480 ml	Combine in bowl. Let rest 30 minutes.
Water, boiling	1 qt	950 ml	
Olive oil, hot	1 c	240 ml	Sauté in heavy pot or steam kettle just until onions are tender.
Onion, minced	2 c	480 ml	
Rice, converted	3½ lb	1.6 kg	Add to onion mixture. Stir over low heat just until rice is coated.
Chicken stock	3 qt	2.8 L	Add to rice. Stir well. Heat to a boil. Boil for 1 minute. Reduce heat to a simmer. Cover tightly. Simmer until rice is cooked and stock is absorbed. Remove from heat. If excess stock remains, cover with towels and let rest. Fluff with a fork, mixing raisins throughout.
Salt	1 T	15 ml	

Nutrient Analysis Per Serving				
	Calories	97	Protein	2.6 gm
	Fat	5 gm	Carbohydrate	10.3 gm
	Cholesterol	0 mg	Calcium	13.3 mg
	Sodium	378 mg	Fiber	0.2 gm

▲ Fried Rice Espagnole

A cross cultural way to feature precooked white rice.

Menu Category:	Side, Starch, Ethnic, Spanish/Mexican
Cooking Method:	Sauté
Preparation Time:	20 minutes
Cooking Time:	20 minutes
Variations:	This procedure will work equally well with precooked, diced potatoes, as well as with countless herb/spice combinations.
Yield:	50 portions (4 oz)

Ingredient	U.S.	Metric	Method
Olive oil, hot	1 c	240 ml	Sauté in heavy pot or tilt kettle just until onions and peppers are tender, about 5 minutes.
Onion, minced	2 c	480 ml	
Green bell peppers, minced	2 qt	1.9 L	
Garlic, minced	2 T	30 ml	
Cumin, ground	¼ c	60 ml	Add to onions. Sauté 1 minute, stirring constantly.
White rice, cooked, cooled	1 gal	3.8 L	Add to onion mixture. Stir-fry over medium heat just until mixture is well combined and rice is slightly golden, about 3 minutes.
Tomatoes, seeded, diced	2 qt	1.9 L	Add to rice mixture. Toss to mix well and heat thoroughly.
Hot pepper sauce	1 T	15 ml	
Chicken broth	2 c	480 ml	

Nutrient Analysis Per Serving	Calories	164	Protein	3.4 gm
	Fat	5 gm	Carbohydrate	27.6 gm
	Cholesterol	0 mg	Calcium	26.7 mg
	Sodium	226 mg	Fiber	0.6 gm

▲ Golden Almond Rice Pilaf

The toasted flavor of almonds is ideal with rice.

Menu Category:	Side, Starch
Cooking Method:	Oven Steam
Preparation Time:	10 minutes
Oven Temperature:	325°F
Cooking Time:	30 minutes
Variations:	Substitute chopped pecans or cashews for almonds.
Yield:	50 portions (4 oz)

Ingredient	U.S.	Metric	Method
Olive oil, hot	1 c	240 ml	Sauté in heavy pot or steam kettle just
Onion, minced	2 c	480 ml	until onions are tender and almonds are
Almonds, slivered	3 c	360 ml	golden.
Rice, converted	3½ lb	1.6 kg	Add to onion mixture. Stir over low heat just until rice is coated. Transfer to one 12″ × 20″ × 4″ insert pan.
Beef or chicken stock	1 gal	3.8 L	Add to rice. Stir well. On stove top, heat to a boil. Boil for one minute. Remove from heat. Cover. Place in preheated 325°F oven. Bake for 25 minutes or until liquid is absorbed. Fluff rice with a fork, mixing almonds throughout.

Nutrient Analysis				
Per Serving	Calories	90	Protein	2.4 gm
	Fat	8 gm	Carbohydrate	2.7 gm
	Cholesterol	0 mg	Calcium	24.5 mg
	Sodium	251 mg	Fiber	0.2 gm

▲ Mediterranean Brown Rice with Almonds

A healthy, hearty side dish for roasted lamb, pork, or poultry.

Menu Category:	Side, Starch, Ethnic, Mediterranean
Cooking Method:	Steam
Preparation Time:	10 minutes
Cooking Time:	60 minutes
Variations:	Substitute pecans for almonds and add some brown sugar.
Yield:	50 portions (4 oz)

Ingredient	U.S.	Metric	Method
Olive oil, hot	1 c	240 ml	Sauté in heavy pot or steam kettle just until onions are tender and almonds are golden.
Onion, minced	2 c	480 ml	
Almonds, toasted	3 c	720 ml	
Golden raisins	3 c	720 ml	
Cinnamon	1 T	15 ml	
Brown rice, raw	3½ lb	1.6 kg	Add to onion mixture. Stir over low heat just until rice is coated. Transfer to one 12″ × 20″ × 4″ insert pan.
Beef stock	1 gal	3.8 L	Add to rice. Stir well. On stove top, heat to a boil. Boil for one minute. Remove from heat. Cover. Place in preheated 325°F oven. Bake for 45 to 60 minutes or until liquid is absorbed. Fluff rice with a fork before service.

Nutrient Analysis Per Serving				
	Calories	234	Protein	5.2 gm
	Fat	9.1 gm	Carbohydrate	34.5 gm
	Cholesterol	0 mg	Calcium	38.5 mg
	Sodium	255 mg	Fiber	0.8 gm

▲ New Delhi Curried Rice

Curry powder adds distinctive color and flavor to traditional steamed rice.

Menu Category:	Side, Starch, Ethnic, Indian
Cooking Method:	Steam
Preparation Time:	10 minutes
Cooking Time:	30 minutes
Variations:	Substitute chili powder, paprika, or fennel for curry powder.
Yield:	50 portions (4 oz)

Ingredient	U.S.	Metric	Method
Olive oil, hot	1 c	240 ml	Sauté in heavy pot or steam kettle just
Onion, minced	2 c	480 ml	until onions are tender.
Curry powder, mild	½ c	120 ml	Add to onions. Sauté for 1 minute. Stir constantly.
Rice, converted	3½ lb	1.6 kg	Add to onion mixture. Stir over low heat just until rice is coated.
Chicken stock	1 gal	3.8 L	Add to rice. Stir well. Heat to a boil. Boil
Salt	1 T	15 ml	for 1 minute. Reduce heat to a simmer. Cover tightly. Simmer until rice is cooked and stock is absorbed. Remove from heat. If excess stock remains, cover with towels and let rest.

Nutrient Analysis Per Serving				
	Calories	97	Protein	2.6 gm
	Fat	5 gm	Carbohydrate	10.3 gm
	Cholesterol	0 mg	Calcium	13.3 mg
	Sodium	378 mg	Fiber	0.2 gm

▲ Pistachio Pilaf with Golden Raisins

Add a light, nutty taste and texture to delicate, versatile rice pilaf.

Menu Category:	Side, Starch
Cooking Method:	Oven Steam
Preparation Time:	10 minutes
Oven Temperature:	325°F
Cooking Time:	30 minutes
Variations:	Substitute chopped pecans or cashews for pistachios.
Yield:	50 portions (4 oz)

Ingredient	U.S.	Metric	Method
Golden raisins	2 c	480 ml	Combine in bowl. Let rest 30 minutes.
Water, boiling	1 qt	950 ml	
Olive oil, hot	1 c	240 ml	Sauté in heavy pot or steam kettle just until onions are tender.
Onion, minced	2 c	480 ml	
Pistachios, chopped	2 c	480 ml	
Rice, converted	3½ lb	1.6 kg	Add to onion mixture. Stir over low heat just until rice is coated. Transfer to one 12″ × 20″ × 4″ insert pan.
Chicken stock	3 qt	2.8 L	Add to rice with reserved raisins and water. Stir well. On stove top, heat to a boil. Boil for one minute. Remove from heat. Cover. Place in preheated 325°F oven. Bake for 25 minutes or until liquid is absorbed. Fluff rice with a fork, mixing raisins and pistachios throughout.

Nutrient Analysis				
Per Serving	Calories	142	Protein	3.1 gm
	Fat	7.5 gm	Carbohydrate	16.3 gm
	Cholesterol	0 mg	Calcium	14.4 mg
	Sodium	189 mg	Fiber	0.3 gm

▲ Orange Rice with Sweet Pepper

Orange juice and zest add a tropical touch to steamed rice.

Menu Category:	Side, Starch, Ethnic, Spanish
Cooking Method:	Steam
Preparation Time:	10 minutes
Cooking Time:	30 minutes
Variations:	Add some orange liqueur to the cooking liquid.
Yield:	50 portions (4 oz)

Ingredient	U.S.	Metric	Method
Olive oil, hot	1 c	240 ml	Sauté in heavy pot or steam kettle just
Onion, minced	2 c	480 ml	until onions and peppers are tender.
Red bell pepper, minced	2 c	480 ml	
Orange zest	1 c	240 ml	Add to onions.
Rice, converted	3½ lb	1.6 kg	Add to onion mixture. Stir over low heat just until rice is coated.
Chicken stock	3 qt	2.8 L	Add to rice. Stir well. Heat to a boil. Boil
Orange juice	1 qt	950 ml	for 1 minute. Reduce heat to a simmer.
Salt	1 T	15 ml	Cover tightly. Simmer until rice is cooked and stock is absorbed. Remove from heat. If excess stock remains, cover with towels and let rest.

Nutrient Analysis Per Serving				
	Calories	106	Protein	2.5 gm
	Fat	4.8 gm	Carbohydrate	13.7 gm
	Cholesterol	0 mg	Calcium	13 mg
	Sodium	347 mg	Fiber	0.2 gm

▲ Steamed Rice with Water Chestnuts

Minced water chestnuts add a nice bite to traditional steamed rice. Great with grilled pork.

Menu Category:	Side, Starch
Cooking Method:	Steam
Preparation Time:	10 minutes
Cooking Time:	30 minutes
Variations:	Add chili powder or turmeric to onion mixture before adding rice.
Yield:	50 portions (4 oz)

Ingredient	U.S.	Metric	Method
Olive oil, hot	1 c	240 ml	Sauté in heavy pot or steam kettle just
Onion, minced	2 c	480 ml	until onions are tender.
Water chestnuts, minced	2 c	480 ml	
Rice, converted	3½ lb	1.6 kg	Add to onion mixture. Stir over low heat just until rice is coated.
Chicken stock	1 gal	3.8 L	Add to rice. Stir well. Heat to a boil. Boil
Salt	1 T	15 ml	for 1 minute. Reduce heat to a simmer. Cover tightly. Simmer until rice is cooked and stock is absorbed. Remove from heat. If excess stock remains, cover with towels and let rest.

Nutrient Analysis Per Serving				
	Calories	96	Protein	2.5 gm
	Fat	4.9 gm	Carbohydrate	10.1 gm
	Cholesterol	0 mg	Calcium	8.1 mg
	Sodium	377 mg	Fiber	0.1 gm

▲ White Rice O'Brien

This is a great plan ahead use for precooked white rice.

Menu Category:	Side, Starch, American Regional
Cooking Method:	Simmer
Preparation Time:	20 minutes
Cooking Time:	20 minutes
Variations:	For entrée preparation, add cooked and sliced shrimp, scallops, chicken, or pork.
Yield:	50 portions (4 oz)

Ingredient	U.S.	Metric	Method
Olive oil, hot	1 c	240 ml	Sauté in heavy pot or tilt kettle just until onions and peppers are tender.
Onion, minced	2 c	480 ml	
Red bell peppers, minced	1 qt	950 ml	
Green bell peppers, minced	1 qt	950 ml	
Garlic, minced	2 T	30 ml	
Chicken broth	2 c	480 ml	Add to onion mixture. Stir over low heat just until well combined and hot for service.
White rice, cooked, cooled	1 gal	3.8 L	
Hot pepper sauce	1 T	15 ml	

Nutrient Analysis Per Serving				
	Calories	136	Protein	2.9 gm
	Fat	2.6 gm	Carbohydrate	25.8 gm
	Cholesterol	0 mg	Calcium	11.8 mg
	Sodium	163 mg	Fiber	0.3 gm

Grains

▲ **Baked Cheese Grits**

This is the traditional southeastern American favorite.

Menu Category:	Side, Starch, American Regional
Cooking Method:	Simmer/Bake
Preparation Time:	20 minutes
Oven Temperature:	350°F
Cooking Time:	1½ hours
Variations:	For a southwestern twist, substitute Monterey Jack cheese with jalapeños and add chili powder or ground cumin to taste.
Yield:	50 portions (3 oz)

Ingredient	U.S.	Metric	Method
Grits	1 qt	950 ml	Combine in large stockpot or steam kettle.
Water, boiling	2 qt	1.9 L	Cook until tender, about 10 minutes. Cool
Milk, lowfat	1 qt	950 ml	to room temperature.
Cheddar cheese, grated	1 lb	454 g	Add to grits. Mix well. Transfer to two
Tabasco sauce	¼ c	60 ml	oiled 12″ × 20″ × 2″ insert pans. Bake
Eggs, beaten	8	8	uncovered in 350°F oven until firm, about 1
Salt	2 t	10 ml	hour. Cool for 20 minutes before cutting.
White pepper, ground	2 t	10 ml	

Nutrient Analysis				
Per Serving	Calories	105	Protein	5.1 gm
	Fat	4.3 gm	Carbohydrate	11.2 gm
	Cholesterol	45 mg	Calcium	95 mg
	Sodium	168 mg	Fiber	0.1 gm

▲ Baked Jamaican Pepper-Herb Grits

This is a Caribbean version of the southeastern American standard.

Menu Category:	Side, Starch, Ethnic, Caribbean
Cooking Method:	Simmer/Bake
Preparation Time:	20 minutes
Oven Temperature:	350°F
Cooking Time:	1½ hours
Variations:	Substitute yellow cornmeal and add diced bell peppers.
Yield:	50 portions (3 oz)

Ingredient	U.S.	Metric	Method
Grits	1 qt	950 ml	Combine in large stockpot or steam kettle.
Water, boiling	2 qt	1.9 L	Cook until tender, about 10 minutes. Cool
Milk, lowfat	1 qt	950 ml	to room temperature.
Hot pepper sauce	¼ c	60 ml	Add to grits. Mix well. Transfer to two
Pickapepper Sauce	¼ c	60 ml	oiled 12″ × 20″ × 2″ insert pans. Bake
Eggs, beaten	8	8	uncovered in 350°F oven until firm, about 1
Salt	2 t	10 ml	hour. Cool for 20 minutes before cutting.
Black pepper	2 t	10 ml	

Nutrient Analysis				
Per Serving	Calories	73	Protein	2.9 gm
	Fat	1.4 gm	Carbohydrate	12 gm
	Cholesterol	35.5 mg	Calcium	32.7 mg
	Sodium	240 mg	Fiber	0.1 gm

▲ Broiled Polenta Marinara

The bright red tomato sauce is a perfect counter for the crisp polenta circles.

Menu Category:	Side, Starch, Ethnic, Italian
Cooking Method:	Simmer/Grill/Broil
Preparation Time:	20 minutes
Setting Time:	Overnight
Cooking Time:	1 hour
Variations:	Add crumbled sautéed Italian sausage to the polenta mixture.
Yield:	50 portions (4 oz)

Ingredient	U.S.	Metric	Method
Water	3 qt	2.8 L	Heat to a boil.
Salt	2 T	30 ml	
Yellow cornmeal	1½ qt	1.4 L	Add very gradually, stirring constantly. Reduce heat to a simmer. Simmer until mixture begins to leave sides of the pot. Remove from heat. Pour into oiled sheet pans. Cool. Cover. Chill overnight. Cut chilled polenta into 2-inch rounds. Place rounds on oiled sheet pans.
Olive oil	1 c	240 ml	Brush the rounds with olive oil. Broil under high heat until dark golden brown on one side. Turn over and repeat for second side. Remove from heat. Keep warm.
Tomato sauce, commercial	3 qt	2.8 L	Combine in stockpot. Heat to a simmer. Simmer 20 minutes. Portion 2 ounces over each polenta portion.
Basil, dried	1 T	15 ml	
Oregano, dried	2 t	10 ml	
Crushed red pepper	1 t	5 ml	

Nutrient Analysis Per Serving				
	Calories	109	Protein	2 gm
	Fat	5 gm	Carbohydrate	15.6 gm
	Cholesterol	0 mg	Calcium	14.8 mg
	Sodium	619 mg	Fiber	0.7 gm

▲ Creole-Style White Hominy

Perfect for any southeastern American menu.

Menu Category:	Side, Starch, American Regional
Cooking Method:	Simmer
Preparation Time:	20 minutes
Cooking Time:	10 minutes
Variations:	Substitute cooked pinto or navy beans.
Yield:	50 portions (3½ oz)

Ingredient	U.S.	Metric	Method
White hominy, canned, drained	10 lb	4.5 kg	Combine in large pot or steam kettle. Heat to a simmer. Simmer 10 minutes, stirring occasionally.
Commercial picante sauce, mild	2 qt	1.9 L	
Onion, minced	1 qt	950 ml	
Green bell pepper, minced	1 qt	950 ml	
Garlic, minced	1 T	15 ml	
Oregano, dried	1 T	15 ml	
Tabasco sauce	¼ c	60 ml	
Salt	1 T	15 ml	
Black pepper	2 t	10 ml	

Nutrient Analysis	Calories	96	Protein	2.4 gm
Per Serving	Fat	1.6 gm	Carbohydrate	19.9 gm
	Cholesterol	0 mg	Calcium	19.4 mg
	Sodium	538 mg	Fiber	0.6 gm

▲ Almond Couscous with Currants

A simple variation on the Mediterranean classic.

Menu Category:	Side, Starch, Ethnic, Mediterranean
Cooking Method:	Simmer
Preparation Time:	20 minutes
Cooking Time:	20 minutes
Variations:	For entrée preparation, add cooked and sliced shrimp, scallops, chicken, or pork.
Yield:	50 portions (4 oz)

Ingredient	U.S.	Metric	Method
Couscous, quick cooking	1 qt	950 ml	Combine in large stockpot or steam kettle.
Water, boiling	2 qt	1.9 L	Cook until tender, about 10 minutes. Cool to room temperature. Reserve.
Currants, dried	2 c	480 ml	Combine in small bowl. Let rest 30
Water, boiling	1 qt	950 ml	minutes to plump currants. Reserve.
Olive oil, hot	½ c	120 ml	Sauté in heavy pot or tilt kettle just until
Onion, minced	2 c	480 ml	onions are tender.
Garlic, minced	2 T	30 ml	
Almonds, slivered	2 c	480 ml	
Chicken broth	2 c	480 ml	Add to onion mixture with reserved
Hot pepper sauce	1 T	15 ml	couscous and currant mixtures. Simmer for 5 minutes.

Nutrient Analysis				
Nutrient Analysis Per Serving	Calories	164	Protein	4.7 gm
	Fat	4.8 gm	Carbohydrate	26 gm
	Cholesterol	0 mg	Calcium	27.3 mg
	Sodium	41 mg	Fiber	0.4 gm

▲ Red Pepper Couscous

An exotic side dish from North Africa.

Menu Category:	Side, Starch, Ethnic, Moroccan
Cooking Method:	Simmer
Preparation Time:	20 minutes
Cooking Time:	20 minutes
Variations:	For entrée preparation, add cooked and sliced shrimp, scallops, chicken, or pork.
Yield:	50 portions (4 oz)

Ingredient	U.S.	Metric	Method
Couscous, quick cooking	1 qt	950 ml	Combine in large stockpot or steam kettle. Cook until tender, about 10 minutes. Cool to room temperature. Reserve.
Water, boiling	2 qt	1.9 L	
Olive oil, hot	½ c	120 ml	Sauté in heavy pot or tilt kettle just until onions are tender.
Onion, minced	2 c	480 ml	
Garlic, minced	2 T	30 ml	
Paprika	2 T	30 ml	Add. Sauté 1 minute, stirring constantly.
Water	1½ qt	1.4 L	Add to onion mixture with reserved couscous. Heat to a simmer. Simmer for 5 minutes.
Tomato paste	¾ c	180 ml	
Pimentos, chopped	2 c	480 ml	
Hot pepper sauce	1 T	15 ml	
Lemon juice	¼ c	60 ml	Add with reserved couscous. Cook over low heat until well heated.

Nutrient Analysis				
Nutrient Analysis Per Serving	Calories	125	Protein	3.6 gm
	Fat	2.4 gm	Carbohydrate	22 gm
	Cholesterol	0 mg	Calcium	12.2 mg
	Sodium	42 mg	Fiber	0.3 gm

Vegetables and Legumes

VEGETABLES

▲ Cajun Barbecued Green Beans

This is a piquant side dish or buffet offering for New South or Gulf Coast menus.

Menu Category:	Side, Vegetable, American Regional
Cooking Method:	Sauté/Simmer
Preparation Time:	20 minutes
Cooking Time:	30 minutes
Variations:	Add chopped smoked ham and substitute cooked navy beans.
Yield:	50 portions (3 oz)

Ingredient	U.S.	Metric	Method
Bacon, lean, diced	8 oz	227 g	Sauté over medium high heat in brazier or large pot just until barely golden.
Onion, diced Garlic, minced	1 qt 2 T	950 ml 30 ml	Add to bacon. Sauté just until onions become golden.
Commercial barbecue sauce Worcestershire sauce	2 qt ½ c	1.9 L 120 ml	Add to onion mixture. Heat to a boil. Reduce heat to a simmer. Simmer 10 minutes.
Black pepper, coarse ground Liquid smoke	1 T 1 t	15 ml 5 ml	
Green beans, IQF, thawed	8 lb	3.6 kg	Add to simmering sauce. Heat to a boil. Reduce heat to a simmer. Simmer 5 minutes.
Tabasco sauce	¼ c	60 ml	Adjust seasoning as desired.

Nutrient Analysis	Calories	64	Protein	2.3 gm
Per Serving	Fat	1.5 gm	Carbohydrate	11.4 gm
	Cholesterol	1.1 mg	Calcium	47.1 mg
	Sodium	379 mg	Fiber	1.1 gm

▲ Chinese Green Beans with Sesame Oil and Almonds

These bright green beans add a festive nutty crunch to Oriental and Polynesian menus.

Menu Category:	Side, Vegetable, Ethnic, Oriental, Polynesian
Cooking Method:	Boil/Sauté
Preparation Time:	20 minutes
Cooking Time:	20 minutes
Variations:	Substitute thinly sliced or julienne broccoli stems for beans.
	Substitute peanuts or toasted pecans.
	Add julienne strips of Chinese cabbage.
Yield:	50 portions (3 oz)

Ingredient	U.S.	Metric	Method
Green beans, IQF, thawed	8 lb	3.6 kg	Blanch beans in boiling water for 3
Water, boiling	as needed	as needed	minutes.
			Shock in ice water. Drain. Reserve.
Peanut oil, hot	1½ c	360 ml	Sauté in preheated 350°F brazier just until
Garlic, minced	¼ c	60 ml	garlic and almonds begin to turn golden.
Almonds, slivered	2 c	480 ml	Add reserved green beans. Stir-fry for 1
Crushed red pepper	1 T	15 ml	minute.
Sugar, granulated	1 c	240 ml	Add to beans. Continue to stir-fry for 2
Sesame oil	¼ c	60 ml	minutes or until beans are crisp and
			tender.

Nutrient Analysis	Calories	97	Protein	3.1 gm
Per Serving	Fat	5.8 gm	Carbohydrate	10.4 gm
	Cholesterol	0 mg	Calcium	49.7 mg
	Sodium	12 mg	Fiber	1.0 gm

▲ Dilled Green Beans

The fresh flavor of the beans is heightened with the touch of dill.

Menu Category:	Side, Salad, Vegetable, Ethnic, Mediterranean
Cooking Method:	Sauté
Preparation Time:	10 minutes
Cooking Time:	5 minutes
Variations:	Mix the color of the beans or add some cooked garbanzos.
	Serve chilled as a salad or warm as a side dish.
Yield:	50 portions (3 oz)

Ingredient	U.S.	Metric	Method
Olive oil	2 c	480 ml	Sauté in preheated 325°F brazier just until
Onion, minced	1 qt	950 ml	onion is golden.
Green beans, cooked, cooled	8 lb	3.6 kg	Add to onions. Stir well to heat completely.
Lemon juice	1 c	240 ml	Add to beans. Toss well. Transfer to
Dill seed	2 T	30 ml	service pieces.
Salt	1 T	15 ml	
Pepper, black	2 t	10 ml	

Nutrient Analysis Per Serving				
	Calories	102	Protein	1.2 gm
	Fat	8.8 gm	Carbohydrate	6.1 gm
	Cholesterol	0 mg	Calcium	41 mg
	Sodium	139 mg	Fiber	0.9 gm

▲ Steamed Broccoli with Sesame Seeds

This refreshing side dish goes well with Oriental entrées.

Menu Category:	Side, Salad, Vegetable, Ethnic, Oriental
Cooking Method:	Sauté
Preparation Time:	10 minutes
Cooking Time:	5 minutes
Variations:	Substitute cauliflower, cucumbers, or zucchini.
Yield:	50 portions (4 oz)

Ingredient	U.S.	Metric	Method
Peanut oil	1 c	240 ml	Sauté in preheated 325°F brazier just until garlic turns golden.
Garlic, minced	2 T	30 ml	
Gingerroot, minced	1 T	15 ml	
Crushed red pepper	2 t	10 ml	
Broccoli florets, steamed	12 lb	5.5 kg	Add to seasoning mixture. Toss and cook 5 minutes or until broccoli is heated thoroughly.
Sherry, dry	2 c	480 ml	
Sugar, granulated	½ c	120 ml	
Soy sauce	½ c	120 ml	
Sesame seeds, toasted	1 c	240 ml	Add to broccoli. Stir well.

Nutrient Analysis	Calories	70	Protein	4.4 gm
Per Serving	Fat	1.6 gm	Carbohydrate	9.4 gm
	Cholesterol	0 mg	Calcium	59.5 mg
	Sodium	192 mg	Fiber	1.3 gm

▲ Swedish Cabbage with Caraway

Serve with roasted or grilled poultry, pork, or beef.

Menu Category:	Side, Vegetable, Ethnic, Scandinavian		
Cooking Method:	Steam		
Preparation Time:	10 minutes		
Cooking Time:	10 minutes		
Variations:	Substitute red cabbage and substitute ground clove for caraway.		
Yield:	50 portions (4 oz)		

Ingredient	U.S.	Metric	Method
Butter, melted	1 c	240 ml	Combine in large bowl. Mix well.
Lemon juice	½ c	120 ml	
Water	½ c	120 ml	
Brown sugar	1 c	240 ml	
Caraway seed	1 T	15 ml	
Green cabbage, shredded	10 lb	4.5 kg	Add to bowl. Mix well. Transfer to four 12″ × 20″ × 2½″ perforated steamer trays. Steam at 15 psi for about 3 minutes. Remove from steamer. Drain as needed.
Cooking apples, peeled, diced	2 qt	1.9 L	

Nutrient Analysis Per Serving	Calories	93	Protein	1.2 gm
	Fat	4 gm	Carbohydrate	14.7 gm
	Cholesterol	10 mg	Calcium	50 mg
	Sodium	56 mg	Fiber	0.9 gm

▲ Red Cabbage with Apple and Cloves

Serve with roasted pork loin or grilled chicken breast.

Menu Category:	Side, Vegetable, Ethnic, German
Cooking Method:	Simmer
Preparation Time:	30 minutes
Cooking Time:	1½ hours
Variations:	Add diced apricots and golden raisins.
Yield:	50 portions (4 oz)

Ingredient	U.S.	Metric	Method
Red cabbage	12 lb	5.5 kg	Combine in steam kettle.
Onion, minced	2 c	480 ml	
Cooking apple, peeled, diced	2 qt	1.9 L	
Red wine vinegar	1 qt	950 ml	
Sugar, granulated	3 c	720 ml	
Water	1 qt	950 ml	
Cloves, whole	10	10	Combine in cloth bag. Add to cabbage mixture. Stir well. Heat to a simmer. Cover kettle. Simmer until cabbage is tender, about 1½ hours.
Allspice, whole	10	10	
Peppercorns, black	1 T	15 ml	
Cornstarch	1 c	240 ml	Combine. Mix well. Add to simmering cabbage. Simmer until juices are thickened. Remove spice bag.
Apple juice, cold	3 c	720 ml	

Nutrient Analysis Per Serving	Calories	109	Protein	1.3 gm
	Fat	0.5 gm	Carbohydrate	47.5 gm
	Cholesterol	0 mg	Calcium	47.5 mg
	Sodium	11.1 mg	Fiber	1.2 gm

▲ Glazed Carrots Grand Marnier

Serve these glistening carrots with grilled or barbecued chicken.

Menu Category:	Side, Vegetable, American Regional
Cooking Method:	Sauté
Preparation Time:	20 minutes
Cooking Time:	20 minutes
Variations:	Substitute cooked, sliced sweet potatoes.
Yield:	50 portions (4 oz)

Ingredient	U.S.	Metric	Method
Butter, melted	2 c	480 ml	Sauté just until carrots are heated and well coated.
Carrots, sliced, cooked	12 lb	5.5 kg	
Orange liqueur	1 c	240 ml	Add. Flame if possible. Simmer 1 minute.
Honey	½ c	120 ml	Add to carrots. Heat to a simmer. Simmer for 5 minutes.
Lemon juice	½ c	120 ml	
Lemon peel, grated	1 T	15 ml	
Salt	1 T	15 ml	
White pepper, ground	1 t	5 ml	

Nutrient Analysis Per Serving				
	Calories	141	Protein	1.3 gm
	Fat	7.6 gm	Carbohydrate	16.2 gm
	Cholesterol	20 mg	Calcium	37.5 mg
	Sodium	276 mg	Fiber	1.6 gm

▲ Sliced Carrots with Apricot Glaze

Serve these ever-popular carrots with roast poultry and pork.

Menu Category:	Side, Vegetable, American Regional
Cooking Method:	Simmer
Preparation Time:	20 minutes
Cooking Time:	30 minutes
Variations:	Substitute a variety of colorful fruit preserves. Add fruit liqueur if desired.
Yield:	50 portions (4 oz)

Ingredient	U.S.	Metric	Method
Butter, melted	1 c	240 ml	Combine in large pot or brazier. Heat to a simmer. Simmer until well combined.
Apricot preserves	2 c	480 ml	
Nutmeg, ground	1 t	5 ml	
Ginger, ground	1 t	5 ml	
Soy sauce	1 c	240 ml	
Orange juice	1 c	240 ml	
Orange rind, grated	¼ c	60 ml	
Carrots, sliced, cooked	12 lb	5.5 kg	Add to simmering sauce. Simmer just until well heated and glazed.

Nutrient Analysis Per Serving				
	Calories	122	Protein	1.6 gm
	Fat	3.9 gm	Carbohydrate	21.5 gm
	Cholesterol	10 mg	Calcium	39.7 mg
	Sodium	440 mg	Fiber	1.7 gm

▲ Oriental-Style Cucumbers with Shredded Carrots

This chilled side dish offers both zesty heat and refreshing cold.

Menu Category:	Side, Vegetable, Ethnic, Oriental
Cooking Method:	None required
Preparation Time:	30 minutes
Marination Time:	Several hours
Variations:	Substitute zucchini for cucumbers.
Yield:	50 portions (3 oz)

Ingredient	U.S.	Metric	Method
Cucumbers	8 lb	3.6 kg	Combine in large bowl. Let rest 2 hours.
Salt	½ c	120 ml	Rinse under cold water. Drain completely. Place in plastic storage container.
Carrots, shredded	4 lb	1.8 kg	Add to cucumbers. Toss well. Cover. Chill
Sugar	1 c	240 ml	several hours.
Soy sauce	2 c	480 ml	
Hot pepper oil	½ c	120 ml	
Sesame oil	½ c	120 ml	

Nutrient Analysis				
Per Serving	Calories	84	Protein	1.4 gm
	Fat	4.5 gm	Carbohydrate	10.6 gm
	Cholesterol	0 mg	Calcium	28.6 mg
	Sodium	1696 mg	Fiber	0.8 gm

▲ Grilled Eggplant with Herbs and Cheese

This is a variation on the Italian vegetable classic.

Menu Category:	Side, Vegetable, Ethnic, Italian
Cooking Method:	Broil
Preparation Time:	20 minutes
Cooking Time:	10 minutes
Variations:	Substitute veal, pork, or chicken for the eggplant.
Yield:	50 portions (5 oz)

Ingredient	U.S.	Metric	Method
Eggplant, stems removed	12 lb	5.5 kg	Cut crosswise into ½-inch thick slices. Carefully cut shallow crisscrosses over the surface of each slice.
Olive oil	2 c	480 ml	Brush both sides of each slice.
Basil, dried Oregano, dried	1 c 1 c	240 ml 240 ml	Sprinkle over eggplant. Place on oiled sheet pans. Broil under medium-high heat for 5 minutes. Turn over. Broil second side for 3 minutes.
Mozzarella cheese, grated	3 qt	2.8 L	Divide over slices. Return to the broiler. Broil until golden brown and bubbly.

Nutrient Analysis Per Serving	Calories	184	Protein	7.8 gm
	Fat	13.4 gm	Carbohydrate	9.7 gm
	Cholesterol	15.3 mg	Calcium	233 mg
	Sodium	130 mg	Fiber	1.5 gm

▲ Ratatouille Nicoise

This Provençale favorite can be served hot or cold.

Menu Category:	Side, Vegetable, Ethnic, French
Cooking Method:	Sauté/Bake
Preparation Time:	60 minutes
Oven Temperature:	400°F then 350°F
Cooking Time:	60 minutes
Variations:	Add capers and substitute cilantro for parsley.
Yield:	50 portions (5 oz)

Ingredient	U.S.	Metric	Method
Eggplant, stems removed	5 lb	2.3 kg	Cut crosswise into ½-inch thick slices.
Salt	1 c	240 ml	Sprinkle over slices. Let rest on paper towels for 30 minutes. Place on oiled sheet pans. Cover. Bake at 400°F for 15 minutes or just until tender. Remove and reserve. Reduce oven temperature to 350°F.
Zucchini, stems removed	5 lb	2.3 kg	Cut lengthwise into ½-inch thick slices. Dry well.
Olive oil, hot	2 c	480 ml	Sauté zucchini in preheated pot or tilt kettle just until golden. Transfer to racks. Reserve oil.
Onions, sliced	2 lb	908 g	Add to reserved hot oil. Sauté until golden.
Green bell pepper, sliced	2 lb	908 g	Add to onions. Sauté until peppers are tender, about 3 or 4 minutes.
Garlic, minced	2 T	30 ml	
Tomatoes, chopped, seeded	3 lb	1.4 kg	Add to onions. Toss well. Set heat to medium high. Simmer uncovered until mixture is fairly thick and dry. Remove from heat. Portion eggplant, zucchini, and onion mixture in layers in 12″ × 20″ × 2″ insert pans. Bake uncovered at 350°F for 30 minutes. Serve hot, warm, or cold.
Italian seasoning blend	¼ c	60 ml	
Parsley, chopped	2 c	480 ml	

Nutrient Analysis Per Serving				
	Calories	121	Protein	1.8 gm
	Fat	9 gm	Carbohydrate	10.2 gm
	Cholesterol	0 mg	Calcium	26.3 mg
	Sodium	154 mg	Fiber	1.0 gm

▲ Szechuan Barbecued Eggplant

Try this as a signature Oriental side dish.

Menu Category:	Side, Vegetable, Ethnic, Oriental
Cooking Method:	Grill/Broil
Preparation Time:	20 minutes
Cooking Time:	10 minutes
Variations:	Substitute sliced zucchini or cucumbers.
Yield:	50 portions (4 oz)

Ingredient	U.S.	Metric	Method
Eggplant, stems removed, sliced	12 lb	5.5 kg	Slice into ½-inch thick slices. Place each slice on aluminum foil square.
Peanut butter	3 c	720 ml	Combine in small bowl. Mix well. Brush mixture over each eggplant slice. Wrap each portion in foil. Cook on preheated medium-high grill for about 6 minutes on each side. Serve in the foil or unwrap.
Soy sauce	2 c	480 ml	
Garlic powder	¼ c	60 ml	
Water	2 c	480 ml	

Nutrient Analysis	Calories	133	Protein	5.2 gm
Per Serving	Fat	7.9 gm	Carbohydrate	10.5 gm
	Cholesterol	0 mg	Calcium	13.1 mg
	Sodium	735 mg	Fiber	1.2 gm

▲ Caribbean Sautéed Mushrooms

Serve this zesty side dish with grilled chicken, beef, and pork entrées.

Menu Category:	Side, Vegetable, Ethnic, Caribbean	
Cooking Method:	Sauté/Simmer	
Preparation Time:	10 minutes	
Cooking Time:	20 minutes	
Variations:	Substitute diced squash for mushrooms.	
Yield:	50 portions (4 oz)	

Ingredient	U.S.	Metric	Method
Smoked bacon, diced	¼ lb	114 g	Sauté in large pot or steam kettle just until barely crisp.
Onion, diced	1 qt	950 ml	Add to bacon. Sauté until vegetables are tender, about 5 minutes.
Red bell pepper, diced	1 qt	950 ml	
Jalapeños, seeded, minced	¼ c	60 ml	
Mushrooms, small, quartered	10 lb	4.5 kg	Add to mixture. Sauté 5 minutes.
Black pepper, coarsely ground	1 T	15 ml	
Dark rum	½ c	120 ml	Add. Flame if possible.
Pickapepper Sauce	½ c	120 ml	Add. Simmer 5 more minutes.

Nutrient Analysis	Calories	63	Protein	3.2 gm
Per Serving	Fat	1.7 gm	Carbohydrate	9.3 gm
	Cholesterol	1.9 mg	Calcium	10.9 mg
	Sodium	159 mg	Fiber	1.0 gm

▲ Roasted Onions with Rubbed Sage

A fragrant side dish to complement roasted poultry and pork.

Menu Category:	Side, Vegetable
Cooking Method:	Bake
Preparation Time:	10 minutes
Oven Temperature:	350°F
Cooking Time:	30 minutes
Variations:	Add fresh or dried thyme to sage.
Yield:	50 portions (4 oz)

Ingredient	U.S.	Metric	Method
Onions, peeled	12 lb	5.5 kg	Slice in half through the middle, not stem end. Place on oiled foil-lined sheets.
Orange marmalade	3 c	720 ml	Brush over each onion half.
Sage, dried	¼ c	60 ml	Sprinkle over onions. Bake at 350°F until tender, about 30 minutes.
Salt	2 T	30 ml	
Black pepper	1 T	15 ml	

Nutrient Analysis Per Serving				
	Calories	95	Protein	1.3 gm
	Fat	0.2 gm	Carbohydrate	23 gm
	Cholesterol	0 mg	Calcium	30.7 mg
	Sodium	261 mg	Fiber	0.9 gm

▲ Acorn Squash with Honey and Maple

This New England specialty is especially popular in the chill of fall.

Menu Category:	Side, Vegetable, American Regional
Cooking Method:	Bake
Preparation Time:	10 minutes
Oven Temperature:	350°F
Cooking Time:	30 minutes
Variations:	Fill split baked squash with sautéed apples and sausage balls.
Yield:	50 portions (8 oz)

Ingredient	U.S.	Metric	Method
Acorn squash, small	25	25	Split in half horizontally. Remove seeds. Trim each end flat. Place on oiled sheet pans.
Honey	1 qt	950 ml	Mix well. Portion 2 ounces into each squash.
Maple syrup	2 qt	1.9 L	
Butter	1 c	240 ml	
Cinnamon, ground	¼ c	60 ml	Sprinkle on top. Bake in preheated 350°F oven until fork tender, about 30 minutes.

Nutrient Analysis Per Serving	Calories	385	Protein	2.7 gm
	Fat	4.1 gm	Carbohydrate	93.2 gm
	Cholesterol	10 mg	Calcium	115 mg
	Sodium	100 mg	Fiber	4.6 gm

▲ Grilled Yellow Squash

Serve this garlic-laced side dish with any grilled or roasted entrée.

Menu Category:	Side, Vegetable, American Regional
Cooking Method:	Grill
Preparation Time:	20 minutes
Cooking Time:	15 minutes
Variations:	Substitute zucchini squash and season with tarragon. Combine all ingredients as directed but sauté instead.
Yield:	50 portions (4 oz)

Ingredient	U.S.	Metric	Method
Yellow squash, ¼-inch slices	8 lb	3.6 kg	Combine in large bowl. Toss well to combine. Portion into individual aluminum foil squares.
Onion, thinly sliced	4 lb	1.8 kg	
Oregano, dried	2 T	30 ml	
Garlic salt	1 T	15 ml	
White pepper, ground	1 T	15 ml	
Butter, soft	1 c	240 ml	Divide among each squash portion. Wrap foil tightly. Grill packets at medium-high heat for about 7 minutes on each side. Turn once during cooking.

Nutrient Analysis Per Serving	Calories	58	Protein	1.3 gm
	Fat	3.9 gm	Carbohydrate	5.5 gm
	Cholesterol	10 mg	Calcium	21 mg
	Sodium	164 mg	Fiber	0.6 gm

▲ Mexican-Style Squash Succotash

Serve with any southwestern American entrée.

Menu Category:	Side, Vegetable, Ethnic, Mexican, American Regional	
Cooking Method:	Sauté/Simmer	
Preparation Time:	10 minutes	
Cooking Time:	20 minutes	
Variations:	Substitute any variety of squash or beans.	
Yield:	50 portions (4 oz)	

Ingredient	U.S.	Metric	Method
Bacon strips, diced	6	6	Sauté in large pot until brown but not crisp.
Onion, diced	2 c	480 ml	Add to bacon. Sauté until tender.
Corn, whole kernel	2 lb	910 g	Add. Sauté until golden brown.
Summer squash, diced	6 lb	2.7 kg	Add. Cover. Simmer until corn and squash are tender, about 15 minutes.
Green chiles, sliced	2 c	480 ml	
Black beans, canned, drained	2 lb	908 g	
Water	3 c	720 ml	

Nutrient Analysis Per Serving				
	Calories	63	Protein	3.1 gm
	Fat	0.9 gm	Carbohydrate	12.1 gm
	Cholesterol	0.6 mg	Calcium	23.6 mg
	Sodium	55 mg	Fiber	0.9 gm

▲ Pureed Squash with Apples and Cinnamon

Serve this New England version with any poultry entrée.

Menu Category:	Side, Vegetable, American Regional
Cooking Method:	Simmer
Preparation Time:	10 minutes
Cooking Time:	20 minutes
Variations:	Use as a filling for a unique dessert double-crust pie.
Yield:	50 portions (4 oz)

Ingredient	U.S.	Metric	Method
Yellow squash, peeled, cooked	7 lb	3.2 kg	Combine in mixer bowl with whip attachment. Mix until well blended. Transfer to a large pot or steam kettle.
Cooking apples, peeled, cooked	3 lb	1.4 kg	
Brown sugar	5 lb	2.3 kg	Add to squash-apple mixture. Heat to a simmer. Simmer for 10 minutes, or until thickened. Serve hot.
Brandy	2 c	480 ml	
Eggs, beaten	12	12	
Cinnamon, ground	2 T	30 ml	
Nutmeg, grated	2 t	10 ml	
Ginger, ground	1½ t	8 ml	
Salt	2 T	30 ml	

Nutrient Analysis Per Serving				
	Calories	236	Protein	2.1 gm
	Fat	1.5 gm	Carbohydrate	50.3 gm
	Cholesterol	51.1 mg	Calcium	65 mg
	Sodium	285 mg	Fiber	0.5 gm

▲ Spaghetti Squash with Basil and Parmesan

When cooked and prepared, this squash looks and tastes much like rich pasta.

Menu Category:	Side, Vegetable, Ethnic, Italian
Cooking Method:	Roast
Preparation Time:	20 minutes
Cooking Time:	60 minutes
Variations:	Substitute spaghetti squash for any thin pasta recipe that calls for a last minute sauté with flavoring ingredients.
Yield:	50 portions (4 oz)

Ingredient	U.S.	Metric	Method
Spaghetti squash, whole	20 lb	9.1 kg	Place on oiled sheet pans. Bake at 350°F for about 45 minutes, turning occasionally. When fork tender, remove from oven. Split in half lengthwise. Remove seeds. Shred lengthwise with fork. Place all shredded squash in large bowl.
Parmesan cheese, grated	2 c	480 ml	Add to squash. Toss well. Serve hot.
Basil, dried	1 T	15 ml	
Salt	1 T	15 ml	
Black pepper	1 T	15 ml	

Nutrient Analysis Per Serving				
	Calories	120	Protein	3.7 gm
	Fat	1.5 gm	Carbohydrate	26.7 gm
	Cholesterol	3.2 mg	Calcium	137 mg
	Sodium	82 mg	Fiber	3.6 gm

▲ Grilled Herbed Zucchini Wafers

A perfect chilled side dish for pork or poultry.

Menu Category:	Side, Vegetable
Cooking Method:	Grill/Broil
Preparation Time:	10 minutes
Cooking Time:	10 minutes
Variations:	Substitute yellow squash.
Yield:	50 portions (4 oz)

Ingredient	U.S.	Metric	Method
Zucchini squash, scrubbed	10 lb	4.5 kg	Bias-cut into ½-inch thick slices. Place in large bowl.
Olive oil	2 c	480 ml	Add to zucchini. Toss well. Place on oiled sheet pans. Broil under high heat for 5 to 6 minutes, turning once. Transfer to large bowl. Cool to room temperature.
Salt	2 T	30 ml	
Black pepper	1 T	15 ml	
Balsamic vinegar	1 c	240 ml	Add to zucchini. Toss gently but well. Serve at room temperature or chilled.
Marjoram, dried	1 T	15 ml	
Tarragon, dried	1 T	15 ml	

Nutrient Analysis Per Serving				
	Calories	96	Protein	0.6 gm
	Fat	8.7 gm	Carbohydrate	4.8 gm
	Cholesterol	0 mg	Calcium	15.8 mg
	Sodium	260 mg	Fiber	0.5 gm

▲ Steamed Zucchini with Carrots and Mint

Serve this zucchini on the side of barbecued poultry or grilled fish.

Menu Category:	Side, Vegetable
Cooking Method:	Steam
Preparation Time:	10 minutes
Cooking Time:	10 minutes
Variations:	Substitute yellow squash for zucchini and tarragon for mint.
Yield:	50 portions (5 oz)

Ingredient	U.S.	Metric	Method
Zucchini squash, scrubbed	5 lb	2.3 kg	Bias-cut into ¼-inch thick slices. Place in large bowl.
Carrots, scrubbed	5 lb	2.3 kg	Bias-cut into ⅛-inch thick slices and add to zucchini.
Chicken broth	2 qt	1.9 L	Heat to a boil in heavy stockpot or steam kettle. Add reserved carrots. Cover. Steam for 4 minutes. Add reserved zucchini. Cover. Continue to steam until carrots and zucchini are tender, about 3 or 4 minutes. Drain as needed.
Mint, dried	2 T	30 ml	Add to vegetables. Toss well.
Salt	1 T	15 ml	
Pepper	2 t	10 ml	

Nutrient Analysis Per Serving				
	Calories	33	Protein	1.8 gm
	Fat	0.4 gm	Carbohydrate	6.2 gm
	Cholesterol	0 mg	Calcium	22.2 mg
	Sodium	270 mg	Fiber	0.7 gm

LEGUMES

▲ Boston Baked Beans

The ever-popular New England classic.

Menu Category:	Side, Vegetable, American Regional	
Cooking Method:	Bake	
Preparation Time:	10 minutes	
Soaking Time:	Overnight	
Oven Temperature:	325°F	
Cooking Time:	6 hours	
Variations:	Substitute a different bean variety or mixture.	
	For a southwestern variation, use pinto beans and add julienne jalapeño peppers.	
Yield:	50 portions (4 oz)	

Ingredient	U.S.	Metric	Method
Navy beans	6 lb	3.6 kg	Cover beans with water. Soak overnight.
Cold water	to cover	to cover	Transfer to stockpot or steam kettle. Heat to a boil. Boil 10 minutes. Drain, reserving water. Transfer beans to a large bowl.
Salt pork, thinly sliced	2 lb	908 g	Add to bowl with beans. Divide mixture
Onion, sliced	2 lb	908 g	between two 12″ × 20″ × 4″ insert pans.
Brown sugar	1 c	240 ml	Top with enough reserved water to cover
Molasses	2 c	240 ml	beans. Cover pans. Bake at 325°F oven for
Mustard, Dijon style	½ c	120 ml	6 hours or until beans are tender. Top with
Ginger, ground	1 T	15 ml	water occasionally. Remove cover for last
Salt	¼ c	60 ml	hour of baking.
Black pepper	1 T	15 ml	

Nutrient Analysis	Calories	140	Protein	6.3 gm
Per Serving	Fat	1.1 gm	Carbohydrate	26.7 gm
	Cholesterol	4.1 mg	Calcium	136 mg
	Sodium	586 mg	Fiber	1.8 gm

▲ Black-Eyed Peas with Spiced Sausage

Serve this southern specialty with a Cajun or other southern pork entrée.

Menu Category:	Side, Vegetable, American Regional
Cooking Method:	Sauté/Simmer
Preparation Time:	10 minutes
Cooking Time:	30 minutes
Variations:	Substitute kidney or pinto beans.
Yield:	50 portions (4 oz)

Ingredient	U.S.	Metric	Method
Bacon, diced	¼ lb	114 g	Sauté in large pot or steam kettle just until
Pork sausage, spicy	2 lb	910 g	bacon and sausage are golden brown.
Onion, diced	1 qt	950 ml	Add to mixture. Sauté until vegetables are
Green bell pepper, diced	1 qt	950 ml	tender, about 5 minutes.
Black-eyed peas, canned, drained	10 lb	4.5 kg	Add to mixture. Simmer for 15 minutes.

Nutrient Analysis	Calories	187	Protein	7.7 gm
Per Serving	Fat	7.3 gm	Carbohydrate	23 gm
	Cholesterol	17 mg	Calcium	126 mg
	Sodium	339 mg	Fiber	1.9 gm

▲ Egyptian-Style Red Lentil Puree

Serve this Mediterranean side dish with grilled poultry, pork, and seafood entrées.

Menu Category:	Side, Vegetable, Ethnic, Mediterranean		
Cooking Method:	Simmer		
Preparation Time:	10 minutes		
Cooking Time:	20 minutes		
Variations:	Convert this to a Mexican dish by substituting pureed pinto beans.		
Yield:	50 portions (4 oz)		

Ingredient	U.S.	Metric	Method
Olive oil, hot	¼ c	60 ml	Sauté just until onions begin to brown.
Onion, minced	1 qt	950 ml	
Garlic, minced	2 T	30 ml	
Lentils, red, rinsed	1½ qt	1.4 L	Add to onions. Stir to mix well.
Cumin, ground	3 T	45 ml	
Coriander, ground	2 T	30 ml	
Chicken stock	1½ gal	5.7 L	Add enough to cover lentils by about 1 inch. Simmer over low heat until lentils begin to break up. Drain well. Puree lentils. Place in large pot. Cook over low heat until fairly dry. Remove from heat. Reserve.
Lemon juice	¼ c	60 ml	Add to lentil mixture. Adjust seasoning.
Cayenne pepper	1 t	5 ml	
Salt	1 T	15 ml	
Black pepper	2 t	10 ml	

Nutrient Analysis Per Serving				
	Calories	125	Protein	9.5 gm
	Fat	2.2 gm	Carbohydrate	17.4 gm
	Cholesterol	0 mg	Calcium	27 mg
	Sodium	377 mg	Fiber	2.3 gm

▲ Herbed Lentils with Tofu

Popular Mediterranean lentils receive the decidedly Oriental touch of tofu.

Menu Category:	Side, Vegetable, Ethnic
Cooking Method:	Simmer/Sauté
Preparation Time:	10 minutes
Cooking Time:	30 minutes
Variations:	Substitute other varieties of cooked legumes.
Yield:	50 portions (4 oz)

Ingredient	U.S.	Metric	Method
Lentils, brown	2 qt	1.9 L	Rinse well. Place in stockpot or steam kettle.
Water, cold	1½ gal	5.7 L	Pour over lentils. Heat to a simmer. Check in 10 minutes. Do not overcook. Strain off liquid. Place lentils in large metal bowl.
Oregano, dried	2 T	30 ml	
Thyme, dried	2 t	10 ml	
Olive oil, hot	1 c	240 ml	Sauté just until golden.
Bacon, minced	1 lb	454 g	
Tofu, drained, diced	2 lb	908 g	Add to bacon. Sauté until golden and crisp.
Red onion, julienne	1 qt	950 ml	Add to pan. Sauté until very tender. Add to lentils.
Parsley, chopped	1 c	240 ml	Add to mixture. Stir gently but well. Serve warm.
Oregano, dried	2 t	10 ml	
Basil, dried	2 t	10 ml	
Black pepper	2 t	10 ml	

Nutrient Analysis Per Serving				
	Calories	212	Protein	12.7 gm
	Fat	10.7 gm	Carbohydrate	17.7 gm
	Cholesterol	7.7 mg	Calcium	65.3 mg
	Sodium	151 mg	Fiber	2.3 gm

▲ Smoky Butter Beans with Chili Sauce

This southern specialty is wonderful when served with roasted or grilled meats or poultry.

Menu Category:	Side, Vegetable, Ethnic, American Regional
Cooking Method:	Sauté/Simmer
Preparation Time:	10 minutes
Cooking Time:	30 minutes
Variations:	Substitute kidney or pinto beans.
Yield:	50 portions (4 oz)

Ingredient	U.S.	Metric	Method
Smoked bacon, diced	¼ lb	114 g	Sauté in large pot or steam kettle just until golden brown.
Onion, diced	1 qt	950 ml	Add to mixture. Sauté until vegetables are tender, about 5 minutes.
Red bell pepper, diced	1 qt	950 ml	
Liquid smoke	½ t	3 ml	
Butter beans, canned, drained	10 lb	4.5 kg	Add to mixture. Simmer for 15 minutes.

Nutrient Analysis Per Serving	Calories	162	Protein	9.6 gm
	Fat	2.2 gm	Carbohydrate	27.3 gm
	Cholesterol	1.9 mg	Calcium	60.1 mg
	Sodium	104 mg	Fiber	1.2 gm

Breads, Muffins, and Biscuits

Breads

▲ Annie's Bakeshop Anadama Bread

A wholesome New England favorite.

Menu Category:	Bread, Breakfast, Brunch, American Regional
Cooking Method:	Bake
Oven Temperature:	350°F
Preparation Time:	20 minutes
Rising Time:	1 to 2 hours
Baking Time:	45 to 50 minutes
Variations:	For a lighter loaf and milder flavor, substitute honey for molasses.
Yield:	50 portions (1 oz)

Ingredient	U.S.	Metric	Method
Cornmeal, yellow	8 oz	227 g	Combine in metal bowl. Stir well until smooth. Let rest for 30 minutes.
Water, boiling	16 oz	454 g	
Yeast, dry	1 T	15 ml	Combine in small bowl. Let rest until foamy, about 5 minutes.
Water, warm	8 oz	227 g	
Molasses, light	8 oz	227 g	Place in mixer bowl with paddle attachment. Add reserved cornmeal and yeast mixtures. Mix at low speed until well blended.
Butter, unsalted	1 oz	28 g	
Salt	1¼ T	19 ml	
Flour, all purpose	2¼ lb	1.02 kg	Add to mixture. Mix at low speed until well blended and dough begins to pull away from sides of the bowl. Portion into four oiled or paper-lined 9″ × 5″ × 3″ loaf pans. Let rise in warm spot until doubled in volume. Bake at 350°F until bread tests done with a hollow thumping sound when tapped, about 45 to 50 minutes. Cool on wire racks.

Nutrient Analysis	Calories	99	Protein	3.1 gm
Per Serving	Fat	1 gm	Carbohydrate	21 gm
	Cholesterol	1.2 mg	Calcium	19.2 mg
	Sodium	168 mg	Fiber	0.5 gm

▲ Apple Bread

A brunch favorite, especially when lightly toasted.

Menu Category:	Bread, Breakfast, Brunch
Cooking Method:	Bake
Oven Temperature:	350°F
Preparation Time:	20 minutes
Rising Time:	2 to 3 hours
Baking Time:	35 to 40 minutes
Variations:	Substitute chopped dried peaches or pears for the apples.
Yield:	50 portions (2 oz)

Ingredient	U.S.	Metric	Method
Apple juice, warm	1 qt	950 ml	Combine in large bowl. Whip well to combine. Cover. Let rest in warm spot until double in volume. Transfer to mixer bowl with dough hook.
Honey	½ c	120 ml	
Yeast, dry	2 T	30 ml	
Flour, whole wheat	1 lb	454 g	
Flour, bread	1 lb	454 g	
Flour, bread	2 lb	908 g	Add to dough in mixer bowl. Knead at low speed until dough is smooth and elastic, about 7 minutes. Portion into four oiled or paper-lined 9″ × 5″ × 3″ loaf pans. Let rise in warm spot until doubled in volume. Bake at 350°F until bread tests done when an inserted knife blade comes out clean, about 35 to 40 minutes. Cool on wire racks.
Dried apples, chopped	8 oz	227 g	
Apple butter	8 oz	227 g	
Butter, unsalted, soft	4 oz	114 g	
Salt	1½ T	23 ml	

Nutrient Analysis Per Serving				
	Calories	177	Protein	5.3 gm
	Fat	2.6 gm	Carbohydrate	35.7 gm
	Cholesterol	17.1 mg	Calcium	5 mg
	Sodium	215 mg	Fiber	0.9 gm

▲ Bishop's Bread

This supposedly originated during a clergyman's surprise Sunday visit to a Kentucky homestead.

Menu Category:	Bread, Breakfast, Brunch, Dessert
Cooking Method:	Bake
Oven Temperature:	350°F
Preparation Time:	20 minutes
Baking Time:	35 to 40 minutes
Variations:	Plump raisins in brandy for 30 minutes before adding.
Yield:	50 portions (2 oz)

Ingredient	U.S.	Metric	Method
Flour, all purpose	1¼ lb	567 g	Combine in mixer bowl with paddle attachment. Mix at low speed until well blended.
Brown sugar	1¾ lb	794 g	
Baking soda	2 t	10 ml	
Raisins, dark	2 c	480 ml	
Pecans, chopped	2 c	480 ml	
Cinnamon, ground	2 t	10 ml	
Salt	1 t	5 ml	
Butter, unsalted, chopped	8 oz	227 g	Add to mixer bowl. Mix until shortening is well blended and mixture appears crumbly.
Buttermilk	2 c	480 ml	Add to mixture. Mix at low speed just until blended. Portion into four oiled or paper-lined 9″ × 5″ × 3″ loaf pans. Bake at 350°F until bread tests done when an inserted knife blade comes out clean, about 35 to 40 minutes. Cool on wire racks.
Eggs, beaten	6 oz	170 g	

Nutrient Analysis				
Per Serving	Calories	188	Protein	2.9 gm
	Fat	7.3 gm	Carbohydrate	30.1 gm
	Cholesterol	24.8 mg	Calcium	38 mg
	Sodium	134 mg	Fiber	0.4 gm

▲ Blueberry Corn Bread

Ideal for brunch, breakfast, or breaktime snacks.

Menu Category:	Bread, Breakfast, Brunch
Cooking Method:	Bake
Oven Temperature:	425°F
Preparation Time:	20 minutes
Baking Time:	25 to 30 minutes
Variations:	Substitute other berries or even chopped raisins or minced dried fruit.
Yield:	50 portions (2 oz)

Ingredient	U.S.	Metric	Method
Cornmeal, yellow	1 lb	454 g	Combine in mixer bowl with paddle attachment. Mix to blend ingredients.
Flour, all purpose	1 lb	454 g	
Baking powder	2½ oz	70 g	
Sugar	8 oz	227 g	
Salt	1 T	15 ml	
Eggs, beaten	8 oz	227 g	Combine in small bowl. Whip well to combine. Add to dry ingredients. Mix at low speed just until ingredients are moistened.
Milk	1 qt	950 ml	
Margarine, melted	8 oz	227 g	
Blueberries, fresh or IQF	2 lb	908 g	Combine in bowl. Toss well. Add to mixture. Mix gently just to combine. Portion into two oiled or paper-lined half-sized sheet pans. Bake at 425°F until corn bread tests done when an inserted knife blade comes out clean, about 18 to 20 minutes. Remove from oven. Cool on wire racks.
Flour, all purpose	4 oz	114 g	

Nutrient Analysis	Calories	149	Protein	3.7 gm
Per Serving	Fat	5.1 gm	Carbohydrate	23.8 gm
	Cholesterol	20.8 mg	Calcium	61 mg
	Sodium	347 mg	Fiber	0.6 gm

▲ Grilled Monkey Bread

This "monkey business" can help build yours! Serve it with warm fruit compote.

Menu Category:	Bread, Breakfast, Brunch, Dessert
Cooking Method:	Bake
Oven Temperature:	325°F
Preparation Time:	20 minutes
Rising Time.	2 to 3 hours
Baking Time:	45 to 60 minutes
Variations:	Add orange or lemon zest and extract.
Yield:	50 portions (2 slices each)

Ingredient	U.S.	Metric	Method
Milk, scalded, warm	24 oz	680 g	Combine in large bowl. Whip well to combine. Cover. Let rest in warm spot until double in volume. Transfer to mixer bowl with dough hook.
Honey	16 oz	454 g	
Yeast, dry	2 T	30 ml	
Flour, all purpose	1½ lb	680 g	
Flour, bread	2 lb	908 g	Add to dough in mixer bowl. Knead at low speed until dough is smooth and elastic, about 7 minutes. Portion into 1-inch balls. Place dough balls next to each other on two oiled or paper-lined half-size sheet pans. Let rise in warm spot until doubled in volume. Bake at 350°F until bread tests done, with a hollow thumping sound when tapped, about 35 to 40 minutes. Cool on wire racks. When cool, slice into ½-inch thick slices. Brush with melted butter. Grill until golden.
Eggs, beaten	10 oz	284 g	
Egg yolks	4 oz	114 g	
Butter, unsalted, soft	4 oz	114 g	
Salt	2 t	10 ml	

Nutrient Analysis Per Serving				
	Calories	191	Protein	6.2 gm
	Fat	4 gm	Carbohydrate	35 gm
	Cholesterol	59.3 mg	Calcium	36.6 mg
	Sodium	122 mg	Fiber	0.7 gm

▲ Iroquois Spoon Bread

Prepare this as close to service as possible.

Menu Category:	Bread, Breakfast, Brunch
Cooking Method:	Bake
Oven Temperature:	350°F
Preparation Time:	20 minutes
Baking Time:	40 to 50 minutes
Variations:	Add chopped pecans and orange extract.
Yield:	50 portions (3 oz)

Ingredient	U.S.	Metric	Method
Cornmeal, white	2¼ lb	1.02 kg	Combine in small bowl. Mix well. Reserve.
Water	3 c	720 ml	
Sugar	3 oz	85 g	
Salt	2 T	30 ml	
Water	1½ qt	1.4 L	Heat to a boil in large pot. Gradually add reserved cornmeal mixture. Stir constantly over medium heat. Simmer 5 minutes. Remove from heat. Cool to barely warm.
Egg yolks	1 lb	454 g	Combine in small bowl. Add to warm cornmeal mixture. Mix well.
Butter, melted	3 oz	85 g	
Buttermilk	1½ qt	1.4 L	
Baking soda	1 T	15 ml	
Egg whites	1 lb	454 g	Place in mixer bowl with wire whip. Whip gradually for 1 minute at low speed. Increase speed to high. Whip until stiff peaks form. Fold one quarter of the mixture into cornmeal mixture. Fold that mixture back into egg whites. Portion into oiled six half-size (12″ × 10″ × 2½″) insert pans. Bake at 350°F until bread is golden brown and puffed, about 40 to 50 minutes. Serve as soon as possible after baking.
Cream of tartar	1 t	5 ml	

Nutrient Analysis Per Serving	Calories	142	Protein	5.1 gm
	Fat	5.2 gm	Carbohydrate	19 gm
	Cholesterol	121 mg	Calcium	51.5 mg
	Sodium	378 mg	Fiber	0.4 gm

▲ **Nut-Rich Boston Brown Bread**

Delightful winter holiday bread.

Menu Category:	Bread, Breakfast, Brunch
Cooking Method:	Steam
Preparation Time:	20 minutes
Cooking Time:	2 hours
Variations:	For a lighter loaf and milder flavor, substitute honey for molasses.
Yield:	50 portions (2 oz)

Ingredient	U.S.	Metric	Method
Flour, rye	8 oz	227 g	Combine in mixer bowl with paddle attachment. Mix to blend well.
Flour, whole wheat	8 oz	227 g	
Cornmeal, yellow	8 oz	227 g	
Baking soda	1½ T	23 ml	
Salt	2 t	10 ml	
Molasses, dark	12 oz	340 g	Add to mixture. Mix at low speed until ingredients are well blended. Portion into four 1-pound capacity molds or coffee cans, no higher than two-thirds the height. Cover molds or cans tightly. Place in large pots or brazier kettles.
Buttermilk	32 oz	908 g	
Raisins, dark	1 lb	454 g	
Pecans, chopped	8 oz	227 g	
Water, boiling	as needed	as needed	Fill to a level halfway up molds or cans. Cover. Simmer/steam over medium heat for two hours. Remove covers. Unmold breads. Cool on wire racks. Slice crosswise for service.

Nutrient Analysis	Calories	135	Protein	2.9 gm
Per Serving	Fat	3.6 gm	Carbohydrate	25 gm
	Cholesterol	0.7 mg	Calcium	48 mg
	Sodium	183 mg	Fiber	0.5 gm

▲ Sweet Potato Nut Bread

Give your bread basket a holiday air all year long.

Menu Category:	Bread, Breakfast, Brunch
Cooking Method:	Bake
Oven Temperature:	350°F
Preparation Time:	20 minutes
Baking Time:	50 minutes
Variations:	Substitute grated zucchini or carrots.
Yield:	50 portions (2 oz)

Ingredient	U.S.	Metric	Method
Flour, whole wheat	1½ lb	680 g	Combine in mixer bowl with paddle attachment. Mix to blend ingredients.
Baking powder	1 t	5 ml	
Baking soda	1 t	5 ml	
Salt	2 t	10 ml	
Cinnamon, ground	1 T	15 ml	
Allspice, ground	2 t	10 ml	
Ginger, ground	1 t	5 ml	
Peanut oil	2 c	480 ml	Combine in small bowl. Mix well. Add to flour mixture. Mix at low speed just until ingredients are moistened.
Brown sugar	2 lb	908 g	
Egg, beaten	8 oz	227 g	
Sweet potatoes, peeled, grated	2 lb	908 g	Add to mixture. Mix at low speed just until blended. Portion into four oiled or paper-lined 9″ × 5″ × 3″ loaf pans. Bake at 350°F until bread tests done when an inserted knife blade comes out clean, about 50 minutes. Cool on wire racks.
Walnuts, chopped	3 c	720 ml	

Nutrient Analysis Per Serving	Calories	211	Protein	6.0 gm
	Fat	7.9 gm	Carbohydrate	31.8 gm
	Cholesterol	193 mg	Calcium	36.3 mg
	Sodium	125 mg	Fiber	1.1 gm

▲ Zucchini Bread with Walnuts and Lemon

Ever-popular—even as a dessert.

Menu Category:	Bread, Breakfast, Brunch, Dessert
Cooking Method:	Bake
Oven Temperature:	350°F
Preparation Time:	20 minutes
Baking Time:	50 to 60 minutes
Variations:	Substitute grated mixed squash or sweet potatoes.
Yield:	50 portions (2 oz)

Ingredient	U.S.	Metric	Method
Flour, whole wheat	1½ lb	680 g	Combine in mixer bowl with paddle attachment. Mix to blend ingredients.
Baking powder	1 t	5 ml	
Baking soda	2 t	10 ml	
Salt	2 t	10 ml	
Cinnamon, ground	1 T	15 ml	
Walnut oil	2 c	480 ml	Combine in small bowl. Mix well. Add to flour mixture. Mix at low speed just until ingredients are moistened.
Sugar, granulated	2 lb	908 g	
Egg, beaten	4 oz	114 g	
Lemon extract	1 t	5 ml	
Zucchini, grated	2 lb	908 g	Add to mixture. Mix at low speed just until blended. Portion into four oiled or paper-lined 9″ × 5″ × 3″ loaf pans. Bake at 350°F until bread tests done when an inserted knife blade comes out clean, about 50 to 60 minutes. Cool on wire racks.
Walnuts, chopped	2 c	480 ml	

Nutrient Analysis	Calories	228	Protein	3.6 gm
Per Serving	Fat	12.1 gm	Carbohydrate	29.3 gm
	Cholesterol	9.7 mg	Calcium	14.8 mg
	Sodium	129 mg	Fiber	0.7 gm

Muffins

▲ Carolina White Corn Hush Puppies

Although legend has it they originated to silence barking, these will have folks talking!

Menu Category:	Bread, Side, Starch, American Regional
Cooking Method:	Deep-fry
Preparation Time:	20 minutes
Cooking Time:	18 to 20 minutes
Variations:	Add grated Monterey Jack cheese and toasted sesame seeds.
Yield:	50 portions (2 oz)

Ingredient	U.S.	Metric	Method
Cornmeal, white	2¼ lb	1.02 kg	Combine in mixer bowl with paddle attachment. Mix to blend ingredients.
Flour, all purpose	1 oz	28 g	
Baking powder	1 oz	28 g	
Sugar	2 oz	57 g	
Salt	1 T	15 ml	
Eggs, beaten	6 oz	170 g	Combine in small bowl. Whip well to combine. Add to dry ingredients. Mix at low speed just until ingredients are moistened. Use spoon or ½-ounce scoop to portion in batches into 375°F frying oil. Cook until hush puppies float and are golden brown, about 3 to 5 minutes. Drain well. Do not salt before service.
Milk	2 c	480 ml	
Buttermilk	2 c	480 ml	
Onion, minced	2 c	480 ml	

Nutrient Analysis				
Per Serving	Calories	117	Protein	2.9 gm
	Fat	3.6 gm	Carbohydrate	19 gm
	Cholesterol	15.6 mg	Calcium	39.5 mg
	Sodium	217 mg	Fiber	0.4 gm

▲ Corn Muffins with Jalapeño and Bacon

Perfect for southwestern menus, or with just about any grilled pork, poultry, or seafood entrée.

Menu Category:	Bread, Breakfast, Brunch, American Regional
Cooking Method:	Bake
Oven Temperature:	425°F
Preparation Time:	20 minutes
Baking Time:	18 to 20 minutes
Variations:	Add grated cheddar cheese and minced scallion or cilantro.
Yield:	50 portions (1½ oz)

Ingredient	U.S.	Metric	Method
Cornmeal, yellow	1¾ lb	794 g	Combine in mixer bowl with paddle attachment. Mix to blend ingredients.
Baking soda	4 t	20 ml	
Bacon, cooked, crumbled	2 c	480 ml	
Jalapeño peppers, minced	¼ c	60 ml	
Sugar	1½ T	23 ml	
Salt	2 t	10 ml	
Egg whites	7 oz	198 g	Combine in small bowl. Whip well to combine. Add to dry ingredients. Mix at low speed just until ingredients are moistened. Portion into oiled or paper-lined 4-ounce muffin pans. Bake at 425°F until muffins test done, about 18 to 20 minutes. Remove muffins from pans. Cool on wire racks.
Picante sauce, hot	2 c	480 ml	
Vegetable oil	8 oz	227 g	
Nonfat yogurt, plain	2 lb	908 g	

Nutrient Analysis	Calories	114	Protein	2.8 gm
Per Serving	Fat	5.3 gm	Carbohydrate	14.6 gm
	Cholesterol	0.3 mg	Calcium	39.1 mg
	Sodium	247 mg	Fiber	0.3 gm

▲ Lemon 'n' Walnut Muffins

Serve these piping hot—with or without butter on the side.

Menu Category:	Bread, Breakfast, Brunch
Cooking Method:	Bake
Oven Temperature:	400°F
Preparation Time:	20 minutes
Baking Time:	15 to 20 minutes
Variations:	Substitute orange for the lemon and pecans for the walnuts.
Yield:	50 portions (2 oz)

Ingredient	U.S.	Metric	Method
Flour, all purpose	2 lb	908 g	Combine in mixer bowl with paddle attachment. Mix to blend ingredients.
Baking powder	¼ c	60 ml	
Sugar	1 lb	454 g	
Salt	2 t	10 ml	
Walnuts, chopped	8 oz	227 g	
Butter, melted	1 lb	454 g	Combine in small bowl. Whip well to combine. Add to dry ingredients. Mix at low speed just until ingredients are moistened. Portion into oiled or paper-lined 4-ounce muffin pans. Bake at 400°F until muffins test done, about 15 to 20 minutes. Remove muffins from pans. Cool on wire racks.
Lemon rind	¼ c	60 ml	
Lemon juice	16 oz	480 ml	
Eggs	1 lb	454 g	

Nutrient Analysis Per Serving				
	Calories	205	Protein	4.8 gm
	Fat	11.3 gm	Carbohydrate	23.8 gm
	Cholesterol	58.6 mg	Calcium	31.7 mg
	Sodium	254 mg	Fiber	0.7 gm

Biscuits

▲ Buttermilk Cinnamon Scones

Delicious and popular—from breakfast to bread basket.

Menu Category:	Bread, Breakfast, Brunch
Cooking Method:	Bake
Oven Temperature:	425°F
Preparation Time:	20 minutes
Cooking Time:	12 minutes
Variations:	Add currants, raisins, or other minced dried fruit.
Yield:	50 portions (2 oz)

Ingredient	U.S.	Metric	Method
Flour, all purpose	2¼ lb	1.02 kg	Combine in mixer bowl with paddle attachment. Mix at low speed until well blended.
Sugar, granulated	11 oz	312 g	
Baking powder	2½ T	38 ml	
Baking soda	1½ t	8 ml	
Cinnamon, ground	2 t	10 ml	
Salt	2¼ t	11 ml	
Butter, cold, chopped	18 oz	510 g	Add to mixer bowl. Mix until butter is well blended and mixture appears crumbly.
Buttermilk	3 c	720 ml	Add to mixture. Mix at low speed until dough is smooth and leaves side of bowl. Transfer to work surface. Pat or roll into ½-inch thick slab. Cut with 2½-inch cutter. Place individual scones 1½ inches apart on oiled or paper-lined sheet pans.
Milk	¼ c	60 ml	Brush over scones.
Sugar, granulated	½ c	120 ml	Combine and sprinkle over scones. Bake at 425°F until puffed and golden, about 12 minutes.
Cinnamon, ground	1 T	15 ml	

Nutrient Analysis **Per Serving**	Calories	181	Protein	3.4 gm
	Fat	8.9 gm	Carbohydrate	24.1 gm
	Cholesterol	23 mg	Calcium	40 mg
	Sodium	272 mg	Fiber	0.5 gm

▲ Cheese and Bacon Biscuits

Perfect accompaniment for southern and southwestern menus.

Menu Category:	Bread, Breakfast, Brunch
Cooking Method:	Bake
Oven Temperature:	450°F
Preparation Time:	20 minutes
Cooking Time:	12 minutes
Variations:	Add minced jalapeños or mild green chilies.
Yield:	50 portions (1 oz)

Ingredient	U.S.	Metric	Method
Flour, all purpose	1 lb	545 g	Combine in mixer bowl with paddle attachment. Mix at low speed until well blended.
Cornmeal, yellow	18 oz	510 g	
Monterey Jack cheese, grated	8 oz	227 g	
Bacon, cooked, crumbled	2 oz	57 g	
Baking powder	2½ T	38 ml	
Baking soda	2 t	10 ml	
Salt	2 t	10 ml	
Shortening	10 oz	284 g	Add to mixer bowl. Mix until shortening is well blended and mixture appears crumbly.
Buttermilk	3 c	720 ml	Add to mixture. Mix at low speed until dough is smooth and leaves side of bowl. Transfer to work surface. Pat or roll into 1-inch thick slab. Cut with 2-inch cutter. Place biscuits 1½ inches apart on oiled or paper-lined sheet pans. Bake at 450°F until puffed and golden, about 12 minutes.

Nutrient Analysis Per Serving				
	Calories	148	Protein	4.0 gm
	Fat	8.3 gm	Carbohydrate	15.3 gm
	Cholesterol	5.5 mg	Calcium	64.1 mg
	Sodium	229 mg	Fiber	0.4 gm

▲ Lemon-Pepper Whole Wheat Biscuits

Hearty biscuits with a twist.

Menu Category:	Bread, Breakfast, Brunch
Cooking Method:	Bake
Oven Temperature:	425°F
Preparation Time:	20 minutes
Cooking Time:	10 minutes
Variations:	Substitute orange rind and add chopped pecans.
Yield:	50 portions (1 oz)

Ingredient	U.S.	Metric	Method
Flour, self-rising	1 lb	454 g	Combine in mixer bowl with paddle attachment. Mix at low speed just until well blended and mixture appears crumbly.
Flour, whole wheat	½ lb	227 g	
Shortening	5 oz	142 g	
Lemon zest	2 T	30 ml	
Black pepper, coarsely ground	2 T	30 ml	
Buttermilk	2 c	480 ml	Add to mixer bowl. Mix just until dry ingredients are barely moist. Transfer to work surface. Pat or roll into ½-inch thick slab. Cut with 2-inch cutter. Place biscuits 1½ inches apart on oiled or paper-lined sheet pans. Bake at 425°F until puffed and golden, about 10 minutes.
Lemon juice	½ c	120 ml	

Nutrient Analysis Per Serving				
	Calories	75.4	Protein	1.9 gm
	Fat	2.8 gm	Carbohydrate	10.9 gm
	Cholesterol	36 mg	Calcium	45.3 mg
	Sodium	126 mg	Fiber	0.2 gm

▲ Mexican Jalapeño Biscuits

Light and flavorful, with just the right touch of heat.

Menu Category:	Bread, Breakfast, Brunch
Cooking Method:	Bake
Oven Temperature:	450°F
Preparation Time:	20 minutes
Cooking Time:	10 to 15 minutes
Variations:	Add grated cheese and toasted pine nuts.
Yield:	50 portions (1½ oz)

Ingredient	U.S.	Metric	Method
Flour, all purpose	2 lb	908 g	Combine in mixer bowl with paddle attachment. Mix at low speed until well blended.
Baking powder	6 oz	170 g	
Salt	1½ T	23 ml	
Chili powder	2 T	30 ml	
Liquid shortening	11 oz	312 g	Add to mixer bowl. Mix just until dough is fairly smooth. Portion with spoon onto oiled or paper-lined sheet pans. Bake at 450°F until puffed and golden, about 10 to 15 minutes.
Milk	2⅔ c	640 ml	
Jalapeño peppers, pickled, chopped	½ c	120 ml	

Nutrient Analysis Per Serving				
	Calories	123	Protein	3 gm
	Fat	6.3 gm	Carbohydrate	15 gm
	Cholesterol	26 mg	Calcium	90.2 mg
	Sodium	595 mg	Fiber	0.5 gm

▲ No-Rise Angel Biscuits

They take their name from the heavenly light texture.

Menu Category:	Bread, Breakfast, Brunch		
Cooking Method:	Bake		
Oven Temperature:	425°F		
Preparation Time:	20 minutes		
Cooking Time:	10 minutes		
Variations:	Add crumbled bacon or finely minced country ham.		
Yield:	50 portions (1½ oz)		

Ingredient	U.S.	Metric	Method
Flour, self-rising	3 lb	1.4 kg	Combine in mixer bowl with paddle attachment. Mix at low speed just until well blended and mixture appears crumbly.
Shortening	10 oz	284 g	
Buttermilk	1 qt	950 ml	Add to mixer bowl. Mix just until dry ingredients are barely moist. Transfer to work surface. Pat or roll into ½-inch thick slab. Cut with 2-inch cutter. Place biscuits 1½ inches apart on oiled or paper-lined sheet pans. Bake at 425°F until puffed and golden, about 10 minutes.

Nutrient Analysis Per Serving	Calories	150	Protein	3.4 gm
	Fat	5.6 gm	Carbohydrate	21 gm
	Cholesterol	0.7 mg	Calcium	115 mg
	Sodium	366 mg	Fiber	0.1 gm

▲ Pepper-Cheese Boarding House Biscuits

These traditional biscuits are a snap to make!

Menu Category:	Bread, Breakfast, Brunch
Cooking Method:	Bake
Oven Temperature:	450°F
Preparation Time:	20 minutes
Cooking Time:	12 minutes
Variations:	Add minced jalapeños or mild green chilies.
Yield:	50 portions (1½ oz)

Ingredient	U.S.	Metric	Method
Flour, all purpose	1 lb	454 g	Combine in mixer bowl with paddle attachment. Mix at low speed until well blended.
Cornmeal, yellow	18 oz	510 g	
Parmesan cheese, grated	8 oz	227 g	
Baking powder	2½ T	38 ml	
Baking soda	2 t	10 ml	
Salt	2 t	10 ml	
Black pepper, coarsely ground	1 T	15 ml	
Shortening	10 oz	284 g	Add to mixer bowl. Mix until shortening is well blended and mixture appears crumbly.
Buttermilk	3 c	720 ml	Add to mixture. Mix at low speed until dough is smooth and leaves side of bowl. Transfer to work surface. Pat or roll into 1-inch thick slab. Cut with 2-inch cutter. Place biscuits 1½ inches apart on oiled or paper-lined sheet pans. Bake at 450°F until puffed and golden, about 12 minutes.

Nutrient Analysis				
Per Serving	Calories	141	Protein	4.5 gm
	Fat	7.2 gm	Carbohydrate	15.5 gm
	Cholesterol	4.1 mg	Calcium	93 mg
	Sodium	271 mg	Fiber	0.4 gm

DESSERTS

FRUIT DESSERTS

▲ Baked Pears with Toasted Almond Butterscotch Sauce

Simple and subtle, just as fruit desserts should be.

Menu Category:	Dessert
Cooking Method:	Bake
Preparation Time:	30 minutes
Oven Temperature:	375°F
Baking Time:	30 to 35 minutes
Variations:	Substitute apples for pears.
	Use canned pears and commercial butterscotch sauce.
Yield:	50 portions (6 oz)

Ingredient	U.S.	Metric	Method
Pears, Anjou or Bartlett	50	50	Peel and core, leaving stems on if possible. Arrange in two buttered 12″ × 20″ × 6″ insert pans.
Sugar, granulated	1 lb	454 g	Sprinkle over pears. Cover. Bake in preheated 375°F oven until pears are barely tender, about 10 to 15 minutes.
Half-and-half	2 qt	1.8 L	Pour over pears. Do not cover. Continue baking until pears are tender, about 15 minutes. Transfer to wire racks set over sheet pans. Reserve all cooking juices. Place pears in shallow dishes for service.
Toasted Almond Butterscotch Sauce, recipe follows	2½ qt	2.4 L	Combine in large pot. Heat to a boil. Reduce heat to a simmer. Simmer for 10 minutes. Portion 2 ounces over each baked pear.
Cooking liquid	1 qt	950 ml	

Nutrient Analysis	Calories	408	Protein	7.6 gm
Per Serving	Fat	13.4 gm	Carbohydrate	63.2 gm
	Cholesterol	45.3 mg	Calcium	92.5 mg
	Sodium	147 mg	Fiber	2.4 gm

Companion Recipe

▲ **Toasted Almond Butterscotch Sauce**

A signature sauce for fruits, poundcake, puddings, or ice cream.

Menu Category:	Sauce
Cooking Method:	Simmer
Preparation Time:	10 minutes
Cooking Time:	15 minutes
Variations:	Substitute walnuts or pecans for almonds.
Yield:	1 gallon

Ingredient	U.S.	Metric	Method
Butter, unsalted	2½ lb	1.2 kg	Combine in heavy pot or steam kettle.
Brown sugar, light	3½ lb	1.6 kg	Heat to a boil, stirring occasionally.
Corn syrup, light	2½ c	600 ml	Remove from heat.
Lemon juice	⅔ c	160 ml	Add to sauce. Stir well. Use as soon as
Almonds, chopped, toasted	2 c	480 ml	possible or chill and reheat for later service.

Nutrient Analysis	Calories	141	Protein	0.5 gm
Per Ounce	Fat	8.3 gm	Carbohydrate	17.1 gm
	Cholesterol	19.4 mg	Calcium	21 mg
	Sodium	82.3 mg	Fiber	0.1 gm

▲ Fresh Apple Sampler with Gingered Yogurt

Crisp slices of sweet apple, served with a tangy sauce.

Menu Category:	Dessert, Brunch
Cooking Method:	None required
Preparation Time:	30 minutes
Variations:	Add raisins and sliced toasted almonds.
	Substitute or blend other fruits.
Yield:	50 portions (4 oz)

Ingredient	U.S.	Metric	Method
Sugar, granulated	1 lb	454 g	Combine in large bowl. Stir well to
Lemon juice	1 c	240 ml	dissolve sugar.
Orange juice	1 c	240 ml	
Lime juice	¼ c	60 ml	
Maraschino liqueur	¾ c	180 ml	
Granny Smith apples,			Add to juice/liqueur mixture. Fold gently
cored, wedged, sliced	3 qt	2.8 L	but thoroughly with large rubber spatula.
Red Delicious apples,			Cover. Chill completely. Stir occasionally.
cored, wedged, sliced	3 qt	2.8 L	Fold gently before portioning into service
			pieces with slotted spoon. Divide liquid
			among each portion.
Sugar, granulated	2 c	480 ml	Combine in large bowl. Mix well. Cover.
Yogurt, lowfat, plain	1 qt	950 ml	Chill completely. Portion 1 ounce over
Orange juice, fresh	1 qt	950 ml	apples just before service.
Orange zest, blanched	½ c	120 ml	
Ginger, grated	2 T	30 ml	

Nutrient Analysis				
Nutrient Analysis	Calories	104	Protein	0.8 gm
Per Serving	Fat	0.3 gm	Carbohydrate	25.2 gm
	Cholesterol	0.2 mg	Calcium	25 mg
	Sodium	8.7 mg	Fiber	0.5 gm

▲ Fresh Fruit with Strawberry-Yogurt Creme Sauce

A delightful end to a meal or a snack in the middle of a busy day.

Menu Category:	Dessert, Brunch
Cooking Method:	None required
Preparation Time:	30 minutes
Variations:	Substitute any mixture of fruit you wish and any of a number of fruit liqueurs.
Yield:	50 portions (6 oz)

Ingredient	U.S.	Metric	Method
Aspartame-based bulk			Combine in large bowl. Stir well.
sweetener	½ c	120 ml	
Lemon juice	2 c	480 ml	
Maraschino liqueur	1½ c	360 ml	
Orange juice	1 c	240 ml	
Oranges wedges	2 qt	1.9 L	Add to juice/liqueur mixture. Fold gently
Apples, peeled, cored,			but thoroughly with large rubber spatula.
sliced	1 qt	950 ml	Cover. Refrigerate for several hours. Fold
Pears, peeled, cored, sliced	1 qt	950 ml	gently before portioning into service
Peaches, peeled, sliced	1 qt	950 ml	pieces. Chill completely.
Plums, seeded, sliced	1 qt	950 ml	
Banana, sliced	1 qt	950 ml	
Grapes, white seedless,			
halved	1 qt	950 ml	
Grapes, red seedless,			
halved	1 qt	950 ml	
Strawberry-Yogurt Creme			Portion 2½ ounces over each serving.
Sauce, recipe follows	1 gal	3.8 L	

Nutrient Analysis	Calories	186	Protein	4.6 gm
Per Serving	Fat	1.3 gm	Carbohydrate	38.1 gm
	Cholesterol	3 mg	Calcium	104 mg
	Sodium	33.8 mg	Fiber	1.1 gm

Companion Recipe

▲ Strawberry-Yogurt Creme Sauce

A topping for fresh fruits.

Menu Category:	Sauce
Cooking Method:	None required
Preparation Time:	30 minutes
Variations:	Substitute other yogurt and fresh fruit.
	Offer with grilled chicken as a refreshing dip.
Yield:	1 gallon

Ingredient	U.S.	Metric	Method
Strawberry yogurt, sugar-free	2 qt	1.8 L	Combine in food processor with metal blade. Process until well pureed. Strain through fine sieve.
Strawberries, fresh or IQF, sliced	2 qt	1.8 L	Chill completely.
Milk, lowfat	1 qt	950 ml	
Vanilla extract	1 T	15 ml	

Nutrient Analysis Per Ounce				
	Calories	21	Protein	0.9 gm
	Fat	0.3 gm	Carbohydrate	3.8 gm
	Cholesterol	1.2 mg	Calcium	32.2 mg
	Sodium	12.2 mg	Fiber	0.1 gm

▲ Guilt-Free Jubilee Cherry Sauce

Serve as a topping for cake, ice cream, and crepes or use as a base for flavoring plain yogurt.

Menu Category:	Sauce
Cooking Method:	Simmer
Preparation Time:	10 minutes
Cooking Time:	10 minutes
Variations:	Substitute other IQF or water-pack fruit and liqueur.
Yield:	1 gallon

Ingredient	U.S.	Metric	Method
Red cherries, sour, IQF	4 lb	1.8 kg	Combine in large pot. Heat to a boil.
Cleargel or arrowroot	½ c	120 ml	Reduce heat to a simmer. Simmer for 1
Water	1 qt	950 ml	minute, stirring constantly. Remove from
Lemon juice	¼ c	60 ml	heat.
Maraschino liqueur	¼ c	60 ml	
Amaretto liqueur	¼ c	60 ml	
Aspartame-based bulk sweetener	½ c	120 ml	Add to sauce mixture. Stir well. Serve hot, warm, or cold.

Nutrient Analysis Per Ounce	Calories	18	Protein	0.7 gm
	Fat	0 gm	Carbohydrate	2.9 gm
	Cholesterol	0 mg	Calcium	2.7 mg
	Sodium	0.6 mg	Fiber	0.1 gm

▲ Mama Clements's Apple Brown Betty

This traditional favorite continues to please.

Menu Category:	Dessert, American Regional		
Cooking Method:	Bake		
Preparation Time:	30 minutes		
Baking Time:	30 to 40 minutes		
Oven Temperature:	350°F		
Variations:	Add chopped toasted almonds or walnuts.		

Yield: 50 portions (5 oz)

Ingredient	U.S.	Metric	Method
Bread crumbs, dry	2 qt	1.9 L	Combine in large bowl. Toss well.
Butter, melted	8 oz	227 g	
Apples, cored, peeled,			Combine in large bowl. Mix well. Portion
diced	1 gal	3.8 L	half the apple mixture into two 12″ × 20″
Maple syrup	2 c	480 ml	× 4″ oiled insert pans. Top with half the
Brown sugar	2 c	480 ml	crumb mixture. Repeat process with
Lemon juice	½ c	120 ml	remaining apple and crumb mixtures.
Cinnamon, ground	2 t	10 ml	
Nutmeg, ground	2 t	10 ml	
Milk	1 qt	950 ml	Pour over top of pans. Bake in lower third of preheated 350°F oven until top is golden and filling is firm, about 30 minutes. Cool for 30 minutes before cutting.

Nutrient Analysis				
Nutrient Analysis	Calories	193	Protein	2.9 gm
Per Serving	Fat	5.1 gm	Carbohydrate	36 gm
	Cholesterol	11.4 mg	Calcium	56.6 mg
	Sodium	176 mg	Fiber	0.3 gm

▲ Marinated Oranges with Mock Rum Cream

Light, refreshing, and incredibly simple.

Menu Category:	Dessert
Cooking Method:	None required
Preparation Time:	30 minutes
Variations:	Substitute any fruit preserve or marmalade.
	Substitute flavored yogurt for sour cream.
Yield:	50 portions (4 oz)

Ingredient	U.S.	Metric	Method
Oranges, navel, peeled	25	25	Cut crosswise into ¼-inch slices. Place in large storage container.
Orange juice	3 qt	2.8 L	Combine. Pour over oranges. Cover. Chill
Lemon juice	2 c	480 ml	completely. Drain well. Portion oranges
Orange liqueur	2 c	480 ml	into shallow desert glasses. Portion 1
Vanilla extract	2 T	30 ml	ounce of liquid over oranges.
Vanilla pudding, sugar-free, prepared	1 qt	950 ml	Combine in mixer bowl with whip attachment. Mix at medium speed until
Milk, additional	3 c	720 ml	well blended. Cover. Chill completely.
Vanilla extract	2 T	30 ml	Portion 1 ounce over oranges.
Rum extract	1 T	15 ml	
Nutmeg, grated	1 T	15 ml	Sprinkle over cream sauce.

Nutrient Analysis	Calories	165	Protein	2 gm
Per Serving	Fat	0.5 gm	Carbohydrate	20 gm
	Cholesterol	1.1 mg	Calcium	72 mg
	Sodium	60 mg	Fiber	0.3 gm

▲ Peach and Pecan Pandowdy

The New England dessert takes on a new southern Georgia flavor.

Menu Category:	Dessert, American Regional
Cooking Method:	Bake
Preparation Time:	30 minutes
Baking Time:	35 to 40 minutes
Oven Temperature:	350°F
Variations:	Substitute chopped toasted almonds or walnuts for pecans.
Yield:	50 portions (5 oz)

Ingredient	U.S.	Metric	Method
Peaches, peeled, sliced	6 lb	2.7 kg	Combine in large bowl. Mix well. Divide among two oiled 12″ × 20″ × 4″ insert pans.
Pecans, chopped	1 lb	454 g	
Brown sugar	3 lb	1.4 kg	
Maple syrup	2 c	480 ml	
Cinnamon, ground	2 t	10 ml	
Cloves, ground	1 t	5 ml	
Nutmeg, ground	1 t	5 ml	
Peach nectar	1 qt	950 ml	Pour over the peach mixture.
Butter, cold, sliced	4 oz	114 g	Divide over the two pans.
Biscuit dough	3 lb	1.4 kg	Divide into two portions. Roll out each portion into 12″ × 20″ rectangle. Layer over peaches. Bake in lower third of preheated 350°F oven until top is golden and filling is firm, about 35 to 40 minutes. Cool for 30 minutes before cutting.

Nutrient Analysis				
Per Serving	Calories	333	Protein	3.1 gm
	Fat	12 gm	Carbohydrate	56.2 gm
	Cholesterol	5 mg	Calcium	33 mg
	Sodium	306 mg	Fiber	0.6 gm

▲ Strawberry Crepes Neapolitan

Simplicity exemplified—and delightful for dessert or your brunch buffet.

Menu Category:	Dessert
Cooking Method:	None required
Preparation Time:	30 minutes
Variations:	Substitute any fruit preserve or marmalade.
	Substitute flavored yogurt for sour cream.
Yield:	50 portions (2 crepes each)

Ingredient	U.S.	Metric	Method
Crepes, 6-inch, commercial	100	100	Arrange on work surface.
Strawberry preserves	3 qt	2.8 L	Portion 1 ounce on each crepe. Spread evenly.
Sour cream	1½ qt	1.4 L	Portion ½ ounce on each crepe. Spread evenly. Roll crepes tightly. Cover. Chill for service.
Sugar, powdered	2 c	480 ml	Immediately before service, sprinkle through decorative doily.

Nutrient Analysis Per Serving				
Calories	355		Protein	5.2 gm
Fat	6.8 gm		Carbohydrate	69 gm
Cholesterol	14 mg		Calcium	81 mg
Sodium	68 mg		Fiber	0.8 gm

▲ Strawberry Shortcake

There's no reason to limit this to summer: Serve it all year long.

Menu Category:	Dessert, American Regional
Cooking Method:	Bake
Preparation Time:	30 minutes
Baking Time:	10 minutes
Oven Temperature:	425°F
Variations:	Substitute peaches or blueberries for strawberries.
	Substitute toasted split croissants for biscuits.
Yield:	50 portions (6 oz)

Ingredient	U.S.	Metric	Method
Flour, self-rising	3 lb	1.4 kg	Combine in mixer bowl with paddle attachment. Mix at low speed just until well blended and mixture appears crumbly.
Shortening	10 oz	284 g	
Sugar, granulated	1 lb	454 g	
Buttermilk	2 c	480 ml	Add to mixer bowl. Mix just until dry ingredients are barely moist. Portion 1½-ounce mounds of biscuit dough 1½ inches apart on oiled or paper-lined sheet pans. Bake in 425°F oven until puffed and golden, about 10 minutes. Cool on wire racks. Slice each biscuit into two halves.
Strawberries, sliced, fresh or IQF	1½ gal	5.7 L	Combine in large bowl. Toss well to combine. Chill completely. Portion 3 ounces over bottom half of biscuit. Top with second biscuit half.
Cream, whipped	3 qt	2.8 L	Portion 2 ounces on top of each portion.

Nutrient Analysis Per Serving				
	Calories	401	Protein	4.3 gm
	Fat	16.8 gm	Carbohydrate	62.3 gm
	Cholesterol	40 mg	Calcium	135 mg
	Sodium	370 mg	Fiber	0.8 gm

CAKES

▲ Choco-Nut Layer Cakes

These rich chocolate cakes are liberally studded with crunchy pecans.

Menu Category:	Dessert
Cooking Method:	Bake
Preparation Time:	30 minutes
Baking Time:	30 to 35 minutes
Oven Temperature:	350°F
Variations:	Substitute commercial chocolate cake mix.
	Add nut or fruit extract to batter.
Yield:	50 portions (4 oz)

Ingredient	U.S.	Metric	Method
Butter, soft	1½ lb	680 g	Place in mixer bowl with whip attachment. Mix at high speed until light and creamy.
Sugar, granulated	4 lb	1.8 kg	Add gradually at high speed.
Eggs	12	12	Add one at a time, mixing well at high speed.
Chocolate, baking, melted	12 oz	340 g	Add. Mix just to blend.
Flour, cake	3 lb	1.4 kg	Combine. Add one third to mixture. Mix at low speed just until combined.
Baking soda	2 T	30 ml	
Salt	1 T	15 ml	
Water, ice cold	1½ qt	1.4 L	Combine. Add one third to mixture. Mix at low speed just until combined. Add second third of dry ingredients. Repeat procedure, mixing at low speed for about 2 minutes or until all ingredients are well mixed. Portion into six greased and floured 9-inch cake pans. Bake in preheated 350°F oven until cakes are firm and test done, about 30 to 35. Cool 10 minutes on wire racks. Remove from pans. Let rest 30 minutes before slicing each cake into two layers.
Vanilla extract	2 T	30 ml	
Chocolate Frosting, commercial	1 gal	3.8 L	Portion one third over three bottom layers. Top with second layer. Repeat with remaining layers, frosting, and pecans. Finish cakes with three top layers.
Pecans, chopped	1 qt	950 ml	
Sugar, powdered	1 c	240 ml	Sprinkle on top, unfrosted layer through decorative doily.

Nutrient Analysis Per Serving	Calories	784	Protein	8.1 gm
	Fat	34 gm	Carbohydrate	123 gm
	Cholesterol	81 mg	Calcium	75.7 mg
	Sodium	639 mg	Fiber	0.7 gm

▲ Cottage Pudding

More a cake than a pudding, it was mentioned in an O. Henry short story way back in 1909.

Menu Category:	Dessert
Cooking Method:	Bake
Preparation Time:	30 minutes
Baking Time:	25 to 30 minutes
Oven Temperature:	400°F
Variations:	Use commercial yellow cake mix with orange extract added.
	Substitute freely with marmalades or preserves.
Yield:	50 portions (3 oz)

Ingredient	U.S.	Metric	Method
Orange marmalade	1½ lb	680 g	Portion into three greased and floured 12″ × 10″ × 2″ insert pans. Reserve.
Flour, all purpose	1½ lb	680 g	Combine in mixer bowl with paddle attachment. Mix at low speed until ingredients are well combined.
Sugar, granulated	27 oz	765 g	
Baking powder	2½ T	38 ml	
Salt	1 T	15 ml	
Butter, melted	8 oz	227 g	Add to mixture. Mix at low speed just until ingredients are well combined.
Milk	24 oz	680 g	
Eggs, beaten	3	3	Add gradually to mixture. Mix at medium speed until mixture is creamy and smooth. Bake in preheated 400°F oven until firm and cakes test done, about 30 to 40 minutes. Cool on wire racks. Let rest 30 minutes before cutting. Serve cake with the marmalade side up.
Vanilla extract	1 T	15 ml	
Rum extract	1 T	15 ml	

Nutrient Analysis Per Serving	Calories	188	Protein	2.8 gm
	Fat	4.5 gm	Carbohydrate	35.8 gm
	Cholesterol	23.8 mg	Calcium	37.3 mg
	Sodium	228 mg	Fiber	0.4 gm

▲ Gingerbread Delight

More than traditional flavor and uncommonly versatile.

Menu Category:	Dessert, American Regional
Cooking Method:	Bake
Preparation Time:	30 minutes
Baking Time:	25 to 30 minutes
Oven Temperature:	375°F
Variations:	Add chopped almonds or pecans.
	Substitute orange extract for vanilla.
Yield:	50 portions (2 oz)

Ingredient	U.S.	Metric	Method
Butter, soft	8 oz	227 g	Place in mixer bowl with whip attachment.
Brown sugar, light	12 oz	340 g	Mix at high speed until light and creamy.
Egg, beaten	2	2	Add to mixture. Mix until well combined.
Vanilla extract	1 T	15 ml	
Molasses	8 oz	227 g	
Milk	16 oz	16 oz	
Flour, cake	1¼ lb	567 g	Add to mixture. Mix at low speed until
Baking powder	2 t	10 ml	well combined. Mixture may appear
Baking soda	2 t	10 ml	curdled. Portion into two paper-lined 12″
Salt	2 t	10 ml	× 10″ × 2″ insert pans. Bake in preheated
Ginger, ground	2 t	10 ml	375°F oven until gingerbread is firm and
Cinnamon, ground	2 t	10 ml	tests done, about 25 to 30 minutes. Cool
Nutmeg, ground	1 t	5 ml	on wire racks. Let rest 30 minutes before
			cutting.

Nutrient Analysis Per Serving				
	Calories	125	Protein	1.6 gm
	Fat	4.2 gm	Carbohydrate	20.3 gm
	Cholesterol	19.2 mg	Calcium	36.1 mg
	Sodium	180 mg	Fiber	0.1 gm

▲ Ginger Pound Cake

This is delightful plain and really super as a base for fruits and sweet sauces.

Menu Category:	Dessert
Cooking Method:	Bake
Preparation Time:	30 minutes
Baking Time:	1½ hours
Oven Temperature:	325°F
Variations:	As many as you want: Just substitute extracts and spices!
Yield:	50 portions (4 oz)

Ingredient	U.S.	Metric	Method
Butter, soft	1½ lb	680 g	Place in mixer bowl with whip attachment.
Shortening	12 oz	340 g	Mix at high speed until light and creamy.
Sugar, granulated	4 lb	1.8 kg	Add gradually at high speed.
Eggs	2½ lb	1.2 kg	Add one at a time, mixing well at high speed.
Flour, all purpose	2¼ lb	1 kg	Combine. Add one third to mixture. Mix at low speed just until combined.
Baking powder	1½ t	8 ml	
Salt	1 t	5 ml	
Ginger, ground	2 t	10 ml	
Nutmeg, ground	1 t	5 ml	
Milk	1½ qt	680 g	Combine. Add one third to mixture. Mix at low speed just until combined. Add second third of dry ingredients. Repeat procedure, mixing at low speed just until all ingredients are well mixed. Portion into three greased and floured 10-inch tube pans. Bake in preheated 325°F oven until pound cakes are firm and test done, about 1½ hours. Cool on wire racks. Let rest 30 minutes before cutting.
Vanilla extract	1 T	15 ml	
Lemon extract	1 T	15 ml	

Nutrient Analysis Per Serving				
	Calories	406	Protein	6.2 gm
	Fat	20.8 gm	Carbohydrate	52.3 gm
	Cholesterol	127 mg	Calcium	40.3 mg
	Sodium	202 mg	Fiber	0.4 gm

▲ Hawaiian Sunset Grilled Pound Cake

Use Lemon Pound Cake or other flavored pound cakes.

Menu Category:	Dessert
Cooking Method:	Simmer/Broil
Preparation Time:	30 minutes
Cooking Time:	30 minutes
Variations:	Add chopped pecans or macadamia nuts.
Yield:	50 portions (5 oz)

Ingredient	U.S.	Metric	Method
Pineapple juice, unsweetened	1¼ qt	1.2 L	Combine in large pot or steam kettle. Heat to a boil. Reduce heat to a simmer.
Orange juice, unsweetened	1¼ qt	1.2 L	
Sugar, powdered	8 oz	227 g	
Orange peel, grated	½ c	120 ml	
Dark rum	1 c	240 ml	
Arrowroot	1 c	240 ml	Combine in small bowl. Mix well. Add gradually to juice mixture. Whip constantly until mixture thickens and becomes clear, about 1 minute. Remove from heat.
Water	2 c	480 ml	
Coconut, toasted	1 c	240 ml	Add to mixture. Stir well. Keep warm.
Lemon Pound Cake, p. 520	3	3	Place slices of pound cake as needed on sheet pans. Broil under medium-high heat until top surface is golden. Turn over. Repeat procedure. Place on service plates. Top with 2 ounces of reserved sauce.

Nutrient Analysis Per Serving	Calories	347	Protein	5.2 gm
	Fat	13.3 gm	Carbohydrate	52.5 gm
	Cholesterol	82 mg	Calcium	43.3 mg
	Sodium	244 mg	Fiber	0.6 gm

▲ Lemon Cheesecake

A tangy, flavorful version.

Menu Category:	Dessert		
Cooking Method:	Bake		
Preparation Time:	30 minutes		
Baking Time:	40 to 50 minutes		
Oven Temperature:	350°F		
Variations:	Add miniature chocolate chips.		
Yield:	50 portions (3 oz)		

Ingredient	U.S.	Metric	Method
Graham cracker crumbs	1½ lb	680 g	Combine in large bowl. Mix well. Divide among three 9-inch springform pans. Press evenly on sides and bottom. Chill until ready to use.
Sugar, granulated	4 oz	114 g	
Butter, melted	12 oz	340 g	
Sour cream	24 oz	680 g	Combine in bowl. Beat well with wire whip. Cover and chill until ready to use.
Sugar, granulated	4 oz	114 g	
Cream cheese, softened	3 lb	1.4 kg	Place in mixer bowl with whip attachment. Mix at medium speed until fluffy and light.
Sugar, granulated	1 lb	454 g	Add one third gradually to mixture.
Eggs, beaten	9	9	Add one third gradually to mixture. Repeat with one third sugar. Repeat procedure until mixture is creamy and smooth. Portion into prepared springform pans. Place on sheet pans. Bake in lower third of preheated 350°F oven until filling is almost set, about 30 minutes. Top with reserved sour cream mixture. Continue baking for 15 more minutes. Remove from oven. Cool on wire racks. Chill several hours before cutting.
Vanilla extract	1 T	15 ml	
Lemon extract	1 T	15 ml	
Lemon peel, grated	½ c	120 ml	

Nutrient Analysis	Calories	295	Protein	4.7 gm
Per Serving	Fat	19.9 gm	Carbohydrate	25.1 gm
	Cholesterol	89.5 mg	Calcium	51.7 mg
	Sodium	221 mg	Fiber	0.2 gm

▲ Lemon Pound Cake with Blueberry Sauce

A full flavored version perfect for dessert and brunch.

Menu Category:	Dessert, Brunch
Cooking Method:	Bake
Preparation Time:	30 minutes
Baking Time:	50 to 60 minutes
Oven Temperature:	325°F
Variations:	Substitute orange extract for lemon.
	Glaze with melted strained marmalade.
Yield:	50 portions (5 oz)

Ingredient	U.S.	Metric	Method
Butter, soft	1½ lb	680 g	Place in mixer bowl with whip attachment. Mix at high speed until light and creamy.
Sugar, granulated	2½ lb	1.2 kg	Add gradually at high speed. Mix until creamy.
Lemon peel, grated	¼ c	60 ml	
Eggs, large	12	12	Add one at a time, mixing well at high speed.
Flour, all purpose	2¼ lb	1 kg	Combine. Add one third to mixture. Mix at low speed just until combined.
Baking powder	1½ t	8 ml	
Baking soda	1½ t	8 ml	
Salt	1½ t	8 ml	
Buttermilk	1½ lb	680 g	Combine. Add one third to mixture. Mix at low speed just until combined. Add second third of dry ingredients. Repeat procedure, mixing at low speed just until all ingredients are well mixed. Portion into three greased and floured 10-inch tube pans. Bake in preheated 325°F oven until pound cakes are firm and test done, about 50 to 60 minutes. Cool on wire racks. Let rest 30 minutes before cutting.
Lemon extract	1 T	15 ml	
Vanilla extract	1 T	15 ml	
Blueberry Sauce, recipe follows	2½ qt	2.4 L	Portion 1½ ounces over each slice.

Nutrient Analysis Per Serving	Calories	330	Protein	5 gm
	Fat	12.9 gm	Carbohydrate	52.2 gm
	Cholesterol	82 mg	Calcium	36.6 mg
	Sodium	244 mg	Fiber	0.7 gm

Companion Recipe

▲ **Blueberry Sauce**

Serve as a topping for Lemon Pound Cake, waffles, pancakes, or ice cream.

Menu Category:	Sauce
Cooking Method:	Simmer
Preparation Time:	10 minutes
Cooking Time:	10 minutes
Variations:	Substitute other IQF or water-pack fruit and liqueur.
Yield:	1 gallon

Ingredient	U.S.	Metric	Method
Blueberries, fresh or IQF	4 lb	1.8 kg	Combine in large pot or steam kettle. Heat
Sugar, granulated	2 lb	908 g	to a simmer. Simmer for 10 minutes,
Cleargel or arrowroot	½ c	120 ml	stirring occasionally. Remove from heat.
Water	1 qt	950 ml	Serve warm or cold.
Lemon juice	¼ c	60 ml	
Amaretto liqueur	¼ c	60 ml	

Nutrient Analysis				
Per Ounce	Calories	38	Protein	0.1 gm
	Fat	0 gm	Carbohydrate	9.7 gm
	Cholesterol	0 mg	Calcium	1.3 mg
	Sodium	1.3 mg	Fiber	0.2 gm

PIES

▲ Washington Pie

This eastern regional specialty isn't a pie at all, but a rich, jam-filled cake.

Menu Category:	Dessert, American Regional
Cooking Method:	Bake
Preparation Time:	30 minutes
Baking Time:	30 to 40 minutes
Oven Temperature:	350°F
Variations:	Add finely chopped pecans or walnuts to the batter.
Yield:	50 portions (4 oz)

Ingredient	U.S.	Metric	Method
Butter	1 lb	454 g	Combine in mixer bowl with whip attachment. Mix at high speed until very light.
Sugar	1½ lb	680 g	
Lemon peel, grated	¼ cup	60 ml	
Eggs, large	12	12	Add one at a time, mixing well at medium speed.
Baking powder	2 T	30 ml	Combine. Add to batter ingredients. Mix at low speed just until well mixed.
Milk	2 c	480 ml	
Flour, all purpose	2 lb	908 g	Add to batter. Mix well at low speed. Portion into six oiled and floured or paper-lined 8-inch cake pans. Place on sheet pans. Bake in lower third of preheated 350°F oven until top is golden and cakes test done, about 30 to 35 minutes. Transfer to wire racks. Cool for 10 minutes before removing from pans. When cool, cut each cake into two layers.
Fruit jam	3 lb	1.4 kg	Spread over bottom layers. Top with second layers. Chill several hours before cutting for service.

Nutrient Analysis Per Serving	Calories	291	Protein	5.4 gm
	Fat	9.7 gm	Carbohydrate	48 gm
	Cholesterol	74 mg	Calcium	75 mg
	Sodium	153 mg	Fiber	0.7 gm

▲ Blackbottom Pie

A rich version of the midwestern American classic.

Menu Category:	Dessert, Ethnic, American Regional		
Cooking Method:	Simmer		
Preparation Time:	30 minutes		
Cooking Time:	10 minutes		
Variations:	Add instant coffee powder to taste to chocolate batter mixture.		
Yield:	50 portions (5 oz)		

Ingredient	U.S.	Metric	Method
Pie crusts, 9-inch, baked	6	6	Place on sheet pans. Reserve.
Gelatin, unflavored Half-and-half	¼ c 2 qt	60 ml 1.9 L	Combine in small saucepan. Let rest 10 minutes. Cook over low heat just until gelatin dissolves. Remove from heat.
Cornstarch Sugar, granulated	2 T 8 oz	30 ml 227 g	Combine in mixer bowl with whip attachment.
Egg yolks	16	16	Add to sugar mixture. Mix at high speed until well blended and pale yellow. Transfer to large pot. Gradually add gelatin mixture. Return mixture to large pot. Cook over low heat until creamy and thickened, about 10 minutes. Divide mixture into two large bowls.
Chocolate, baking, melted Vanilla extract	5 oz 1 T	142 g 15 ml	Add to half the custard. Mix well. Portion into pie shells.
Egg whites Cream of tartar	16 1 t	16 5 ml	Beat in mixer bowl with whip attachment at low speed until frothy. Increase speed to medium. Beat until peaks just begin to form.
Sugar, granulated	2 c	480 ml	Add gradually to egg whites. Beat at high speed until stiff peaks form. Fold in one fourth of remaining custard mixture. Fold this mixture back into egg whites. Portion over chocolate layers in pie shells. Cover. Chill completely before cutting.

Nutrient Analysis	Calories	338	Protein	6.5 gm
Per Serving	Fat	20.6 gm	Carbohydrate	35.4 gm
	Cholesterol	82.4 mg	Calcium	50.8 mg
	Sodium	336 mg	Fiber	0.I gm

▲ Cannoli Tarts with Strawberry Sauce

Serve as a bright, tempting Italian dessert.

Menu Category:	Dessert, Ethnic, Italian
Cooking Method:	Simmer
Preparation Time:	30 minutes
Cooking Time:	20 minutes
Variations:	Substitute prepared pudding for ricotta filling.
	Substitute blueberries or other fruit.
Yield:	50 tarts

Ingredient	U.S.	Metric	Method
Ricotta cheese	3 c	720 ml	Combine in large bowl. Mix well.
Whipped cream	3 c	720 ml	
Rum extract	1 t	5 ml	
Chocolate chips	1 c	240 ml	
Powdered sugar	1 c	240 ml	
Tart shells, baked (3 oz)	50	50	Arrange on sheet pans. Portion with 3 ounces of the filling. Chill well for service.
Strawberry slices	50	50	Place on top of each tart.
Strawberry puree, unsweetened	3 qt	2.8 L	Combine in large pot. Heat to a simmer. Cook over low heat to dissolve sugar and thicken sauce. Remove from heat. Chill. Portion about 2 ounces of sauce on plate. Top with tarts.
Powdered sugar	2 lb	908 g	

Nutrient Analysis Per Serving				
	Calories	425	Protein	4.6 gm
	Fat	23 gm	Carbohydrate	51.7 gm
	Cholesterol	39 mg	Calcium	55.6 mg
	Sodium	232 mg	Fiber	0.3 gm

▲ Clafouti

An open-face fruit tart.

Menu Category:	Dessert, Ethnic, French
Cooking Method:	Bake
Preparation Time:	30 minutes
Baking Time:	30 to 40 minutes
Oven Temperature:	350°F
Variations:	Add chopped toasted almonds to the batter mixture.
Yield:	50 portions (5 oz)

Ingredient	U.S.	Metric	Method
Flour, all purpose	8 oz	227 g	Combine in mixer bowl with whip
Sugar, granulated	12 oz	340 g	attachment.
Milk	5 c	1.2 L	With mixer at low speed, add gradually.
Eggs, large	10	10	Add to mixer bowl. Mix at medium speed
Sour cream	3 c	720 g	until well blended. Reserve.
Vanilla extract	3 T	45 ml	
Almond extract	1 T	15 ml	
Pie crust shells, 9-in	6 each	6 each	Prick shells with fork. Portion cherries into
Cherries, tart, IQF	5 lb	2.3 kg	each shell. Divide filling over cherries. Place on sheet pans. Bake in lower third of preheated 350°F oven until top is golden and filling is firm, about 30 to 40 minutes. Cool for 30 minutes before cutting.

Nutrient Analysis				
Per Serving	Calories	381	Protein	5.6 gm
	Fat	20 gm	Carbohydrate	46.5 gm
	Cholesterol	66 mg	Calcium	57.8 mg
	Sodium	243 mg	Fiber	0.3 gm

▲ Grasshopper Pie

A delightful, fluffy chilled pie.

Menu Category:	Dessert, American Regional
Cooking Method:	Simmer
Preparation Time:	30 minutes
Cooking Time:	10 minutes
Variations:	Substitute other liqueurs and/or extracts.
Yield:	50 portions (4 oz)

Ingredient	U.S.	Metric	Method
Gelatin, unflavored Milk, cold	3 T 2 c	45 ml 480 ml	Combine in small saucepan. Let rest 10 minutes. Cook over low heat just until gelatin dissolves. Remove from heat. Cool to room temperature.
Egg yolks	24	24	Put in mixer bowl with whip attachment. Mix at high speed until pale and yellow, about 5 minutes.
Sugar, granulated Crème de menthe liqueur, green Crème de cocoa	12 oz 12 oz 12 oz	340 g 340 g 340 g	Add to egg mixture with reserved gelatin mixture. Mix at high speed until well blended. Chill until thickened.
Cream, whipped	1½ qt	1.4 L	Add to mixture. Mix at low speed just until well mixed.
Commercial chocolate pie crusts, 9-in	6	6	Portion filling into pie shells. Cover with plastic wrap. Chill completely before cutting.

Nutrient Analysis Per Serving				
	Calories	355	Protein	3.8 gm
	Fat	18.4 gm	Carbohydrate	37.5 gm
	Cholesterol	121 mg	Calcium	26.6 mg
	Sodium	223 mg	Fiber	0 gm

▲ Pennsylvania Shoofly Pie

This is the classic Pennsylvania Dutch dessert.

Menu Category:	Dessert, American Regional
Cooking Method:	Bake
Preparation Time:	30 minutes
Baking Time:	30 to 40 minutes
Oven Temperature:	350°F
Variations:	Add chopped pecans and golden raisins.
Yield:	50 portions (5 oz)

Ingredient	U.S.	Metric	Method
Brown sugar	3 lb	1.4 kg	Combine in food processor with metal
Flour, all purpose	2¼ lb	1.02 kg	blade. Process until mixture is crumbly.
Salt	1 t	5 ml	Reserve.
Butter, cold, chopped	12 oz	340 g	
Molasses	3 c	720 ml	Combine in large bowl. Add 1½ qt of
Baking soda	1 T	15 ml	reserved crumb mixture. Toss gently but well.
Pie crust shells, 9-in	6 each	6 each	Prick shells with fork. Portion filling into shells. Top with remaining crumb mixture. Place on sheet pans. Bake in lower third of preheated 350°F oven until top is golden and filling is firm, about 30 to 40 minutes. Cool for 30 minutes before cutting.

Nutrient Analysis				
Per Serving	Calories	508	Protein	4.8 gm
	Fat	21 gm	Carbohydrate	77.5 gm
	Cholesterol	30 mg	Calcium	63.7 mg
	Sodium	370 mg	Fiber	0.4 gm

▲ State Fair Blueberry Pie

This should put blue ribbon smiles on patrons' faces!

Menu Category:	Dessert, American Regional
Cooking Method:	Bake
Preparation Time:	30 minutes
Baking Time:	45 to 60 minutes
Oven Temperature:	375°F
Variations:	Try with blackberries, huckleberries, or elderberries.
Yield:	50 portions (6 oz)

Ingredient	U.S.	Metric	Method
Flour, all purpose	8 oz	227 g	Combine in large bowl. Mix well.
Sugar, granulated	2½ lb	1.2 kg	
Lemon rind, grated	½ c	120 ml	
Cinnamon, ground	1½ T	23 ml	
Ginger, ground	1 t	5 ml	
Blueberries, fresh or IQF	8 lb	3.6 kg	Add to dry ingredients. Toss gently to mix well.
Pie crust shells, 9-in	6	6	Prick shells with fork. Portion filling into shells.
Butter, cold, sliced	4 oz	114 g	Divide over filling.
Pie crust circles, 10-in	6 each	6 each	Top filling with crusts. Crimp edges to seal well. Cut several small slits in top crust.
Milk	½ c	120 ml	Brush over top crust. Place pies on sheet pans. Bake in lower third of preheated 375°F oven until top is golden and filling is firm, about 45 to 60 minutes. Cool for 30 minutes before cutting.

Nutrient Analysis				
Per Serving	Calories	429	Protein	3.5 gm
	Fat	19.1 gm	Carbohydrate	64 gm
	Cholesterol	22 mg	Calcium	13.3 mg
	Sodium	260 mg	Fiber	1.1

Puddings

▲ Mohawk Valley Indian Pudding

Also called "hasty pudding," this country inn version comes from New Hampshire.

Menu Category:	Dessert
Cooking Method:	Bake
Preparation Time:	30 minutes
Baking Time:	35 to 40 minutes
Oven Temperature:	350°F
Variations:	Substitute maple syrup for part of the molasses.
	Add chopped pecans or walnuts.
	Serve with whipped cream or vanilla ice cream.
Yield:	50 portions (6 oz)

Ingredient	U.S.	Metric	Method
Eggs, beaten	8	8	Combine in mixer bowl with whip attachment. Mix at medium speed until well combined.
Cornmeal, yellow	20 oz	567 g	
Flour, all purpose	8 oz	227 g	
Molasses	16 oz	454 g	
Vanilla extract	1 T	15 ml	
Salt	1 T	15 ml	
Ginger, ground	2 t	10 ml	
Cinnamon, ground	2 t	10 ml	
Nutmeg, ground	1 t	5 ml	
Milk, scalded, hot	2 gal	7.6 L	Add gradually, whipping constantly. Portion into three greased and floured 12″ × 10″ × 2″ insert pans. Bake in preheated 350°F oven until pudding is puffed and golden, about 35 to 40 minutes. Remove from oven. Cool on wire racks. Let rest 30 minutes before serving.

Nutrient Analysis Per Serving				
	Calories	179	Protein	7.7 gm
	Fat	4.3 gm	Carbohydrate	28.1 gm
	Cholesterol	45.6 mg	Calcium	220 mg
	Sodium	222 mg	Fiber	0.3 gm

▲ New Bedford Corn and Sweet Potato Pudding

A classic corn pudding, often served with ice cream.

Menu Category:	Dessert
Cooking Method:	Bake
Preparation Time:	60 minutes
Baking Time:	50 to 60 minutes
Oven Temperature:	300°F
Variations:	Substitute maple syrup for part of the molasses.
	Substitute pumpkin for sweet potatoes.
	Add dark rum to batter or sprinkle on top while pudding cools.
Yield:	50 portions (3 oz)

Ingredient	U.S.	Metric	Method
Milk	1½ qt	1.4 L	Combine in large pot or steam kettle. Heat
Butter	6 oz	170 g	just to a simmer.
Molasses	12 oz	340 g	
Cornmeal, yellow	1 lb	454 g	Place in mixer bowl with paddle attachment. Slowly add scalded milk mixture, mixing at low speed until well blended. Cover. Let rest until all liquid is absorbed.
Eggs, beaten	9	9	Combine. Add to cornmeal mixture in
Sweet potatoes, mashed	3 c	720 ml	mixer bowl. Mix at low speed until well
Cinnamon, ground	2 T	30 ml	blended. Portion into greased and floured
Nutmeg, ground	2 t	10 ml	muffin pans (6 ounce). Bake in preheated
Ginger, ground	2 t	10 ml	300°F oven until puffed and firm, about 50 to 60 minutes.

Nutrient Analysis	Calories	131	Protein	3.2 gm
Per Serving	Fat	4.7 gm	Carbohydrate	19.8 gm
	Cholesterol	48 mg	Calcium	65.1 mg
	Sodium	62 mg	Fiber	0.4 gm

▲ Spanish Flan

The popular Mexican and southwestern caramel custard pudding.

Menu Category:	Dessert
Cooking Method:	Bake
Preparation Time:	60 minutes
Baking Time:	50 to 60 minutes
Oven Temperature:	350°F
Variations:	Substitute maple syrup for the caramelized sugar. Vary the flavor by substituting different extracts.
Yield:	50 portions (6 oz)

Ingredient	U.S.	Metric	Method
Sugar, granulated	1½ lb	680 g	In heavy pot, cook sugar until it begins to turn golden. Divide immediately among 50 buttered 6-ounce custard cups or ramekins. Place prepared cups in 12″ × 20″ × 4″ insert pans. Reserve.
Milk	2 gal	7.6 L	Combine in heavy pot or steam kettle.
Cinnamon sticks	3	3	Heat just to a simmer. Remove from heat.
Vanilla extract	¼ c	60 ml	Let rest until cool. Discard cinnamon sticks.
Eggs	2 dozen	2 dozen	Place in mixer bowl with whip attachment. Mix at high speed until foamy and light.
Sugar, granulated	2 lb	908 g	Add gradually, mixing at medium speed. When well combined, gradually add reserved milk. Mix at medium speed until well blended. Divide among prepared cups or ramekins.
Water, boiling	as needed	as needed	Pour into insert pans to a level half way up side of cups. Bake in preheated 350°F oven until custards test done, about 1 hour. Remove from oven. Place cups on wire racks. Serve warm.

Nutrient Analysis Per Serving				
	Calories	228	Protein	7.5 gm
	Fat	4.8 gm	Carbohydrate	40 gm
	Cholesterol	88.8 mg	Calcium	201 mg
	Sodium	101 mg	Fiber	0.1 gm

Cookies

▲ Choco-Mint Brownies

These rich brownies combine two flavors patrons love.

Menu Category:	Dessert, American Regional
Cooking Method:	Bake
Preparation Time:	30 minutes
Baking Time:	30 to 35 minutes
Oven Temperature:	425°F
Variations:	Substitute nut or brandy extract for mint.
	Substitute pecans or almonds, for walnuts.
Yield:	50 brownies (3 oz)

Ingredient	U.S.	Metric	Method
Eggs	10	10	Combine in mixer bowl with whip
Sugar, granulated	3½ lb	1.6 kg	attachment. Mix at high speed until very
Instant coffee powder	¼ c	60 ml	light and fluffy, about 10 minutes.
Vanilla extract	2 T	30 ml	
Mint extract	2 T	30 ml	
Chocolate, baking, melted	1 lb	454 g	Add gradually to mixture, mixing at low
Butter, melted	1 lb	454 g	speed.
Flour, all purpose	14 oz	397 g	Add to mixture. Mix only until combined.
Pecans, chopped	1 lb	454 g	Portion batter into two paper-lined 12″ ×
Salt	½ t	3 ml	10″ × 2″ insert pans. Bake in preheated 425°F oven until brownies are firm, about 30 to 35 minutes. Cool in the pans. Let rest 2 hours before cutting.

Nutrient Analysis				
Per Serving	Calories	336	Protein	4.1 gm
	Fat	19.5 gm	Carbohydrate	42.2 gm
	Cholesterol	62.5 mg	Calcium	21.2 mg
	Sodium	111 mg	Fiber	0.5 gm

▲ Gingersnap Giants

These spicy, oversized cookies will be big hits.

Menu Category:	Dessert, American Regional
Cooking Method:	Bake
Preparation Time:	30 minutes
Baking Time:	10 to 12 minutes
Oven Temperature:	350°F
Variations:	Add finely chopped almonds or pecans.
Yield:	100 Cookies

Ingredient	U.S.	Metric	Method
Butter, soft	1½ lb	680 g	Place in mixer bowl with whip attachment.
Sugar, granulated	1½ lb	680 g	Mix at medium speed until light and creamy.
Molasses	6 oz	170 g	Add to mixture. Mix until well combined.
Egg, beaten	3	3	
Vanilla extract	1 T	15 ml	
Flour	1½ lb	680 g	Add to mixture. Mix at low speed until well combined. Form into 1-inch balls.
Baking soda	3 T	45 ml	
Salt	1 t	5 ml	
Cinnamon, ground	1 T	15 ml	
Cloves, ground	1 T	15 ml	
Ginger, ground	2 t	10 ml	
Sugar, granulated	2 c	480 ml	Place in large bowl. Roll dough balls to coat well. Place sugared balls 2 inches apart on sheet pans. Bake in preheated 350°F oven until cookies are firm, about 10 to 12 minutes. Cool on sheet pans. Remove with spatula when cool.

Nutrient Analysis Per Cookie				
	Calories	242	Protein	2.4 gm
	Fat	11.7 gm	Carbohydrate	34.7 gm
	Cholesterol	43 mg	Calcium	20.2 mg
	Sodium	309 mg	Fiber	0.3 gm

▲ Kiss O' Chocolate Drop Cookies

From the midwest, a variation on the classic American cookie.

Menu Category:	Dessert, American Regional
Cooking Method:	Bake
Preparation Time:	30 minutes
Baking Time:	10 to 12 minutes
Oven Temperature:	375°F
Variations:	Add chopped pecans and golden raisins.
Yield:	100 Cookies

Ingredient	U.S.	Metric	Method
Butter, soft	1 lb	454 g	Combine in mixer bowl with whip attachment. Mix at medium speed until light and creamy.
Sugar, granulated	10 oz	285 g	
Brown sugar	10 oz	285 g	
Egg, beaten	2	2	Add to mixture. Mix at medium speed until light and creamy.
Vanilla extract	1 T	15 ml	
Chocolate extract	2 t	10 ml	
Chocolate, semisweet, melted	12 oz	340 g	Add to mixture. Mix until well combined.
Flour, all purpose	1¼ lb	567 g	Add to mixture. Mix at low speed until well combined. Portion 1 T drops 1½ inches apart on oiled or paper-lined sheet pans. Press flat. Bake in preheated 375°F oven until cookies are firm, about 10 to 12 minutes. Cool on wire racks.
Baking powder	2 t	10 ml	
Salt	1 t	5 ml	

Nutrient Analysis Per Cookie				
	Calories	183	Protein	2.4 gm
	Fat	10 gm	Carbohydrate	23.7 gm
	Cholesterol	28.4 mg	Calcium	21.7 mg
	Sodium	162 mg	Fiber	0.3 gm

▲ Luscious Lemon Nutcrunch Bars

Traditional favorites with uncommonly wonderful flavor.

Menu Category:	Dessert, American Regional
Cooking Method:	Bake
Preparation Time:	30 minutes
Baking Time:	40 to 45 minutes
Oven Temperature:	350°F
Variations:	Substitute nut or brandy extract for mint.
	Substitute pecans, almonds, or peanuts for walnuts.
Yield:	50 bars

Ingredient	U.S.	Metric	Method
Flour, all purpose	1 lb	454 g	Combine in large bowl. Mix well. Press firmly into two paper-lined 12″ × 10″ × 2″ insert pans. Bake in preheated 350°F oven until golden, about 25 to 30 minutes. Cool on wire racks. Reserve.
Butter, soft	12 oz	340 g	
Salt	½ t	3 ml	
Sugar, powdered	8 oz	227 g	
Flour, all purpose	14 oz	397 g	Combine in mixer bowl with whip attachment. Mix at low speed to combine well.
Sugar, granulated	1½ lb	681 g	
Pecans, chopped	12 oz	340 g	
Eggs, beaten	6	6	Add to dry ingredients. Mix at medium speed just until well combined. Portion over two baked crusts. Bake in preheated 350°F oven until golden, about 25 to 30 minutes. Cool on wire racks. Let rest 1 hour before cutting.
Lemon juice	¾ c	180 ml	

Nutrient Analysis Per Serving				
	Calories	197	Protein	3.7 gm
	Fat	11.1 gm	Carbohydrate	23 gm
	Cholesterol	40.5 mg	Calcium	13.4 mg
	Sodium	100 mg	Fiber	0.5 gm

▲ Oatmeal-Date Delights

Healthy, crunchy treats for dessert or breaktime.

Menu Category:	Dessert, American Regional
Cooking Method:	Bake
Preparation Time:	30 minutes
Baking Time:	10 to 12 minutes
Oven Temperature:	375°F
Variations:	Substitute golden raisins for dates.
Yield:	100 Cookies

Ingredient	U.S.	Metric	Method
Butter, soft	8 oz	227 g	Place in mixer bowl with whip attachment. Mix at medium speed until light and creamy.
Sugar, granulated	8 oz	227 g	Add to butter. Mix at medium speed until light and creamy.
Brown sugar	8 oz	227 g	
Eggs, beaten	2	2	Add to mixture. Mix until well combined.
Vanilla extract	1 T	15 ml	
Flour	8 oz	227 g	Add to mixture. Mix at low speed until well combined.
Baking powder	1 t	5 ml	
Baking soda	1 t	5 ml	
Salt	1 t	5 ml	
Oats, quick cooking	4 oz	114 g	Add to mixture. Mix just until well combined. Portion 1 t drops 1½ inches apart on oiled or paper-lined sheet pans.
Dates, pitted, minced	8 oz	227 g	
Coconut, grated	4 oz	114 g	Sprinkle over cookie drops. Bake in preheated 375°F oven until cookies are firm, about 10 to 12 minutes. Cool on wire racks.

Nutrient Analysis Per Cookie				
	Calories	58	Protein	0.7 gm
	Fat	2.5 gm	Carbohydrate	8.8 gm
	Cholesterol	9.2 mg	Calcium	6 mg
	Sodium	54 mg	Fiber	0.2 gm

BREAKFAST AND BRUNCH

EGGS AND CHEESE

▲ Baked Eggs with Ham and Jarslberg Cheese

Prepare this the night before you need it so all the ingredients blend just right.

Menu Category:	Brunch
Cooking Method:	Bake
Preparation Time:	20 minutes
Chilling Time:	Overnight
Baking Time:	1 hour
Oven Temperature:	350°F
Variations:	Substitute freely with type of ham and flavor of cheese.
Yield:	50 portions (6 oz)

Ingredient	U.S.	Metric	Method
Bread slices, toasted	3 lb	1.4 kg	Cut into ½-inch strips. Divide half of the toast strips among two 12″ × 10″ × 2″ insert pans prepped with nonstick spray.
Boiled ham, ¼″ dice	3 lb	1.4 kg	Divide half of the ham and cheese over toast strips. Top with remaining toast strips then with remaining ham and cheese.
Jarlsberg cheese, grated	3 lb	1.4 kg	
Eggs, beaten	1½ qt	1.4 L	Combine in mixer bowl with whip attachment. Mix at medium speed until well blended. Divide this mixture over each of the filled pans. Cover. Chill overnight. When ready to cook, place covered pans in preheated 350°F oven. Bake 45 minutes. Remove covers. Bake 10 minutes more or until top is golden brown. Let rest 10 minutes before cutting.
Milk, lowfat	3½ qt	3.3 L	
Mustard, Dijon style	¼ c	60 ml	
Salt	2 t	10 ml	
Black pepper	2 t	10 ml	

Nutrient Analysis				
Per Portion	Calories	305	Protein	229 gm
	Fat	14 gm	Carbohydrate	20 gm
	Cholesterol	161 mg	Calcium	401 mg
	Sodium	762 mg	Fiber	0.2 gm

▲ Breakfast Pizza with Sausage and Cheese

Why wait until later in the day?

Menu Category:	Brunch, Ethnic, Italian
Cooking Method:	Sauté/Bake
Preparation Time:	30 minutes
Cooking Time:	30 minutes
Oven Temperature:	450°F
Variations:	For a southwestern version, substitute picante sauce for half of the tomato sauce and top with grated Monterey Jack cheese with jalapeños.

Yield: 50 portions (7 oz)

Ingredient	U.S.	Metric	Method
Pizza dough, 16″ × 24″ sheets (approx. 6 lb of dough)	4	4	Press into the bottom and up the sides of four 12″ × 20″ × 2″ sheet pans. Prick with fork.
Tomato sauce, unsalted	3 qt	2.8 L	Spread over pizza dough.
Eggs, scrambled	1 gal	3.8 L	Combine in large bowl. Mix well. Distribute evenly over sauce-topped crusts.
Bell pepper, minced	3 c	720 ml	
Mozzarella cheese, skim, grated	4 lb	1.8 kg	Distribute over eggs. Bake in preheated 450°F oven until crust is crisp and top is bubbly, about 8 to 10 minutes.
Pork sausage, sautéed, crumbled	2 lb	906 g	

Nutrient Analysis Per Serving	Calories	386	Protein	22.2 gm
	Fat	21.6 gm	Carbohydrate	27.5 gm
	Cholesterol	258 mg	Calcium	252 mg
	Sodium	761 mg	Fiber	0.8 gm

▲ Brunch Blintzes

Perfect for tailgate catering or everyday breakfast fare.

Menu Category:	Brunch
Cooking Method:	Griddle
Preparation Time:	20 minutes
Cooking Time:	20 minutes
Variations:	Substitute any fruit preserve for filling.
Yield:	50 portions (2 per portion)

Ingredient	U.S.	Metric	Method
Cream cheese, softened	3 lb	1.4 kg	Combine in mixer bowl with whip attachment. Mix at medium speed until well blended and fluffy. Reserve.
Strawberry preserves, melted	2 lb	908 g	
Orange juice	2 c	240 ml	
Milk	2 qt	1.9 L	Combine in mixer bowl with whip attachment. Mix at medium speed until well blended. Transfer to storage container. Cover. Chill at least 1 hour. Pour 1-ounce portions onto preheated, oiled 350°F griddle. Cook until top surface begins to appear dry. Transfer to sheet pans. Keep warm in 250°F oven. To finish, spread uncooked side of blintz with 1 ounce of filling. Fold over two ends. Roll tightly.
Flour, all purpose	1½ lb	680 g	
Eggs, beaten	24	24	
Sugar, powdered	1 c	240 ml	Sprinkle over top.

Nutrient Analysis Per Portion				
	Calories	259	Protein	8.3 gm
	Fat	13 gm	Carbohydrate	28.5 gm
	Cholesterol	135 mg	Calcium	91 mg
	Sodium	134 mg	Fiber	0.5 gm

▲ Huevos Rancheros

These are breakfast and brunch traditions in Mexico and the southwestern United States.

Menu Category:	Brunch, Ethnic, Mexican, American Regional
Cooking Method:	Sauté/Bake
Preparation Time:	30 minutes
Cooking Time:	10 minutes
Oven Temperature:	350°F
Variations:	For an Italian variation, substitute fennel-enhanced tomato sauce for the picante mixture and top with grated Mozzarella cheese.
Yield:	50 portions (5 oz)

Ingredient	U.S.	Metric	Method
Tortillas, wheat, 6-inch Olive oil	50 as needed	50 as needed	Brush with olive oil. Place on oiled sheet pans.
Commercial picante sauce	3¼ qt	3.1 L	Portion 1 ounce on each tortilla.
Eggs, poached soft, cold	50	50	Place in center of tortilla.
Monterey Jack cheese, grated	3¼ qt	3.1 L	Portion 1 ounce on each egg. Bake in preheated 350°F oven until cheese is bubbly and golden, about 5 to 10 minutes.
Commercial picante sauce, heated	3¼ qt	3.1 L	Portion 1 ounce over top of each.

Nutrient Analysis Per Serving	Calories	305	Protein	16.6 gm
	Fat	17.5 gm	Carbohydrate	22 gm
	Cholesterol	243 mg	Calcium	290 mg
	Sodium	758 mg	Fiber	0 gm

▲ Mediterranean Scrambled Eggs with Mint Yogurt Sauce

A fresh new specialty brunch selection.

Menu Category:	Brunch, Ethnic, Mediterranean
Cooking Method:	Sauté/Simmer
Preparation Time:	20 minutes
Cooking Time:	1 hour
Variations:	For a Mexican touch, add chopped chilies to the eggs and picante sauce to the yogurt.
Yield:	50 portions (4 oz)

Ingredient	U.S.	Metric	Method
Yogurt, lowfat, plain	2 qt	1.9 L	Combine in mixer with whip attachment.
Scallion, minced	1 c	240 ml	Mix at medium speed until well blended.
Mint, dried	3 T	45 ml	Transfer to storage container. Cover. Chill
Lemon juice	⅓ c	80 ml	well.
Hot pepper sauce	2 t	10 ml	
Butter, melted	6 oz	170 g	Sauté at medium high heat in large pot or
Scallions, minced	2 c	480 ml	brazier. Cook, stirring, for 2 minutes.
Green bell pepper, minced	2 c	480 ml	Reduce heat to medium low.
Eggs, beaten	3 qt	2.8 L	Combine in large bowl. Mix well. Add to
Water	1 c	240 ml	vegetable mixture. Cook at medium-low
Parsley, chopped	2 c	480 ml	heat, stirring occasionally, until eggs are
Salt	1 T	15 ml	well set. Transfer to service pans. Top each
Sugar	1 T	15 ml	serving with 1½ ounces reserved mint yogurt sauce.

Nutrient Analysis				
Per Portion	Calories	136	Protein	9 gm
	Fat	8.8 gm	Carbohydrate	4.9 gm
	Cholesterol	242 mg	Calcium	102 mg
	Sodium	253 mg	Fiber	0.1 gm

▲ Stuffed French Toast with Honey Ricotta

Serve as a brunch or light lunch selection.

Menu Category:	Brunch	
Cooking Method:	Griddle/Bake	
Preparation Time:	20 minutes	
Cooking Time:	30 minutes	
Variations:	Add miniature chocolate chips and chopped pecans to cheese mixture.	
Yield:	50 portions (6 oz)	

Ingredient	U.S.	Metric	Method
French bread, bias-sliced, 2-inch thick	100	100	Cut pockets through the side of each.
Eggs, beaten	4	4	Combine in large bowl. Mix well. Spoon this mixture into the pocketed bread slices. Cover and chill if desired.
Ricotta cheese	2 lb	908 g	
Honey	6 oz	170 g	
Orange rind	2 T	30 ml	
Eggs, beaten	8	8	Combine in large bowl. Mix well. Dip stuffed bread slices into this mixture.
Milk	2 qt	1.9 L	
Vanilla extract	¼ c	60 ml	
Cinnamon, ground	2 T	30 ml	
Nutmeg, grated	1 T	15 ml	
Butter, melted	1 c	240 ml	Pour onto preheated 350°F griddle. Add stuffed bread slices. Cook until golden brown on both sides. Transfer to sheet pans. Bake in preheated 350°F oven for about 20 minutes, or until bread slices are puffed and filling is hot.
Strawberry Sauce Grand Marnier, recipe follows	1½ gal	5.7 L	Portion 2 ounces over top of each.

Nutrient Analysis Per Serving	Calories	526	Protein	12.3 gm
	Fat	19.5 gm	Carbohydrate	67.2 gm
	Cholesterol	95.5 mg	Calcium	190 mg
	Sodium	560 mg	Fiber	0.8 gm

Companion Recipe

▲ **Strawberry Sauce Grand Marnier**

Serve with Stuffed French Toast with Honey Ricotta, ice cream, crepes, or pound cake.

Menu Category:	Sauce
Cooking Method:	Sauté/Simmer
Preparation Time:	20 minutes
Cooking Time:	20 minutes
Variations:	Substitute any of a number of berries and liqueurs.
Yield:	1 gallon

Ingredient	U.S.	Metric	Method
Butter, melted	12 oz	240 g	In heavy pot or brazier kettle, sauté over high heat until berries are tender and juices form in the pan.
Strawberries, sliced	8 lb	3.6 kg	
Powdered sugar	3 c	720 ml	Add to berries. Simmer and stir to dissolve sugar.
Grand Marnier	3 c	720 ml	Add to berries. Flame if possible. Stir over high heat until flames subside.

Nutrient Analysis	Calories	54	Protein	0.2 gm
Per Ounce	Fat	2.3 gm	Carbohydrate	6.4 gm
	Cholesterol	5.8 mg	Calcium	4.4 mg
	Sodium	23 mg	Fiber	0.1 gm

▲ Southwestern Rarebit

A spirited version of the Welsh classic.

Menu Category:	Brunch, American Regional
Cooking Method:	Simmer
Preparation Time:	30 minutes
Cooking Time:	30 minutes
Variations:	Substitute toasted split croissants or English muffins for toast. Top each portion with crisply-fried tortilla strips.
Yield:	50 portions (4 oz)

Ingredient	U.S.	Metric	Method
Cheddar cheese, mild, diced	3 lb	1.4 kg	Combine in large pot or steam kettle. Cook over low heat, stirring constantly, until cheese melts.
Monterey Jack cheese, diced	3 lb	1.4 kg	
Butter	6 oz	170 g	
Mustard, dry	2 T	30 ml	
Chili powder	2 T	30 ml	
Eggs, beaten	12	12	Combine with 2 cups of cheese mixture. Whip well. Add to cheese mixture. Whip well.
Beer	1 qt	950 ml	Combine. Add to cheese mixture. Simmer over low heat for 5 minutes. Whip gently. Transfer to storage containers. Keep warm.
Commercial picante sauce	2 c	480 ml	
Toast triangles	150	150	Place on plates. Portion cheese mixture over the middle.

Nutrient Analysis Per Serving				
	Calories	316	Protein	16.7 gm
	Fat	23.3 gm	Carbohydrate	11.3 gm
	Cholesterol	111 mg	Calcium	428 mg
	Sodium	519 mg	Fiber	0.2 gm

Pancakes and Waffles

▲ Blini

Yeasty, light miniature pancakes.

Menu Category:	Brunch
Cooking Method:	Griddle
Preparation Time:	20 minutes
Rising Time:	3 hours
Cooking Time:	10 minutes
Variations:	Traditionally served with caviar, these are wonderful with sour cream or plain yogurt.
Yield:	50 portions (3 per portion)

Ingredient	U.S.	Metric	Method
Water, warm	1 c	240 ml	Combine in large bowl. Let rest in warm spot until foamy.
Sugar, granulated	1 T	15 ml	
Active dry yeast	½ oz	15 g	
Milk, scalded, warm	2 c	480 ml	Combine in mixer bowl with paddle attachment. Mix at low speed until well blended. Add reserved yeast mixture. Mix at low speed for 1 minute. Cover bowl. Let rest until doubled in volume, about 2 hours. Return mixture to mixer with paddle attachment.
Sugar, granulated	¼ c	60 ml	
Butter, melted	¼ c	60 ml	
Buckwheat flour	8 oz	227 g	
Milk, lukewarm	2 c	480 ml	Add to mixture. Mix at low speed for 1 minute. Cover bowl. Let rest until doubled in volume and bubbly, about 1 hour. Return mixture to mixer with paddle attachment.
Flour, all purpose	8 oz	227 g	
Egg yolks	4	4	
Salt	2 t	10 ml	
Heavy cream, whipped	2 c	480 ml	Add to mixture. Mix at low speed just until blended.
Egg whites, whipped stiff	4	4	Add to mixture. Mix at low speed just until blended. Pour ½-ounce portions onto preheated oiled 350°F griddle. Cook 1 minute on each side. Transfer to sheet pans. Keep warm in 250°F oven.

Nutrient Analysis Per Portion				
	Calories	93	Protein	2.7 gm
	Fat	5.4 gm	Carbohydrate	9.2 gm
	Cholesterol	34 mg	Calcium	36.1 mg
	Sodium	114 mg	Fiber	0.2 gm

▲ German Apple Pancakes

Dramatic and rich, these put a crowning touch on any brunch menu.

Menu Category:	Brunch
Cooking Method:	Sauté/Bake
Preparation Time:	20 minutes
Cooking Time:	20 minutes
Oven Temperature:	425°F
Variations:	Substitute any sautéed fruit or fruit preserve for filling.
Yield:	50 portions (8 oz)

Ingredient	U.S.	Metric	Method
Milk	2 qt	1.9 L	Combine in mixer bowl with whip attachment. Mix at medium speed until well blended. Transfer to storage container. Cover. Chill at least 1 hour.
Flour, all purpose	2 lb	908 g	
Eggs, beaten	1 gal	3.8 L	
Honey	1 c	240 ml	
Baking powder	3 T	45 ml	
Butter, melted	1 lb	454 g	
Vanilla extract	⅓ c	80 ml	
Cinnamon, ground	2 t	10 ml	
Nutmeg, ground	1 t	5 ml	
Butter, melted	2 lb	908 g	Divide among three 12″ × 10″ × 2″ insert pans. Coat bottom and sides well.
Sugar, granulated	3 c	720 g	Sprinkle over the three prepared pans.
Apples, peeled, sliced	3 qt	2.8 L	Combine well. Divide among the three prepared pans. Place over high heat and cook until mixture bubbles. Divide reserved batter over apples. Place in preheated 425°F oven. Bake 15 minutes. Reduce heat to 350°F. Bake for 10 minutes more. Transfer to wire racks. Let cool 5 minutes before slicing.
Sugar, granulated	2 lb	2 lb	
Cinnamon, ground	3 T	45 ml	
Sugar, powdered	2 c	480 ml	Sprinkle over top.

Nutrient Analysis Per Portion				
	Calories	571	Protein	13.2 gm
	Fat	30.7 gm	Carbohydrate	64.2 gm
	Cholesterol	372 mg	Calcium	116 mg
	Sodium	398 mg	Fiber	0.8 gm

▲ Holiday Pumpkin-Nut Pancakes

These are especially popular in the golden days of autumn.

Menu Category:	Brunch
Cooking Method:	Griddle
Preparation Time:	20 minutes
Cooking Time:	20 minutes
Variations:	Serve these with maple syrup—and be sure to warm it!
Yield:	50 portions (6 oz)

Ingredient	U.S.	Metric	Method
Flour, all purpose	4 lb	1.8 kg	Combine in mixer bowl with paddle attachment. Mix at low speed until well combined.
Sugar, brown	1 c	240 ml	
Baking powder	½ c	120 ml	
Cinnamon, ground	2 T	30 ml	
Nutmeg, ground	1 T	15 ml	
Ginger, ground	1 T	15 ml	
Salt	2 T	30 ml	
Milk	3½ qt	3.3 L	Combine. Add to dry ingredients. Mix at low speed just until ingredients are blended. Pour 2 ounce portions onto preheated oiled 350°F griddle. Cook first side until top surface bubbles. Turn over. Cook second side 1 minute. Transfer to sheet pans. Keep warm in 250°F oven.
Vegetable oil	1 c	240 ml	
Eggs, beaten	8	8	
Pumpkin puree	2 lb	908 g	
Pecans, chopped	1 qt	950 ml	

Nutrient Analysis Per Portion	Calories	291	Protein	9.1 gm
	Fat	13.1 gm	Carbohydrate	37.8 gm
	Cholesterol	39.1 mg	Calcium	144 mg
	Sodium	462 mg	Fiber	1.3 gm

▲ Kentucky Griddle Cakes

From the rich heritage of American home cooking.

Menu Category:	Brunch, American Regional
Cooking Method:	Griddle
Preparation Time:	20 minutes
Cooking Time:	20 minutes
Variations:	Serve these with molasses, syrup, or sorghum.
Yield:	50 portions (4 oz)

Ingredient	U.S.	Metric	Method
Flour, all purpose	1½ lb	680 g	Combine in mixer bowl with paddle attachment. Mix at low speed until well combined.
Cornmeal, yellow	3½ lb	1.6 kg	
Baking powder	2 T	30 ml	
Baking soda	2 T	30 ml	
Sugar, granulated	¼ c	60 ml	
Salt	3 T	45 ml	
Buttermilk	3 qt	2.8 L	Combine. Add to dry ingredients. Mix at low speed just until ingredients are blended. Pour 1-ounce portions onto preheated oiled 350°F griddle. Cook first side until top surface bubbles. Turn over. Cook second side 1 minute. Transfer to sheet pans. Keep warm in 250°F oven.
Vegetable oil	1½ c	360 ml	
Eggs, beaten	12	12	

Nutrient Analysis Per Portion				
	Calories	264	Protein	7.9 gm
	Fat	9.6 gm	Carbohydrate	38.3 gm
	Cholesterol	53.3 mg	Calcium	90.4 mg
	Sodium	610 mg	Fiber	0.9 gm

▲ New York Cheddar Pancakes

A delightful, savory pancake to serve with grilled pork sausage.

Menu Category:	Brunch
Cooking Method:	Griddle
Preparation Time:	20 minutes
Cooking Time:	20 minutes
Variations:	Use commercial pancake mix, adding cheddar cheese as directed. Serve with cinnamon-flavored applesauce.

Yield:	50 portions (5 oz)

Ingredient	U.S.	Metric	Method
Applesauce, commercial	3 qt	2.8 L	Combine in pot or steam kettle. Heat to a simmer. Simmer for 5 minutes, stirring occasionally. Remove from heat. Reserve.
Brown sugar	1 lb	454 g	
Cinnamon	2 T	30 ml	
Flour, all purpose	4½ lb	2 kg	Combine in mixer bowl with paddle attachment. Mix at low speed until well combined.
Sugar, granulated	1½ c	360 ml	
Baking powder	¼ c	60 ml	
Baking soda	3 T	45 ml	
Salt	2 T	30 ml	
Buttermilk	1 gal	3.8 L	Combine. Add to dry ingredients. Mix at low speed just until ingredients are blended.
Butter, melted	1½ lb	680 g	
Eggs, beaten	12	12	
Cheddar cheese, grated	1 qt	950 ml	Add to mixture. Mix at low speed just until cheese is well distributed. Pour 2-ounce portions onto preheated oiled 350°F griddle. Cook first side until top surface bubbles. Turn over. Cook second side 1 minute. Transfer to sheet pans. Keep warm in 250°F oven. Serve with 2 ounces of cinnamon applesauce.
Caraway seed, whole	2 T	30 ml	

Nutrient Analysis Per Portion	Calories	406	Protein	12.2 gm
	Fat	16.8 gm	Carbohydrate	55.3 gm
	Cholesterol	93.4 mg	Calcium	210 mg
	Sodium	755 mg	Fiber	1.3 gm

▲ Whole Wheat Honey Pancakes

Sure to be a hit on your healthy brunch buffet or any breakfast menu.

Menu Category:	Brunch
Cooking Method:	Griddle
Preparation Time:	20 minutes
Cooking Time:	20 minutes
Variations:	Serve these with blueberry syrup or strawberry sauce. Use egg substitute instead of whole eggs.
Yield:	50 portions (6 oz)

Ingredient	U.S.	Metric	Method
Flour, all purpose	3 lb	1.4 kg	Combine in mixer bowl with paddle attachment. Mix at low speed until well combined.
Flour, whole wheat	1 lb	454 g	
Baking powder	¾ c	180 ml	
Baking soda	1 T	15 ml	
Salt	2 T	30 ml	
Milk	1 gal	3.8 L	Combine. Add to dry ingredients. Mix at low speed just until ingredients are blended. Pour 2-ounce portions onto preheated 350°F griddle. Cook first side until top surface bubbles. Turn over. Cook second side 1 minute. Transfer to sheet pans. Keep warm in 250°F oven.
Butter, melted	2 c	480 ml	
Eggs, beaten	36	36	
Honey	1 lb	454 g	

Nutrient Analysis				
Per Portion	Calories	312	Protein	12.1 gm
	Fat	13.2 gm	Carbohydrate	38.5 gm
	Cholesterol	179 mg	Calcium	171 mg
	Sodium	704 mg	Fiber	0.8 gm

▲ Golden Waffles with Nantucket Cranberry Syrup

Crisp orange waffles offer the perfect base for the tangy sweet syrup.

Menu Category:	Brunch
Cooking Method:	Waffle Iron
Preparation Time:	20 minutes
Cooking Time:	Manufacturer's guidelines
Variations:	Add chopped pecans to batter.
	Substitute virtually any fruit sauce or melted preserve.
Yield:	50 portions (7 oz)

Ingredient	U.S.	Metric	Method
Flour, all purpose	4 lb	1.8 kg	Combine in mixer bowl with paddle
Sugar, granulated	1 c	240 ml	attachment. Mix at low speed until well
Baking powder	½ c	120 ml	combined.
Salt	2 T	30 ml	
Milk	2 qt	1.9 L	Combine. Add to dry ingredients. Mix at
Butter, melted	1 lb	454 g	low speed just until ingredients are
Eggs, beaten	36	36	blended. Pour 1 cup batter onto preheated
Orange rind, grated	2 c	480 ml	oiled waffle iron. Cook according to
Orange extract	1 T	15 ml	manufacturer's directions. Transfer to sheet
			pans. Keep warm in 250°F oven.
Nantucket Cranberry Syrup, recipe follows	3¼ qt	3.1 L	Portion over each waffle.
Sugar, powdered	2 c	480 ml	Sprinkle over top.

Nutrient Analysis Per Portion	Calories	388	Protein	11 gm
	Fat	12.5 gm	Carbohydrate	62.5 gm
	Cholesterol	176 mg	Calcium	119 mg
	Sodium	563 mg	Fiber	1.1 gm

Companion Recipe

▲ **Nantucket Cranberry Syrup**

Serve with waffles, pancakes, blintzes, pound cake, or ice cream.

Menu Category:	Sauce
Cooking Method:	Simmer
Preparation Time:	20 minutes
Cooking Time:	30 minutes
Variations:	Substitute strawberries or blueberries for cranberries.
	Substitute orange juice for cranberry juice.

Yield:	1 gallon

Ingredient	U.S.	Metric	Method
Cranberry juice	1½ qt	1.4 L	Combine in large pot or steam kettle. Heat to a boil. Boil without stirring until sugar dissolves.
Sugar, granulated	1½ lb	680 g	
Cranberries, whole	3 lb	1.4 kg	Add to pot. Heat to a simmer. Simmer just until cranberries pop open, about 5 to 10 minutes. Remove from heat. Keep warm for service.
Maple syrup	2 c	480 ml	
Orange rind, grated	2 T	30 ml	

Nutrient Analysis Per Ounce	Calories	45	Protein	0.1 gm
	Fat	0.1 gm	Carbohydrate	11.8 gm
	Cholesterol	0 mg	Calcium	1.6 mg
	Sodium	3.6 mg	Fiber	0.1 gm

OTHER BRUNCH DISHES

▲ Broiled Citrus Mélange

Delicately crisp fruit with a simple rum sauce.

Menu Category:	Brunch, Dessert
Cooking Method:	Broil
Preparation Time:	20 minutes
Cooking Time:	10 minutes
Variations:	Substitute rum extract and orange juice if no alcohol is desired.
Yield:	50 portions (6 oz)

Ingredient	U.S.	Metric	Method
Vanilla pudding, prepared	1 qt	950 ml	Combine in mixer bowl with whip
Milk	1 qt	950 ml	attachment. Mix at medium speed until
Vanilla extract	2 T	30 ml	well blended. Cover. Chill completely.
Dark rum	½ c	120 ml	Reserve.
Orange liqueur	½ c	120 ml	
Oranges, seedless, sectioned	2 qt	1.9 L	Combine in large plastic storage container. Cover. Chill completely. Drain well.
Tangerines, seedless, sectioned	2 qt	1.9 L	Portion fruit into casserole dishes. Place on sheet pans. Broil under medium high heat
Grapefruit, white, sectioned	2 qt	1.9 L	until crisp edges form, about 8 to 10 minutes. Top with 1½ ounces of reserved
Grapefruit, red, sectioned	2 qt	1.9 L	sauce. Serve warm.
Dark rum	1 qt	950 ml	

Nutrient Analysis Per Portion	Calories	149	Protein	2.1 gm
	Fat	1.2 gm	Carbohydrate	18.7 gm
	Cholesterol	4.2 mg	Calcium	70.8 mg
	Sodium	46.3 mg	Fiber	0.4 gm

▲ Strawberries and Oranges with Cointreau and Mint

Serve as an elegant dessert or fruit salad.

Menu Category:	Dessert, Salad, Ethnic, Italian
Cooking Method:	None required.
Preparation Time:	20 minutes
Marination Time:	Several hours
Variations:	Substitute grapefruit for orange or mix a variety of seeded citrus fruits.
	Substitute dark rum for Cointreau.
	Add diced pineapple.
Yield:	50 portions (6 oz)

Ingredient	U.S.	Metric	Method
Strawberries, halved	2 qt	1.9 L	Toss to combine. Chill at least one hour.
Honey	1 c	240 ml	
Orange juice	1 qt	950 ml	
Navel oranges, sections	2 qt	1.9 L	Add to strawberries. Toss well. Chill
Mint, fresh, chopped	1 c	240 ml	several hours.
Cointreau	½ c	120 ml	

Nutrient Analysis Per Serving				
	Calories	51	Protein	0.6 gm
	Fat	0.2 gm	Carbohydrate	12.6 gm
	Cholesterol	0 mg	Calcium	19.3 mg
	Sodium	1.7 mg	Fiber	0.3 gm

▲ Tropical Marinated Fruit Cocktail

For that special brunch buffet or whenever you want the tropical touch.

Menu Category:	Brunch, Dessert
Cooking Method:	None required
Preparation Time:	20 minutes
Variations:	Substitute rum extract and orange juice if no alcohol is desired.
Yield:	50 portions (6 oz)

Ingredient	U.S.	Metric	Method
Sugar, brown	1 lb	908 g	Combine in large bowl. Stir well to
Lemon juice	2 c	480 ml	dissolve sugar.
Maraschino liqueur	1 c	240 ml	
Orange liqueur	1 c	240 ml	
Orange juice	1 c	240 ml	
Red grapes, seedless, split	2 qt	1.9 L	Add to juice/liqueur mixture. Fold gently but thoroughly with large rubber spatula.
Green grapes, seedless, split	2 qt	1.9 L	Cover. Refrigerate for several hours. Serve very cold.
Oranges, seedless, sectioned	2 qt	1.9 L	
Grapefruit, red, sectioned	2 qt	1.9 L	

Nutrient Analysis	Calories	107	Protein	0.6 gm
Per Serving	Fat	0.2 gm	Carbohydrate	23.4 gm
	Cholesterol	0 mg	Calcium	27.5 mg
	Sodium	5.8 mg	Fiber	0.4 gm

▲ Toasted Almond Granola

A wholesome, popular alternative to traditional breakfast offerings.

Menu Category:	Brunch
Cooking Method:	Bake
Preparation Time:	30 minutes
Baking Time:	30 minutes
Oven Temperature:	350°F
Variations:	Substitute whatever mixture of dried fruits and extracts you like.
Yield:	50 portions (3 oz)

Ingredient	U.S.	Metric	Method
Rolled oats	7 lb	3.2 kg	Combine in mixer bowl with paddle
Sunflower seeds, roasted	3 c	720 ml	attachment. Mix at low speed until
Vegetable oil	2 c	480 ml	ingredients are thoroughly blended and
Honey	2 c	480 ml	coated, about 7 to 10 minutes. Transfer
Sugar, brown	2 c	480 ml	mixture to four 12″ × 20″ × 2″ insert pans.
Vanilla extract	1 T	15 ml	Bake in preheated 350°F oven for 30
Almond extract	1 T	15 ml	minutes. Stir frequently. Remove from
Cinnamon, ground	2 t	10 ml	oven. Cool. Transfer mixture to large bowl.
Nutmeg, ground	2 t	10 ml	
Almonds, slivered, toasted	3 c	720 ml	Add to mixture. Using a large rubber
Raisins	3 c	720 ml	spatula, toss mixture to combine well.
Apricots, dried, diced	3 c	720 ml	Store in airtight containers.
Coconut, toasted	2 c	480 ml	

Nutrient Analysis	Calories	549	Protein	14 gm
Per Serving	Fat	22 gm	Carbohydrate	78.7 gm
	Cholesterol	0 mg	Calcium	74.5 mg
	Sodium	10 mg	Fiber	1.5 gm

▲ Peppered Roast Beef Hash

Let your leftover inventory do double duty with this winner.

Menu Category:	Brunch
Cooking Method:	Sauté
Preparation Time:	30 minutes
Cooking Time:	30 minutes
Variations:	This procedure works wonderfully with any cooked meat or chicken. For ethnic diversity, substitute herbs and spices.
Yield:	50 portions (4 oz)

Ingredient	U.S.	Metric	Method
Roast beef, minced	8 lb	3.6 kg	Combine in mixer bowl with paddle
Bell pepper, minced	1 lb	454 g	attachment. Mix at low speed just until
Onion, minced	8 oz	227 g	well combined. Form into 5 ounce patties.
Potatoes, cooked, diced	3 lb	1.4 kg	Cook patties on preheated, oiled 350°F
Beef stock	1 qt	950 ml	griddle until golden brown on first side,
Worcestershire sauce	2 c	480 ml	about 5 to 7 minutes. Turn over. Cook
Hot pepper sauce	½ c	120 ml	second side until golden, about 5 to 7
Commercial picante sauce,			minutes more. Transfer with spatula to
mild	2 c	480 ml	oiled sheet pans. Keep warm in 250°F
Salt	2 T	30 ml	oven.
Black pepper	2 T	30 ml	

Nutrient Analysis	Calories	307	Protein	16.9 gm
Per Serving	Fat	22.1 gm	Carbohydrate	10 gm
	Cholesterol	62.4 mg	Calcium	26.3 mg
	Sodium	570 mg	Fiber	0.2 gm

▲ Philadelphia Scrapple

A Pennsylvania Dutch dish.

Menu Category:	Brunch, American Regional
Cooking Method:	Simmer/Griddle
Preparation Time:	1 hour
Cooking Time:	1 hour
Variations:	Serve with maple syrup and fried eggs.
	For country style cornmeal mush, simply eliminate the pork and spices.
Yield:	50 portions (6 oz)

Ingredient	U.S.	Metric	Method
Pork, lean, diced	6 lb	2.7 kg	Combine in large pot or steam kettle. Heat to a boil. Reduce heat to simmer. Simmer for 30 minutes. Remove from heat. Cool. Drain and reserve liquid. Puree pork in food processor or food chopper. Return pork and reserved liquid to pot or steam kettle. Heat to a boil.
Pork stock	1 gal	3.8 L	
Sage, rubbed	1 T	15 ml	
Salt	2 T	30 ml	
Black pepper	1 T	15 ml	
Cornmeal, yellow	3½ lb	1.6 kg	Combine in large bowl. Add gradually to boiling pork mixture. Stir constantly until mixture returns to a boil. Reduce heat to a simmer. Simmer for 20 minutes, stirring occasionally. Remove from heat. Portion mixture into six oiled 9″ × 5″ × 3″ pans. Cool to room temperature. Cover. Chill completely. When ready to cook, invert pans onto cutting board. Cut each loaf into 16 slices.
Pork stock, cold	3 qt	2.8 L	
Flour, all purpose	as needed	as needed	Dredge slices in flour. Sauté slices on oiled preheated 350°F griddle until golden on both sides, about 10 to 15 minutes.

Nutrient Analysis Per Serving	Calories	294	Protein	18 gm
	Fat	13.4 gm	Carbohydrate	24.8 gm
	Cholesterol	50 mg	Calcium	10.4 mg
	Sodium	550 mg	Fiber	0.6 gm

▲ Toasted Bagels with Apples and Cheddar

A quick side bread.

Menu Category:	Bread, Breakfast, Brunch
Cooking Method:	Broil
Preparation Time:	20 minutes
Cooking Time:	20 minutes
Variations:	Substitute tomatoes for apples and add strips of grilled bacon.
Yield:	50 portions (3 oz)

Ingredient	U.S.	Metric	Method
Bagels, split	50 each	50 each	Brush cut sides of bagels with butter. Place
Butter, melted	1 lb	454 g	on oiled or paper-lined sheet pans.
Apples, cored, peeled	8 lbs	3.6 kg	Cut into 100 ½-inch slices.
Cheddar cheese, grated	2 lbs	908 g	Divide over apple slices. Broil under medium-high heat until cheese is golden brown and bubbly. Serve hot.

Nutrient Analysis Per Serving				
	Calories	343	Protein	10.7 gm
	Fat	15 gm	Carbohydrate	41.9 gm
	Cholesterol	47 mg	Calcium	159 mg
	Sodium	386 mg	Fiber	0.5 gm

Index

Page numbers in **boldface** indicate recipes.

Acorn Squash with Honey and Maple, **469**
African foods, 51
Almond
  Couscous with Currants, **449**
  Granola, Toasted, **558**
  Toasted, Butterscotch Sauce, **504**
American regional food, 396
  appetizers, **238**, **240**
  beef, **217**, **218**, **248**, **345**
  breads, **483**, **492**, **493**
  breakfast and brunch, **542**, **546**, **550**, **560**
  chicken, **252**, **254**, **373**, **375**, **378**, **380**, **383**, **384**
  desserts, **509**, **511**
    pies, **522**, **523**, **526**
    cookies, **532**, **533**, **534**, **535**, **536**
    cakes, **516**
  grains, **437**, **438**, **446**, **447**, **450**
  pork, **359**, **364**
  potatoes, **282**, **425**, **431**, **434**, **435**
  salads and dressings, **292**, **305**
  sampler menu, 183–189
  seafood, **256**, **336**
    crabmeat, **229**, **230**, **313**
    shrimp, **318**, **233**, **322**, **323**, **324**
  soups, **250**, **255**, **260**, **263**, **268**, **270**
  terms, 88–100
  turkey, **293**, **297**, **389**, **392**, **393**, **394**, **395**
  vegetables
    beans, **455**, **476**, **477**, **488**
    carrots, **461**, **462**
    mushrooms, **241**
    squash, **469**, **470**, **471**, **472**
Anadama Bread, **483**
Anglo-Indian food, 261

Appetizers, **211–244**
  beef
    Empanadas, Argentine Spiced, **213**
    Greek-Style Herbed Cocktail Meatballs, **215**
    Hungarian Goulash Stew, **249**
    Mandarin, with Sesame-Mustard Dressing, **284**
    Mexican Carne Picadillo, **217**
    Nachos, Mexican Stuffed, **216**
    Oriental Flank Steak Spirals, **219**
    Quesadillas Con Carne, **218**
    Ragout, **247**
    Skewered Swedish Meatballs, **220**
    Stew, Green Chile, **248**
  chicken
    Chili, Green, **254**
    Drumsticks with Jalapeño Jelly, **224**
    Grilled, Salad with Chopped Pecans, **290**
    Grilled, Strips with Red Chile Marinade, **225**
    Jambalaya, Cajun, **252**
    Salad, **287**
    Salad Bali Hai with Mango Chutney Dressing, **288**
    Salad Bombay with Curry and White Grapes, **289**
    Salad, Mexican Fiesta, **291**
    Wings, Chinese, **227**
    Wings, Shanghai, **226**
    Yakitori, **228**
  Chimichurri Sauce, **214**
  Crostini with Caponata, Grilled, **237**

  Guacamole Pancho Villa, **238**
  meat, **213–223**
  menu suggestions, 169–170, 176–177, 181, 183–184, 189, 192–193, 197, 200, 204–205
  Mushrooms, Spicy Marinated, **241**
  pasta
    Chilled Linguine with Ginger and Peanuts, **413**
    Cold Cheese Tortellini with Mustard Yogurt Sauce, **416**
    Cold Noodles with Shredded Vegetables, **417**
    Salad Mexicana, **418**
    Szechuan Noodles with Bean Sauce and Chicken, **419**
  Pecans, Spiced Cocktail, **240**
  Pita Wedges with Red Lentil Hummus, **239**
  pizza
    Cheese Calzone, **235**
    Crust Dough, Italian, **236**
    Mushroom Snacks, **243**
    Sicilian Vegetarian, **242**
  Polynesian *Pu Pu*, **222**
  pork
    Grilled, with Ginger and Burgundy, **360**
    Sates, Spicy Indonesian, **223**
    Salad, Venetian, with Walnuts, **286**
    Toasts, Grilled, with Mango Chutney, **221**
  poultry, **224–228**
  salad(s)
    Catalonian Tomato, with Lentils and Olives, **278**
    Chicken, **287**

Appetizers (cont.)
Chicken, Bali Hai with Mango Chutney Dressing, 288
Chicken, Bombay with Curry and White Grapes, 289
Chicken, Mexican Fiesta, 291
Chinese Shrimp Shells with Broccoli Florets, 415
Granny Smith's Turkey, 293
Green Lentil, with Red Wine Vinaigrette, 279
Grilled Chicken, with Chopped Pecans, 290
Indian-Style Coleslaw with Orange Mayonnaise, 277
Mediterranean Lentil, with Grilled Peppers, 280
Mediterranean New Potato, 281
Mexican Emperor French Dressing, 305
Moroccan-Style Turkey, 294
Nicoise, Provençale-Style, 302
Paella, 300
Pasta, Mexicana, 418
Pork, Venetian, with Walnuts, 286
Potato, 282
Southwestern Duck, with Melon and Pecans, 292
Smoked Turkey, Calypso, 295
Smoked Turkey with Honey and Soy Sauce, 296
Sweet Potato, with Pineapple and Ginger, 283
Warm Shrimp, with Sesame Vinaigrette, 301
Yogurt Vinaigrette with Cumin and Cilantro, 310
seafood, 229–234
Baked Shrimp Italiano, 232
Beer-Batter Coconut Shrimp with Orange Sauce, 318
Broiled Roughy with Orange Sauce and Pecans, 336
Broiled Scallops with Spiced Orange Sauce, 314
Broiled Shrimp with Chinese-Style Basting Sauce, 320
Ceviche of Scallops Veracruz, 231
Chilled Shrimp with Rotini and Olives, 298
Chinese Fried Shrimp, 234
Chinese Shrimp Shells with Broccoli Florets, 415
Crabmeat Norfolk, 229
Crabmeat Remick with Chile Mayonnaise, 230
Curried Scallops with Spiced Apple Relish, 316
Glazed Shrimp with Chilies and Sesame, 321
Louisiana Shrimp Pilau, 322

Louisiana-Style Barbecued Shrimp, 233
Low Country White Corn Crab Cakes, 313
Provençale-Style Salade Nicoise, 302
San Francisco Bayside Cioppino, 256
for seafood menu, 203
Shrimp Americaine, 323
Shrimp Creole, 324
Shrimp and Vegetable Teriyaki, 325
Warm Caribbean Shrimp Salad, 299
Warm Shrimp Salad with Sesame Vinaigrette, 301
soup(s)
Calalou, 257
Caribbean Red Bean and Lentil, 258
Chilled and Spiced Melon, 259
Corn Chowder with Grilled Pepper, 260
Fresh Mushroom Cream Bisque, 262
Fresh Mushroom, with Vermouth, 264
Manhattan Clam Chowder with Dry Sherry, 255
Mexican-Style Gazpacho, 265
Minestrone, 266
Peach Chilled Bisque with Brandy, 263
Philadelphia Pepper Pot, 250
Pistou Provençale, 267
Southwestern Herbed Meatball, 251
Squash Bisque with Ginger, 268
Tortilla, Monterey, 269
Wisconsin Cheese, 270
turkey salad
Granny Smith's, 293
Moroccan-Style, 294
Smoked, Calypso, 295
Smoked, with Honey and Soy Sauce, 296
Vegetable Frittata, 244
vegetarian, 235–244
Apple(s)
Bread, 484
Brown Betty, 509
and Cheddar, Toasted Bagels with, 561
Granny Smith's Turkey Salad, 293
Bread with Pecans, 484
Pancakes, German, 548
Pureed Squash with, and Cinnamon, 472
Relish, Spiced, 317
Sampler, Fresh, with Gingered Yogurt, 505
Walnut Vinaigrette Dressing, 303

Argentine Spiced Beef Empanadas, 213
Austin-Style Chicken Burritos, 373
Austrian food, 429
Avocado, Guacamole Pancho Villa, 238

Bacon
Biscuits, Cheese and, 496
Mashed Potatoes, Cheese 'n', 424
Bacteria, food temperatures and, 47
Bagels, Toasted, with Apples and Cheddar, 561
Bakery products, 39
Barbecue
Chicken, 374
Eggplant, Szechuan, 466
Green Beans, Cajun, 455
Haddock, Oriental, 331
Pork with Apricots, 357
Shrimp, Louisiana-Style, 233
Turkey Breast, Oven-Smoked, 394
Bar requirements, 165
Bavarian Meat Loaf with Ginger Glaze, 347
Beans. See Legumes
Beef, 33–34, 63
Baked Meat Loaf with Creole Tomato Sauce, 345
Bavarian Meat Loaf with Ginger Glaze, 347
Bracciole, 349
Bul-Kogi, 350
Creole Tomato Sauce, 346
Empanadas, Argentine Spiced, 213
Greek-Style Herbed Cocktail Meatballs, 215
Green Chile Stew, 248
Hash, Peppered Roast, 559
Hungarian Goulash Stew, 249
Jamaican Marinated Flank Steak, 351
Mandarin, with Sesame-Mustard Dressing, 284
Mexican Carne Picadillo, 217
Nachos Campeche, Mexican Stuffed, 216
Oriental Flank Steak Spirals, 219
Ragout, 247
Roestbraten, 353
Salad, Thai, 285
Skewered Swedish Meatballs, 220
Southwestern Herbed Meatball Soup, 251
Sukiyaki, 354
Tenderloin, Oriental Smoke-Roasted, 352
timetables for cooking, 6–7, 12, 14, 18, 23, 27
Beer, yields per keg, 166–167
Beer-Batter Coconut Shrimp with Orange Sauce, 318
Beverages, 61

Biscuits, 493–500
    Buttermilk Cinnamon Scones,
        495
    Cheese and Bacon, 496
    Lemon-Pepper Whole Wheat, 497
    Mexican Jalapeño, 498
    No-Rise Angel, 497
    Pepper-Cheese Boarding House,
        500
Bishop's Bread, 485
Black Bean Salad, Spiced, 273
Blackbottom Pie, 523
Black Currant Sauce, 390
Black-Eyed Peas with Spiced
        Sausage, 477
Blini, 547
Blintzes, 541
Blueberry
    Corn Bread, 486
    Pie, 528
    Sauce, 521
Boston Baked Beans, 476
Boston Brown Bread, Nut-Rich, 489
Bowl capacities, 55–56
Bracciole, 349
Bread(s), 483–491. See also Biscuits;
        Muffins; Quick Breads; Yeast
        Breads
    Boston Brown, Nut-Rich, 489
    menu suggestions, 178, 180, 187,
        191, 195–196, 199, 202
    Spoon, Iroquois, 488
    Toasted Bagels with Apples and
        Cheddar, 561
Breakfast. See Brunch
Broccoli
    Cold Cheese Tortellini with
        Mustard Yogurt Sauce, 416
    Florets, Chinese Shrimp Shells
        with, 415
    Herbed, with Mixed Peppers, 276
    Steamed, with Sesame Seeds, 458
Broiling, 5–9
Brownies, Choco-Mint, 532
Brunch
    breads
        Anadama, 483
        Apple, 484
        Bishop's, 485
        Blueberry Corn, 486
        Buttermilk Cinnamon Scones,
            495
        Cheese and Bacon Biscuits, 496
        Corn Muffins with Jalapeño
            and Bacon, 493
        Grilled Monkey, 487
        Iroquois Spoon, 488
        Lemon 'n' Walnut Muffins, 494
        Lemon-Pepper Whole Wheat
            Biscuits, 497
        Mexican Jalapeño Biscuits, 498
        No-Rise Angel Biscuits, 497
        Nut-Rich Boston Brown, 489
        Pepper-Cheese Boarding
            House Biscuits, 500

    Sweet Potato Nut, 490
    Toasted Bagels with Apples
        and Cheddar, 561
    Zucchini, with Walnuts and
        Lemon, 491
eggs. See Eggs
fruit. See Fruit
Lemon Pound Cake with
    Blueberry Sauce, 520
menu suggestions, 176, 178,
    180–181, 183, 188–189, 192,
    196–197, 200, 202–203, 207
Nantucket Cranberry Syrup, 554
pancakes (see Pancakes)
Peppered Roast Beef Hash, 559
Philadelphia Scrapple, 560
Strawberry Sauce Grand Marnier,
    545
Strawberry-Yogurt Creme Sauce,
    507
Toasted Almond Granola, 558
Waffles with Nantucket
    Cranberry Syrup, 553
Bul-Kogi, 350
Butter Beans, Smoky, with Chili
    Sauce, 480
Buttermilk Cinnamon Scones, 495
Butterscotch Sauce, Toasted
    Almond, 504

Cabbage
    Indian-Style Coleslaw with
        Orange Mayonnaise, 277
    Red, with Apples and Cloves,
        460
    Swedish, with Caraway, 459
Cajun Chicken Jambalaya, 252
Cake(s), 514–522
    Choco-Nut Layer, 514–515
    Cottage Pudding, 515
    Gingerbread Delight, 516
    Ginger Pound, 517
    Hawaiian Sunset Grilled Pound,
        518
    lemon
        Cheesecake, 519
        Pound, with Blueberry Sauce,
            520
        Washington Pie, 522
Calalou, 257
Calzone, Cheese, 235
Cannoli Tarts with Strawberry
    Sauce, 524
Can sizes, 58
Cantonese Braised Potatoes, 423
Cantonese Sweet and Sour Trout,
    339
Capacities of equipment, 55–57
Caribbean food, 257, 258, 315, 346,
    351, 433, 448, 467
    poultry, 374, 295
    seafood, 299, 314
Carolina White Corn Hush
    Puppies, 492

Carrots
    Glazed, Grand Marnier, 461
    Sliced, with Apricot Glaze, 462
    Steamed Zucchini with, and
        Mint, 475
Catalanian Tomato Salad with
    Lentils and Olives, 278
Catering equipment, 163
Centigrade/Fahrenheit conversions,
    45–46
Cereals, 61
    Toasted Almond Granola, 558
Ceviche of Scallops Veracruz, 231
Cheese, 52–54, 539–546
    and Bacon Biscuits, 496
    'n' Bacon Mashed Potatoes, 424
    Calzone, 235
    Grits, Baked, 447
    Jarlsberg, Baked Eggs with Ham
        and, 539
    Manicotti
        Mixed, with Pimento Cream
            Sauce, 407
        Pasta Rolls with, and Spinach,
            406
    New York Cheddar Pancakes,
        551
    Pepper-, Boarding House
        Biscuits, 500
    Pizza with Sausage and, 540
    Soup, Wisconsin, 270
    Southwestern Rarebit, 546
    Toasted Bagels with Apples and
        Cheddar, 561
    Tortellini
        Cold, with Mustard Yogurt
            Sauce, 416
        with Roma Tomato Sauce, 401
Cheesecake, Lemon, 519
Cherry
    Clafouti, 525
    Sauce, 508
Chicken, 371–388
    Barbecued, Blue Mountain, 374
    Braised, Mexican-Style, 375
    breasts
        Country Captain, 380
        Grilled, with Lemon and
            Capers, 382
        Peach-Basted Broiled, 384
        Tandoori-Style Roasted, 387
    Burritos, Austin-Style, 373
    chili
        Green, 254
        with Tortilla "Pasta," 376
    Drumsticks with Jalapeño Jelly,
        224
    grilled
        with Apricot Glaze, 380
        Lime-Marinated, 383
        Salad with Chopped Pecans,
            290
        Strips, with Red Chile
            Marinade, 225
    Jambalaya, Cajun, 252

Chicken (cont.)
  Legs, Thai-Style, **388**
  with Orange Sauce Orlando, **378**
  Salad, **287**
    Bali Hai with Mango Chutney
      Dressing, **288**
    Bombay with Curry and White
      Grapes, **289**
    Mexican Fiesta, **291**
    Paella, **300**
  Sesame, with Mild Chilies, **385**
  Smoked, Fettuccine with, **402**
  Szechuan Noodles with Bean
    Sauce and, **419**
  Szechuan Velvet, **386**
  Tetrazzini Milano, **377**
  timetables for cooking, **10**
  wings
    Chinese, **227**
    Shanghai, **226**
  Yakitori, **228**
Chili
  Chicken, with Tortilla "Pasta,"
    376
  Green Chicken, **254**
Chilled pastas. See Salad(s), pasta
Chilled soups
  Chilled and Spiced Melon, **259**
  Creme Senegalaise, **261**
  Curry, **261**
  Mexican-Style Gazpacho, **265**
  Peach Chilled Bisque with
    Brandy, **263**
Chimichurri Sauce, **214**
Chinese food, **50, 253, 342, 456, 466**
  beef, **284**
  pork, **358, 365, 367**
  poultry, **226, 227, 385, 386, 391,
    419**
  seafood, **234, 328, 339, 341, 415**
Chocolate
  Blackbottom Pie, **523**
  Choco-Mint Brownies, **532**
  Choco-Nut Layer Cakes, **514–515**
  Drop Cookies, Kiss O', **534**
Cioppino, San Francisco Bayside,
  256
Clafouti, **525**
Clam
  Chowder, Manhattan, with Dry
    Sherry, **255**
  Sauce, White, Linguine with, **405**
Coconut Shrimp, Beer-Batter, with
  Orange Sauce, **318**
Cod, Broiled, with Jalapeño Onion
  Marmalade, **327**
Coleslaw, Indian-Style, with
  Orange Mayonnaise, **277**
Conversions
  Fahrenheit/Centigrade, **45–46**
  microwave time, **46**
  recipes yields, **68–71**
  weights and measures, **33–46**
Cookies, **532–536**
  Choco-Mint Brownies, **532**

Gingersnap Giants, **533**
  Kiss O'Chocolate Drop, **534**
  Lemon Nutcrunch Bars, **535**
  Oatmeal-Date, **536**
Cooking methods, **3–36**
Corn
  Chowder, with Grilled Pepper,
    260
  and Sweet Potato Pudding, **530**
Corn bread, Blueberry, **486**
Cornmeal
  Blueberry Corn Bread, **486**
  Broiled Polenta Marinara, **449**
  Carolina White Corn Hush
    Puppies, **492**
  Corn Muffins with Jalapeño and
    Bacon, **493**
  Indian Pudding, **529**
  Iroquois Spoon Bread, **488**
  Kentucky Griddle Cakes, **550**
  New Bedford Corn and Sweet
    Potato Pudding, **530**
  Pepper-Cheese Boarding House
    Biscuits, **500**
Corn Muffins with Jalapeño and
  Bacon, **493**
Cottage Pudding, **515**
Country Captain Chicken Breasts,
  380
Couscous
  Almond, with Currants, **449**
  Red Pepper, **452**
Crab(meat)
  Cakes, Low Country White
    Corn, **313**
  Norfolk, **229**
  Remick with Chile Mayonnaise,
    230
Crackers, **61**
Cranberry Sauce, Spiced, **396**
Creme Senegalaise, **261**
Creole-Style White Hominy, **450**
Creole Tomato Sauce, **346**
Crepes, Neapolitan, Strawberry,
  512
Cucumbers, Oriental-Style, with
  Shredded Carrots, **463**
Curry
  Rice, **442**
  Sauce, Indonesian, Baked
    Haddock with, **330**
  Scallops with Spiced Apple
    Relish, **316**
  Soup, Chilled, **261**
  and White Grapes, Chicken
    Salad Bombay with, **289**
  Yams, Jamaican, **433**

Dairy products, **40, 62**
Decor, for events, **167–169**
Deep-frying, **9–10**
Definitions of food terms, **88–119**
Desserts, **503–536**
  Grilled Monkey Bread, **487**

menu suggestions, **176, 178, 180,
  183, 187–188, 191–192, 196,
  199, 202**
  Zucchini Bread with Walnuts and
    Lemon, **491**
Dilled Green Beans, **457**
Down-South White Rice with
  Raisins, **438**
Dry-heat cooking methods, **5–22**
Duck Salad, Southwestern, with
  Melon and Pecans, **292**

Eggplant
  Grilled, with Herbs and Cheese,
    464
  Grilled Crostini with Caponata,
    237
  Ratatouille Nicoise, **465**
  Szechuan Barbecued, **466**
Eggs, **539–546**
  Baked, with Ham and Jarlsberg
    Cheese, **539**
  Blintzes, **541**
  Chinese Eggdrop Soup, **253**
  Huevos Rancheros, **542**
  Mediterranean Scrambled, with
    Mint Yogurt Sauce, **543**
  Pizza with Sausage and Cheese,
    540
  Southwestern Rarebit, **546**
  Stuffed French Toast with Honey
    Ricotta, **544**
  Vegetable Frittata, **244**
Egyptian-Style Red Lentil Puree,
  478
Empanadas, Argentine Spiced Beef,
  213
Entrees
  beef
    Bavarian Meat Loaf with
      Ginger Glaze, **347**
    Bracciole, **349**
    Broth, Oriental Noodles with,
      409
    Bul-Kogi, **350**
    Empanadas, Argentine, **213**
    Greek-Style Herbed Cocktail
      Meatballs, **215**
    Jamaican Marinated Flank
      Steak, **351**
    Meat Loaf with Creole Tomato
      Sauce, **345**
    Mexican Carne Picadillo, **217**
    Mexican Stuffed Nachos
      Campeche, **216**
    Quesadillas Con Carne, **218**
    Roestbraten, **353**
    Sukiyaki, **354**
    Tenderloin, Oriental Smoke-
      Roasted, **352**
    Yakitori, **228**
  chicken
    Blue Mountain Barbecued
      Chicken, **374**
    Braised, Mexican-Style, **375**

Breast, Grilled, with Lemon and Capers, 382
Breasts, Country Captain, 380
Breasts, Peach-Basted Broiled, 384
Breasts, Tandoori-Style Roasted, 387
Burritos Austin-Style, 373
Chili with Tortilla "Pasta," 376
Drumsticks with Jalapeño Jelly, 224
Grilled, with Apricot Glaze, 380
Legs, Thai-Style, 388
Lime-Marinated Grilled, 383
with Orange Sauce Orlando, 378
Salad, 287
Sesame, with Mild Chilies, 385
Strips, Grilled, with Red Chile Marinade, 225
Szechuan Velvet, 386
Tetrazzini Milano, 377
Wings, Chinese, 227
Wings, Shanghai, 226
Chimichurri Sauce, 214
Creole Tomato Sauce, 346
Grilled Crostini with Caponata, 237
lamb
Roast, with Ginger Baste, 355
Skewered, with Cinnamon-Pepper Marinade, 356
pasta
Cheese Tortellini with Roma Tomato Sauce, 401
Chinese Shrimp Shells with Broccoli Florets, 415
Cold Noodles with Shredded Vegetables, 417
Fettuccine with Tomato and Capers, 403
Fusilli with Meatless Marinara Sauce, 404
Linguine with White Clam Sauce, 405
Manicotti Rolls with Cheese and Spinach, 406
Mixed Cheese Manicotti with Pimento Cream Sauce, 407
Rainbow Primavera, 414
Spaghetti with Mixed Herbs, 411
Stir-Fried Noodles with Ginger and Scallions, 412
Szechuan Noodles with Bean Sauce and Chicken, 419
Pita Wedges with Red Lentil Hummus, 239
pizza
Cheese Calzone, 235
Dough, Italian, 236
Sicilian Vegetarian, 242
pork
Barbecued, with Apricots, 357

Loin, Chinese, 358
Loin Sante Fe, Grilled 359
Medallions Barcelona, 361
Polynesian Pu Pu Appetizer, 222
Roast Loin Florentine, 363
Ribbons with Spinach, Velvet 367
Salad, Venetian, with Walnuts, 286
Sautéed, with Bourbon and Mustard, 364
Szechuan, with Peanuts, 365
Tenderloin with Orange and Ginger, 362
Tuscan-Style, with Herbed Lentils, 366
salad
Chicken, 287
Mediterranean Lentil, with Grilled Peppers, 280
Nicoise, Provençale-Style, 302
Pork, Venetian, with Walnuts, 286
Smoked Turkey, Calypso, 295
Southwestern Duck, with Melon and Pecans, 292
Turkey, Moroccan-Style, 294
Turkey, with Wild Rice and Mandarin Orange, 297
Warm Shrimp, with Sesame Vinaigrette, 301
seafood
Beer-Batter Coconut Shrimp with Orange Sauce, 318
Cantonese Sweet and Sour Trout, 339
Chinese Fried Shrimp, 234
Cod with Jalapeño Onion Marmalade, 327
Crabmeat Norfolk, 229
Crabmeat Remick with Chile Mayonnaise, 230
Curried Scallops with Spiced Apple Relish, 316
Glazed Shrimp with Chilies and Sesame, 321
Italian-Style Baked Trout, 340
Haddock with Herbs and Chablis, 329
Haddock with Indonesian Curry Sauce, 330
Louisiana Shrimp Pilau, 322
Louisiana-Style Barbecued Shrimp, 233
Low Country White Corn Crab Cakes, 313
Mixed Seafood Paella, 326
Oriental Barbecued Haddock, 331
Poached Salmon with Aromatic Vegetables, 337
Polynesian Baked Monkfish with Sweet 'n' Sour Sauce, 332

Red Snapper Veracruz, 333
Roughy with Orange Sauce and Pecans, 336
Scallops with Spiced Orange Sauce, 314
for seafood menu, 203
Shrimp Americaine, 323
Shrimp with Chinese-Style Basting Sauce, 320
Shrimp Creole, 324
Shrimp Italiano, 232
Shrimp with Rotini and Olives, 298
Shrimp and Vegetable Teriyaki, 325
Sole with Mixed Peppers and Fruit, 334
Sweet and Sour Whitefish Fillets, 341
Szechuan Broiled Flounder, 328
Trout Romano, 338
Turban of Sole Florentine, 335
Warm Shrimp Salad with Sesame Vinaigrette, 301
turkey
Breast with Black Currant Sauce, 389
Breast, Chinese-Style Roasted, 391
Breast, Oven-Smoked Barbecued, 394
Grilled, for Fajitas, 392
Marsala with Mushrooms, 397
Medallions of, in Mustard Sauce, 393
Roast, with Spiced Cranberry Sauce, 395
Salad, Moroccan-Style, 294
Salad with Wild Rice and Mandarin Orange, 297
Smoked, Salad Calypso, 295
Veal
Braised, Saltimbocca, 368
Piccata Milanese, 369
Equipment, 55–58, 163, 165
European food, 360
Events, themes and decor for, 167–169

Fahrenheit/Centigrade conversions, 45–46
Fajitas, Grilled Turkey for, 392
Fettuccine Pasta with Tomato and Capers, 403
Fifty servings, food amounts for, 61–68
Finfish, 327–342. See also specific fish
Fish. See Seafood
Flan, Spanish, 531
Flavor substitutes, 50–51
Flounder, Szechuan Broiled, 328

Food
    language of, 73–159
    quantities, 59–71
    safety, temperature guidelines, 47
    terms, 88–159
Foodservice planning, 161–207
French Dressing, Mexican Emperor, 305
French fries, deep-frying timetable, 10
French food, 50, 127–142, **247, 267, 298, 302, 329, 465, 525**
French Toast, Stuffed, with Honey Ricotta, **544**
Fried Rice Espagnole, **439**
Fruit, 62, 120–121. See also specific fruits
    Broiled Citrus Mélange, **555**
    Cocktail, Tropical Marinated, **557**
    desserts, 503–513
    Fresh, with Strawberry-Yogurt Creme Sauce, **506**
    weight to measure conversions, 40–41
Full-service bar requirements, 165
Fusilli with Meatless Marinara Sauce, **404**

German food, 50, **347, 353, 460, 548**
Gingerbread Delight, **516**
Ginger Glaze Basting Sauce, **348**
Ginger Pound Cake, **517**
Gingersnap Giants, **533**
Glaze, Ginger, Basting Sauce, **348**
Gnocchi, **426**
Grains, 61, **447–452**. See also specific grains
    weight to measure conversions, 41–42
Granola, Toasted Almond, **558**
Grasshopper Pie, **526**
Greek food, 50, **215**
Green Beans
    Cajun Barbecued, **455**
    Chinese, with Sesame Oil and Almonds, **456**
    Dilled, **457**
    with Dill and Garlic Vinaigrette, **275**
    Hot Three Bean Salad, **274**
    Provençale-Style Salade Nicoise, **302**
Green Chile Beef Stew, **248**
Green Lentil Salad with Red Wine Vinaigrette, **279**
Grilled Chicken with Apricot Glaze, **380**
Grilled Chicken Breast with Lemon and Capers, **382**
Grilled Chicken Salad with Chopped Pecans, **290**
Grilled Chicken Strips with Red Chile Marinade, **225**

Grilled Crostini with Caponata, **237**
Grilled Eggplant with Herbs and Cheese, **464**
Grilled Herbed Zucchini Wafers, **474**
Grilled Monkey Bread, **487**
Grilled Pork with Ginger and Burgundy, **360**
Grilled Pork Loin Santa Fe, **359**
Grilled Pork Toasts with Mango Chutney, **221**
Grilled Potatoes O'Brien, **425**
Grilled Turkey for Fajitas, **392**
Grilled Yellow Squash, **470**
Grits
    Baked Cheese, **447**
    Baked Jamaican Pepper-Herb, **448**
Guacamole Pancho Villa, **238**

Haddock
    Baked, with Herbs and Chablis, **329**
    Baked, with Indonesian Curry Sauce, **330**
    Oriental Barbecued, **331**
Ham
    cooking timetables, 8, 20
    and Jarlsberg Cheese, Baked Eggs with, **539**
Hasty pudding, **529**
Hawaiian Sunset Grilled Pound Cake, **518**
Herbed Broccoli with Mixed Peppers, **276**
Herbed Lentils with Tofu, **479**
Herbs, 48–49, 125–126
    weight to measure conversions, 42–43
Hominy, Creole-Style White, **450**
Hot and spicy menu, 204–207
Huevos Rancheros, **542**
Hungarian food, 50, **249**
Hush Puppies, Carolina White Corn, **492**

Indian Pudding, **529**
Indian food, 50, **277, 289, 316, 317, 387, 442**. See also Curry
Indonesian food, 51, **223, 330**
Ingredients
    key, 50–51
    substitutes, 50–52
International food terms, 101–119
International sampler ethnic menu, 169–190
Iroquois Spoon Bread, **488**
Italian food, 51, **237, 244, 266, 449, 464, 473**
    beef, **349**
    desserts, **524, 556**
    menu suggestions, 178–180
    pasta. See Pasta, Italian
    pizza. See Pizza
    pork, **286, 363, 366**

potatoes, **281, 426, 430**
poultry, **377, 382, 397**
seafood, **232, 335, 338, 340**
terms, 120–126, 142–152
veal, **368, 369**

Jamaican food. See Caribbean food
Japanese food, **228, 325, 354**
Jewish food, **428**

Kentucky Griddle Cakes, **550**
Kentucky Sweet Potatoes, **434**
Key ingredients, 50–51
Kidney beans, Hot Three Bean Salad, **274**
Kiss O'Chocolate Drop Cookies, **534**
Korean food, **350**

Lamb, 34, 63–64, **355–356**
    cooking timetables, 7, 15, 19, 25, 27
    Roast, with Ginger Baste, **355**
    Skewered, with Cinnamon-Pepper Marinade, **356**
Legumes, **476–480**
    Black-Eyed Peas with Spiced Sausage, **477**
    Boston Baked Beans, **476**
    Caribbean Red Bean and Lentil Soup, **258**
    Egyptian-Style Red Lentil Puree, **478**
    Hot Three Bean Salad, **274**
    for international ethnic sampler menu, 175
    Mexican Stuffed Beef Nachos Campeche, **216**
    Mexican-Style Squash Succotash, **471**
    Pistou Provençale, **267**
    Pita Wedges with Red Lentil Hummus, **239**
    Red Pepper Couscous, **452**
    salads, 273–283
Lemon
    Cheesecake, **519**
    Nutcrunch Bars, **535**
    -Pepper Whole Wheat Biscuits, **497**
    Pound Cake with Blueberry Sauce, **520**
    'n' Walnut Muffins, **494**
Lentil(s)
    Herbed, with Tofu, **479**
    Herbed, Tuscan-Style Pork with, **366**
    red
        Hummus, Pita Wedges with, **239**
        Puree, Egyptian-Style, **478**
    salad
        Catalanian Tomato Salad, **278**

Mediterranean with Grilled
    Peppers, **280**
  with Red Wine Vinaigrette, **279**
Soup, Caribbean Red Bean and,
    258
Light Fresh Mushroom Soup with
    Vermouth, **264**
"Light Lunch" Warm Caribbean
    Shrimp Salad, **299**
Light Vinaigrette Dressing, **304**
Lime-Marinated Grilled Chicken,
    383
Linguine with White Clam Sauce,
    405
Liquor, 165, 166
Lobster, Mixed Seafood Paella, **326**
Louisiana Shrimp Pilau, **322**
Louisiana-Style Barbecued Shrimp,
    233
Low Country White Corn Crab
    Cakes, **313**

Mandarin Beef with Sesame-
    Mustard Dressing, **284**
Manhattan Clam Chowder with
    Dry Sherry, **255**
Manicotti
  Mixed Cheese, with Pimento
      Cream Sauce, **407**
  Pasta Rolls with Cheese and
      Spinach, **406**
Marinades
  Apple Walnut Vinaigrette
      Dressing, **303**
  Light Vinaigrette Dressing, **304**
  Orange Yogurt Sauce, **306**
  Russian Salad Dressing, **308**
Marinated Oranges with Mock
    Rum Cream, **510**
Measure to weight conversions,
    39–44
Meatball(s)
  Greek-Style Herbed Cocktail, **215**
  Soup, Southwestern Herbed, **251**
Meat Loaf
  Baked, with Creole Tomato
      Sauce, **345**
  Bavarian, with Ginger Glaze, **347**
Meats, 32–36, 122–123, **343–369.**
    See also Beef; Lamb; Pork;
    Veal
  appetizers, **213–223**
  cooking timetables, 10, 32
  menu suggestions, 173–174, 179,
      186, 190, 194, 198, 201, 206
  salads, **284–286**
  soups, **247–251**
Medallions of Turkey in Mustard
    Sauce, **393**
Mediterranean food, **382, 457, 543**
  grains, **441, 449**
  lentils, **239, 279, 280, 478**
  salads, **281, 294, 300, 310**
Melon
  Soup, Chilled and Spiced, **259**

Southwestern Duck Salad with,
    292
Menu
  concepts, 169–207
  writing, terms for, 75–88
      American regional, 88–100
      international, 101–119
Methods of cooking, 3–36
Metric conversions, 44–46
Mexican food, **214, 238, 241, 305,**
    418, 439, 471, 498, 531, 542
  beef, **216, 217, 218**
  chicken, **224, 225, 290, 291, 375,**
      376
  menu suggestions, 176–178
  seafood, **231, 327, 333**
  soup, **251, 265, 269**
Microwave time conversions, 46
Minestrone, **266**
Mixed Cheese Manicotti with
    Pimento Cream Sauce, **407**
Mixed Seafood Paella, **326**
Moist-heating cooking methods,
    22–32
Monkfish, Polynesian Baked, with
    Sweet 'n' Sour Sauce, **332**
Moroccan food, **294, 356, 452**
Muffins, **492–494**
  Carolina White Corn Hush
      Puppies, **492**
  Corn, with Jalapeño and Bacon,
      493
  Lemon 'n' Walnut, **494**
Mushroom(s)
  Cream Bisque, Fresh, **262**
  Pizza Snacks, **243**
  Soup, with Vermouth, **264**
  Spaghettini Porcini with Garlic
      and Herbs, **410**
  Spicy Marinated, **241**
  Turkey Marsala with, **397**

Nachos, Mexican Stuffed Beef, **216**
Nantucket Cranberry Syrup, **554**
Navy beans, Pistou Provençale, **267**
New Bedford Corn and Sweet
    Potato Pudding, **530**
New Delhi Curried Rice, **442**
New York Cheddar Pancakes, **551**
Noodles, **399–420**
No-Rise Angel Biscuits, **497**
Northeastern U.S. menu, 189–192
Nut-Rich Boston Brown Bread, **489**

Oatmeal-Date Delights, **536**
Okra, Calalou, **257**
Onion rings, deep-frying timetable,
    10
Onions, Roasted, with Rubbed
    Sage, **468**
Orange Rice with Sweet Pepper,
    444
Orange roughy, Broiled, with
    Orange Sauce and Pecans,
    336

Orange(s)
  Broiled Citrus Mélange, **555**
  Marinated, with Mock Rum
      Cream, **510**
  Sauce, **319**
      Orlando, **379**
      and Pecans, Broiled Roughy
          with, **336**
      Yogurt, **306**
  Strawberries and, with Cointreau
      and Mint, **556**
Oriental food, **423.** *See also* Chinese
    food; Japanese food; Korean
    food; Thai food
  beef, **219, 352, 355**
  menu suggestions, 181–183
  Noodles. *See* Pasta, Oriental
  seafood, **301, 320, 321, 331, 391**
  vegetables, **456, 458, 463, 466**
Origins of food terms, 88–119
Oven-Smoked Barbecued Turkey
    Breast, **394**

Pacific Coast U.S. menu, 192–197
Paella
  Mixed Seafood, **326**
  Salad, **300**
Panbroiling, 11–13
Pancakes, **547–552**
  Blini, **547**
  German Apple, **548**
  Kentucky Griddle Cakes, **550**
  New York Cheddar, **551**
  Pumpkin-Nut, **549**
  Whole Wheat Honey, **552**
Pan capacities, 55
Pandowdy, Peach and Pecan, **511**
Panfrying, 13–16
Pasta, **399–420**
  Italian
      Cheese Tortellini with Roma
          Tomato Sauce, **401**
      Chicken Tetrazzini Milano, **377**
      Fettuccine with Smoked
          Chicken, **402**
      Fettuccine with Tomato and
          Capers, **403**
      Fusilli with Meatless Marinara
          Sauce, **404**
      Linguine with White Clam
          Sauce, **405**
      Manicotti Rolls with Cheese
          and Spinach, **406**
      Mixed Cheese Manicotti with
          Pimento Cream Sauce, **407**
      Rainbow Pasta Primavera, **414**
      Salad Mexicana, **418**
      Shrimp with Rotini and Olives,
          298
      Spaghetti with Mixed Herbs,
          411
      Spaghettini Porcini with Garlic
          and Herbs, **410**
  menu suggestions, 173–174, 177,
      179, 182, 186, 203, 206–207

Pasta (cont.)
  Oriental
    Chinese Shrimp Shells with
      Broccoli Florets, **415**
    Cold Noodles with Shredded
      Vegetables, **417**
    Linguine with Ginger and
      Peanuts, **413**
    Noodles with Beef Broth, **409**
    Stir-Fried Noodles with Ginger
      and Scallions, **412**
    Szechuan Noodles with Bean
      Sauce and Chicken, **419**
    Vermicelli with Chili Oil and
      Cashews, **420**
  salads. *See* Salad(s), pasta
Peach(es)
  -Basted Broiled Chicken Breasts,
    384
  Chilled Bisque with Brandy, **263**
  and Pecan Pandowdy, **511**
Pear(s)
  Baked, with Toasted Almond
    Butterscotch Sauce, **503**
  Swiss-Style Mashed Potatoes
    with, **432**
Pecans, Spiced Cocktail, **240**
Pennsylvania Shoofly Pie, **527**
Pepper(s)
  -Cheese Boarding House Biscuits,
    500
  Mixed, and Fruit, Baked Sole
    with, **334**
Peppered Roast Beef Hash, **559**
Philadelphia Pepper Pot Soup, **250**
Philadelphia Scrapple, **560**
Pies, **522–528**
  Blackbottom, **523**
  Blueberry, **528**
  Cannoli Tarts with Strawberry
    Sauce, **524**
  Grasshopper, **526**
  Pennsylvania Shoofly, **527**
Pimento Cream Sauce, **408**
Pistachio Pilaf with Golden Raisins,
  443
Pistou Provençale, **267**
Pita Wedges with Red Lentil
  Hummus, **239**
Pizza. *See also* Calzone
  Crust Dough, Italian, **236**
  Sicilian Vegetarian, **242**
  with Sausage and Cheese, **540**
  Snacks, Mushroom, **243**
Planning, **161–207**
Poached Salmon with Aromatic
  Vegetables, **337**
Poaching, **25–26**
Polenta, Marinara, Broiled, **449**
Polynesian Baked Monkfish with
  Sweet 'n' Sour Sauce, **332**
Polynesian food, **456**
  pork, **221, 222**
  salads, **283, 288**
  seafood, **332**

Pork, **35**, **64–65**, **357–367**. *See also*
  Bacon
  Barbecued, with Apricots, **357**
  Bavarian Meat Loaf with Ginger
    Glaze, **347**
  cooking timetables, **8, 12, 15, 19,**
    24, 28
  Grilled, with Ginger and
    Burgundy, **360**
  Loin
    Chinese Firecracker, **358**
    Grilled, Sante Fe, **359**
    Roast, Florentine, **363**
  Medallions Barcelona, **361**
  Mexican Carne Picadillo, **217**
  Philadelphia Scrapple, **560**
  Polynesian *Pu Pu* Appetizer, **222**
  Ribbons, Velvet, with Spinach,
    367
  Salad, Venetian, with Walnuts,
    286
  Sates, Spicy Indonesian, **223**
  Sautéed, with Bourbon and
    Mustard, **364**
  Szechuan, with Peanuts, **365**
  Tenderloin, with Orange and
    Ginger, **362**
  Toasts, Grilled, with Mango
    Chutney, **221**
  Tuscan-Style, with Herbed
    Lentils, **366**
Potato(es), **423–436**. *See also* Sweet
    Potato(es)
  Cantonese Braised, **423**
  Crisps, Saratoga, **431**
  Croquettes with Garlic and
    Cheese, **427**
  Gnocchi, **426**
  Kugel with Golden Raisins, **428**
  mashed
    Cheese 'n' Bacon, **424**
    Swiss-Style, with Pear, **432**
  O'Brien, Grilled, **425**
  Pancakes *Roesti*, **429**
  Provençale-Style Salade Nicoise,
    302
  Roasted, with Garlic and Herbs,
    430
  Salad, **282**
    New, Mediterranean, **281**
Pot capacities, **56–57**
Poultry, **66, 124–128, 371–397**. *See*
    also Chicken; Duck; Turkey
  appetizers, **224–228**
  cooking timetables, **8, 15, 20, 32**
  menu suggestions, **172–173, 177,**
    179, 182, 185–186, 190, 194,
    198, 201, 206
  salads, **287–297**
  soups, **252–254**
Pound Cake
  Ginger, **517**
  Hawaiian Sunset Grilled, **518**
  Lemon, with Blueberry Sauce,
    520

Praline Yams, **435**
Pressureless steaming, **28–30**
Pressure steaming, **29**
Provençale-Style Salade Nicoise,
  302
Puddings, **529–531**
Pumpkin-Nut Pancakes, **549**
Pureed Squash with Apples and
  Cinnamon, **472**

Quesadillas Con Carne, **218**
Quick breads. *See also* Muffins
  Apple, **484**
  Bishop's, **485**
  Blueberry Corn, **486**
  Iroquois Spoon, **488**
  Sweet Potato Nut, **490**
  Zucchini, with Walnuts and
    Lemon, **491**

Ratatouille Nicoise, **465**
Recipe yields, **68–71**
Red Beans
  and Lentil Soup, Caribbean, **258**
  Pistou Provençale, **267**
Red Cabbage with Apples and
  Cloves, **460**
Red Pepper Couscous, **452**
Red Snapper, Veracruz, **333**
Red Wine Vinaigrette Salad
  Dressing, **307**
Relish, Spiced Apple, **317**
Rice, **437–446**. *See also* Wild Rice
  Baked Chile-Cheese, **437**
  Down-South White, with Raisins,
    438
  Espagnole, Fried, **439**
  Louisiana Shrimp Pilau, **322**
  Mediterranean Brown, with
    Almonds, **441**
  Mixed Seafood Paella, **326**
  New Delhi Curried, **442**
  Orange, with Sweet Pepper, **444**
  Paella Salad, **300**
  Pilaf, Golden Almond, **440**
  Pistachio Pilaf with Golden
    Raisins, **443**
  Steamed, with Water Chestnuts,
    445
  White, O'Brien, **446**
Roasting, **16–21**
Roestbraten, **353**
Russian Salad Dressing, **308**

Salad(s), **271–310**
  Catalanian Tomato, with Lentils
    and Olives, **278**
  Ceviche of Scallops Veracruz, **231**
  Chicken, **287**
    Bali Hai with Mango Chutney
      Dressing, **288**
    Bombay with Curry and White
      Grapes, **289**

Grilled, with Chopped Pecans, 290
Mexican, 291
Dilled Green Beans, 457
dressings, 303–310
Green Beans with Dill and Garlic Vinaigrette, 275
Green Lentil, with Red Wine Vinaigrette, 279
Herbed Broccoli with Mixed Peppers, 276
Hot Three Bean, 274
Indian-Style Coleslaw with Orange Mayonnaise, 277
Mandarin Beef with Sesame-Mustard Dressing, 284
meat, 284–286
Mediterranean Lentil, with Grilled Peppers, 280
Mediterranean New Potato, 281
menu suggestions, 170–171, 177, 178, 181, 184, 189, 193, 200, 203, 205
Mexican Emperor French Dressing, 305
Nicoise, Provençale-Style, 302
Paella, 300
pasta
Chilled Linguine with Ginger and Peanuts, 413
Chilled Shrimp with Rotini and Olives, 298
Chinese Shrimp Shells with Broccoli Florets, 415
Cold Cheese Tortellini with Mustard Yogurt Sauce, 416
Cold Noodles with Shredded Vegetables, 417
Mexicana, 418
Rainbow Pasta Primavera, 414
Szechuan Noodles with Black Bean Sauce and Chicken, 419
Vermicelli with Chili Oil and Cashews, 420
Potato, 282
poultry, 287–297
seafood, 298–302
Southwestern Duck, with Melon and Pecans, 292
Spiced Black Bean, 273
Spicy Marinated Mushrooms, 241
Steamed Broccoli with Sesame Seeds, 458
Strawberries and Oranges with Cointreau and Mint, 556
Sweet Potato, with Pineapple and Ginger, 283
Thai Beef, 285
Turkey, 293
Moroccan-Style, 294
Smoked, Calypso, 295
Smoked, with Honey and Soy Sauce, 296
with Wild Rice and Mandarin Orange, 297

Warm Caribbean Shrimp, 299
Venetian Pork, with Walnuts, 286
Warm Shrimp, with Sesame Vinaigrette, 301
Salad dressings
Apple Walnut Vinaigrette, 303
Light Vinaigrette, 304
Mexican Emperor French, 305
Orange Yogurt Sauce, 306
Red Wine Vinaigrette, 307
Russian, 308
Sesame-Mustard, 309
Yogurt Vinaigrette with Cumin and Cilantro, 310
Salmon, Poached, with Aromatic Vegetables, 337
Saltimbocca, Braised Veal, 368
Sandwich fillings
Chicken Salad, 287
Crabmeat Remick with Chile Mayonnaise, 230
Greek-Style Herbed Cocktail Meatballs, 215
San Francisco Bayside Cioppino, 256
Saratoga Potato Crisps, 431
Sates, Spicy Indonesian Pork, 223
Sauce. See also Salad dressings
Black Currant, 390
Blueberry, 521
Cherry, 508
Chimichurri, 214
Creole Tomato, 346
Ginger Glaze Basting, 348
Nantucket Cranberry Syrup, 554
Orange, 319
Orlando, 379
Yogurt, 306
Pimento Cream, 408
Spiced Apple Relish, 317
Spiced Cranberry, 396
Spiced Orange, 315
Strawberry, Grand Marnier, 545
Strawberry-Yogurt Creme, 507
Sweet and Sour, 342
Toasted Almond Butterscotch, 504
Sausage
and Cheese, Pizza with, 540
Spiced, Black-Eyed Peas with, 477
Sautéing, 21–22
Scallops
Broiled, with Spiced Orange Sauce, 314
Ceviche of, Veracruz, 231
Curried, with Spiced Apple Relish, 316
Paella Salad, 300
Scandinavian food, 220, 459
Scones, Buttermilk Cinnamon, 495
Scoop capacities, 57

Seafood, 66–67, 123–124, 309–342. See also specific finfish and shellfish
appetizers, 229–234
cooking timetables, 9, 10, 13, 16, 20–21, 32
menu suggestions, 172, 177, 182, 185, 194, 197, 201, 203–204, 206
salads, 298–302
soups, 255–256
Sesame Chicken with Mild Chilies, 385
Sesame-Mustard Salad Dressing, 309
Shanghai Chicken Wings, 226
Shoofly Pie, Pennsylvania, 527
Shortcake, Strawberry, 513
Shrimp
Americaine, 323
Barbecued, Louisiana-Style, 233
Beer-Batter Coconut, with Orange Sauce, 318
Broiled, with Chinese-Style Basting Sauce, 320
Chilled, with Rotini and Olives, 298
Creole, 324
Fried, Phoenix-Style Chinese, 234
Glazed, with Chilies and Sesame, 321
Italiano, Baked, 232
Mixed Seafood Paella, 326
Paella Salad, 300
Pilau, Louisiana, 322
salad, warm
Caribbean, 299
with Sesame Vinaigrette, 301
Shells, Chinese, with Broccoli Florets, 415
and Vegetable Teriyaki, 325
Sicilian Vegetarian Pizza, 242
Side dishes
grains
Almond Couscous with Currants, 449
Baked Cheese Grits, 447
Baked Jamaican Pepper-Herb Grits, 448
Broiled Polenta Marinara, 449
Carolina White Corn Hush Puppies, 492
Creole-Style White Hominy, 450
pasta
Cheese Tortellini with Roma Tomato Sauce, 401
Manicotti Pasta Rolls with Cheese and Spinach, 406
Mixed Cheese Manicotti with Pimento Cream Sauce, 407
Oriental Noodles with Beef Broth, 409
Spaghettini Porcini with Garlic and Herbs, 410

Side dishes (*cont.*)
  Vermicelli with Chili Oil and
    Cashews, 420
  potatoes. *See* Potato(es)
  rice. *See* Rice
  vegetables
    Acorn Squash with Honey and
      Maple, 469
    Black-Eyed Peas with Spiced
      Sausage, 477
    Boston Baked Beans, 476
    Cajun Barbecued Green Beans,
      455
    Caribbean Sautéed
      Mushrooms, 467
    Chinese Green Beans with
      Sesame Oil and Almonds,
      456
    Dilled Green Beans, 457
    Egyptian-Style Red Lentil
      Puree, 478
    Glazed Carrots Grand Marnier,
      461
    Herbed Lentils with Tofu,
      479
    Jamaican Curried Yams, 433
    Kentucky Sweet Potatoes, 434
    Mexican-Style Squash
      Succotash, 471
    Oriental-Style Cucumbers with
      Shredded Carrots, 463
    Pureed Squash with Apples
      and Cinnamon, 472
    Ratatouille Nicoise, 465
    Red Cabbage with Apples and
      Cloves, 460
    Red Pepper Couscous, 452
    Roasted Onions with Rubbed
      Sage, 468
    Sliced Carrots with Apricot
      Glaze, 462
    Smoky Butter Beans with Chili
      Sauce, 480
    Spaghetti Squash with Basil
      and Parmesan, 473
    Steamed Broccoli with Sesame
      Seeds, 458
    Steamed Zucchini with Carrots
      and Mint, 475
    Swedish Cabbage with
      Caraway, 459
    Szechuan Barbecued Eggplant,
      466
Simmering, 26–28
Skewered Lamb with Cinnamon-
  Pepper Marinade, 356
Skewered Swedish Meatballs, 220
Skirting requirements for tables,
  164
Sliced Carrots with Apricot Glaze,
  462
Smoked ham, broiling timetable, 8
Smoked Turkey Salad Calypso, 295
Smoked Turkey Salad with Honey
  and Soy Sauce, 296

Smoky Butter Beans with Chili
  Sauce, 480
Snacks, Mushroom Pizza, 243
Sole
  Baked, with Mixed Peppers and
    Fruit, 334
  Baked Turban of, Florentine, 335
Sopa Albondiga, 251
Soups, 245–270. *See also* Chili
  meat, 247–251
  menu suggestions, 171–172, 177,
    178–179, 181, 184–185,
    189–190, 193–194, 197, 200,
    203, 205
  poultry, 252–254
  seafood, 255–256
  vegetable, 257–270
South American food, Argentine
  Spiced Beef Empanadas,
  213
Southern U.S. menu, 197–200
Southwestern Duck Salad with
  Melon and Pecans, 292
Southwestern Herbed Meatball
  Soup, 251
Southwestern Rarebit, 546
Southwestern U.S. menu, 200–203
Spaghetti with Mixed Herbs, 411
Spaghettini Porcini with Garlic and
  Herbs, 410
Spaghetti Squash with Basil and
  Parmesan, 473
Spanish food, 51, 120–126,
    153–159, 265, 278, 531
  pork, 357, 361
  rice, 439, 444
Spanish Flan, 531
Spices, 48–49, 125–126
  weight to measure conversions,
    42–43
Spinach
  Baked Turban of Sole Florentine,
    335
  Calalou, 257
  Manicotti Pasta Rolls with
    Cheese and, 406
  Velvet Pork Ribbons with, 367
Spoon Bread, Iroquois, 488
Squash. *See also* Acorn Squash;
    Yellow Squash; Zucchini
  Bisque with Ginger, 268
  Pureed, with Apples and
    Cinnamon, 472
  Spaghetti, with Basil and
    Parmesan, 473
  Succotash, Mexican-Style, 471
Starches. *See also* Grains; Potatoes;
    Rice; Side dishes
  menu suggestions, 174–175, 177,
    180, 183, 186, 190, 194–195,
    198, 201, 207
Steamed Broccoli with Sesame
  Seeds, 458
Steamed Rice with Water
  Chestnuts, 445

Steamed Zucchini with Carrots and
  Mint, 475
Steaming, 28–32, 57
Stewing, 26–28
Stews
  Beef Ragout, 247
  Green Chile Beef, 248
  Hungarian Goulash, 249
Stir-fried Noodles with Ginger and
  Scallions, 412
Stovetop steaming, 28–30
Strawberry
  Crepes Neapolitan, 512
  and Oranges with Cointreau and
    Mint, 556
  sauce
    Cannoli Tarts with, 524
    Grand Marnier, 545
    -Yogurt Creme, 507
  Shortcake, 513
Stuffed French Toast with Honey
  Ricotta, 544
Substitutes, flavor, 50–51
Sukiyaki, 354
Summer squash. *See also* Zucchini
  Bisque with Ginger, 268
  Grilled Yellow, 470
  Pureed, with Apples and
    Cinnamon, 472
  Succotash, Mexican-Style, 471
Swedish food, 51, 459
Sweet Potato(es)
  Jamaican Curried Yams, 433
  Kentucky, 434
  Nut Bread, 490
  Praline Yams, 435
  Pudding, Corn and, 530
  Salad with Pineapple and
    Ginger, 283
Sweet and Sour
  Sauce, 342
  Whitefish Fillets, 341
Swiss food, 429, 432
Szechuan Barbecued Eggplant, 466
Szechuan Broiled Flounder, 328
Szechuan food. *See* Chinese food;
    Oriental food
Szechuan Noodles with Black Bean
  Sauce and Chicken, 419
Szechuan Pork with Peanuts, 365
Szechuan Velvet Chicken, 386

Table skirting requirements, 164
Tandoori-Style Roasted Chicken
  Breasts, 387
Temperature
  conversions, Fahrenheit/
    Centigrade, 45–46
  food safety and, 47
Terms, for menu writing, 75–88
Thai food, 285, 388
Themes for events, 167–169
Thesaurus, menu writing, 75–88
Timetables
  braising, 23–25

broiling, 6–9
deep-frying, 10
panbroiling, 12–13
panfrying, 14–16
pressureless steaming, 30
pressure steaming, 30–32
roasting, 18–21
simmering, 27–28
Tomato
　Salad, Catalanian, with Lentils
　　and Olives, 278
　Sauce, Creole, 346
Tortellini, cheese
　Cold, with Mustard Yogurt
　　Sauce, 416
　with Roma Tomato Sauce, 401
Tortilla(s)
　Soup Monterey, 269
　with Spiced Meat, 218
Translations of food terms, 120–126
Tripe, Philadelphia Pepper Pot
　Soup, 250
Tropical food, 362, 557
Trout
　baked
　　Italian-Style, 340
　　Romano, 338
　Cantonese Sweet and Sour, 339
Tuna, Provençale-Style Salade
　Nicoise, 302
Turkey, 389–397
　breast
　　Broiled, with Black Currant
　　　Sauce, 389
　　Chinese-Style Roasted, 391
　　Oven-Smoked Barbecued, 394
　Grilled, for Fajitas, 392
　Marsala with Mushrooms, 397
　Medallions of, in Mustard Sauce,
　　393
　Roast, with Spiced Cranberry
　　Sauce, 395

Salad, 293
　with Wild Rice and Mandarin
　　Orange, 297
smoked
　Salad Calypso, 295
　Salad with Honey and Soy
　　Sauce, 296
Tuscan-Style Pork with Herbed
　Lentils, 366

Veal, 35–36, 65, 368–369
　cooking timetables, 7, 12, 14, 18,
　　24, 27
　Piccata Milanese, 369
　Saltimbocca, Braised, 368
Vegetable(s), 67–68, 121–122,
　455–475. See also specific
　vegetables
　Aromatic, Poached Salmon with,
　　337
　Frittata, 244
　menu suggestions, 175, 180, 183,
　　186–187, 190–191, 195,
　　198–199, 201–202, 207
　pressure steaming timetables, 31
　salads, 273–283
　soups, 257–270
　Teriyaki, Shrimp and, 325
　weight to measure conversions,
　　43–44
Vegetarian food, 242
Venetian Pork Salad with Walnuts,
　286
Vermicelli with Chili Oil and
　Cashews, 420
Vinaigrette. See Salad dressings
Volume conversions, U.S./metric,
　44

Waffles with Nantucket Cranberry
　Syrup, 553

Warm Shrimp Salad with Sesame
　Vinaigrette, 301
Washington Pie, 522
Weight conversions, 39–45
Whitefish Fillets, Sweet and Sour,
　341
White Rice O'Brien, 446
Whole Wheat Honey Pancakes, 552
Wild Rice, Turkey Salad with, and
　Mandarin Orange, 297
Winter squash, Acorn Squash with
　Honey and Maple, 469
Wisconsin Cheese Soup, 270

Yakitori, 228
Yams. See Sweet Potato(es)
Yeast breads
　Anadama, 483
　Monkey, Grilled, 487
Yellow beans, Hot Three Bean
　Salad, 274
Yields
　beer per keg, 166–167
　liquor per quart, 165
　of recipes, 68–71
Yogurt
　Strawberry-, Creme Sauce, 507
　Vinaigrette with Cumin and
　　Cilantro, 310

Zucchini
　Bread with Walnuts and Lemon,
　　491
　Ratatouille Nicoise, 465
　Steamed, with Carrots and Mint,
　　475
　Vegetable Frittata, 244
　Wafers, Grilled Herbed, 474